HAVE THE AUDACITY®

How to Record, Mix and Produce with Audacity

By

R.N. Roller

Audacity® software is copyright © by the Audacity Team.

The name Audacity® is a registered trademark. This is not an offical product of Audacity.

HAVE THE AUDACITY: **How to Record, Mix and Produce with Audacity**

Published by RBK Studios a division of PAH Publishing Monett, MO 65708

No part of this publication may be reproduced, stored in a retrieval system, or transmitted in any form or by any means electronic, mechanical, photocopying, recording, scanning or otherwise, except as permitted under Sections 107 or 108 of the 1976 United States Copyright Act, without prior written permission of the Publisher. Request to the Publisher for permission should be addressed to PAH PUBLISHING 711 Hillcrest St. Monett, MO 65708.

Trademarks: Audacity is a registered trademark and like other items in this guide, they are used only for identification. The same applies to references to musical artists and music including song titles. Other titles and lyrics are the property of Paul A. Herd and are used with permission. Any references to products and companies are made solely on part of the author, and no compensation was received.

LIMIT OF LIABILITY/DISCLAIMER OF WARRANTY: THE PUBLISHER (ALL DIVISIONS) AND AUTHOR MAKE NO REPRESENTATIONS OR WARRANTIES WITH RESPECT TO THE ACCURACY OR COMPLETENESS OF THIS WORK AND SPECIFICALLY DISCLAIM ALL WARRANTIES, INCLUDING WITHOUT LIMITATION WARRANTIES OF FITNESS OF A PARTICULAR PURPOSE. NO WARRANTY MAY BE CREATED OR EXTENDED BY SALES OR PROMOTIONAL MATERIALS. THE ADVICE AND STRATEGIES CONTAINED HEREIN MAY NOT BE SUITABLE FOR EVERY SITUATION. THIS WORK IS SOLD WITH UNDERSTANDING THAT THE PUBLISHER IS NOT ENGAGED IN RENDERING LEGAL, ACCOUNTING, OR OTHER PROFESSIONAL SERVICES. IF PROFESSIONAL ASSISTANCE IS REQUIRED, THE SERVICES OF A COMPETENT PROFESSIONAL PERSON(S) SHOULD BE SOUGHT. NEITHER THE PUBLISHER OR AUTHOR SHALL BE LIABLE FOR DAMAGES ARISING HEREFROM, THE FACT THAT AN ORGANIZATION, WEBSITE OR PRODUCT IS REFERRED TO IN THIS WORK AS A CITATION AND/OR A POTENTIAL SOURCE OF FURTHER INFORMATION DOES NOT MEAN THAT THE AUTHOR OR THE PUBLISHER ENDORSES THE INFORMATION, THE ORGANIZATION, PRODUCTS, WEBSITE MAY PROVIDE OR RECOMMENDATIONS IT MAY MAKE, FURTHER READERS SHOULD AWARE THAT ANY WEBSITE LISTED IN THIS GUIDE MAY HAVE CHANGED OR DISAPPEARED BETWEEN THE TIME THIS WAS WRITTEN AND READ. ALSO BE AWARE THE METHODS, SHORT CUTS IN AUDACITY IT'S SELF MAY HAVE CHANGED.

PAH Publishing books are also available at bulk discount for industrial or sale promotional use. Write to Trade Desk-Wholesale Department at the Publisher's address.

PAH PUBLISHING
711 Hillcrest
Monett, MO 65708
Email: infor@pahpub.com

Printed and Published in the USA

Have the Audacity! How to Record, Mix and Produce with Audacity
R.N. Roller

p. cm. Includes index
ISBN: 9798986686806
1. Music Recording 1. Title 2022   Podcasting

CONTENTS

MULTIPLE-TRACK RECORDING INTRODUCTION 6

PART 1 Introduction to Audacity

CHAPTER 1   STARTING AUDACITY AND AN INTRODUCTION TO THE PROGRAM... 12

CHAPTER 2 THE EFFECTS 24

CHAPTER 3 ANALYZE AND TOOLS 61

CHAPTER 4   GETTING CONNECTED WITH AUDACITY 74

Part 2 Recording

CHAPTER 5   SETTING UP A RECORDING STUDIO 81

CHAPTER 6 MICROPHONES AND MIXING BOARDS 93

CHAPTER 7 CONNECTING INSTRUMENTS AND MICROPHONE PLACEMENT...104

CHAPTER 8 LAYING DOWN A TRACK 119

Part 3 Mixing

CHAPTER 9 GETTING READY TO MIX THE TRACKS... 146

CHAPTER 10 WHAT IS MIXING?... 149

CHAPTER 11 MIX IT UP AND MIX WELL PART 1 155

CHAPTER 12 MIX IT UP AND MIX WELL PART 2 177

Part 4 Mastering

CHAPTER 13 DO THE MASTER MIX 189

CHAPTER 14 MAKING AN ALBUM 196

Part 5 The Business

CHAPTER 15 THE BUSINESS OF MUSIC 215

Appendix 1 Audacity Short Cuts..218
Appendix II Studio Log Sheet..221
Appendix III Vocal Booth Plans...222
Appendix IV Record Pressing Plants..228
Appendix V Sound Examples..229
INDEX...231

Hillcrest Studios nd Books

ABOUT THIS BOOK: The purpose of this book is to provide a guide to how download, install and use the free audio recording program known as Audacity ®. It is widely available on the internet for download. It is one of the most useful programs available and simple to use once you understand how to use it. That is the purpose of this book. This book will guide through the process step- by-step to create an album, we also give you tips of producing a podcast. To avoid problems with copyrights we have used songs that I have created and own the copyrights. The songs were created for the purpose of this book.

Unlike other books on this on this subject we have loaded this guide with photos taken from the actual application. We have also included information on setting up a recording studio, plus tips in recording, - mixing, and mastering a full album. In addition, we have also included instructions on how to assemble items that will help in recording. At the end we even cover the legal aspects of protecting your recording.

While we have focused on recording music, we also discuss using Audacity for a podcast or religious services, which it excels at. While we used Audacity's information in this guide it is not an official publication from Audacity, so we will cover the good, the bad, and the ugly of the program. Because it can get overwhelming at times, we have tried to write a guide with simple to understand instructions, with a touch of humor at times. If there are important things to remember, we will point that out. Failure to not follow this could result in damage to equipment or your hearing. The author and the publisher assume no responsibility whatsoever and assume no liability. All products and companies mention in this guide are from personal recommendation, and in no way were we compensated for these recommendations.

One last thing, music, and the recording of your own music can be addictive, and you will want more and more stuff. You may find yourself clearing out a room, may even move the kids into the garage so you can have their room, and turn it into a full-time recording studio. Then you will walk inside and disappear forever. Seriously, recording, music you write (or doing your own podcast) can be one of the greatest rewarding things in your life. So, I wish you all luck, and go reach for your dreams. Note we make no guarantee that the links in this guide have no change, or no longer exist.

Dedication: This book is dedicated in memory of my dear mother-in-law Christine who passed during the writing of this book. You may see her name on the guitar in the photos of this guide. This is because as I told you music can be addictive. it was her that started this for with a guitar and amp for a Christmas present that lead to another guitar, a bass, a keyboard and where ever tomorrow brings. She was never a mother-in-law, just a second mother.

Multiple-Track Recording Introduction

Fig 0-1 Thomas Edison with his phonograph (Library of Congress)

Fig 0-2 **The "Godfather of Sound' Les Paul** in front of his invention the 8 track multiple track recorder. *(Les Paul)*

Fig 0-3 A typical 4-track recorder for the 1960's Shown is the Studer J37 4-track (Creative Commons Attribution 2.0 Generic license.*)*

In the beginning there was Thomas Edison (fig 0-1) with his new invention he called-phonograph. It was a simple contraption that involved a diaphragm, a metal stylus, and a cylindrical drum wrapped in a tin foil sheet with a handle to rotate it laterally. But it allowed one to record a voice. It was by all definitions it was crude compare the crystal-clear recording, but later experiments would lead to wax cylinders that would improve the sound. In 1887 Emile Berliner patented the gramophone which was a flat wax disc that could be recorded on which would be considered the first record.

The method to record was that it had to be done all in one take with the entire band being recorded all at once. So, you might imagine the anxious band members when the **singer just can't hit that last note at the end**, and they had to go back and do it all over again. So many times, mistakes would go through on published records.

Until 1948 all recordings were done on a 10-inch record that was played back at 78 rpm. After that due to introduction of the first commercial tape recorder by Ampex and Columbia Records released 12-inch vinyl record that turned at 33-1/3 rpm and compared to the old 78's it was step forward into hi-fidelity. But still recording was only a single track, meaning the entire band had to be record all at the same time. This caused some instruments and sound to be loss.

As early as in 1949 there was sort of a way of recording a track on top of another, by playing it back through a speaker and recording the new track. You can duplicate this by recording one track, then play it back on another playback machine, while recording your new track, and the old track together. It was still recording on a single track, but it was like the first recording was just another member in the studio. It was great break through, but it had its drawbacks. One mistake after laying the first track down, recording back on top of the second track added noise to the track. Plus, more than a couple passes the sound would drop off significantly.

This would be a catalyst for a legendary guitarist Les Paul's (0-2) idea of having several recorders record right over on top of each other each using a specific portion of the tape, allowing you to control the sound of each track. This would be the break-through that the recording industry needed. This way if the rest of the band laid down a perfect track and the guitars missed a note you didn't have to have everyone back only the guitarist. But the real reason Paul wanted this was that he was able to play guitar with himself. He could lay down a smooth rhythm track and then come back and add a shattering lead guitar on top of it and both could be heard. What refrigeration to food storage, multiple tracks, was to be recording.

As the industry caught on to Paul's invention other companies began to improve on the design, making recording heads smaller and more compact so that it could fit all into one tape deck. At first was the four - track record machine that used reel-to-reel one-inch-wide tape. (fig 0-3). Most of the 1960's bands including the Beatles and the Doors used this to record some of their famous songs.

They also learned that they could use an old from of multiple tracking, by allowing the machine to record the pervious tracks to one single track and the erasing the other tracks allowing you to record other tracks on top of the first one. This process in known as' bouncing'. And it is still used today and can be used in Audacity. However, if this done too many times the sound will start to distort or become weak, and the new tracks will overpower the previously recorded ones. So there is a limit to how many times this can be done.

So, the natural thought was if you add more tracks, you could add more depth and keep the quality of the sound. So as technology improved in the 1970's we got 8 tracks and then 16 tracks, and 32 tracks near the end of the decade. It was the 16 track that Queen recorded the famous Bohemian Rhapsody on, and this was done by recording by 'bouncing' the tracks- we will get into later in the book, and how it works.

In the 1980's and 1990's even more tracks were added. This was great for the professionals with a record company backing them but the machines cost over 10K, which would be close to 100K into today's money and some even close to a million. The average song writer, and music hobbyist could not afford it.

Let the horns be sounded as in 1972 TASCAM released an inexpensive recorder. The A3340 4-track recorder (0-4) with 10.5" tape reels, with 7½ and 15 ips speeds w/ manual direction toggle lever. This was just a recorder, and a mixing board was also needed. And even though it was cheaper than most of the professional equipment in recording studios, it was still out of the reach of many hobbyists.

Fig 0-4 The TASCAM A3340 4-track recorder

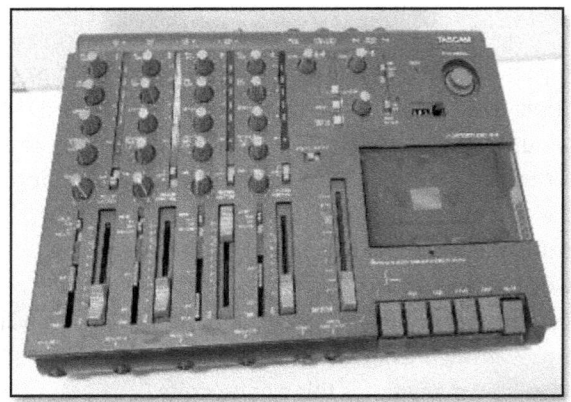

Fig 0-5 TASCAM PORTASTUDIO 4-track Recorder allow even hobbyist musicians to own a multi-track recorder.

Fig 0-6 TASCAM DP-006 digital recorder

Fig 0-7 The 24 track TASCAM Digital recorder

In the 1980's semiconductors, transistors were becoming the norm, and reducing the size all electrical equipment. Compare the size of a calculator in the 1970's to one in the 1980's. Teachers in the 1970's banned them from math classes. Unless you had a 300-pound six-foot-five center for the football team in front of you, you could not hide one of the things. By the next decade they were small enough to fit in your palm. Also at this time was a takeover in the audio world- cassette tapes.

TASCAM released the Porta One Ministudio. Fig. (0-5) This all in one was a multiple-track recording studio with a mixing board and it did not use reel-to-reel tape, but a standard cassette tape that you go get at your local discount store. However, after you polished the sound to perfection and you took the tape out from the Ministudio and put it into you it into your car's tape player to show off to your best bud's you would become a laugh, as play back speeds were different. So,to get the sound right you had to record to a standard two track recorder. Other companies also followed TASCAM and offered simple to use multiple track recorders for the home studio. Including *Yamaha* and *Cutec,* but TASCAM was the leader in this and still is today.

In the 2000's tape of any kind was deleted, and the sound was stored on a SD Card. At first the digital recorders were expensive but have dropped in price and they can be found for a few hundred dollars. They come in 4, 6, 8 16, 24 (fig 0-6 and 0-7) and even more tracks. The DP-006 is battery powered and can go with you anywhere. The big plus the tracks can be downloaded on the computer to use with Audacity®.

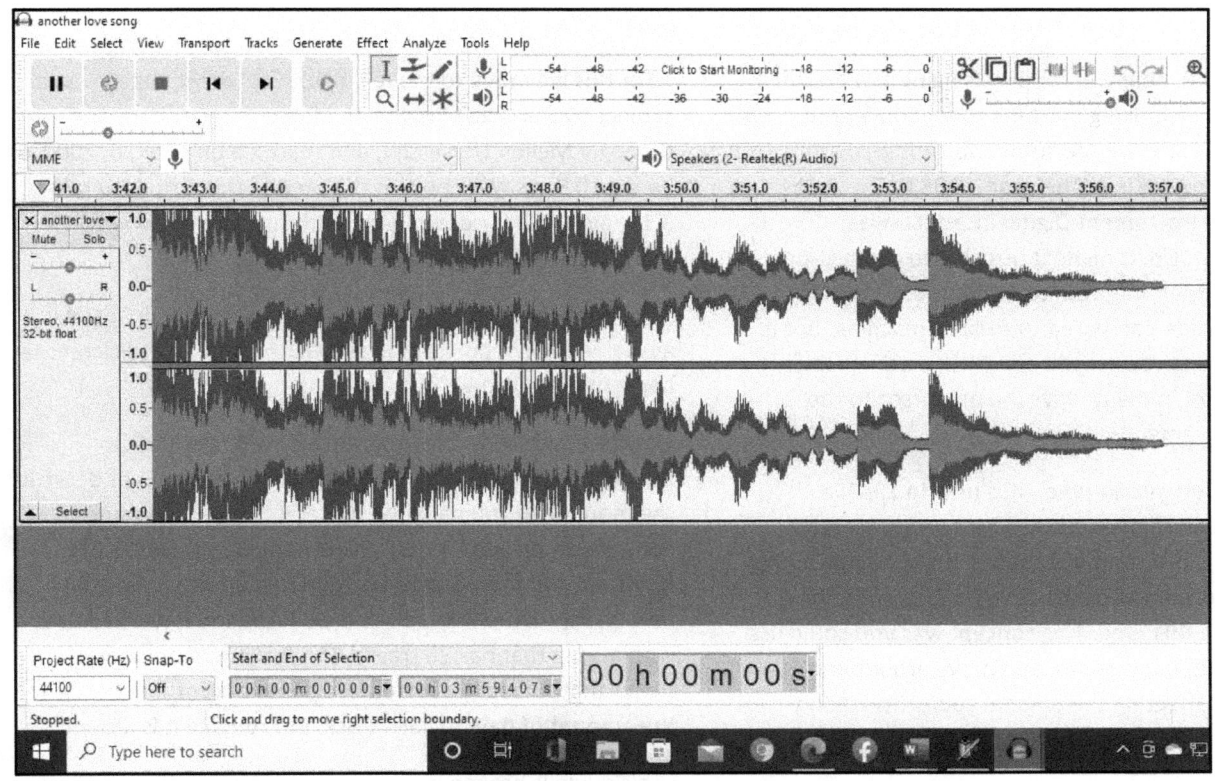

Fig 0-8 A typical Audacity screen shot. Showing the master mix of the song, Another Love Song.

DAW

There was a time when if you said, "I going to build recording studio in my house", eyebrows would come up and hands would go out...for they wanted a handout. "Because man, you had to be rich." You would have thousands even hundreds of thousands of dollars in a studio. Today, all you will get "Hey, that's cool!" For all you need now is a computer and way of getting the sound to the computer, and a digital audio workstation — DAW for short. It has become staple for today's home and even professional studios.

For a few hundred bucks you have access of powerful recording, editing, and mixing of both audio and MIDI tracks. You don't have the have the mixing console that looks like you're aboard the *Starship Enterprise.* It and digital recorders have completely replaced the analog machines, but these still have their fans.

The debate is still out which sounds better, and just like which is better ice cream-chocolate or vanilla- it is a matter of personal choice. When it comes to the ease to work with digital wins hands down, it is easy to manipulate a tone by tweaking the sound wave on the computer by changing the pitch and easily add effects to it. While with analog it requires do it to the tape yourself.

So where did it start? Well find yourself a DeLorean and rev up 1.21 gigawatts and get that hair as high as you can get it, as we are going into the past. Way back into the 1980's.

As we land you, we hear Def Leppard singing *"Photograph"* blaring out of strange looking machine that people drop coins in. It is called a jukebox; we see someone eating *Croissan'wich* at Burger King. The year is 1983. This is the year MIDI- Musical Instrument Digital Interface-was introduced to the world. It made it possible to connect one keyboard with another and even to a computer. The computers were crude compared to today's machine. But it did allow musicians to record and edit MIDI tracks in their computers and were in many ways the precursor to the modern DAW programs.

We move a little forward in time - it is now In 1989, a company called Digidesign released a Mac product called Sound Tools. This was a computer-based stereo digital audio recorder that featured non-destructive editing, something that missing before this time. This concept was you could use the computer to cut, copy, paste, and move around the recording without affecting the original audio. You didn't have to slice and paste tape together.

We forward to 1991, when Digidesign introduced a four-track successor to the stereo-only of the Sound Tools. It was called *Pro Tools* which remain a very popular DAW to this very day.

But this book is about Audacity. It technically is not a DAW. But instead, is a DAE- digital audio editor and recording application software. It is available for Windows, macOS, Linux, and other Unix-like operating systems.

For this we move to the fall of 1999 where it began n as a project by Dominic Mazzoni and Roger Dannenberg at Carnegie Mellon University, and released on May 28, 2000, as version 0.8. As were now at the time of this writing version 3.1 is available for download. Audacity remains one of the most popular downloads there is.

It is available at: www.audacityteam.org/download/ it is available for Windows, Mac and GNU/Linux. Just click on the appropriate button.

It is free, but it is a big program and will take time to download and install. While it can run on a laptop or desktop, the more RAM you have the better it runs. For Windows recommended RAM 4 GB / 2 GHz minimum is GB / 1 GHz. However, the more tracks you add to a file you create will require more memory. I have 8 GB RAM and it worked fine with a song that has 30 tracks. The maximum number of tracks that Audacity can hold is up the RAM of the device and the amount of data in each track. But roughly it is around 30.

This guide is broken into several different parts. Installing and working with Audacity; Recording, showing up how to record each instrument including microphone placement and what you will need. Mixing, there many built in effects in the Audacity program, and we go through each one giving basic guideline to things like compression and reverb that can make your track god from dull to outstanding. Then mastering to make a demo or an album. With the last section production and legal aspects of music. So, if you have yet done so go to the website and download the program. I will get a cup of coffee and meet you in the next chapter.

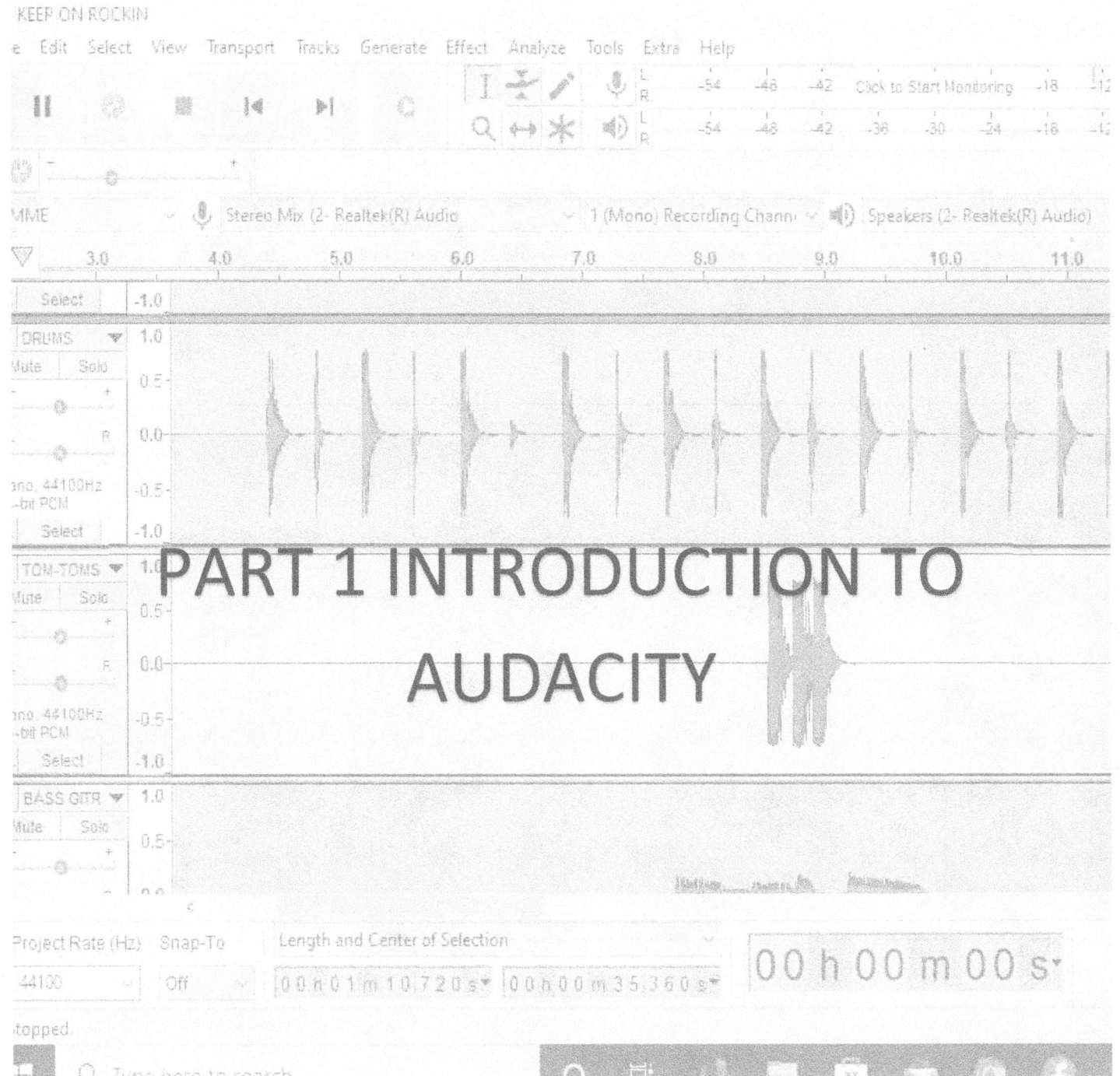

PART 1 INTRODUCTION TO AUDACITY

CHAPTER 1   Starting Audacity and an Introduction to the Program

To open Audacity Click on this logo on your home page, if it is not there, go the start button find it and click on it there, you might want to click and drag it on to the home screen for the next time.   When it opens the home screen for Audacity will appear (fig 1.1)

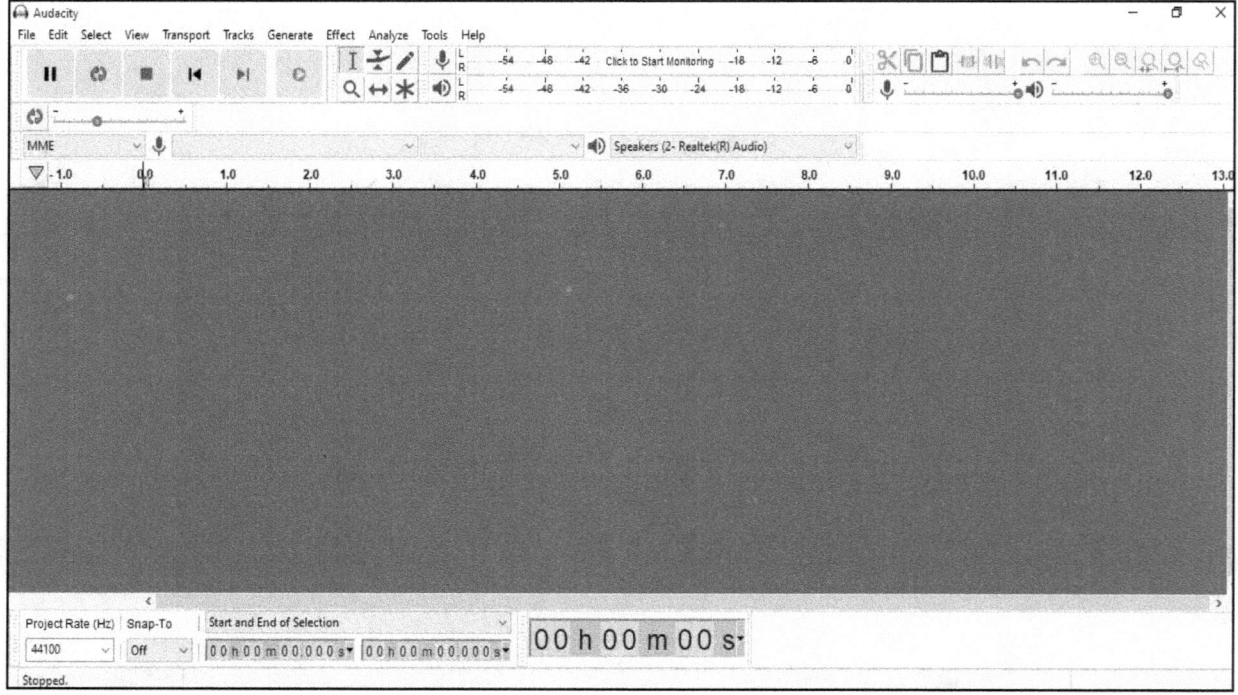

Fig 1.1 The home screen of Audacity.

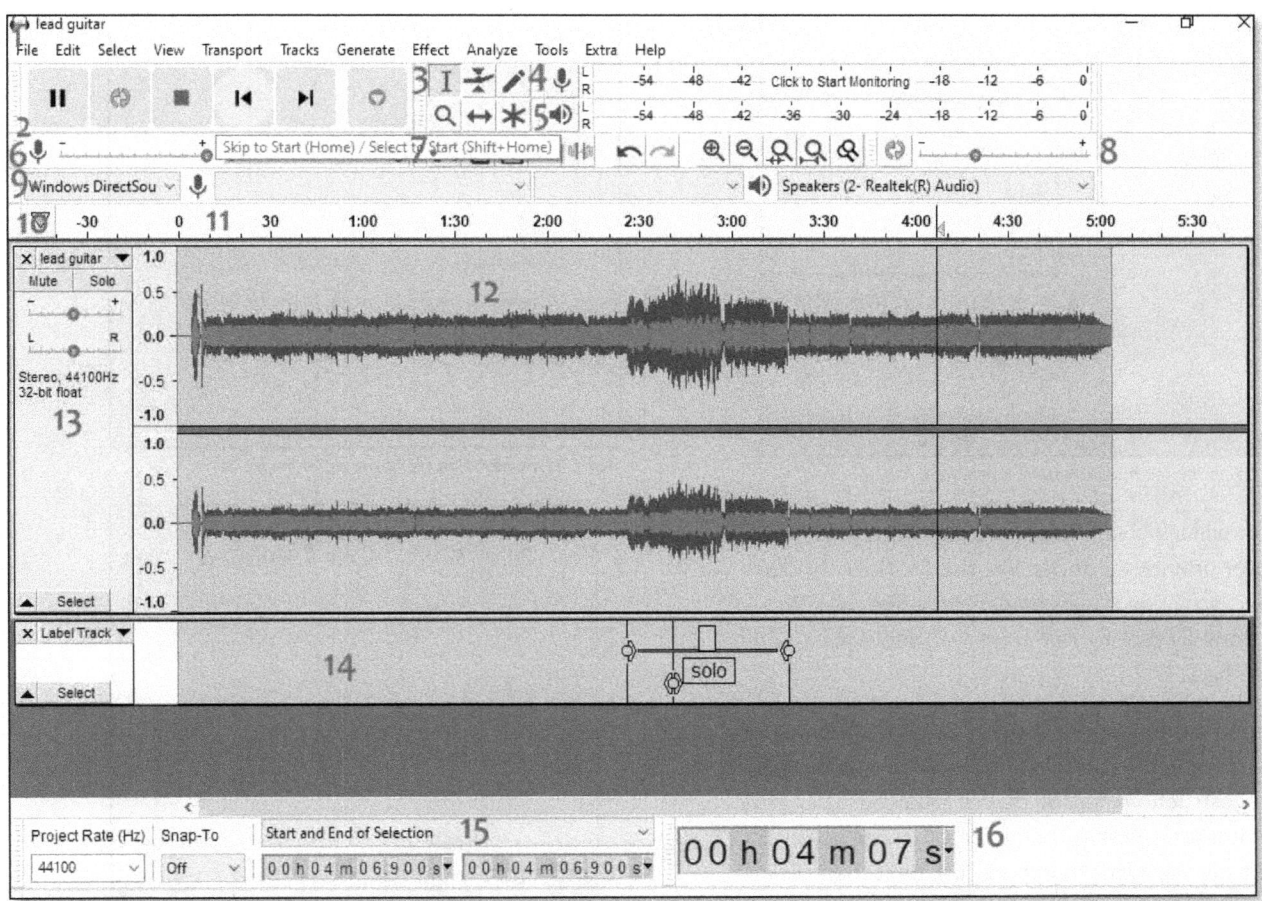

1 Menu Bar 2 Transport Toolbar 3 Tools Toolbar 4 Recording Meter 5. Playback Meter Toolbar 6 Mixer Toolbar 7 Edit Toolbar 8 Play-at-Speed Toolbar 9 Device Toolbar 10 Unpinned Play/Recording Head 11 Timeline 12 Audio track 13 Track Control Panel 14 Label Track 15 Selection Toolbar 16 Time Toolbar

There are several different menu bars that are of the Audacity program. It is important that you under where these are before attempting to use the program. See fig 1.2 for their locations, and location of other items. A photo of a track is shown to show all the locations.

To start a new project you have to use the top menu bar (Number 1 in fig 1.2) . Click FILE and another box will appear that looks like fig 1.3. New will open a new project, Open…will bring up your file folder where you have saved as a project. Recent Files will take you to the last few projects you worked on. This can be a great time saver. Close will close the project you are working but will not close Audacity.

To close the program, use the red X at the far top right-hand corner. Save project will come up if you changed anything. Clicking *Save Project,* clicking on this will bring up another box that will have the choices of save (which can also be short cut to pressing 'Control S" on the keyboard as in many programs). Save as, all files will still be saved as .aup3 file. You cannot save them as any other type of file here, but it does allow you to use a different file.

Clicking on *Export* will bring up another box. This will allow you to export the file in several different forms. Including **exporting the aup3 files themselves by clicking on Export Multiple… Note that if the export is not available it will not be highlighted.** For you cannot export a multiple track recording to MIDI, thus MIDI will not be highlighted.

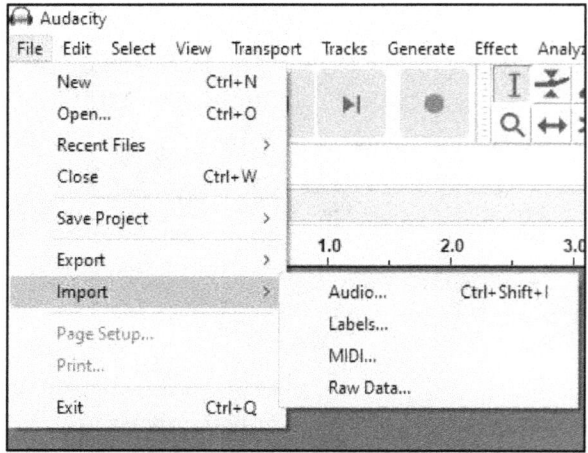

Fg 1-2 Items on the file menu. Import is selected.

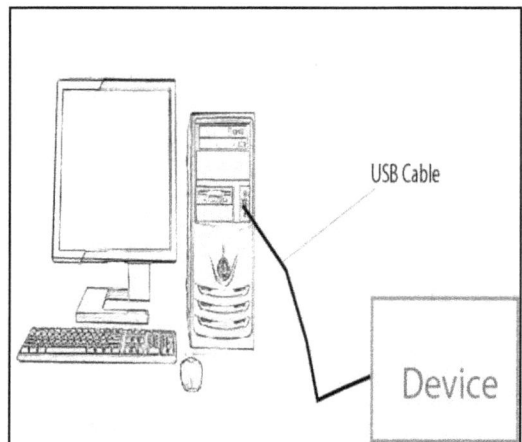

Fig 1.3 Downloading files from another device

Import will allow you to import files from your computer or another device like the TASCAM DP-006 recorder, provided it uses loadable file like .wav files. This is done by clicking Audio this will allow you to do this. See fig 1.3

To import from a device like the TASCAM recorder. It must be connected to the computer with a UBS cable, and the instructions for the device followed. Then click on File>Import> Audio. Then look for the device and then the file you want to import click on it then click Open. The file then will be imported into open Audacity screen.

Clicked on *Edit* and a new menu box will appear (see fig 1.4). If nothing is selected some of the links in this box will remain light gray. We will cover these later.

In most other programs clicking *Ctrl P* will bring up the printer program, but since this is not available in Audacity, doing this will bring up the Preferences window (fig 1.5). In the preference window are many applications that control the input devices like microphones and interfaces which will be need to input sound into the program. We will cover that in chapter 7. It also controls the output devices like headphone and monitors.

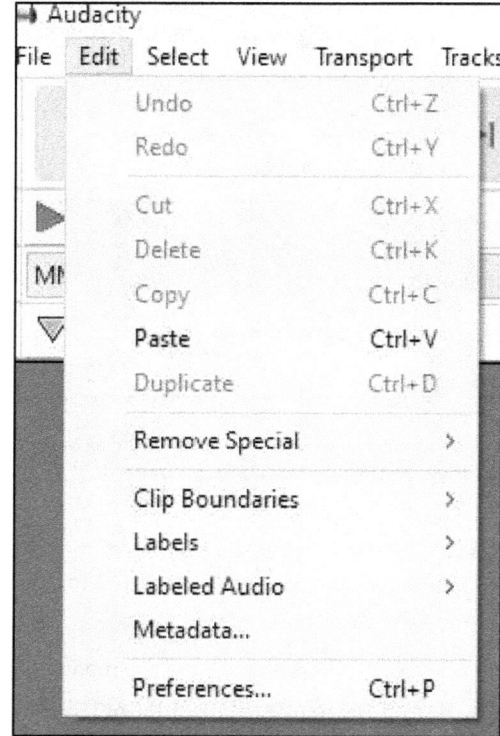

Fig 1.4 Items on the Edit menu.

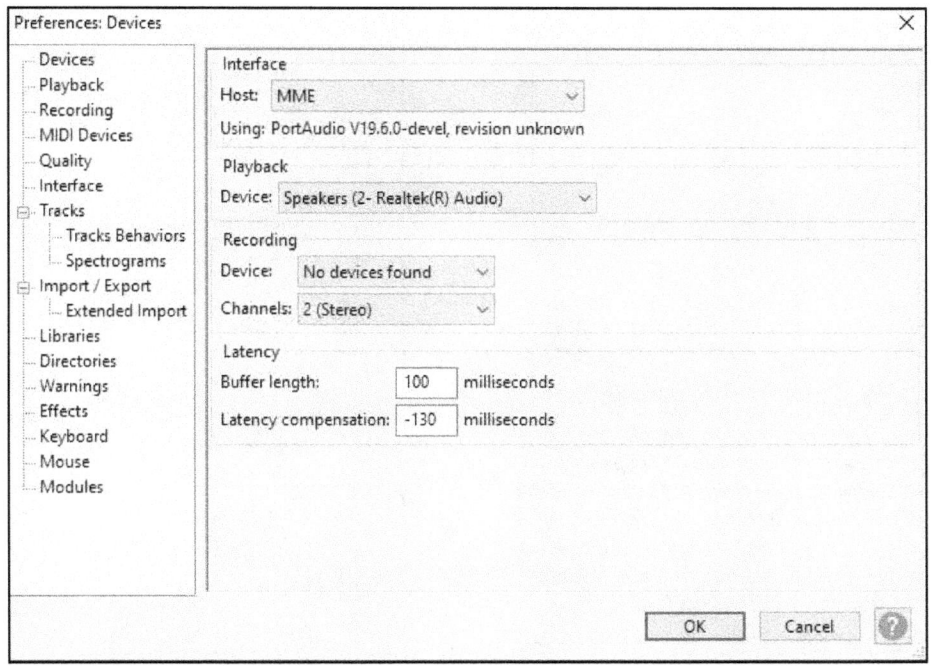

Fig 1.5 The preferences box Device is selected.

It also controls the recording, MIDI devices, the tracks, import and export options, directories and libraries effects, keyboard, mouse, modules, and warnings-such to warn you about saving a project before closing.

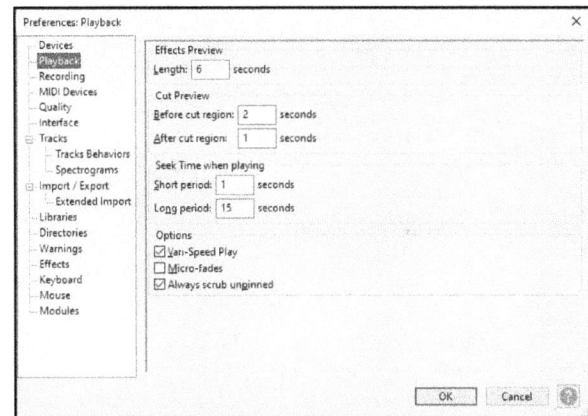

Fig 1.6 Playback menu in Preference box

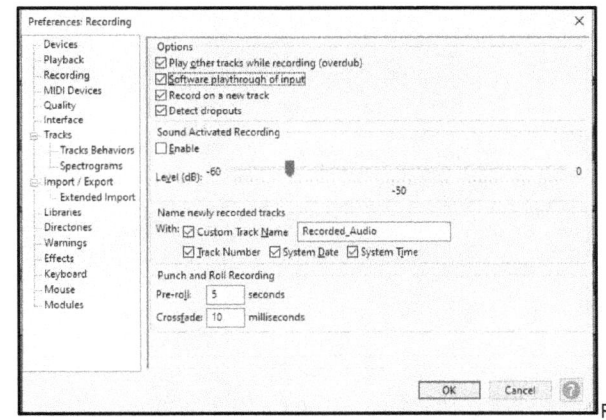

Fig 1.7 Recording menu in Preference box.

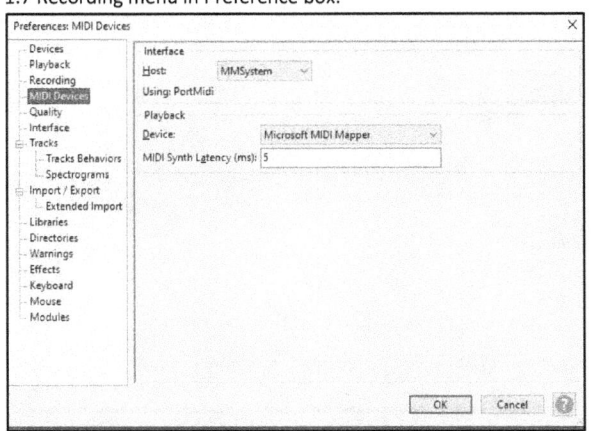

Fig 1.8 MIDI menu in the Preference box.

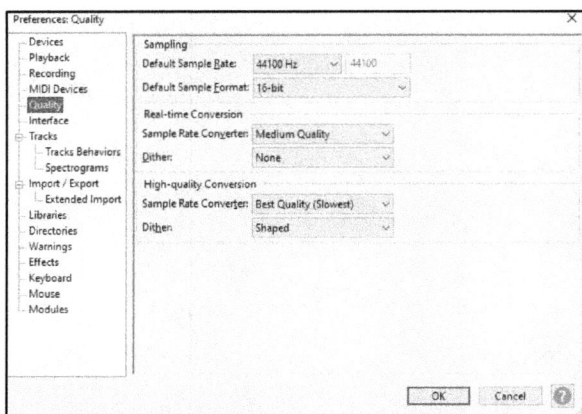

Fig 1. 9 The Quality menu in the Preference box. Controls the sample rate, which will useful when you have record to a CD or upload your work. Plus, if you have Dither which is the process of adding noise to a signal in order to reduce quantization distortion when reducing the bit depth of a file. Dithering should only be applied during the mastering stage when bouncing from 24 or 32-bit down to 16-bits. This will be covered in more detail in the master section of this guide.

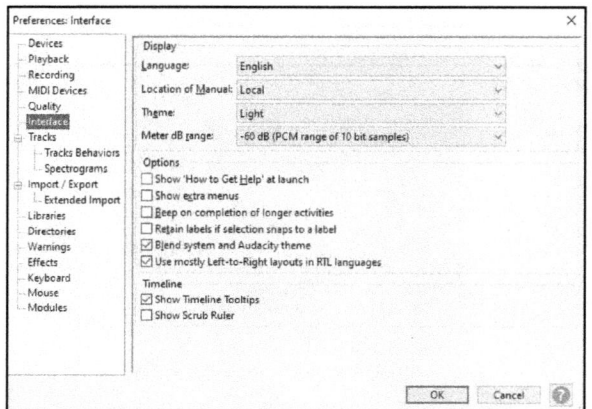

Fig. 1-10 Interface menu on the Preference box. This controls the units used to allow you make a guitar work with the computer. We will cover this in chapter XX in the recording section.

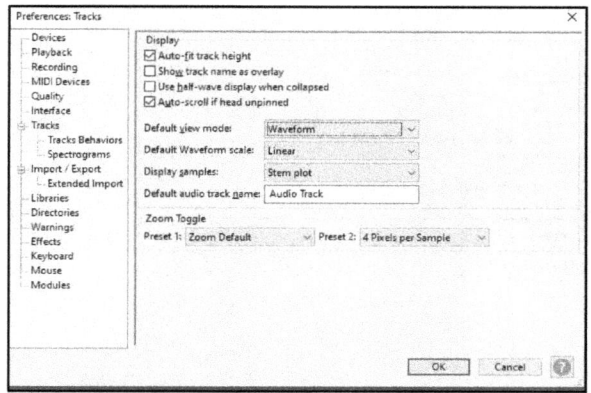

Fig 1-11 Main track menu on the preference box. This can control the type of wave pattern, size and the name it is called.

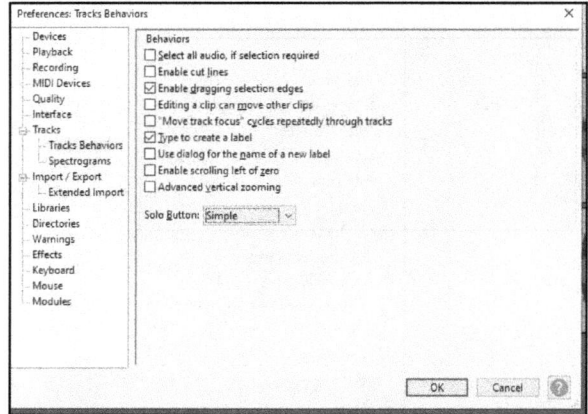

Fig 1-12 Track behavior menu

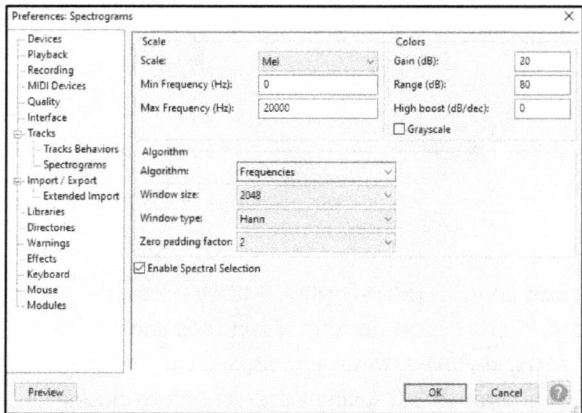

Fig 1-13 Spectrograms menu.

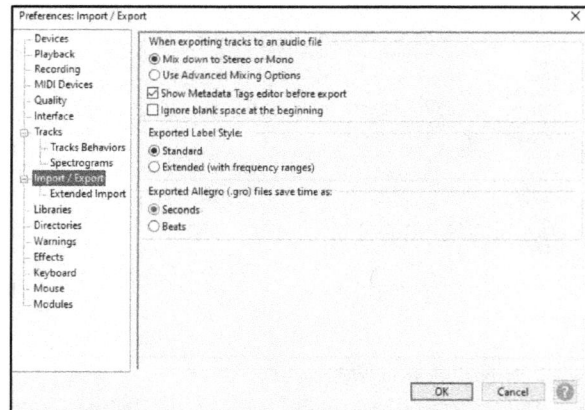

Fig 1-14 Import and export options in the preference box.

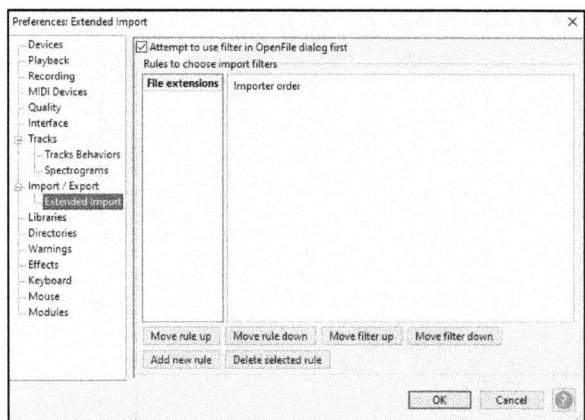

Fig 1-15 Advance import options.

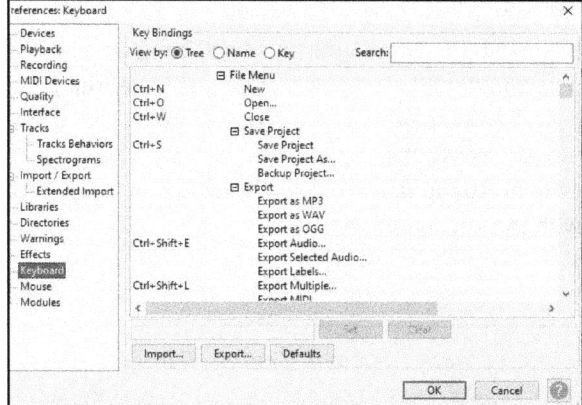

Fig 1-18 Keyboard menu, list the short cuts to use on the keyboard.

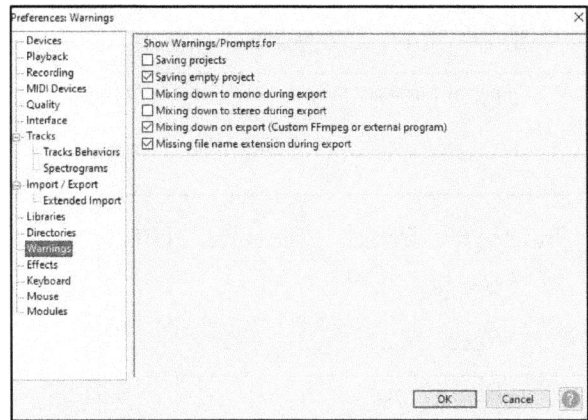

Fig 1-16 Setting the warning that will pop up.

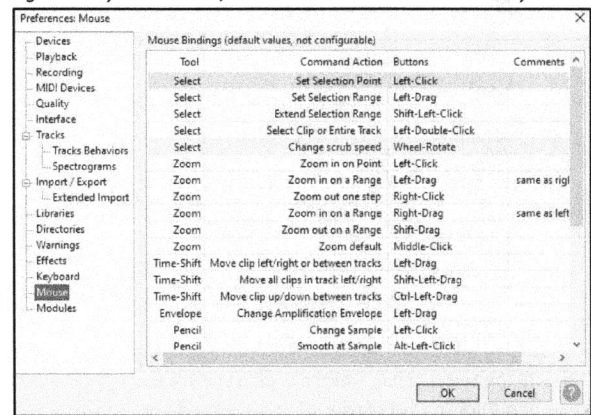

Fig 1-19 Menu for mouse actions. Under the Preference box.

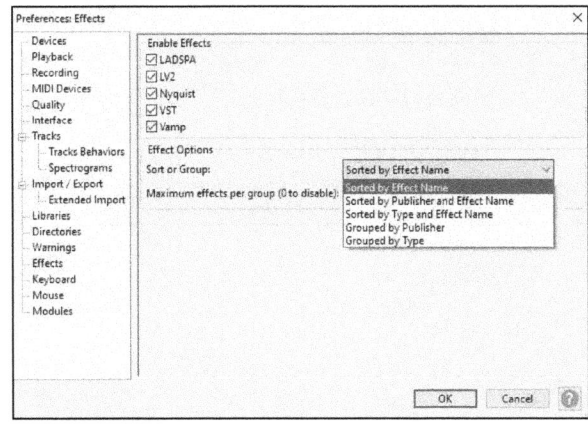

Fig 1-17 The Effect menu in the Preference menu.

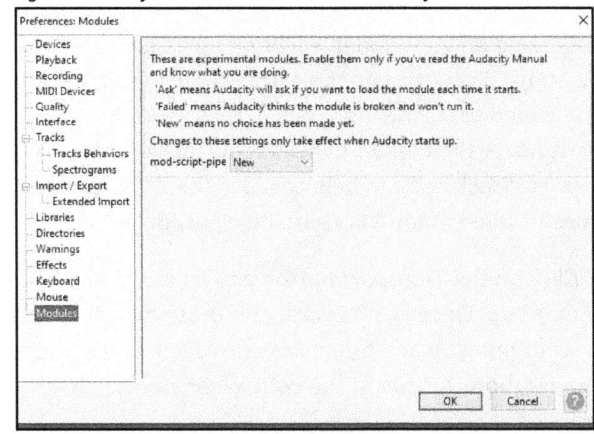

Fig 1-20 The modules menu should NOT be access and most recording applications will have no need for this.

Clicking on the *Select* button will bring up the menu box. Fig 1-21   Those with an '>' will bring up another box. You don't have to click on it, just hover the point over it and the other box will come. Then slide the mouse over to the application you want. The words or symbols to the side are the short cuts that can be used with the keyboard.

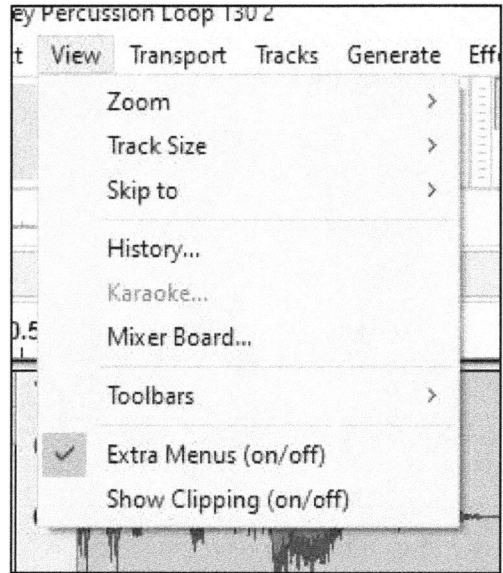
Fig 1-22 the View Menu box the check mark next Extra menu show it is on.

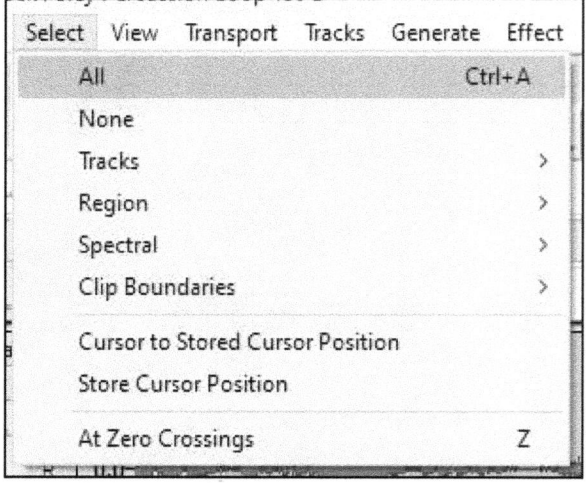
Fig 1-21 the Select menu, which can assist where you want the cursor to be or a track to start playing at.

Clicking on *View* and it will bring up its menu box fig 1-22.box. If you turn on the extra Menu another box will be added to the header. Again, those with an '>' you just hover the pointer over to bring up those additional boxes. Track size can help collapse the width of track, useful when many tracks are being used.

Click on the *Transport* button and its menu box fig 1-23 comes up. Once again Clicking on those marked with an > with bring up additional boxes. We will cover these applications further in the book when need.

Fig 1-23 the transport menu

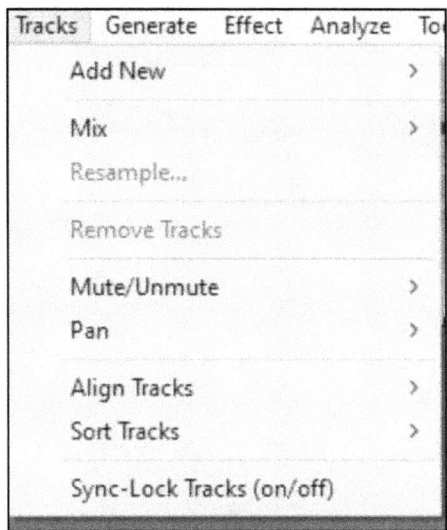

Fig 1-24 The track menu. This button will be use most of the time, in order to create a new track or mix down the track.

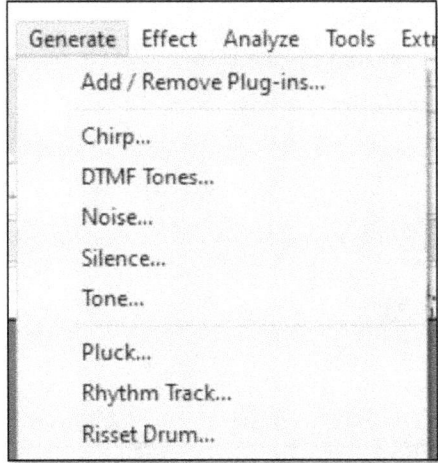

Fig 1-25 another useful menu button, this is good to produce a click track or reduce noise in a track. In the mixing section of this guide, we will show you how to use this.

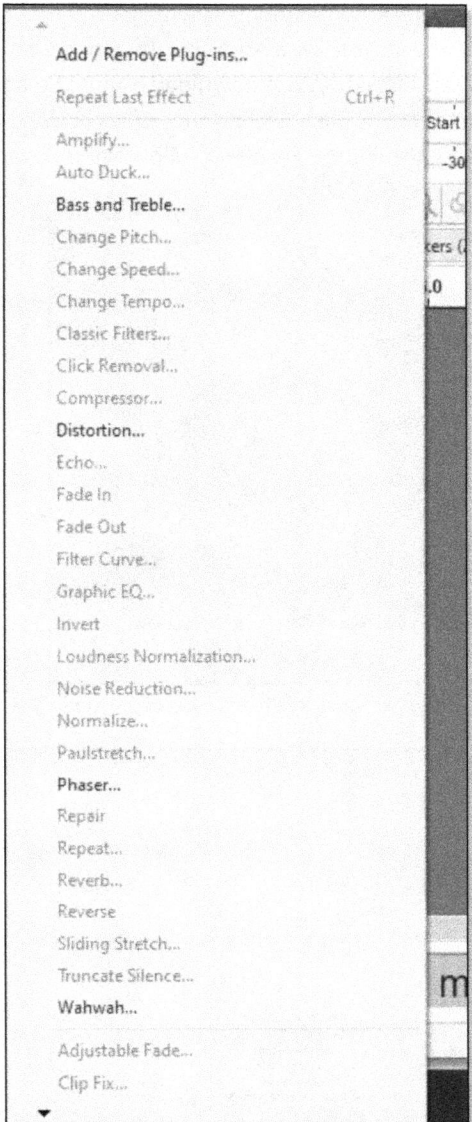

Fig 1-26 One half of the effects menu.

Of all the buttons that will be used it will the *Effects* fi 1-26 and 27 is the most useful of these boxes and is the longest with a lot of choices for all the effects that will help you create that studio sound. Including compression, EQ, reverb, even studio fade out so can get that fade out sound that is on records. Plus, much more. You can also add other effects here.

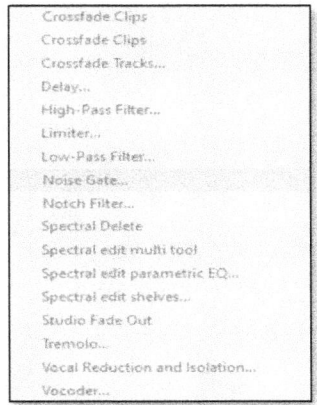

Fig 1-27 More effects

There are several other effects available on the internet that will work with Audacity. They must be downloaded. Once they are download it must be added to the *Program 86X* files. To find these files on a PC window and install the new effect follow the following photographers. Fig 1-28 to 1-32.

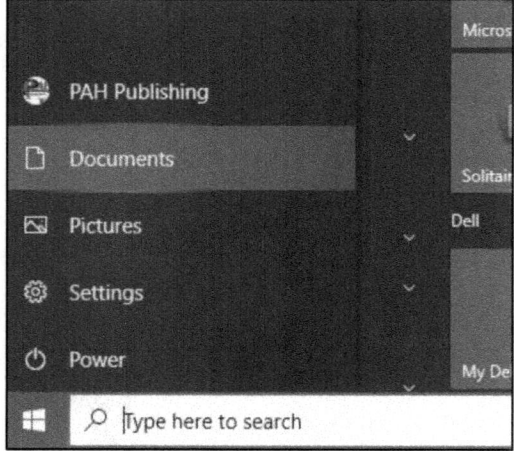

Fig 1-28 Click document on the on the side bar of your home screen.

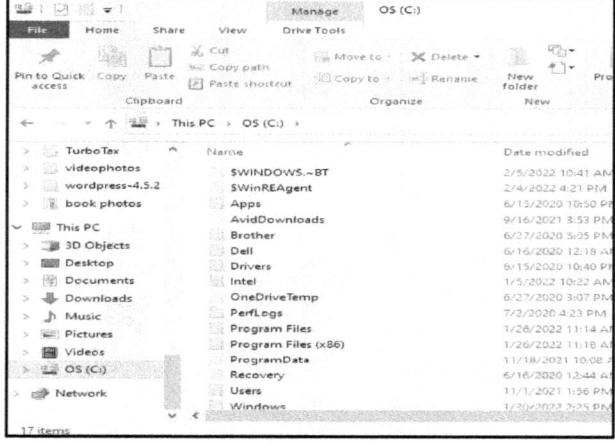

Fig 1-29 Click OS C: then click Program files(X86)

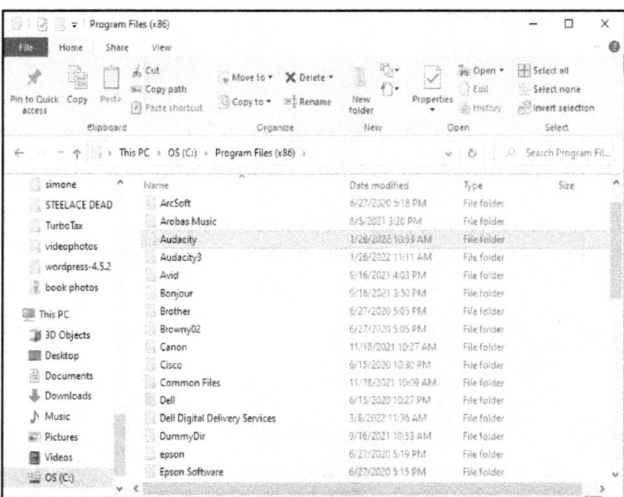

Fig 1-30 Next find and click open the Audacity file.

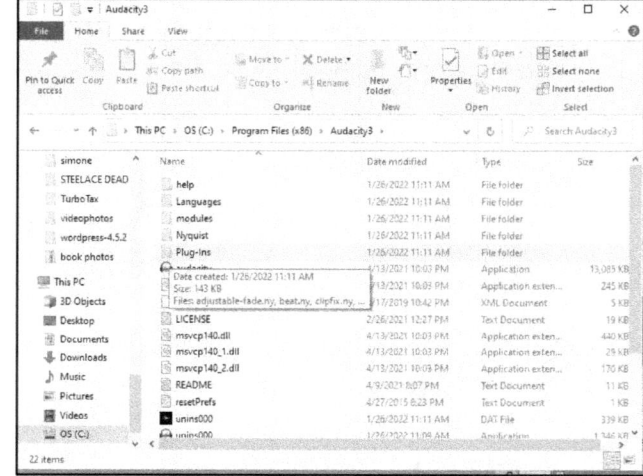

Fig 1-31 Next click and open the file marked plug ins.

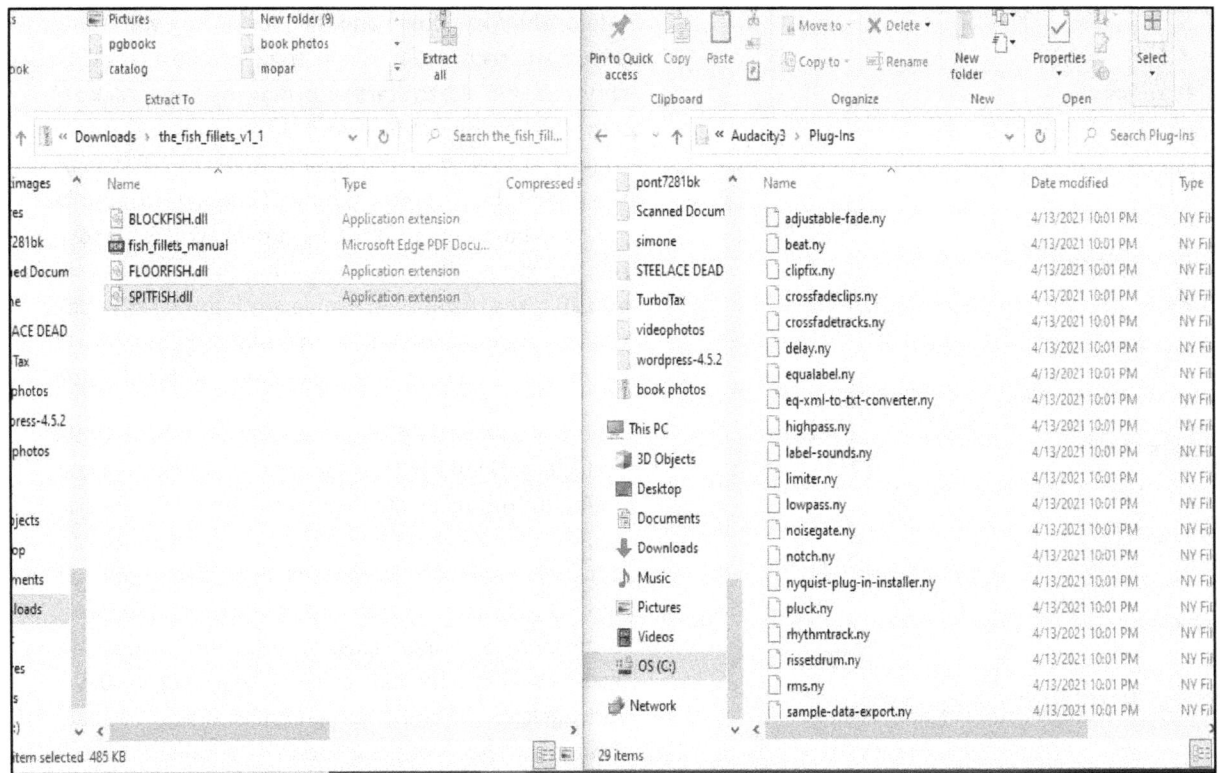

Fig 1-32 Now with the downloads and the plug-in files open grab the download (SPITFISH is a de-sser program.) and drag and drop it into the Plug in file. To activate it you may have to reboot Audacity it is on.

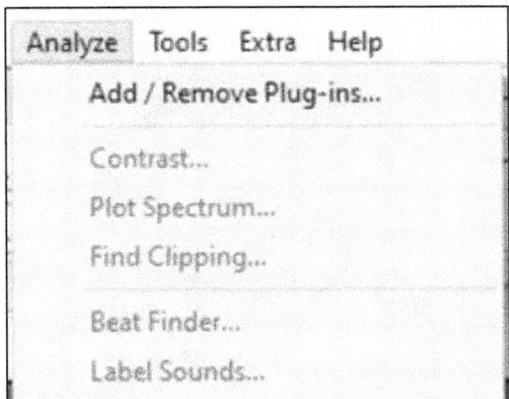

Fig 1-33 Click on Analyze and this box appears, this good for finding unwanted noise which we will describe in the mixing section of this guide.

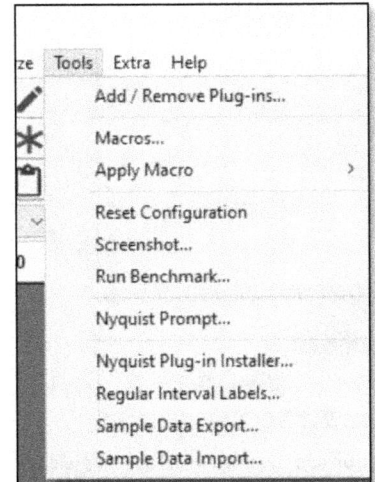

Fig 1-34 Tools menu will allow you to add more items to like effects to Audacity. For example, the Spitfish we just downloaded

Hold 'Shift' key down and the play button will change to a loop and record will change to record next track. Or use shortcut Shift + R to start recording in a new track at either the current cursor position or at the beginning of the current selection. By default, Audacity will record at the end of the currently selected (or only) track, so be sure you have cursor at the right place you want to record, or it could record over something that has taken you 20 takes to get right. However, if this does happen use the Undo button on the tool bat at the number 7 position in the photo at the beginning of this chapter.

There are several different looks you can have to the Audacity screen. For this guide we are using the Light theme for produces the imagines. Default is the classic fig 1-38 the one that most people use. It is tones of blue and grays, there is a lighter version of this theme also. And a darker version with darker grays and the wave forms by default are orange fig 1-39. For those that have trouble seeing is the high contrast theme fig 1-40, with dark background and bright green lettering. You can also create your own. This is all done by clicking *EDIT>INTERFACE>Theme*. Or you can create your own by selecting Custom in the drop-down menu.

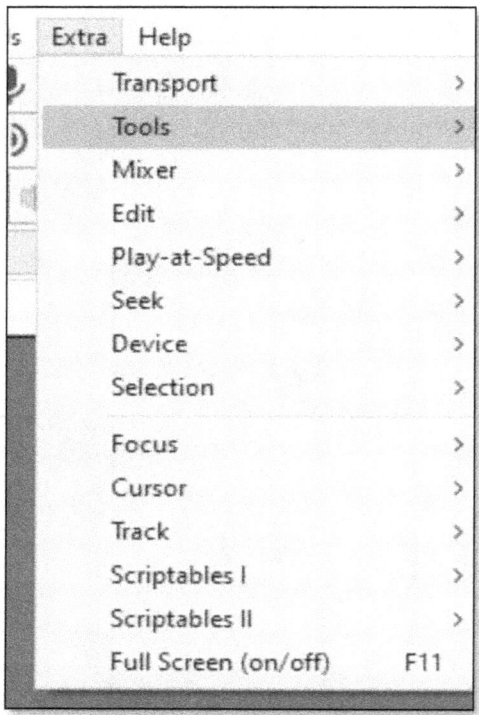

Fig 1-35 If you clicked the 'Extra menu' under View this box will appear. It does not appear on default.

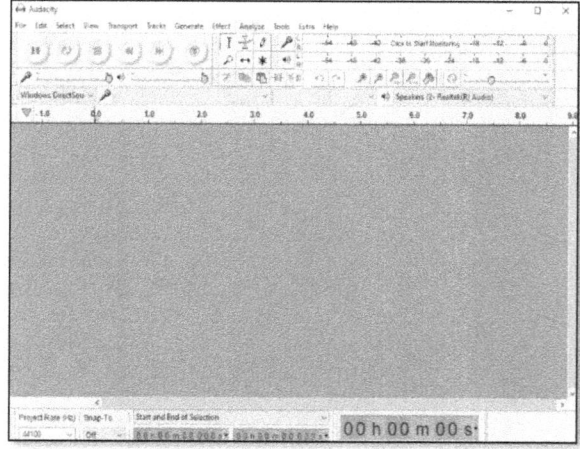

Fig 1-38 The classic look

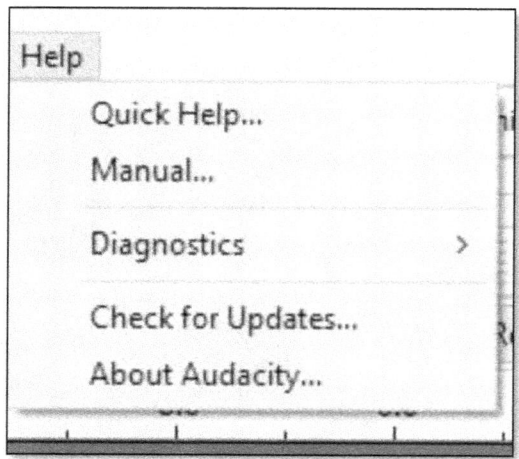

Fig 1-36 Click on the help button and this box comes up. This will take you to online manual.

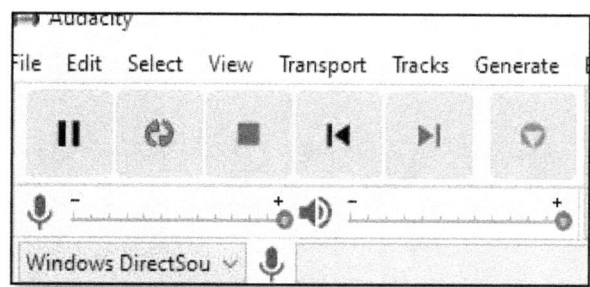

Fig 1-37 The main playback and record menu.

22

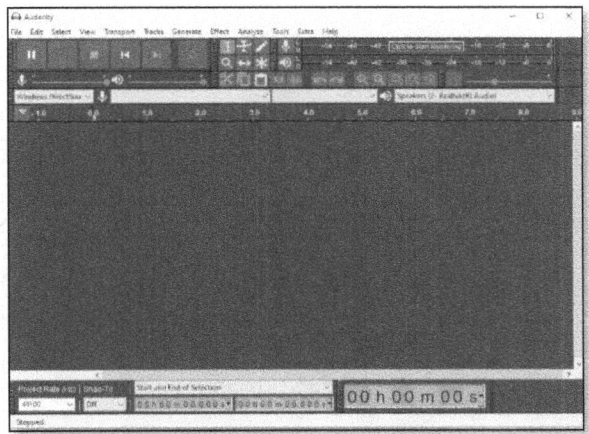

Fig 1-39 The dark theme

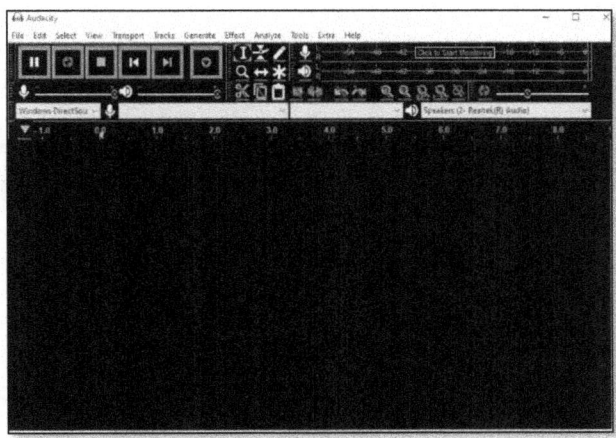

Fig 1-40 High contrast uses black background and bright green lines and lettering.

CHAPTER 2 The Effects

We will cover how to use these effects in detail in the mixing section of this guide, this is just to give you a general idea of what they are and how they work.

What Effects Can Do

Using things compression can make a track that was being hidden be brought out from the others. Adding reverb can make dull track have depth and life. By changing pitch, you can create a backing vocal or change that one note that just isn't just right. Have, a bass track that was not recorded loud enough? Amplify can help increase the sound. Too loud? Use Loudness normalization.

By using EQ, you can increase or decrease the low or high sound. Vocals just a little too low or too high? Changing speed can do this. You can distortion an instrument with distortion. You can change Bass and Treble. Unwanted buzz from a microphone or guitar effect box? This can be removed with noise reduction. But you better be careful, just as too much of one ingredient can spoil the soup, so can too much of these effects.

What Effects Can't Do

No number of effects is going to turn your voice into **Freddie Mercury's, or your guitar playing into Eddie Van Halen's or make your band the next Beatles.** These were God given talents, you just must use what is given to you. Nothing takes the place of some talent and lots of practice. The more you work with Audacity, the better you will get.

You can change pitch to voice to where it can hit the high notes, but you are going to sound like a chipmunk or some other cartoon character. You can speed up a guitar riff some, but there comes a point where it will sound unnatural. Unless this is the sound you are looking for, it is best to avoid this. While effects can make a good recording sound great, no effect can make a crappy sounding record sound good. Fig 2-1.

Fig 2-1 Effects can take the ordinary and create it into art. Effect can take a dull tack and become it become great. **But can't make a bad track great.**

Fig 2-2: A rack of studio effects, Audacity contains these as digital effects, but they do the same thing.

We will go through each effect that is listed under the menu heading effect as they appear. This only a description of what they are and how they work. In the Mixing Section we will discuss how to use them in detail, using actual examples.

AMPLIFY

What is it?: Basically a output booster. It boosts the selected tracks. Yes, unlike many other effects one track can be selected and used at the same time. with this effect. If more than one track is boosted it will boost according to the loudest track while it preserves the relative volumes of the tracks and/or channels. You can also use the "Amplification (dB)" box in Amplify as a quick check of the current peak level of the selection.

TOOLS:

Input Box: Type a value for the amount of amplification you would like to apply. Positive values make the sound louder, negative values make it quieter. Fig 2-3 As you type, the New Peak Amplitude input box will be updated. When a track is selected this effect will automatically produce the peak dB need to boost the sound. In most cases, you will not have to change this.

If you put in a negative value in the Amplification (dB) box, it will give you the current peak amplitude of the selection. For example, in fig 2-4 it will be lowered by this much.

Slider: Drag the slider right to make the sound louder, or to the left to make it quieter. As you drag, your selected value will be updated in the input box, and the New Peak Amplitude input box will be updated.

New Peak Amplitude (dB): Type in the value you would like for the new peak amplitude of your track. As you type, the Amplification input box will be updated. *Allow Clipping*: If this box is not checked, and you attempt to enter an Amplification value that will result in a New Peak Amplitude of greater than 0 dB, the OK button will become inactive. This will prevent you from applying too much amplification. If this box is checked you can apply as much amplification as you want, possibly creating a horribly distorted sound-if that is what you want. In most cases you will not.

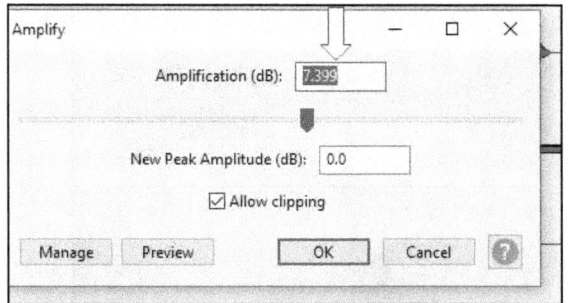

Fig 2-3 The amplification box show the amplification need to boost the loudest track. In this case it is 7.4 dB, in most cases you can just click OK

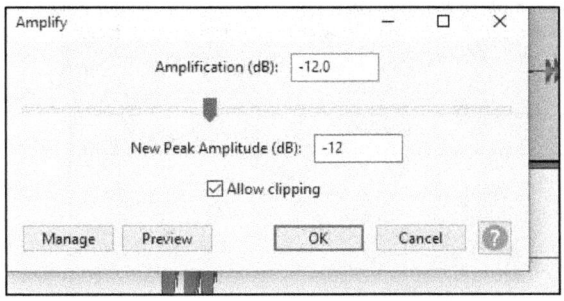

-Fig2-4 Amplify can also be used to make a track quieter, thus is useful if one is so loud it is cause clipping to occur.

AUTO DUCK

Chances are if you are using Audacity for recording your own music, this will be one effect you have never heard of. And when hear it you fall to the ground and look for low flying ducks. However, it has nothing to do with our fine feathered friends.

What is it? What it does is reduces (ducks) the volume of one or more selected tracks whenever the volume of a single unselected "control track" placed underneath reaches a particular threshold level.

What is it Use for?

The effect can be used to create voice-overs for podcasts or DJ sets, for automatic "ramping" of background music in radio productions and for turning down a voice in original language as soon as its translation kicks in. For example, The music builds in exactment and then lowers as you shout out your name and the name of your show, "and we will be back shortly." then the music builds again. Then you use fades to fade the music out and begin your show. Auto duck will create a dip in the music as you begin to speak but will still play softly in the background, see fig 2-5 for example.

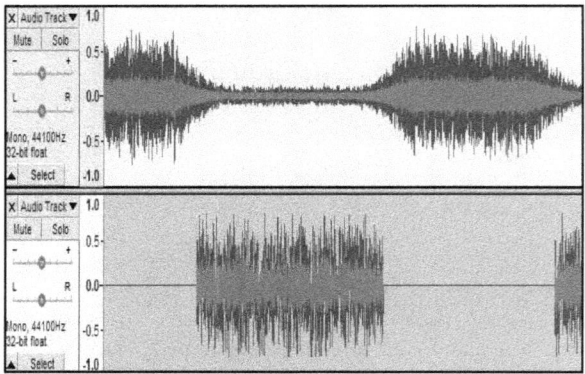

Fig 2-5 An example of the Auto Duck effect in use in use. Notice how the top music track fade in and out with the bottom control track.

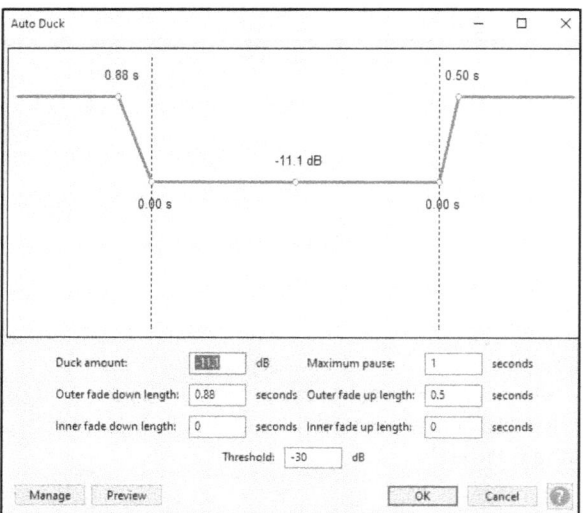

Fig 2-6 Auto Duck box, is the automatic suggested setting. Each can be changed.

Duck Amount: The amount (default: -12 dB) of volume reduction in the selected track when a signal above the threshold level is detected

Maximum Pause: Avoids over-rapid volume changes by setting a length of time following the ramp down that must be exceeded before the volume is ramped up again. The default value is 1 second, but irrespective of the setting, volume will not ramp up unless the pause is at least as long as the fade down length plus the fade up length.

Fade Down Lengths: The length of time over which the selected tracks fade down to the ducked volume (default: 0.5 seconds).

Fade Up Lengths: The length of time over which the selected tracks fade up from the ducked volume (default: 0.5 seconds). The "outer" and "inner" fade lengths both adjust the perceived speed of the fade. In effect, the inner length controls the length of time the ducked track is attenuated by the full Duck amount. If you play with the fade lengths, you will be able to see this in the graph.

Threshold: The level (0 to -100 dB RMS. Default: -30 dB RMS) used for detecting a signal in the control track.

BASS AND TREBLE

What it is? This is one of the oldest methods of equalization. It controls the amount of bass (low frequencies) and treble (higher frequencies) of your audio independently see fig 2-7. It the same thing as the bass, treble and volume controls on your domestic stereo system. There are no set values to use, you just must use again your ears.

Bass (dB): The amount of gain (amplification above 0 dB or attenuation below 0 dB) to low (bass frequencies). Set this to a positive amount to boost the bass, or a negative amount to reduce the bass. Bass gain is applied to frequencies lower than 1,000 Hz, with the most gain being applied to frequencies about 100 Hz or lower.

Treble (dB): The amount of gain (amplification above 0 dB or attenuation below 0 dB) to high frequencies. Set this to a positive amount to boost the treble, while a negative amount will reduce the treble. Treble gain is applied to frequencies higher than 1,000 Hz, with the most gain being applied to frequencies above 10,000 Hz.

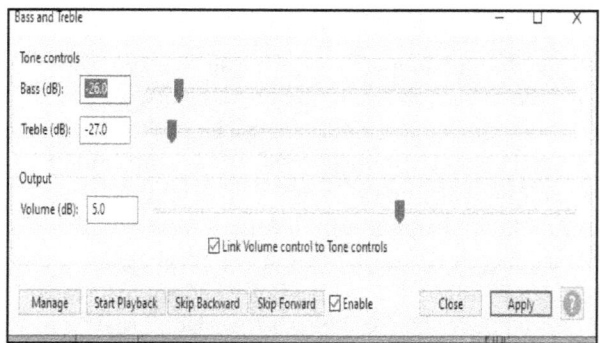

Fig 2-7 Bass and treble box

Volume (dB): This increases or reduces the overall level by up to +/- 30 dB. If you apply a boost to the bass or treble, it will tend to increase the overall level. As a result, the final level may be pushed so high that it distorts (clips). To avoid clipping, reduce the level by setting the Volume control lower. While if you reduce the bass or treble it may make the final level too quiet. To compensate for the lower level, set the Volume control higher.

If both the treble and bass frequencies are increased and the overall volume lowered, the overall effect is a reduction in the middle frequencies. Similarly, reducing both the bass and treble and increasing the volume has an overall effect of boosting the middle frequencies.

Link Volume control to Tone controls: When this is enabled (checked), adjusting either the Bass or Treble controls will automatically adjust the Volume control so as to lessen the change in the resulting output level approximately the same.

Even if you do link the Volume control, the overall output level may still change a little, depending on the frequency content depending on how much the bass or treble are changed. Therefore, always check the Playback Meter Toolbar for possible clipping when trying out different bass and treble settings. Even when linked, you can still adjust the Volume control independently of the tone controls.

CHANGE PITCH

What is it? It changes the pitch of a selected tone. It can lower or raise it. By changing the pitch, you can make a singer sound lower or higher. Of all effects this one can quickly go over done and you will end sounding like a chipmunk or a demon and create an unnatural sound. It can also be used to create a chorus effect.

Back in the old days of analog recording to change the pitch you had to change speed that the tape was recording or played back. This took great skill because too much of a change and the voice or sound unnatural quickly.

To change the pitch and not affect the track layout use Change pitch effect. Change Pitch works by applying an up or down percentage change to the existing pitch of a selection. As well as choosing the percent change directly you can define it as: a change from one pitch to another a change in semitones or a change from one frequency to another.

Note: Change Pitch senses the first detectable pitch in a selection and sets "Pitch from" and "Frequency (Hz) from" accordingly. These two controls are not a detection of the "key" or "tonality" of music.

TOOLS:

Pitch: If you know both the key the original recording is in and the key you want to change it to, change both the Pitch "from" and "to" values. If you don't Audacity will estimate starting pitch. This appears at the top of the box when it opens, which it takes form the selected part of the track. It lists it on both the tone letter and the Hz reading. It is best to zoom in on the track and change pitch by single note, especially on vocals, instead of a large selection this because Audacity attempts to detect the pitch of the most meaningful note, if this is large selection it will be at the start of the selection or the loudest note. For example, if you have a very short, quiet note on A3 followed by a longer, louder note on C4 Audacity will probably detect C4 but if the second note is the same volume, then Audacity will probably detect A3.

Semitones (half-steps): If you do not know the key the original recording is in, but you know how many semitones it needs to be changed, enter that value here. For example: you could duplicate a vocal track and then apply Change Pitch with a value of +7 semitones (a major fifth) to create a harmony vocal. We will cover this more later in another chapter.

If you change the Pitch "to" note when the "from" and to" octaves are the same, this could mean either an increase or decrease in pitch depending on the "from" Pitch. So, it is recommended to check in the "Semitones (half-steps)" box if the value is going down (minus sign) or up (no sign) as you intend. If you need to change pitch in the other direction you can change the semitones value instead (see the example below) or change the "to" octave number.

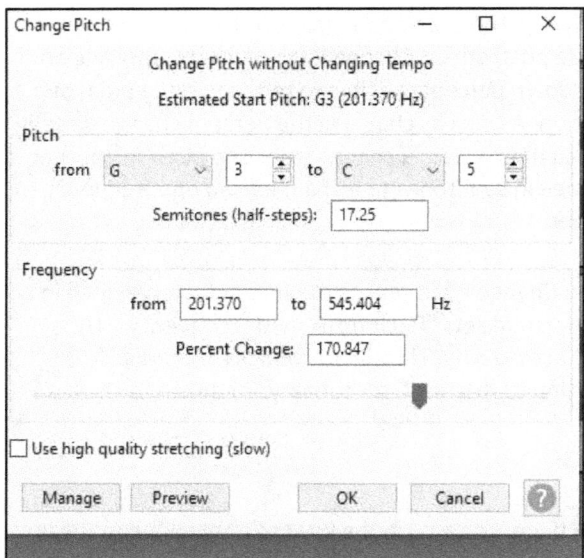

Fig 2-8 Change Pitch box and controls

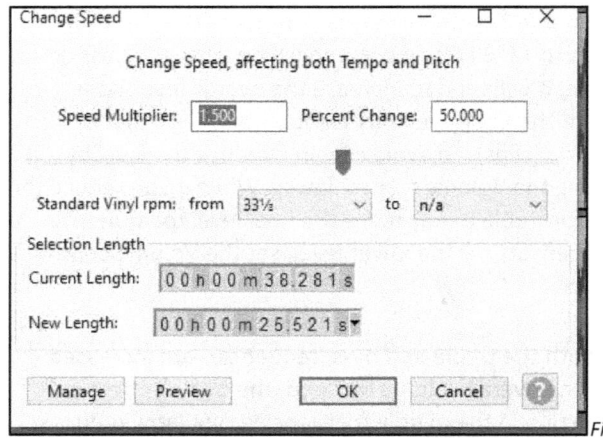

Fig 2-9 change speed box.

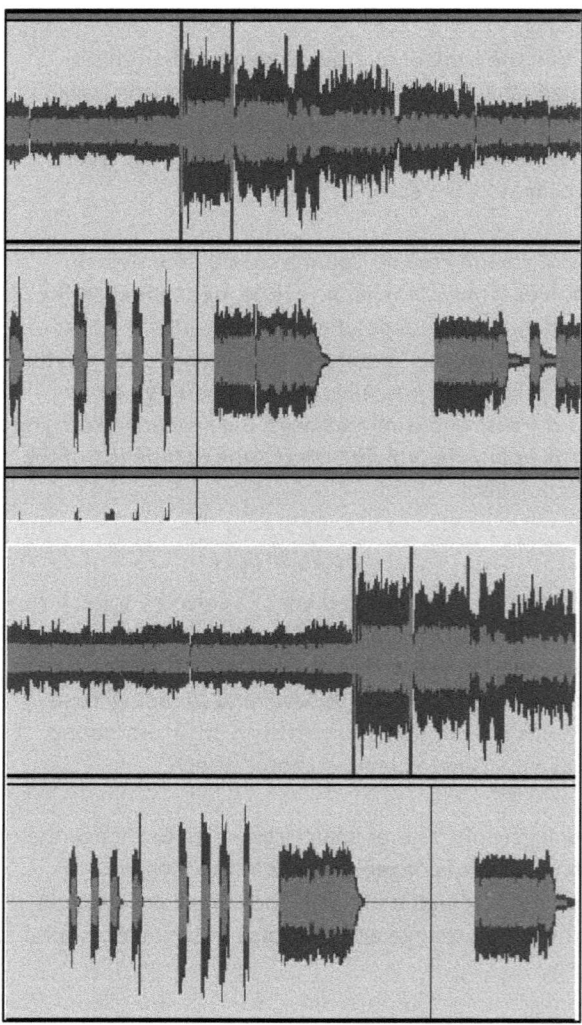

Fig 2-10 How speed change can affect the track layout. The above photo is the lead guitar track before the speed change was applied. The bottom photo is with a 1.5 speed change (yes this is a larger change, but we wanted it to be noticeable). Notice how before the lead guitar riff is embedded in the track of the rhythm guitar, but after the change the lead guitar riff is now in front of the rhythm guitar. This sounds awful. The change this back click Control Z or click the undo button on the menu bar.

Frequency (Hz): The "from" input box initializes to the first meaningful detected pitch in the selection and does not update if the other controls are changed. However, if you know the original frequency and the frequency you want to change to, you can enter these in the "from" and "to" boxes. Detection of a steady sine tone will often be very accurate (with the upper frequency limitation noted below) in which case you may only need to change the "to" input box to the desired frequency for the tone.

Percent Change: If you would like to change the pitch by a given percent, enter a value in this input box or use the slider.

Use High Quality Stretching (slow): If this checkbox is enabled, the same SBSMS high quality algorithm is used that is used in the Sliding Stretch effect. Change Pitch will process much more slowly if this checkbox is enabled, but the exact length of the selection will be preserved. For small to moderate tempo changes, the resulting quality will usually be higher, especially with percussive music (such as piano music). Vocals are not affected that much with this.

CHANGE SPEED

What is it? It changes the speed fig 2-9 and 2-10 of the playback of the recording. It does not change the speed of the recording itself. But it will simulate this. Again, this is one of those tricky effects, and has to be added like hot sauce, small little does is what you use. This is because using change speed will greatly affect the tempo, pitch and frequency content. So, use it very wisely and it little amounts or your project will quickly become the foundation for cartoon land.

This effect is the play back not the recording speed and thus is the opposite that effect. Slowing down the recording speed will increase the tone when played back, however when reducing playback speed all frequencies become lower. Like when increasing playback speed, all frequencies become higher.

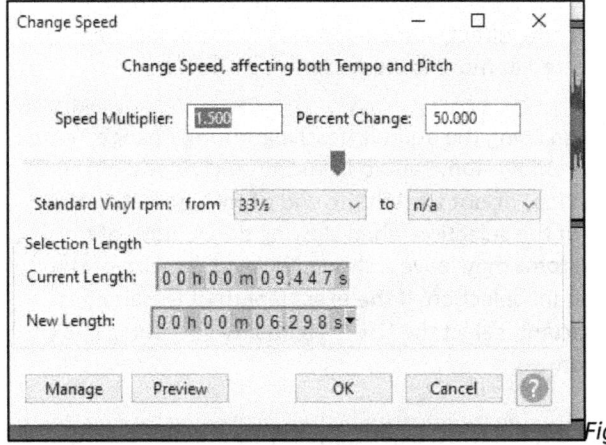

Fig 2-11 The change speed effect box.

To change tempo without affecting pitch or frequency range, see Change Tempo or Sliding Stretch. Note all controls are linked, so if you change one the others will change. Another drawback to this effect is when it is used it will throw timing off from the other tracks. See figure 2-10.

TOOLS

Speed Multiplier: This sets how many times faster or slower the audio will play. For example, setting this to "2.000" will double the speed (and raise the pitch by one octave), or setting this to "0.500" will halve the playback speed (and lower the pitch by one octave).

Values between 0.010 (1/100th of the original speed) and 50.000 (50 times faster) are permitted. Values outside of this range will gray out the OK and Preview buttons showing this value cannot be applied.

Percent Change: If you know how much you want to change the speed of the audio in percent, enter that value here. You can also drag the slider to choose a Percent Change - the input box and the Speed Multiplier will update as you drag the slider.

Values between -99.000 % (equivalent to 1/100th of the original speed) and 4900.000 % (equivalent to 50 times faster) are permitted. Values outside of this range will gray out the OK and Preview buttons and cannot be applied.

Standard Vinyl RPM: If you have ever owned a record player you have played a 33-1/3 record at 45 RPM and "Oh Sweet." come out sounding like 'Chicky by Bo'. Or you played a 45 RPM single at 33-1/3 and a blazing guitar solo sound like a funeral march. This will be the same thing here, where you use the drop-down menu to select which one you want to use.

Selection Length: The Current Length time control indicates the length of the current selection. This control is for information only and cannot be modified.: **The New Length Time:** control sets the length that the selection will be after applying the effect.

The Selection Format may be changed by selecting the required option from the dropdown menu of the New Length control. To access the dropdown menu, click the little black downwards-pointing triangle on the right end of the time control, right-click over any of its time digits, or select any of the digits then use the keyboard Menu Key. Changing the format in the New Length control will also update the digits in the Current Length control.

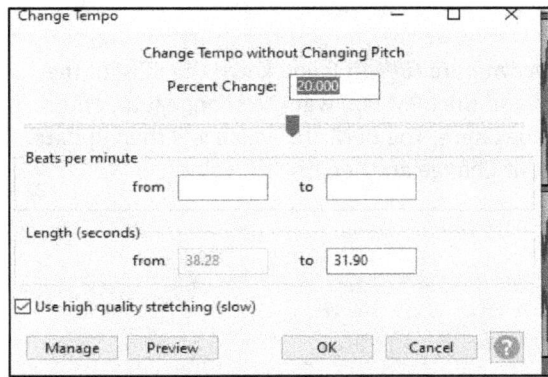

Fig 2-12 Tempo change box

CHANGE TEMPO

What is it? It boosts the channel make it sound faster while not changing the speed of the playback, meaning you won't sound like a cartoon character. Oh, a blessing huh? One big drawback it does by changing the length of the selected track. This can throw the timing off from the other tracks, causing it to sound awful. See fig 2-13. So, it is best to use the effect on one track and make other match or apply to all track or better used during mastering.

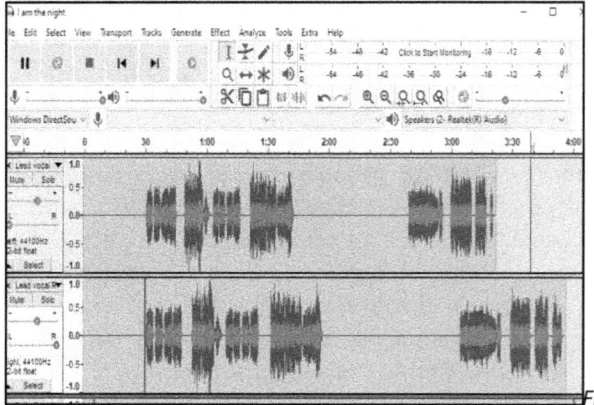

Fig 2-13 Notice we applied a temp change of 20% to just one vocal track (top) and left the other one unchanged to show how much it shrinks the original track. Now when played back the music will be in line with the bottom track but ay out of step with the track that the effect was applied to.

Note like the Change Speed effect the input boxes are linked. Therefore, changing the value in one box will change the values in other boxes as appropriate.

Percent Change: If you know the amount you want to change the tempo of the selection, enter that value in the input box. You can also drag the slider to select a value: the input box will update as you drag the slider.

Beats per minute (BPM): If you know the BPM of the selection and the BPM you want to change it to, enter those values here. The BPM "to" value will then update the Percent Change and Length "to" values.

Length: If you know what you would like the new length of the selection to be, enter that value in the to input box. The from box shows the current length of the selection and cannot be changed. This is useful if you have a piece of narration that is just a little bit too long or too short to fit where you want it.

Use High Quality Stretching (Slow): If this checkbox is enabled, the same SBSMS high quality algorithm is used that is used in the Sliding Stretch effect. Change Tempo will process much more slowly if this checkbox is enabled but will retain the complete content. For small to moderate tempo changes, the resulting quality will usually be higher, especially with percussive music (such as piano music).

Limitations: Change Tempo is a time-stretching effect because it defies the normal expectation that reducing the speed of the audio (thus increasing its length) will reduce the pitch and vice versa. As with any time-stretching effect, some audible distortions will be expected at more extreme settings.

When using the default (fast) algorithm, Change Tempo may remove some audio from the start or end of the selection, or not stretch the end of the content to the end of the selection when slowing down. Both of these symptoms may leave a short silence at the end of the resultant selection. If the exact length of the audio is important, select the Use high quality stretching (slow) option.

The default (fast) algorithm may sometimes sound echoey, especially when slowing down percussive music. For small to moderate tempo changes, use the "high quality" option to avoid this problem.

Fig 2-14 classic filters contains several differ filters that are obtained from the drop down menu under filter type.

The "high quality" algorithm is only suitable for small to moderate tempo changes and the sound quality will deteriorate very badly for extreme changes. For extreme slowing down, consider using the *Paulstretch* effect.

CLASSIC FILTERS

WHAT IS IT? Classic Filters offers three different types of filters which together emulate the vast majority of analog filters, providing a useful graphical tool for analysis and measurement. It is used to control the high and low frequencies. This effect is not enabled by default. To enable it, use Effect > Add / Remove Plug-ins... to open the Plug-in Manager box.

TOOLS

On the Vertical Scale: is in dB and shows the amount of gain (amplification above 0 dB or attenuation below 0 dB) that will be applied to the audio at any given frequency. See fig 2-14

The Horizontal Scale: This shows the frequencies in Hz to which volume adjustments will be applied. Dragging the Classic Filters window wider displays some additional points on the scale. Fig 2-14

On the far-right hand side are the vertical scale sliders: By default, the vertical scale reads from 0 dB to -10 dB, but these two sliders to left of the scale let you adjust the upper- and lower-dB values so as to change the visible range on the graph. Note that moving either slider may change the horizontal position of the 0 dB line.

Filter Type

Butterworth: An analog Butterworth filter provides a "maximally flat" passband (ie. no ripples), the magnitude response at the cutoff frequency is -3 dB, and above (for low pass) or below (for high pass) the cutoff frequency, the attenuation increases at approximately 6 dB per octave times the filter order (so for example 60 dB per octave for 10th order).

Chebyshev Type I: Chebyshev Type I filters are similar to Butterworth filters, except that a) the magnitude response of the passband has "ripples" in it (usually small), b) at the cutoff frequency the magnitude response is equal to the ripple value, and c) above (below for high pass) the cutoff frequency, the stopband attenuation increases more rapidly, for a given filter order, than Butterworth.

Chebyshev Type II: Chebyshev Type II filters are similar to Butterworth, including the flat passband response, except that a) at the cutoff frequency the magnitude response is equal to the ripple value, b) above (below for high pass) the cutoff frequency, the stopband attenuation increases more rapidly, for a given filter order, than Butterworth, and c) the stopband attenuation varies from infinite to the ripple value. (Here it is common to use a ripple value of 20, 30 or more dB).

Subtype: Lowpass: The filter passes low frequencies and attenuates high frequencies. Highpass: The filter passes high frequencies and attenuates low frequencies.

Order Choose a value between 1 and 10. "1" - first-order filters - have the most gradual cutoff slope.

Cutoff Enter the cutoff frequency. Anything above this number will be cut off.

Passband Ripple: For Butterworth filters no value can be entered and any value displayed is ignored. For Chebyshev Type I filters type in the acceptable amount of passband ripple. Higher values of passband ripple will also increase the cutoff slope For Chebyshev Type II filters no value can be entered, and any value displayed is ignored.

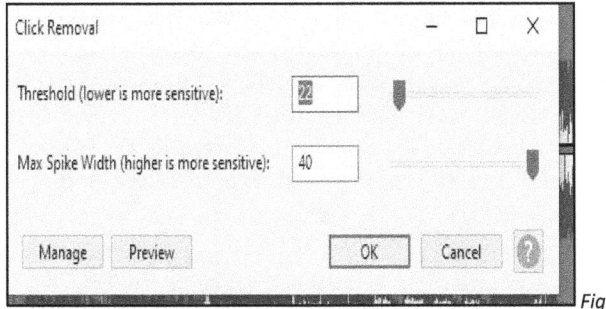

Fig 2-15 Click removal box.

CLICK REMOVAL

What Is it? What is to remove the click track that you created? *Buzz wrong answer.* It might seem that would be the correct answer, or question If we are playing *Jeopardy*. Remove that click track is simple as clicking on the X and it is gone.

What this effect does I much more than that. No instead it attempts to remove clicks on audio tracks and is especially suited to '*declicking'* recordings made from vinyl records, without damaging the rest of the audio. However, it is beneficial to other types of tracks like guitar tracks which can tone down the spikes that are causing the track to clip.

Threshold: Entering a lower value or moving the slider left will detect softer clicks. Setting this too low may cause false click detection and damage the audio. Setting it too high may leave audible clicks that you would rather it removed.

TOOLS

Max Spike Width: Enter a value or move the slider to set the length of the spike that is considered to be a click. Setting this too high may cause false click detection and damage the audio. Setting it too low may leave audible clicks that you would rather it removed.

If Click Removal displays a message that the algorithm is not effective on the audio and nothing changed, try making a larger selection. Lowering the Threshold value or increasing the Max Spike Width may also enable Click Removal to act on the audio. Note that click Removal requires an audio selection of more than 4096 samples. This is about 93 milliseconds at 44,100 Hz project rate as shown in Selection Toolbar. The Click Removal algorithm does not work on all clicks, and so may trigger the "not effective" message above even on a full selection that has some clicks.

Very soft and rapid light ticks that sound like crackle from static electricity (often heard on recordings from vinyl records) will not be effectively removed. For this type of noise, you should use the Noise Reduction effect.

If individual brief or subtle clicks are not dealt with by Click Removal, try the Repair effect on those individual clicks. Repair can work on a selection up to 128 samples wide (about three milliseconds at 44,100 Hz project rate).

Broader clicks of 10 milliseconds or longer may not be removed. In this case there are a couple of optional Nyquist Plugins that you can install. Use *PopMute* to heavily attenuate loud clicks and pops to make them less obtrusive. Really loud and wide glitches that still sound too bad can be repaired by using EZ-Patch to replace the glitch with adjacent undamaged audio.

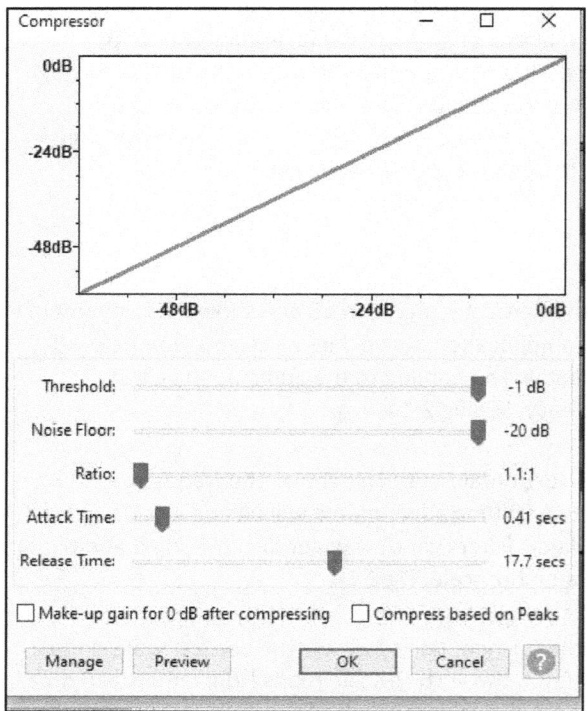

Fig 2-16 the Compressor is one of the most valuable effects there is. The right amount can be a lifesaver to drowning track, but too much can destroy it.

COMPRESSOR

What is it? A device that compresses an audio signal. To make a section louder and stand out. It was first invented to make live music fit into the parameters of TV and radio or vinyl record and tape. For this reason, it was thought that compression would die in the digital age. Instead, the compressor is more popular than ever, with more variations on the basic concept than ever before.

Want to know what it sounds like? Ever notice you are listening to an old TV show, late at night while everyone else is asleep and you must crank it a way up to hear the show, then a commercial comes on and BOOM it wakes up everyone in the house. Well, that is just because it is an old show and wasn't recorded with Dolby sound, possible. However, this happens even if it is a new show. Are commercials louder? It is not your imagination, nor it is not due to your equipment. As I have heard experts in electronics tell me. It is due to the signal on the ad being compressed and the other not. Yes, this is done on purpose for this reason, to make it stand out. And this is used recording to make a track stand out.

Compression is often misused because of the way we hear. Our ear/brain combination can differentiate among very fine pitch changes, but not amplitude. So, there is a tendency to over compress until you can "hear the effect," this usually gives everything an unnatural sound and most beginners will do this.

Until you've trained your ears to recognize subtle amounts of compression, you should watch the compressor's gain reduction meter, which shows how much the signal is being compressed. You may be surprised to find that even with 6dB of compression, you don't hear much apparent difference—therefore it is important to listen to it again without compression, then you will notice the change.

Graph: Is the biggest item in the box and moving or changing the controls will affect this graph. Move the control sliders around and watch how the line on the graph responses. The higher the bar goes the more compression is being applied. The lower the less. You may have notice that only when moving the threshold or the ratio sliders does the graph line move, however they will greatly affect the sound output.

The graph shows the input level along the bottom (horizontal axis) and the output level scale on the left (vertical axis) to illustrate the dynamic range compression effect.

TOOLS

Threshold: sets the level at where compression will begin. Above this level, the output increases at a lesser rate than the corresponding input change. As a result, with lower thresholds, more of the signal gets compressed. Again, push the slider to the left and then the right and watch how the line changes. See fig 2-17.

Noise Floor: The compressor adjusts the gain on audio below this background level to prevent it being unduly amplified in processing. This is mainly useful when compressing speech, for like a podcast to prevent the gain increasing during pauses and so over-amplifying the background noise. It really does not have much use in music or singing tracks.

Ratio: The amount of compression applied to the audio once it passes the threshold level. The higher the Ratio the more the loud parts of the audio will be compressed. The Ratio sets the slope of the blue line on the graph above the threshold. For example, with 4:1 compression, a 16dB increase at the input gives a 4dB increase at the output. With "infinite" compression, the output remains constant no matter how much you pump up the input. Bottom line: Higher ratios increase the effect of the compression

Attack Time: How soon the compressor starts to compress the dynamics after the threshold is exceeded. If volume changes are slow, you can push this to a high value. Short attack times will result in a fast response to sudden, loud sounds; however, it will make the changes in volume much more obvious to listeners.

Release Time: also called Decay is how soon the compressor starts to release the volume level back to normal after the level drops below the threshold. A long-time value will tend to lose quiet sounds that come after loud ones but will avoid the volume being raised too much during short quiet sections like pauses in speech. Short time is also good on special effects, like the 1960's psychedelic '60s drum sounds.

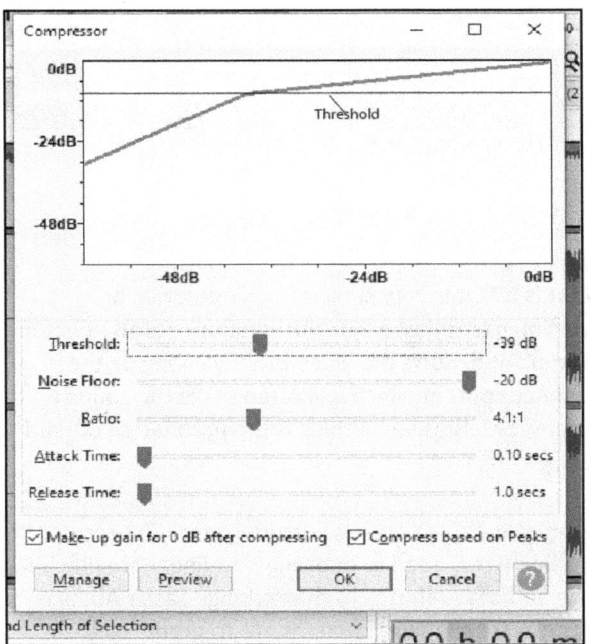

Fig 2.17 The point where the blue line bends is the threshold.

Make-up gain for 0 dB: After compressing: Amplifies the resultant audio in all selected tracks after compression to a peak level of 0 dB. All tracks are amplified by the same amount as in the Amplify effect. This is great to use in the final mix down and all tracks are selected or in the mastering section.

Compress Based on Peaks: Base the threshold and gain adjustment on peak values of the waveform rather than the average (RMS) value used when in default (unchecked) state. When using RMS, the compressor uses "downward" compression, making louder sounds above the threshold quieter while leaving quieter ones below it untouched. When using peak values, "upwards" compression is applied which makes the audio louder but amplifies the louder sounds above the threshold progressively less than those below it. When the original (input) level is 0 dB there is no amplification.

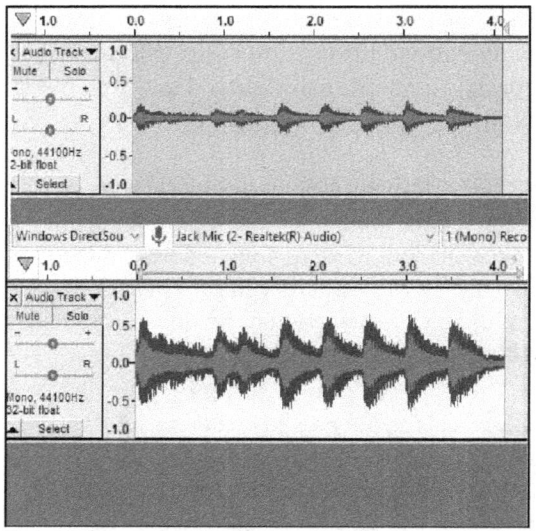

Fig 2-18 The top photo is without added distortion, below is with distortion. Notice the increase in sound.

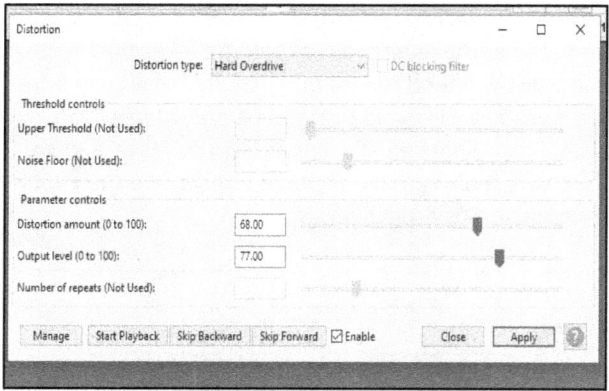

Fig 2-18 The distortion effect box

DISTORTION

What is it? It is very similar to an overdrive or distortion pedal that used with a guitar or is an effect on the amp. It distorts the waveform by changing the frequency content which will often make the sound 'crunchy' or 'abrasive'. Which is the foundation of hard rock.

Technically this effect is a '*wave-shaper*'. The result of wave being reshaped to applying non-linear amplification to the audio waveform. To make things easier Audacity added preset shaping functions are to produces a different types of distortion.

For more "analog" sounding distortion, the track should be resampled to a high sampling rate so as to reduce aliasing-an error in the wave. So, make sure it is sampled at last 44k. Equalization may also be applied, before or after applying the distortion effect to modify the timbre of the distorted audio.

TOOLS

DISTORTION TYPE: These are the shaping functions. Each type defines how the input signal is mapped to the output level. You notice when you through the list of the output boxes change according to the type of distortion. Each one will have set parameters for each type of distortion. However, you can change these by moving the sliders or typing in an amount   These include:

1. **Hard Clipping**
2. **Soft Clipping**
3. **Soft Overdrive**
4. **Medium Overdrive**
5. **Hard Overdrive**
6. **Odd Harmonic**
7. **Even Harmonic**
8. **Expand and Compress**
9. **Leveller**
10. **Rectifier Distortion**
11. **Hard Limiter 1413**

Hard Clipping: This type of distortion cuts off peaks at the top and bottom of the waveform. Note that hard clipping is very likely to cause aliasing distortion, which may be undesirable. It boxes include:

Clipping level (-100 to 0 dB): Peaks greater than this level are cut off. The slider control has a logarithmic scale to allow settings close to 0 dB to be made more easily and accurately.

Drive (0 to 100): When set to greater than 0, the waveform is amplified this amount (dB) prior to being clipped.

Make-up Gain (0 to 100): When set greater than 0, the output from the effect is amplified. When set to 100, the amplification is such that an input level of 0 dB (full track height) will produce an output level of 0 dB.

Soft Clipping This type of distortion is similar to Hard Clipping except that 'corners' where clipping intersects with the waveform are rounded. This is achieved by progressively reducing the gain when the input is above the clipping threshold. The softer the clipping, the more rounded the clipped peaks and the less risk of aliasing distortion.

Threshold (-100 to 0 dB): The level at which gain reduction (clipping) starts. The slider control has a logarithmic scale to allow settings close to 0 dB to be made more easily and accurately.

Hardness (0 to 100): The 'hardness' of the clipping (100 % being "hard").

Make-up Gain (0 to 100): When set greater than 0, the output from the effect is amplified. When set to 100, the amplification is such that an input level of 0 dB (full track height) will produce an output level of 0 dB.

Note that even without "Make-up Gain", the output level may be higher than the clipping threshold because the peaks are in effect 'squashed' flatter rather than being completely cut off.

Soft Overdrive: This is the "softest" of the overdrive types and produces the least amount of high harmonics. It can be useful for reducing the dynamic range (thus increasing the sustain of musical instruments) while adding the least amount of "crunch" to the sound.

Distortion Amount (0 to 100): The amount / strength of the distortion.

Output level (0 to 100): An output level adjustment. When set to 0 the output is silent.

Medium Overdrive: *Distortion* amount (0 to 100): The amount / strength of the distortion.

Output level: (0 to 100): An output level adjustment. When set to 0 the output is silent.

Hard Overdrive: This is the "hardest" of the overdrive types and produces the greatest number of high harmonics. This would typically be used for producing a heavily distorted effect. Like heavy metal sound.

Distortion Amount (0 to 100): The amount / strength of the distortion.

Output Level (0 to 100): An output level adjustment. When set to 0 the output is silent.

Harmonic Distortion: These types of distortion create a series of odd or even harmonics. "Odd" harmonics have frequencies that are an odd number of times higher than the fundamental frequency, whereas even harmonics are an even number of times higher than the fundamental frequency. For example, the second harmonic of a 440 Hz sine wave is a sine wave with a frequency of 880 Hz. Note that because real world sounds contain many frequencies, these distortion effects are unlikely to create recognizable "harmony" type sounds, but rather will produce distortion with a unique tonal character. This type of distortion is similar to the warm tube sound.

Cubic Curve (odd harmonics): This shaping function is often used in electric guitar distortion effects as it is possible to avoid aliasing distortion with only a modest amount of oversampling. This implementation does not use oversampling, though oversampling can be applied manually by resampling the track to a higher rate prior to applying this distortion effect.

One limitation of this type of distortion is that even when applied fully, the effect is still quite mild. Stronger effects can be achieved by applying the algorithm multiple times, which can be achieved by setting the "Repeat processing" control greater than 0.

When applied once only, each frequency component of the sound gains one harmonic overtone that is 3 times the original frequency. When the effect is applied multiple times, additional odd numbered harmonics are created.

Distortion Amount (0 to 100): The amount / strength of the distortion.

Output Level (0 to 100): An output level adjustment. When set to 0 the output is silent.

Repeat Processing (0 to 5): The number of times to repeat the distortion algorithm. When set to 0 the effect is applied once only.

Even Harmonics: This type of distortion produces a series of harmonics that are 2, 4, 6... times the frequency of the original waveform (even numbers). Producing even harmonics requires that the waveform is distorted asymmetrically, which if not corrected will produce substantial DC offset. To counter the DC offset, a DC blocking filter is provided.

DC blocking filter When this box is checked, a low frequency filter is applied which will reduce the DC component of the processed audio.

Distortion Amount (0 to 100): The amount / strength of the distortion.

Harmonic Brightness (0 to 100): Higher values produce a greater number of harmonics.

Expand and Compress: It distorts by compressing or expanding the signal. It contains these boxes:

Distortion Amount (0 to 100): The amount / strength of the distortion.

Output Level (0 to 100): An output level adjustment. When set to 0 the output is silent.

Leveller: The Leveller effect makes quiet passages louder and loud passages quieter. It does this in a way that is different from the Compressor effect and will add some distortion to the processed audio. Tools include.

Noise floor (-80 to -20): [default = -70] This is equivalent to the "Noise Threshold" setting in the original "Leveller" effect. It sets the noise threshold for the effect. For audio that is not already at maximum volume, higher threshold settings tend to amplify the audio by a lesser amount and may reduce the chance of background noise becoming obtrusive.

Parameter Controls:

Levelling Fine Adjustment (0 to 100): [default = 0] This is an additional control that was not available in the original effect. It allows fine adjustment of the amounts of "levelling".

Degree of Levelling (0 to 5): [default = 1] Controls the amount of levelling that is applied to the signal. When the fine adjustment is at zero, the amounts 0 to 5 are equivalent to the original effect choices: 1 = Light, 2 = Moderate, 3 = Heavy, 4 = Heavier, 5 = Heaviest.

Rectifier Distortion: This type of distortion is modeled on a simple electronic component called a rectifier. The boxes include on it are:

DC Blocking Filter When this box is checked, a low frequency filter is applied which will reduce the DC component of the processed audio.

Distortion Amount (0 to 100): The amount / strength of the distortion. From 0 to 50 % the lower half of the waveform is progressively clipped (hard clipping) until at 50 % only the upper half of the waveform remains (equivalent to half wave rectification. From 50 to 100 %, the lower half of the input waveform is progressively reproduced on the positive side (upper half) of the audio channel, until at 100% the waveform comprises of the upper half plus the inverted lower half of the original waveform (equivalent to full wave rectification)

Hard Limiter 1413: This type of distortion is modeled on the "Hard Limiter" LADSPA plug-in that was included in older versions of Audacity. The default settings are different from the original effect (the original defaults would produce no effect). The boxes here include:

dB Limit (-100 to 0dB): [default = -6] This is the amplitude level above which the input signal is processed. If the Wet level is 100% and Residue level 0%, the peak level of the result will be clipped down to this level.

Wet Level (-100 to 0dB): [default = 50] This is the percentage of the clipped signal that is fed to the output. It thus acts as a volume control for audio below the dB limit. When set to 100%, all sounds below the dB limit are fed to the output. At lower settings, the volume of the result will be reduced.

Residue Level (-100 to 0dB): [default = 50] This allows a proportion of the signal that has been removed by clipping to be added back to the output and so soften the effect. When set to 0%, all of the clipped signal is discarded. At the higher settings, some of the clipped signal will be restored, making the limit softer. More peaks and troughs of the original waveform will be retained, and the resultant volume level will be higher than that set in the dB limit.

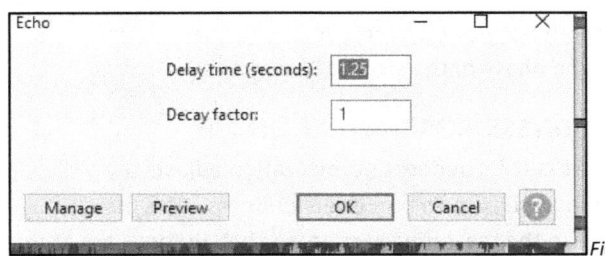

Fig 2-19 Echo effect box

ECHO

What is it?: This effect repeats the audio you have selected again and again, normally softer each time. The delay time between each repeat is fixed, with no pause in between each repeat. It only has two tools to work with. Fig 2-19

Delay: The amount of delay between the echoes, in other words the length of each echo.

Decay Factor: Usually a number between 0 and 1. A value of 0 means no echo, and a value of 1 means that each echo is exactly as loud as the original, so this merely extends the current selection unchanged. A value of 0.5 reduces the amplitude or loudness of each echo by half each time, so the audio dies out quite slowly. Smaller values make it die out more quickly. Values above 1 increase the amplitude of the echo each time, which you could use as a special effect.

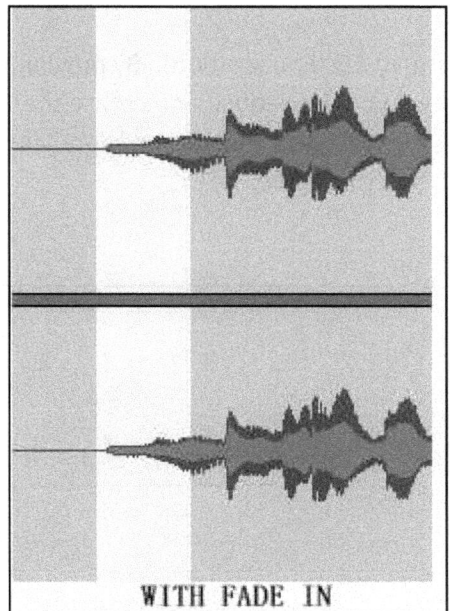

Fig 2-20 Fade In effect

FADE IN

What is it? Simple fades in fig 2-20 a selected track. No tools, automatically happens.

FADE OUT

What is it? Simple fades in fig 2-21 a selected track. No tools, automatically happens.

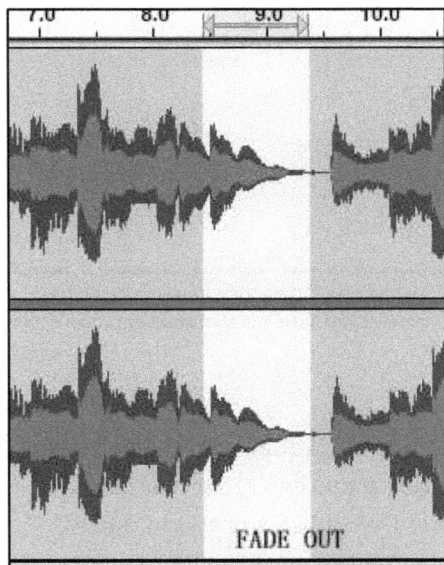

Fig 2-21 Fade out effect

FILTER CURVE

What is it? A form of EQ (Equalization). By moving the line up or down you can reduce or increase the different tones. We will cover this in more detail in the mixing section of this guide.

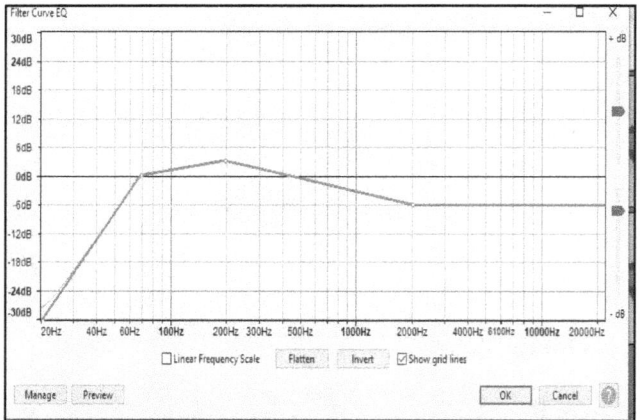

Fig 20-22 Filter curve is a form of EQ

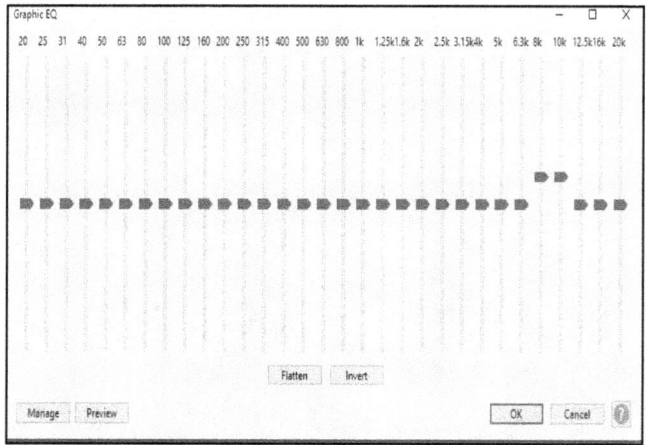

Fig 2-23 The Graphic EQ works much like a traditional mixing board, move the sliders up to increase the output of that Frequency and down to soften or remove it.

GRAPHIC EQ

What is it? A form of EQ (Equalization). By moving the sliders up or down you can reduce or increase the different tones. We will cover this in more detail in the mixing section of this guide.

Fig 2-24 Invert simply switch the top part and the bottom half of the signals.

INVERT

What is it? It cuts the signal in half and the bottom part is now the top and the top is the bottom. Fig 2-24. Why would this be important?

Phase is a simple solution to a common audio problem. Sometimes the signal on a particular track is out of phase with the rest of the music, leading it to sounding thin and without body or presence. So, it becomes important to flip the phase of the signal 180 degrees.

LOUDNESS NORMALIZATION

What is it? Loudness normalization adjusts the recording based on perceived loudness. This mainly done in the mastering section, so that all songs are at the same level, and the listener does not have to switch volume up and down. Normalization differs from dynamic range compression, which applies varying levels of gain over a recording to fit the level within a minimum and maximum range. Fig 2-25 normalization adjusts the gain by a constant value across the entire recording.

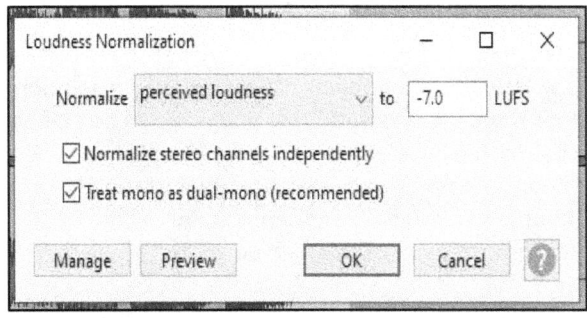

Fig 2-25 Loudness normalization can figure by Perceived loudness or the RMS factor. There are certain guidelines to what the value should be, we will cover this in the mastering section.

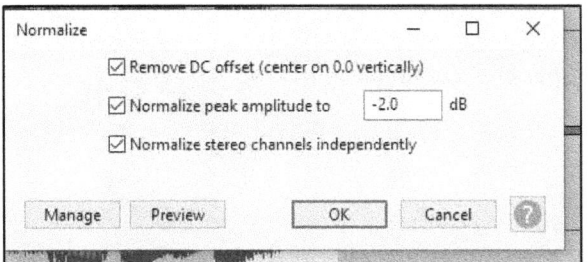

Fig 2-26 Normalize is not usually used in music production and can destroy work.

NORMALIZE

What is it? Audio normalization is a process that increases the level of a recording by a constant amount so that it reaches a target—or norm. Normalization applies the same level increase to the entire duration of an audio file. Normalization is typically used to scale the level of track or file to just within its available maximum. Fig 2-26

It is not used much in music production except to sample music as in Rap and Hip Hop. Too many beginners are looking for the easiest way to make their songs loud. It's a common mistake to think that normalization plays a role. There are many better methods, to accomplish this and it will be covered in the Mastering section.

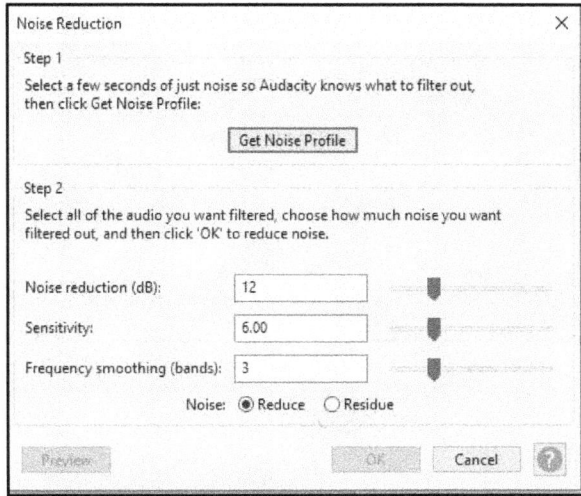

Fig 2-27 Noise reduction box.

NOISE REDUCTION

What is it? Just as the name implies It removes background noise like hum and buzz that is so common in recording. Fig 2-27

TOOLS

Get Noise Profile: This tool analyzes a selected selection of noise to make recommendation of the amount of noise that will become the threshold for the remove of noise. This will appear in the boxes below.

Reduce button will reduce the selected amount of noise, to hear the amount that will be reduced, but not have it take place. Click the *Residue* button than Preview. If the track has been harmed by the reduction, decrease the *sensitivity* amount

Frequency Smoothing can reduce the perception of noise artifacts by spreading them out over one or more frequency bands. This parameter goes from 0 to 12, there are no set guidelines. As a pod cast will use different level then a Rap song, and Rap song will used different levels then a heavy rock song. Use the preview button to listen to what the changes are. a podcast the spoken voices all settings should be between 5-7. For the music each time is going to be different you will just have to find 'the sweet spot'.

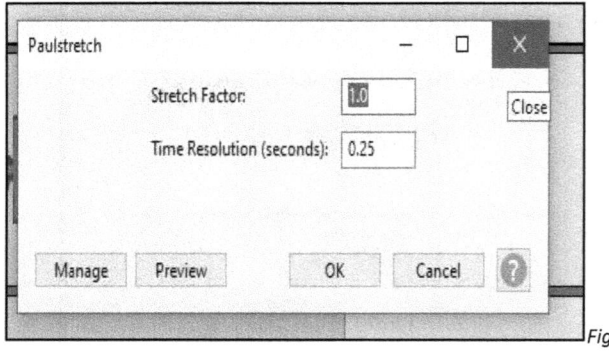

2-28 Paulstretch Box

PAULSTRETCH

What is It? No this is not some dude named Paul stretching to get the last doughnut in the box. No instead, the slows down the audio without changing the pitch. It is a straightforward effect if only two things that can be changed.

Stretch Factor: This sets how much longer the processed sound will be relative to the original. For example, setting this to 10 will stretch 1 minute of audio into approximately 10 minutes of audio, somewhat less at higher Time Resolutions.

Time Resolution (Seconds): In order for the effect to work, this value must be smaller than the selected area in the waveform. Small values have good time resolution, but poor frequency resolution, so you may still be able to detect a rhythm (albeit a very slow rhythm). Large values have poor time resolution, but have great frequency resolution, so transients will disappear, but pitch differences may be better preserved.

Usually, a value of 0.25 seconds is good for most music. Very large values (greater than 2 seconds) can be used for special effects such as "smearing" a song into a sound-texture, even if the Stretch Factor is close to 1.0 run it with a 'phaser effect on the guitar, and with the Reverse effect in Audacity you can really create some wild special effect sounds.

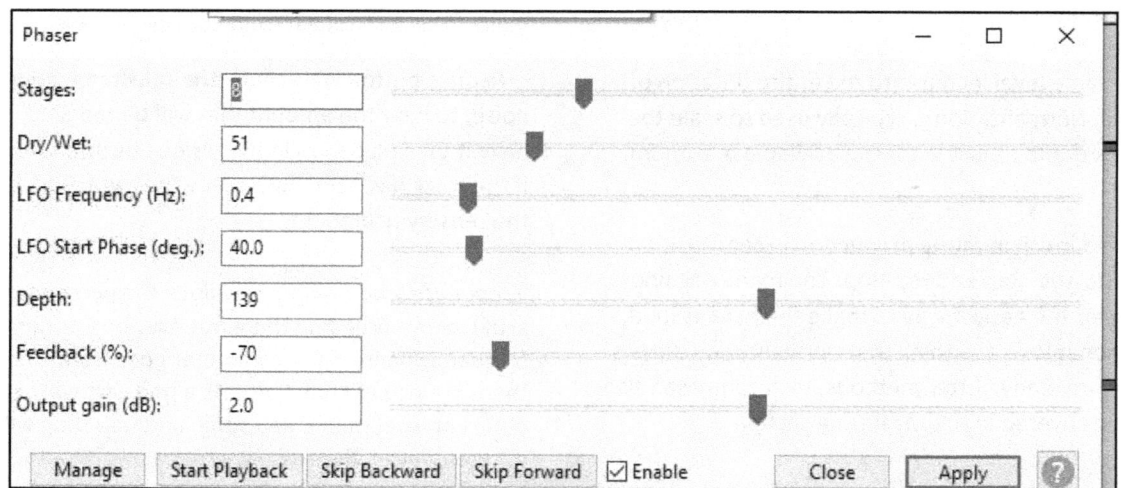

Fig 2-29 Phaser effect box

PHASER

What is it? This is one of those words that depending on who you are is to what you see. The average individual thinks of Star Trek ° thinks of the laser gun on the TV show. To a guitarist it is an effect pedal that create some awesome effects. In audio mixer it is a special effect that can be used to create unique sounds. It is called a Phaser because it works by combining phase-shifted signals with the original signal. The movement of the phase-shifted signals is controlled using a Low Frequency Oscillator (LFO). Fig 2-29.

TOOLS:

Stages: The Phaser effect consists of a series of filters that each produce a frequency-dependent delay. By mixing some of the original signal with the delayed signal, phase cancellation will occur at a particular frequency, creating a marked notch (reduction in level) at that frequency. When the original and delayed signals are "in phase" with each other, that frequency will be boosted to a higher level, creating a peak at that frequency. Each "stage" in the effect adds more notches and peaks in the frequency response, giving more complexity to the sound.

Dry/Wet: When set to 0, only the "Dry" (unprocessed) signal is produced. When set to 255 (maximum), only the delayed signals are produced. Because the effect's sound results from phase interaction, the effect sounds strongest when the Dry/Wet mix is set at the default halfway position (128).

LFO Frequency (Hz*):* This is a low frequency oscillator (LFO) control that adjusts the rate at which the effect sweeps up and down across the frequency range.

LFO Start Phase (deg.*):* The start position of the low frequency oscillator is adjustable between 0 and 360 degrees. When set at zero (the default) the filters begin sweeping from high frequency down to low frequency. When set at 180 degrees, the filters begin by sweeping up from low frequency.

Depth: The depth control governs how high the filter frequencies sweep. At a low setting the phaser will primarily affect bass frequencies. At higher settings the phaser effect can sweep high into the treble.

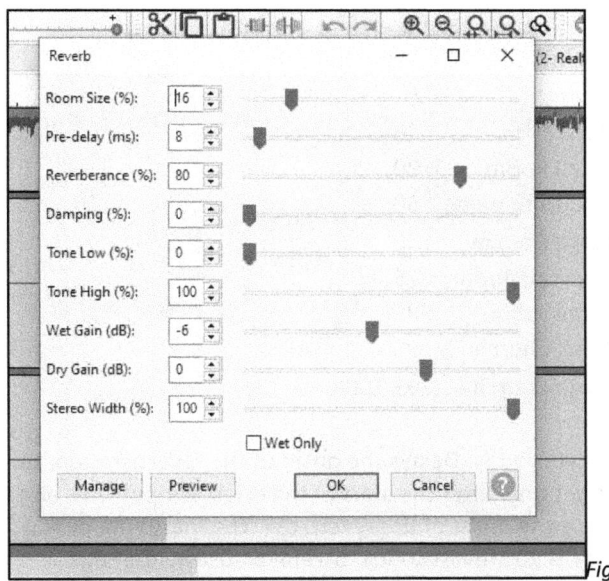

Fig 2-30 Reverb effect box.

REVERB

What Is it? Ever notice you sound better singing in the bathroom than you do outside? That is do to reverb. Reverb adds reverberation (rapid, modified repetitions blended with the original sound that gives an impression of ambience). The Reverb effect is based on the original "*freeverb*" algorithm. Applying a small amount of stereo reverb to an untreated mono signal duplicated into a two-channel stereo track will usually make it sound more natural. It also makes drums bigger and a guitar more powerful, along with creating outstanding vocal presence. Fig 2-30

TOOLS

Room Size: Every notice how different your voice sounds in the bathroom or how even the smallest voice in a big church seems to get echoed? This is what this is about the percentage (%) set s the room size. 0% is like a closet, while 100% is like a huge cathedral or large auditorium. The higher the value the more the reverberation effect.

Reverb Room Size Settings

Room Size	Percentage Setting
Closet	0
Bathroom	16
Small Room	30
One car garage	50
Large Garage	70
Medium Room	75
Large room	85
Med. Church	90
Large Church	95-100

Pre-delay (ms): Delays the onset of the reverberation for the set time after the start of the original input. This also delays the onset of the reverb tail. The maximum pre-delay is 200 milliseconds. Careful adjustment of this parameter can improve the clarity of the result.

Reverberance (%): Sets the length of the reverberation tail. This determines how long the reverberation continues for after the original sound being reverbed comes to an end, and so simulates the "liveliness" of the room acoustics. For any given reverberance value, the tail will be greater for larger room sizes.

Damping (%): Increasing the damping produces a more "muted" effect. The reverberation does not build up as much, and the high frequencies decay faster than the low frequencies. Simulates the absorption of high frequencies in the reverberation.

Tone Low (%): Setting this control below 100% reduces the low frequency components of the reverberation, creating a less "boomy" effect.

Tone High (%): Setting this control below 100% reduces the high frequency components of the reverberation, creating a less "bright" effect.

Wet Gain (dB) and Dry Gain (dB) Applies volume adjustment to the reverberation. Pushing the sliders to the right will increase the volume of the reverb pushing the both of them to the right can make a distorted lead guitar scream.

If the *Wet Gain and Dry Gain* values are the same, then the mix of wet effect and dry audio to be output to the track will be made louder or softer by exactly this value (assuming "Wet Only" below is not checked).

Stereo Width (%): Sets the apparent "width" of the Reverb effect for stereo tracks only. Increasing this value applies more variation between left and right channels, creating a more "spacious" effect. When set at zero, the effect is applied independently to left and right channels.

Wet Only: When this control is checked, only the wet signal (added reverberation) will be in the resulting output, and the original audio will be removed. This can be useful when previewing the effect, but in most cases, you should uncheck this when applying the effect for you will not be pleased with the sound.

One use is to create a "reverb only" track that you can then mix in greater or lesser proportion with the original track. See the mixing section.

Luckily you don't have to worry about all of this as under the tab marked Manage, you will see one marked Factory presets The following presets are provides available from the Manage menu:

Defaults (the default settings),Vocal I, Vocal II, Bathroom, Small Room Bright, Small Room Dark, Medium Room, Large Room, Church Hall, Cathedral. Each of these have presets for all the above boxes, and are pretty useful. You can use them or tweak them and then save your own preset. Or you can do your own setting and save that.

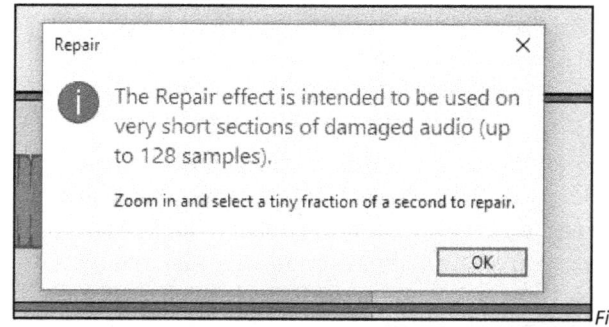

Fig 2-31 The repair tool can repair only small sections of audio. If you select too much this box will pop up.

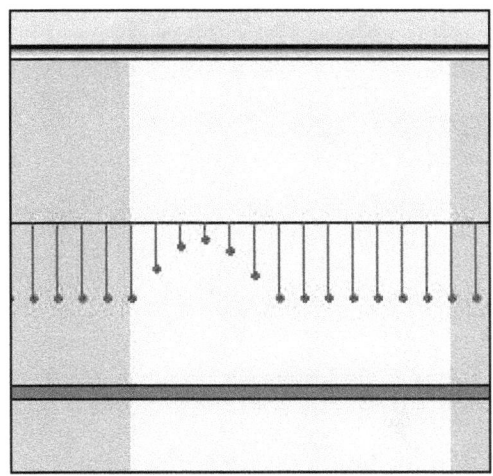

Fig 2-32 you will have in to zoom in until the wave appears in individual dots to utilize the repair function

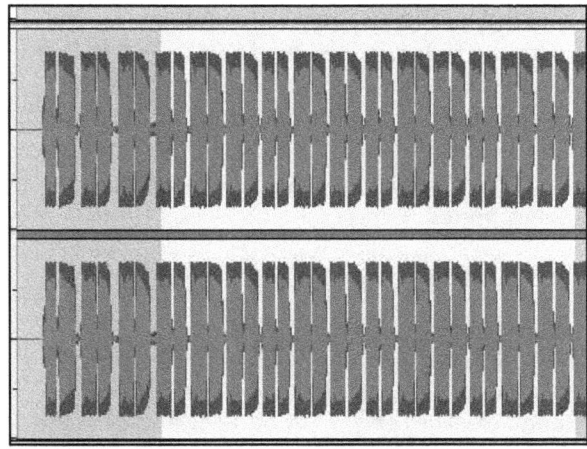

Fig 2-35 The selected part of the track is repeated.

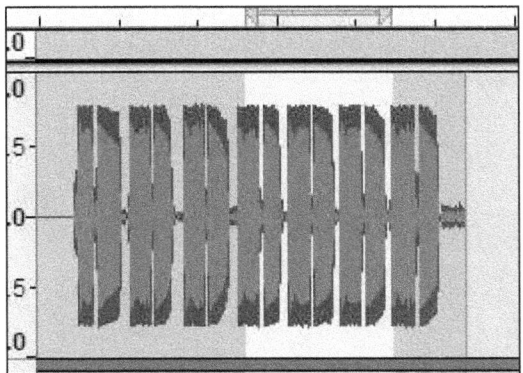

Fig 2-33 REPEAT EFFECT useful in repeating a short audio track that that Repeat over and over (like drum track). Select the track you want to repeat then click on Effect> Repeat.

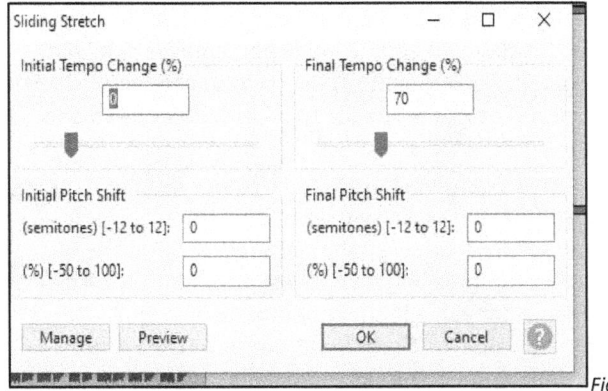

Fig 2-36 Sliding stretch effect box

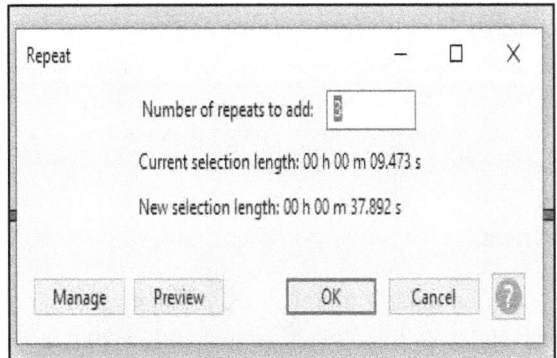

Fig 2-34 Repeat effect box. Select the number of repeats you want. Click OK.

REVERSE

What Is it? Ever heard if you play some record backwards it says something? That is what reverse is it will take a selected section of audio and reverse it. It is great for special effects. There are setting, just select the audio and click on the effect and the audio will automatically flip.

SLIDING STRETCH

What Is it? Allows you to make a continuous change to the tempo and/or pitch of a selection by choosing initial and/or final change values. Tempo changes made without selecting a pitch change preserve the original pitch, and pitch changes made without selecting a tempo change preserve the original tempo. Fig 2-36. In short you can either slow it down by pushing the sliders to the left or speed it up by pushing the sliders to the right. Push them to all the right and voice will sound like a chipmuck sucking up helium while taking speed.

Now you may ask why would I want that sound? Well just like most effects it follows the *"Goldilocks Rule"* too much or too little is not good, only the right amount is good, and works well. Say you have an outro recorded, but it was record at a tempo that is just a little too slow, or too fast. By using small changes, you can make the outro sound better.

TOOLS

Tempo Change: Initial and final tempo change values can be managed using the slider (which will move in whole number values only) or by entering a value in the box, which can be either a whole number or a number including a fraction. They range from -90 to plus 500.

The percentage of the original rate required for the beginning of the processed audio. Positive percentages speed the audio up and negative percentages slow the audio down: -50% is half-speed, 0% is unchanged, 50% is 1.5 times the original speed, 100% is double speed and so on.

Pitch Shift: The two "Initial" input boxes are interdependent. Entering the required value in one of the boxes for Initial Pitch Shift will automatically display the equivalent value in the other Initial box. Similarly, **entering a value in "Final" input box will display the equivalent value in the other Final box.** Each box goes from -12 to +12, these boxes work in conjunction with the boxes below.

Initial (semitones): Enter the pitch shift in semitones (half steps) required for the beginning of the processed audio. Art of this group is also the percentage.

Initial (%): Alternatively, enter the pitch shift as a percentage of the original frequency as required for the beginning of the processed audio. Changing these will also have an effect on how the pitch change sounds. Again, the only way to learn is to play around with the controls. And remember the Goldilocks rule.

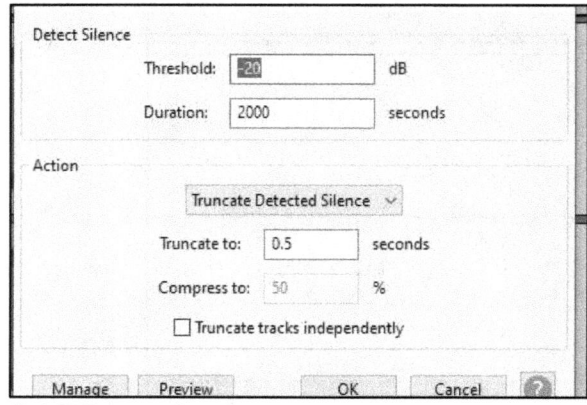

Fig 2-37 Truncate silence box

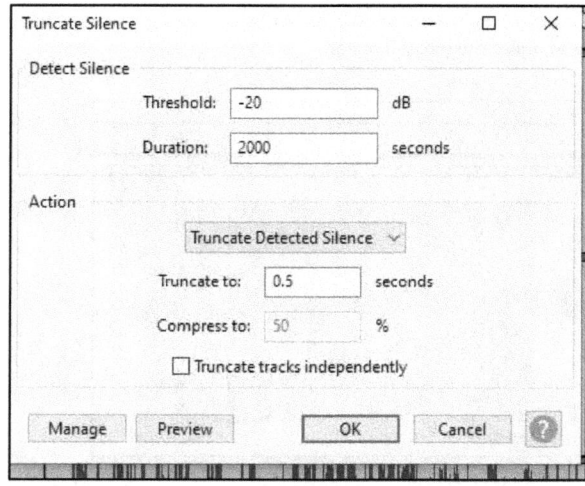

Fig 2-38 Truncate silence has two tools to use. One is to detect and shorten the silence by a selected time as shown

TRUNCATE SILENCE

What Is it? It is a wonderful and time saving audio editing tool for Podcasters and Voiceover Artist but has very little use for music recordings. What is basically does it detects silence between speaking parts and truncates-shortens-it. Fig 2-37 to 2-39.

For example, you have a podcast and you are discussing the subject but you stumble for a word for a couple of seconds then remember it, or you are reading something but slowly and it sounds **"uh…as…if…you don't what are** speaking about. Using this effect, will make it sound uh, as if you **don't** know what your speaking about.

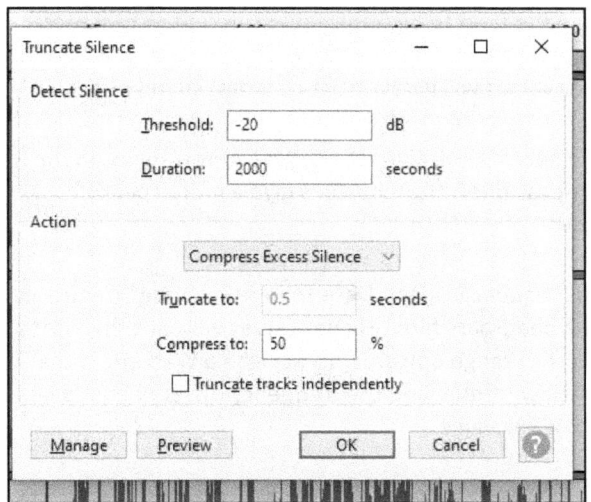

Fig 2-39 the other tool is Compress the silence. Notice how the time box is grayed out and not useable, be the percentage box is now useable.

TOOLS

Truncate Detected Silence: When this method is selected, silences are simply shortened to the "Detect Silence" duration se fig 2-38 When this method is selected, the "Truncate to:" (seconds) control is available lower down the interface and the "Compress to:" (percent) control is grayed out.

All detected silences are shortened to the same duration. When the audio remains below the "Detect Silence" threshold level for at least the "Detect Silence" duration, it will be reduced to the "Truncate to" duration entered here.

Compress Excess Silence: This is a more advanced mode that allows silences to be shortened proportionally according to their original duration. When this method is selected, silence in excess of the "Detect Silence" duration is reduced to a percentage of its original duration (see example below). When this method is selected, the "Compress to:" (percent) control is available lower down the interface and the "Truncate to:" (seconds) control is grayed out. Because silences are reduced by a specified percentage, the final duration of each detected silence varies according to its original length.

When the audio remains below the "Detect Silence" threshold for at least the "Detect Silence" duration, any silence in excess of the "Detect Silence" duration is reduced to the "Compress to" percentage entered here. The entire detected silence is not proportionally reduced.

Truncate Tracks Independently: When the effect is run on multiple selected tracks the unchecked checkbox Truncate tracks independently checkbox determines whether to treat the tracks as a mix that must be kept synchronized or to process the tracks independently one after the other.

When checked "off" (default), silence is only removed where it occurs in the same place in all the selected tracks. If the silence is in different places in each selected track, running the effect with this option enabled will not remove any silence. This is good when you have stopped speaking but the music track is playing softly in the background. Even though it is detecting silence on the vocal track, it is not cutting it, for the music is playing.

When checked "on", each selected track is processed individually. All the specified silence will be removed but different parts in each track may no longer be synchronized with each other. Choose this option to truncate silence in multiple different songs which you imported into separate Audacity tracks, and so are not part of a mix.

WAH-WAH

What Is it? Let us step back in time for a little while. **The decade is the 1970's** -the sound the Wah-Wah pedal. The great guitarists were all use them no more so than Peter Frampton. Nearly everyone had his album, and every want to be guitarist if they had one pedal it was this pedal. Fig 2-40

Now we are back in the modern-day times, and this effect can be used on any instrument that can be recorded with Audacity. It creates a rapid tone quality variation like that guitar sound so popular in the 1970's. It can be used to create spooky sounds from the Bass and piano. And pure out creepy sounds with vocals. And of course, for the electric guitar to create that famous sound.

TOOLS

LFO Frequency: Sets the speed at which the band-pass filter is swept back and forth.

LFO Start Phase: The start position of the LFO cycle. This determines whether the band-pass filter starts at its lowest, mid, or highest frequencies. Another way to look at it is that it determines whether at the start of the effect the pitch is rising or falling.

Depth: Determines the range of frequencies that are swept through by the band-pass filter. Higher values will sweep the filter to higher frequencies and so give more variation to the sound quality over a complete LFO cycle. Lower values will give a more constant sound effect.

Resonance: Determines the degree of resonance in the band-pass filter. **Higher values give a more "peaky"** effect.

Wah Frequency Offset: Determines the "base" frequency of the band-pass filter. Higher values will shift the filter's frequency range upwards. To achieve a Wah effect that is in the low frequencies the frequency offset needs to be set to a low value.

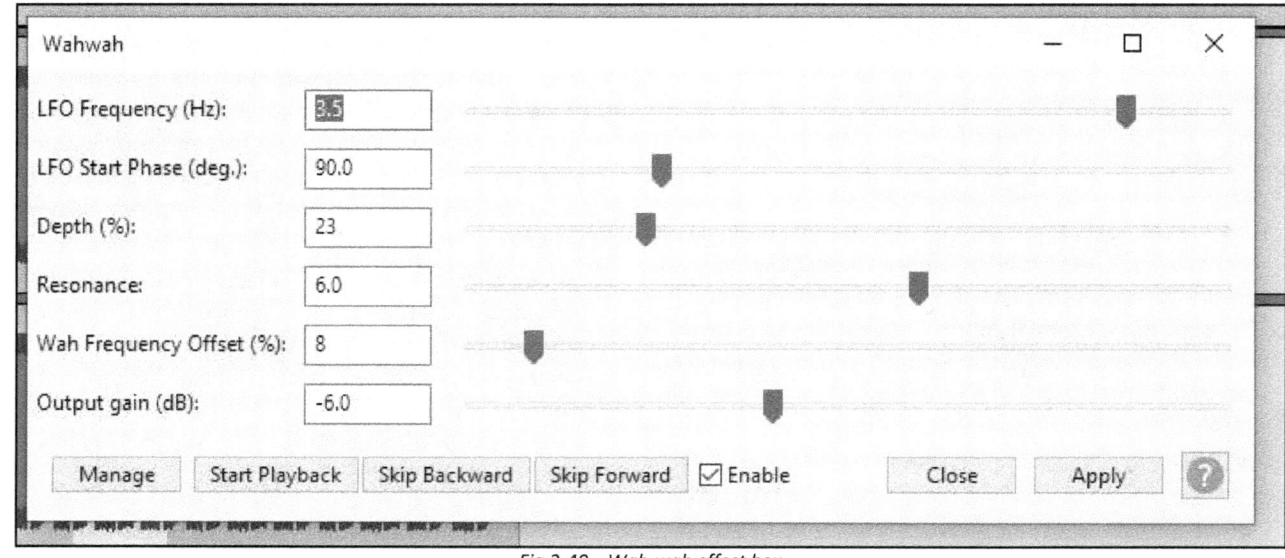

Fig 2-40   Wah-wah effect box

Output gain (dB): Controls the amount of gain (volume) positive or negative that will be applied by the effect.

This effect supports Real-time preview - effect settings can be changed while playing and listening to the result in real-time. Text-based button controls are provided as in the image above. The Enable checkbox acts like a live "Bypass" control. Uncheck the checkbox unchecked checkbox Enable to hear the audio without the effect applied, and recheck the box checked checkbox Enable to hear the effect applied at its current settings.

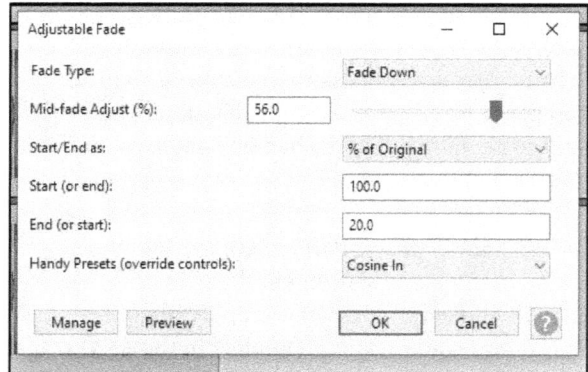

Fig 2-41 Adjustable Fade

ADJUSTABLE FADE

What Is it? *Adjustable Fade* increases or reduces the audio volume by a varying amount. This effect is more versatile than *Fade In* and *Fade Out* in that it can fade to or from any amplification level rather than only between silence and the original level. For example you are going from verse to chorus where more volume is needed, instead of have a sudden change we can fade it in. Or we are going from chorus to another verse, we can *fade out*. Another use in it is when you remove noise for a track and there is a sudden cut of in sound. Fig 2-41

TOOLS

FADE TYPE:

Fade Up: provides a linear or simple curve fade up from a low gain setting to a higher gain setting.

Fade Down: provides a linear or simple curve fade down from a high gain setting to a lower gain setting.

S-Curve Up: provides a "double" curve that bends one way and then the other. The level will rise gradually at first, then progressively more steeply toward the middle of the fade before gradually leveling out.

S-Curve Down: The level will fall gradually at first, then progressively more steeply toward the middle of the fade before gradually leveling out.

Mid-fade Adjust: This slider control has a range of +/- 100 (default 0). It allows the shape of the fade that has been selected in the "Fade Type:" menu to be modified. Setting this control greater than zero will tend to push up the center of fade, whereas negative values will tend to pull down the level in the middle of the fade.

When used with "*Fade Type/Fade Up*", a value of zero (default) will produce a linear fade. Values greater than zero will cause the fade to rise more rapidly at first before leveling out to the higher amplification level. Values less than zero will cause the fade to rise slowly at first then gradually rise more rapidly. The further away from zero that this is set, the more curved the fade will be. The mid fade amplification will never be less than the start of the fade or greater than the end of the fade.

If used with "*Fade Type/Fade Down*", a value of zero (default) will produce a linear fade. Values greater than zero will cause the fade to fall gradually at first then progressively more steeply as it approached the final level. Values less than zero will cause the fade to fall rapidly at first then progressively level out. The further away from zero that this is set, the more curved the fade will be. The mid fade amplification will never be greater than the start of the fade or less than the end of the fade.

When used with "*Fade Type/ S-Curve Up or S-Curve Down*", halfway through the fade the gain will be exactly half way between the starting point and end point.

With values greater than zero the fade will retain its "double curve" character but will be a bit higher at the mid-point. With values greater than zero the fade will retain its "double curve" character but will be a bit lower at the mid-point.

Start/End as: This dropdown enables you to choose between percentage or dB as the units to be used in the Start and End gain parameter boxes below.

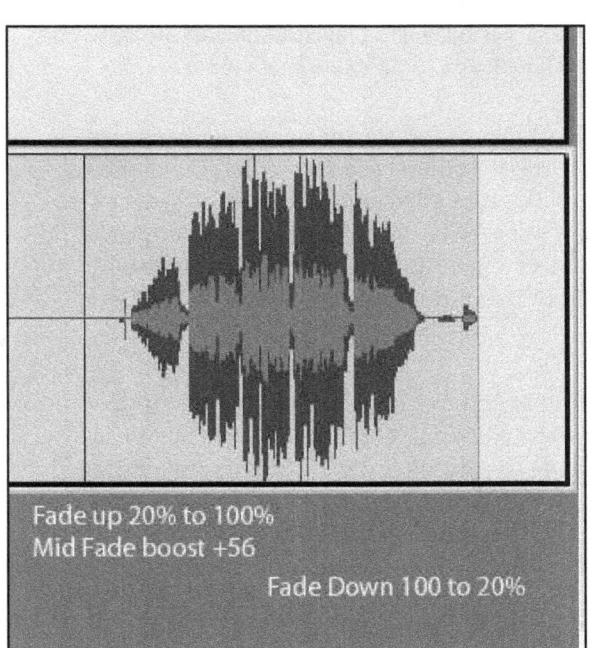

Fig 2-42 Each fade must be done separately then combined.

With values greater than zero the fade will retain its "double curve" character but will be a bit higher at the mid-point. With values greater than zero the fade will retain its "double curve" character but will be a bit lower at the mid-point.

Start/End as: This dropdown enables you to choose between percentage or dB as the units to be used in the Start and End gain parameter boxes below.

Warning: The start and end boxes must both be fill in or you will get an error code. They define the initial and final gain (amplification amount) of the fade. It is unimportant if these are entered with the initial gain in the first text box and the final gain in the last, or the other way around as the direction of the fade is determined by the Fade Type: selection. Start/End. If you are using percentage units, the default value of 0 (silence) will give you the start of a fade up from silence.

End/Start): Enables you to set the End (or start) gain. If you are using percentage units, the default value of 100 (the original level or unity gain) will give you the final gain for a fade up to full volume.

Before you start on you own track and possible destroy. Instead create a new project. *Click Generate> Nosie* select White Nosie and click okay and play around with the controls with this. It will help you understand them more.

Handy Presets: A number of fixed preset curve shapes are available from this dropdown selector: Linear, Exponential, Logarithmic, Rounded, Cosine and S-Curve. If you select a preset curve it will override all other parameter settings dialog box for this effect. To make the other parameters operable you will need to set "None Selected" from this dropdown.

All presets either fade in from silence to the original level or fade out from the original level to silence. Note that unlike the Fade In and Fade Out effects in the top section of the Effect menu, this effect will treat empty space in the selected region as silence, It is therefore important to select exactly the region that you want the effect to be applied to.

None Selected: Manual settings. Fade Type, Mid Fade Adjust, Start and End settings are all functional.

Linear In: Same as the Fade In effect.

Linear Out: Same as the Fade Out effect.

Exponential In: The level rises exponentially, similar to using the Envelope Tool.

Exponential Out: The level falls exponentially, similar to using the Envelope Tool.

Logarithmic In: A "convex" curve that rises moderately steeply from silence and progressively less steeply.

Logarithmic: A "convex" curve that falls gently initially then progressively more rapidly.

Rounded In: A "convex" curve that rises abruptly from silence then progressively less steeply.

Rounded Out: A "convex" curve that falls gradually from the initial level, then progressively more steeply to a fairly abrupt end.

Cosine In: A "convex" curve that rises moderately steeply from silence and gradually levels out to create a smooth transition to the original level

Cosine Out: A "convex" curve with a smooth transition from the original level, progressively falling more steeply to silence.

S-Curve In: A "double" curve that creates a smooth transition from silence, gradually rising more steeply, then leveling out to create a smooth transition to the original level.

S-Curve Out: A "double" curve that creates a smooth transition from the original level, gradually falling more steeply, then leveling out to create a smooth transition to silence. Similar to the Studio Fade Out effect.

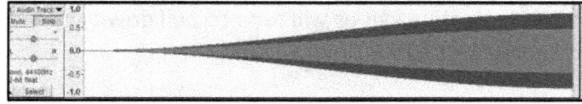
Fig 2-43 An example of an S-curve

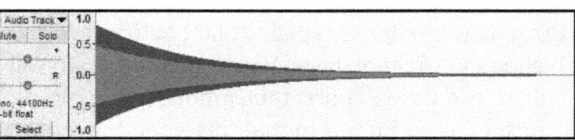
Fig 2-44 Example of Exponential Out

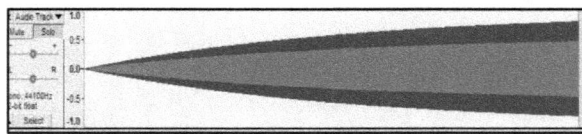
Fig 2-45 An example of Logarithmic

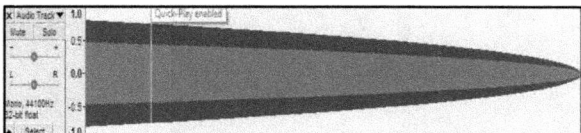

Fig 2-45 An Example of Rounded Out

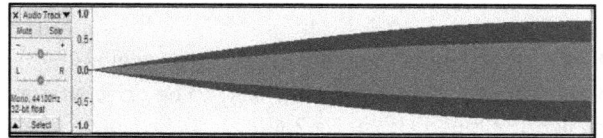

Fig 2-46 An Example of Cosine In

Desired Effect	Fade Type	Mid-Fade Adjust (%)	Start/End)	End Start
Linear fade-in from silence to original level	Fade Up	0	0	100
Linear fade-out from original level to silence	Fade Down	0	0	100
Linear fade from original level to half volume	Fade Down	0	50	100
Exponential fade-out similar to using Envelope Tool	Fade Down	Less than 0	0	100
Fade-out for 'Equal Power' crossfade	Fade Down	+50	0	100
Fade-in for 'Equal Power' crossfade	Fade Up	+50	0	100
Similar to 'Studio Fade Out' effect	S-Curve Down	0	0	100
Smooth change from half of original volume to twice original volume	S-Curve Up	0	50	200

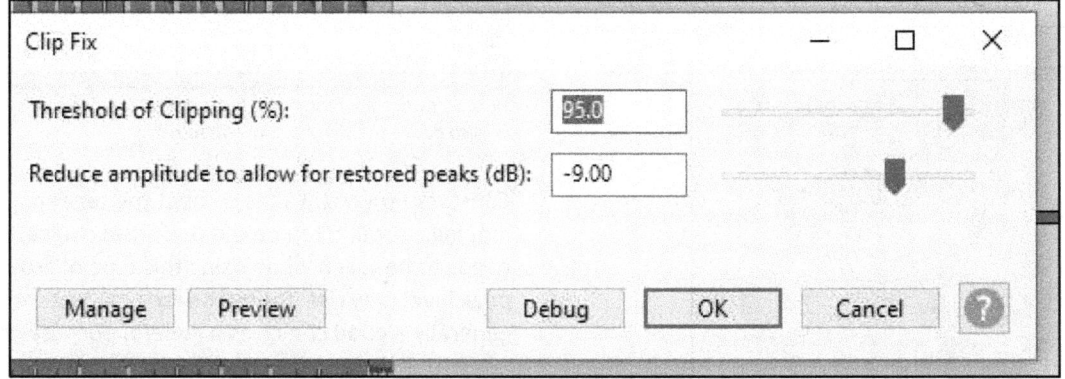

Fig 2-47 Clip Fix box

CLIP FIX

What Is it? It attempts to reconstruct clipped regions by interpolating the lost signal. It is only likely to be effective for repairing lightly clipped audio. Fig 2-47

CROSS FADE CLIPS

What Is it? Attempts to cross between two different clips on the SAME TRACK. Say we have a guitar track but we di d the solo and a pasted it into the track and we have the notice click and it changes. Cross fading can help remove this. There are no tools when it is clicked on it will automatically fade out the front clip and fade in the rear clip. Fig 2-48 to 2-49

CROSS FADE TRACKS

What Is it? Attempts to cross between two clips on two different tracks. Say we have a guitar track but we redid the solo and instead of pasting we have it playing under the other track and silence the other solo in the first track, this will help it ease out of the first track and into the second track. Fig 2-50 to 2-51.

TOOLS:

Fade Type:

Constant Gain: This is the default. It fades out the upper track, and fade in the lower track with linear fades (the same type of fade as is achieved by using the Fade In / Fade Out effects). "Constant Gain" ensures that, as long as the original audio is not clipped, the crossfade will not clip - this is the default. However, "Constant Gain" crossfades may cause the overall volume to dip slightly during the fade.

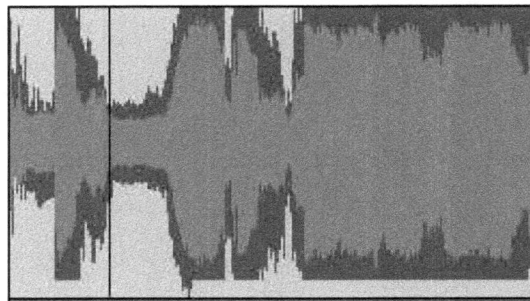

Fig 2-49 Notice how the fade works, the weaker side grows in loudness and the loud side at the first goes down and they flow together.

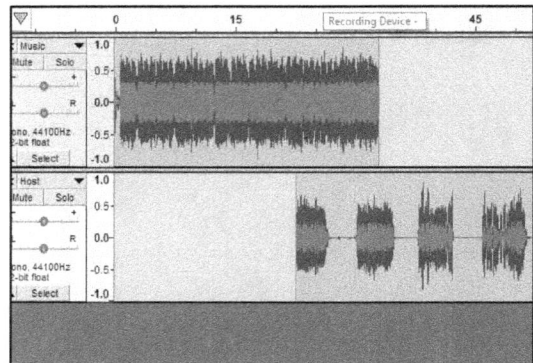

Fig 2-50 Notice in this podcast we have the music still going strong when the host comes in Cross fade tracks can take care of that.

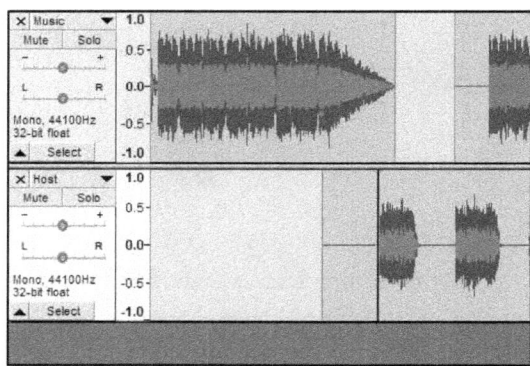

Fig 2-51 Notice how the music fades slowly and the host's voice quickly fades in. Also notice the sharp cut in with music.

Constant Power 1: Fades combat the tendency of the volume dipping, so will often be the preferred choice, though care needs to be taken when using this type of crossfade as the peak level may rise during the fade. "Constant Power 1" is generally a good choice as a general purpose crossfade effect.

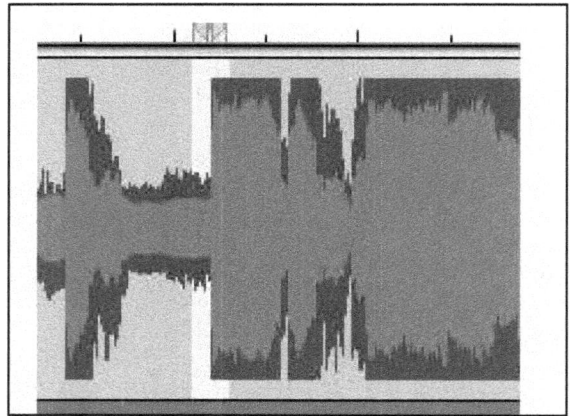

Fig 2-48 Cross fade Clips. Here we have a new clip that was pasted in we select only a small amount of each side of the clips. Otherwise, the change will be too greatly known. You just want to ease into the change.

Constant Power 2: This option is also designed to maintain a fairly constant volume through the course of the fade. This variation of the constant power fade starts to fade in a little more rapidly than "Constant Power 1" and the crossfading may sound a bit abrupt in the first or last moments of the fade, though it may be preferred when crossfading songs that are beat-matched. This version is based on the legacy "Cross Fade In" and "Cross Fade Out" effects of previous versions of Audacity.

Custom Curve: The preset options will cater for most crossfading tasks, but if fine control over the effect is required, the custom curve option may be useful. This option enables the "Custom Curve" slider control, which allows the rate at which the tracks crossfade to be manually adjusted. This text box / slider control has no effect unless "Custom Curve" is selected as the "Fade Type". When enabled, it controls the curvature of the fade in a similar way to the "curve" control on a DJ mixer.

High settings are useful if you want both tracks to be strongly present during the crossfade time, though it is not likely that the maximum setting will be often required. At maximum (1.0), the upper track will maintain close to full volume until close to the end of the crossfade, and will then fade out rapidly, while the lower track will fade in very rapidly to almost full volume. The overall volume is likely to be noticeably higher during the crossfade period.

When set to the halfway position (0.5), the fade is approximately a "constant power" type curve and will usually maintain a fairly steady volume throughout the crossfade.

Fade Direction

Automatic: The effect will attempt to automatically work out whether a fade-in or fade-out is required. This is the default and will usually give the correct result. If you get a fade-out where you want a fade-in, or vice versa, then undo the operation Ctrl + Z and use one of the other two choices listed below.

How automatic fade direction works: The automatic setting is based on the proximity of the ends of the selection to the ends of the selected audio clip(s). If the start of the selection is closer to the start of the selected audio clip than the end of the selection is to the end of the audio clip, the effect creates a fade-in. Conversely, if the end of the selection is at or near the end of the selection, and the start of the selection is not at or near the start of the audio clip. then a fade-out will occur. In the unlikely event that both ends of the selection are exactly the same distance from the ends of the selected audio clip, the effect will fade out.

Alternating Out / In: The selected region in the first selected track will fade out. If more than one track is selected, the selected region in the next selected track will fade in. If more than two tracks are selected, the fade direction will continue to alternate fade-out / fade-in / fade-out.

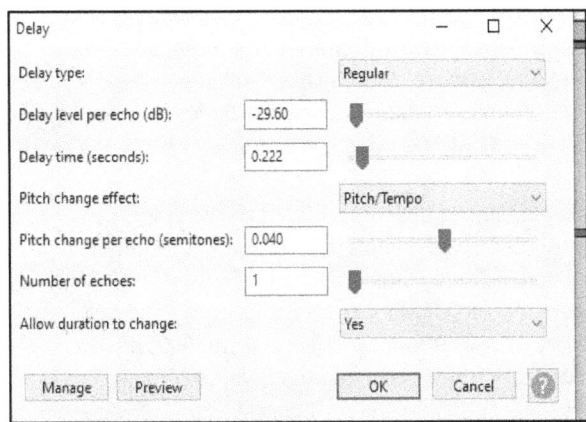

Fig 2-52 Delay effect box

The selected region in the first selected track will fade in. If more than one track is selected, the selected region in the next selected track will fade out. If more than two tracks are selected, the fade direction will continue to alternate fade-in / fade-out / fade-in.

DELAY

What is it?: You can use Delay to create a multiple echo effect with options for variable delay times between successive echoes and the number, amplitude and pitch of successive repeats. This could create a sustain note for vocals or a guitar. Fig 2-52

TOOLS

Delay Type

Regular: In this selection each echo is delayed by the same amount.

Bouncing ball: Makes the echoes occur increasingly close together (faster).

Reverse bouncing ball: Makes the echoes occur increasingly far apart (slower).

Delay level Per Echo (dB): This controls the amount in dB by which each successive echo will change loudness. The more negative this value, the more the echoes will die away. Positive values cause successive echoes to be louder. When set to 0.0, all echoes will be the same volume.

Note, because echoes are often added to the original audio, the processed audio will often have a higher peak level than the original. If the output exceeds 0 dB (full track height) and so triggers the red clipping warning lights in Playback Meter Toolbar, you should open Effect > Amplify..., ensure "Amplification (dB)" shows a negative dB value (not "0.0 dB") then click OK.

Delay time (Seconds): This controls the time between echoes. For the Bouncing Ball types of delay, this sets the delay time for the longest (slowest) echo.

Pitch Change Effect

Pitch/Tempo: Changes the pitch in the same way that the Change Speed effect causes a change in pitch. The sound quality of each echo is very good, but an increase in pitch speeds up the delayed audio and a decrease in pitch slows it down. The echoes will be noticeably desynchronized with any comparable echoes in other tracks where "Pitch/Tempo" was not applied.

LQ Pitch Shift: Changes the pitch while maintaining the same tempo in a similar way to the Change Pitch effect. The sound quality of each echo is of lower quality than the "Pitch/Tempo" effect (including a short additional echo on percussive sounds) and the delay time will often be a little longer than specified. However, interesting "spiraling" effects can be produced.

Pitch Change Per echo (Semitones): This controls the amount in semitones by which each successive echo will change pitch. The change can be set to fractions of a semitone which can produce a "glissando"- a continuous slide upward or downward between two notes-type of delay. When set to zero, the pitch change effect is disabled.

Number of Echoes: This controls how many echoes are produced. It is here that this effect can really over whelming, unless you want to go for special effect sound 1 or 2 is the most you want to use.

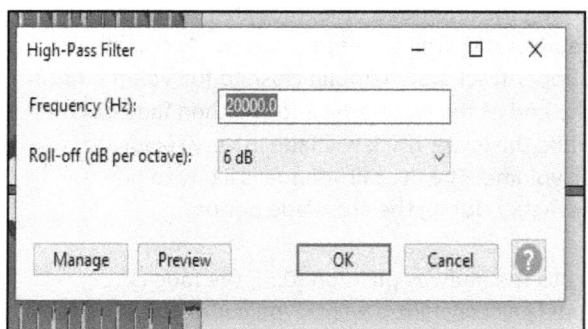

Fig 2-53 High pass Filter

Allow Duration to Change: Yes: (Default). Allows the processed audio to lengthen so to accommodate all the requested echoes. No: The processed audio is trimmed to the same length as the original selection. Any echoes that would have occurred after the end of the original selection will be deleted. Choose this option if you need to keep the delayed track synchronized with other tracks in the project.

HIGH AND LOW PASS FILTERS

What is it?: High pass and low pass filters are also a form of EQ.

A *High-Pass Filter* passes frequencies above a selected cutoff frequency. It does not eliminate all the sound below but attenuates frequencies below its cutoff frequency. This effect can therefore be used to reduce low frequency noise. Fig 253

A *Low-Pass Filter* passes frequencies below a selected cutoff frequency. Like the High Pass filter, it does not eliminate all the sound above but attenuates frequencies above its cutoff frequency. This effect can therefore be used to reduce high frequency noise. Each is a different effect but use the same tools.

TOOLS

Frequency (Hz): Sound below this cutoff frequency in Hz is not eliminated but increasingly attenuated as the frequency falls further below the cutoff. The cutoff frequency (sometimes also called corner frequency) defines the point at which the audio is reduced by 3 dB. Thus, there will also be a small and decreasing amount of attenuation just above the cutoff frequency as in the following image.

Roll-off (dB per octave): sets the steepness of the attenuation below the corner frequency. Higher roll-off values give a steeper slope to the attenuation. For example, with a roll-off of 6 dB per octave, the sound decreases by 6 dB in amplitude for each octave below the cutoff frequency (an octave above is double the frequency). To achieve more attenuation, run the effect again or use a greater roll-off.

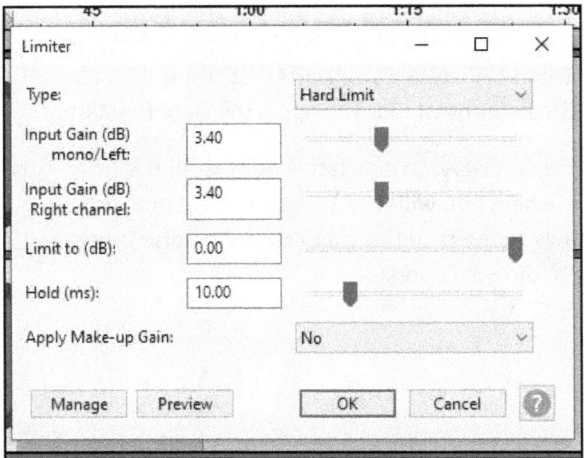

Fig 2-54 Limiter Box

LIMITERS

What is it?: Use the Limiter effect to pass signals below a specified input level unaffected or gently reduced, while preventing the peaks of stronger signals from exceeding this threshold. Mastering engineers often use limiting combined with make-up gain to increase the perceived loudness of an audio recording during the audio mastering process. FIg 2-54

This limiter effect provides two basic types of effect; "*limiting*" and "*clipping*". The "limiting" effect is a special kind of dynamic compression that responds very rapidly to peaks in the waveform. The "clipping" effect is a kind of distortion that changes the shape of the waves by "clipping" off the high and low peaks.

TOOLS

Soft Limit: This progressively reduces the gain as the amplitude of the waveform approaches the "Limit to (dB)" threshold and prevents the waveform from exceeding that level.

Hard Limit: Makes no change to the audio until the peaks reach the "Limit to (dB)" threshold. Where the input level (after applying optional input gain) exceeds the threshold, an equal amount of negative gain is applied so that the peaks never exceed the threshold.

Hard Clipping: Is the simplest method for reducing peaks. It just chops off the peaks at the "Limit to" threshold. Note that clipping causes distortion. Hard clipping may be useful for purposefully introducing distortion on high peaks, for example to add high harmonics to percussive sounds.

Warning excessive use of hard clipping creates a harsh distortion that is usually unpleasant. For heavier use of distortion, the "Soft Clipping" option may be preferable. When it is applied heavily, the effect is similar to a "Fuzz Box" effect.

Input Gain: Amplifies the audio before applying the limiter. As the limiter acts on audio peaks that exceed the Limit to (dB) threshold, it will clearly have little or no effect on audio tracks in which all of the audio is below the threshold level. In such cases, the audio should be amplified before limiting so that the limiter can work properly. Amplification could be applied using Audacity's Amplify effect, or more conveniently using the "Input Gain" controls.

For mono tracks, only the "mono/Left" gain control has any affect. For stereo tracks the left and right channel gains may be adjusted independently of each other.

Limit to (dB): Limits the amplitude (after optional amplifying) to this level. Whichever type is selected, the limiter prevents the waveform from exceeding this level. (Note that makeup gain, if used, is applied to the waveform after it has been limited.)

Hold: This applies only to the "Hard Limiter" and "Soft Limiter" settings. It has no effect when using either of the "Clip" settings. In order to catch even the most sudden peak, the limiter "looks ahead" to see when the next peak is coming and begins to reduce the gain just a little in advance of the peak. The gain level is then held at the reduced level for a short while before being released back to the normal level. Looking ahead and holding the gain level allows the gain to adjust more smoothly and reduces the amount of distortion. The shorter the "Hold" duration, the faster the limiter responds to changes in input level. It is generally desirable for the limiter to respond very rapidly, but responding too rapidly will produce distortion, especial when processing low frequency sounds such as a double bass. Normally this control can be left at the default (10 ms) setting.

Apply Makeup Gain: Amplifies the output (post limiter) close to 0 dB (usually just a little below 0 dB). This is useful when using the limiter to maximize loudness.

NOISE GATE

What is it?: A Noise Gate is a type of "audio gate" that is "open" and allows sounds to pass unaltered when the level is above a certain "threshold" level. When the audio signal is below the threshold level, the gate "closes" and stops, or reduces the signal making it substantially quieter. A Noise Gate does not eliminate noise from a signal it only reduces the noise level during the quiet periods between sounds. There are many situations where this can be useful. Fig 2-55

If there is very low-level noise that is effectively masked by the recorded material, a Noise Gate can lower the noise level during silent parts of the recording where the low-level noise would otherwise be apparent.

When noise reduction by other methods causes unacceptable degradation of the sound quality, a Noise Gate can reduce the noise level to some extent between sounds without affecting the actual recorded sounds.

Where there is low level intermittent noise of a similar type to the actual recorded sound (for example, if sound from a distant television or radio is audible during pauses in a speech recording or music recording) a Noise Gate can make the pauses more silent. This can happen with items like unshielded or interface devices. One thing that Noise gate can take care of is breaths in a vocal track. We all have to breath, if we don't, we die. And when we are singing a powerful track, we must take in that deep breath before the next line-the microphone hears this. Nosie gate can remove some of it.

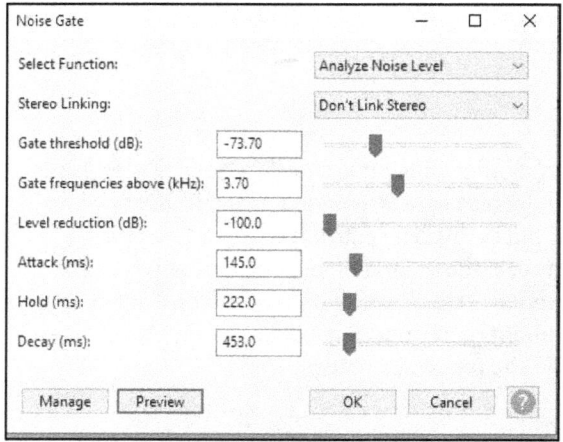

Fig 2-55 Noise gate box. Select Analyze Noise level from the drop-down menu in the Select function box. Click Preview.

A Noise Gate may be used after the Audacity Noise Reduction effect to further reduce the noise level during periods that should be silent.

TOOLS:

Select Function: There are two functions *Analyze Noise Level* and *Gate*. Choose Analyze Noise Level first this will determine the gate threshold. The apply the Gate function.

Gate Threshold is always in a negative number and is from -6 to -96 this is where you will type to recommendation in. Listen carefully to the result to check that the noise is being cut and the audio is still present.

Gate Frequencies: **are listed in kHz's for 0- 10.**

Level of Reduction: goes from -100 to 0.

Attack: is how long the gate acts in most case you will want a fairly quick attack it rages from 14 to 1000 ms seconds.

Hold goes from 0-2000ms, this determines how long the gate will last.

Decay: the ms of the effect after it lets go. It lasts from to 10-4000 ms.

There are no set guide lines and you will just have to play around with the sliders.

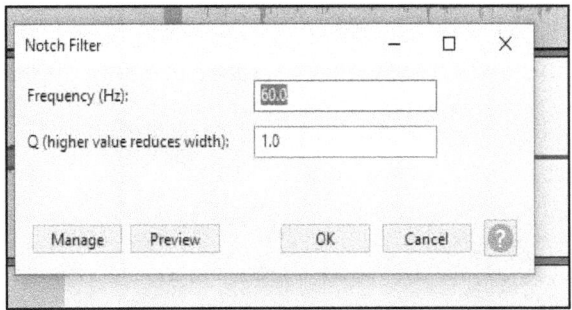

Fig 2-56 Notch filler

NOTCH FILTER

What is it?: Suppose you have track and you listened to it, only to be disappointed to find it is contaminated with a continuous, pure tone of some kind such as ceiling fan. This is a case where you can get good results. using the Notch Filter, Fig 2-56, effect which you will find underneath the divider in the Effect menu.

TOOLS

Frequency Enter any amount that up to half the sample rate. A rate greater than half the sample rate of the track are not valid because a track can only contain frequencies up to half its sample rate. The sample rate is found on the left-hand side of track and is displaced as Hz. For example, 44100 samples per second can be expressed as either 44,100 Hz, or 44.1 kHz.

Q factor: This determines the width of the notch cut from your audio (default value is 1). Values above 1 create a narrower notch, and values below 1 create a wider notch. The Q Factor must be at least 0.10.

SPECTRAL DELETE

What is it?: Before you can do anything with this effect you must convert it to either multi view or Spectrogram fig 2-57 . The Spectral Delete is used with a Spectral Selection to delete that spectral selection from the audio.

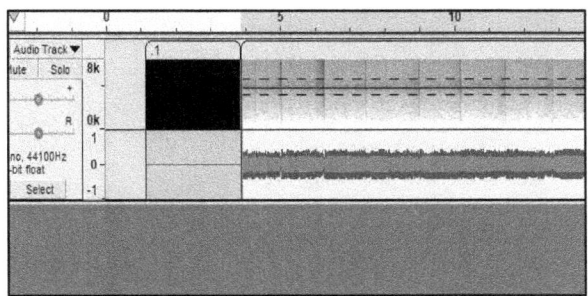

Fig 2-57 A form of mixed tracks top the multicolored spectrum band and the bottom the stand waveform.

A spectral selection has been made in the spectrogram part of the track from 5 kHz to 7 kHz. After applying the Spectral Delete command we can see that Audacity has removed that part of the spectrum for the time range of the selection

Note: For technical reasons this effect is not suitable for selecting very low frequencies. The actual lower limit depends on the track sample rate. For a sample rate of 44,100 Hz, if the lower frequency bound goes below about 100 Hz, then all frequencies below the upper bound will be removed (as if the selection extended down to zero Hz).

SPECTRAL EDIT MULTI TOOL

Before you can do anything with this effect you must convert it to either multi view or Spectrogram. Depending on how the track is displayed and what spectral selection has been made, this effect will do one of the following:

When the track is not in a Spectrogram View with Spectral Selection enabled, an error message will be displayed. When the spectral selection has a center, upper and lower frequency this effect performs as a notch filter with the center frequency defined by the center frequency of the spectral selection and the width defined by the upper and lower frequencies of the spectral selection

If the spectral selection begins at 0 Hz this effect performs a high pass filter with a roll-off of 12 dB/octave and with the cutoff frequency defined by the upper frequency of the spectral selection

When the spectral selection ends at the Nyquist frequency of the track this effect performs a low pass filter with a roll-off of 12 dB/octave and with the cutoff frequency defined by the lower frequency of the spectral selection

If both the upper and lower frequency bound of the spectral selection are undefined, an error message will be displayed. You should go back and define one or both frequency bounds. Note: If the attenuation is not sufficient, you can use Ctrl + R to repeat the effect.

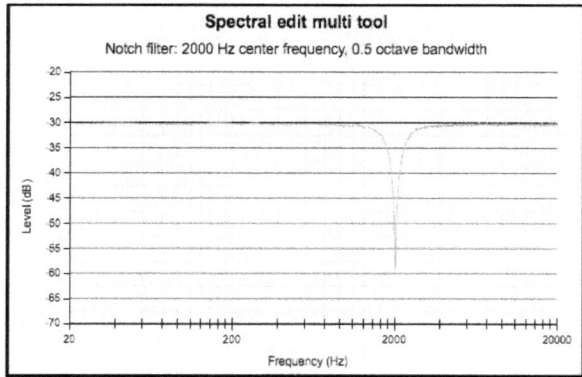

Fig 2-58. If you make a spectral selection that has both an upper and lower boundary, selecting Effect > Spectral edit multi tool will apply a notch filter. The above is an example the spectral selection had a center frequency of 2,000 Hz and a bandwidth of 0.5 octave. Audacity

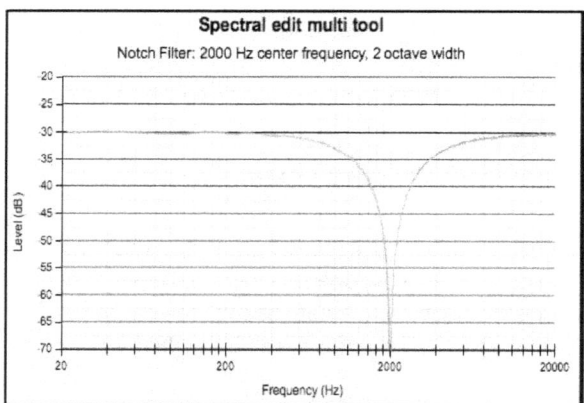

Fig 2-59 In the following example the spectral selection had a center frequency of 2,000 Hz and a bandwidth of 2 octaves. Audacity

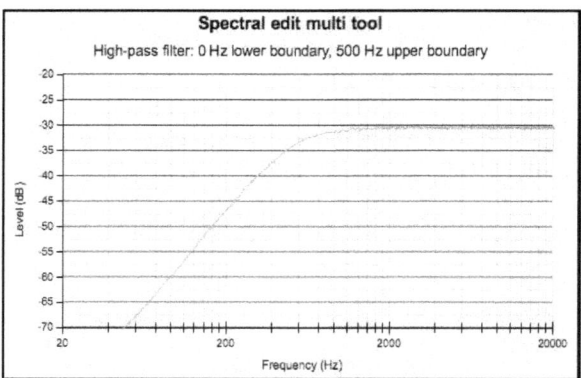

Fig 2-59 If you make a spectral selection that has the lower boundary at 0 Hz, selecting Effect > Spectral edit multi tool will apply a high-pass filter. Audacity

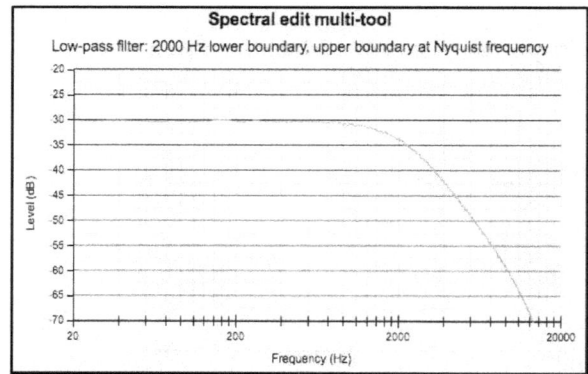

Fig 2-60. If you make a spectral selection that has the upper boundary at the Nyquist frequency of the track, selecting Effect > Spectral edit multi tool will apply a low-pass filter. Audacity

SPECTRAL EDIT PARAMETRIC EQ

The Spectral edit parametric EQ tool is used with a Spectral Selection to apply either a band boost filter, or band-cut filter to the selection. Accessed by: Effect > Spectral edit parametric EQ fig 2-61

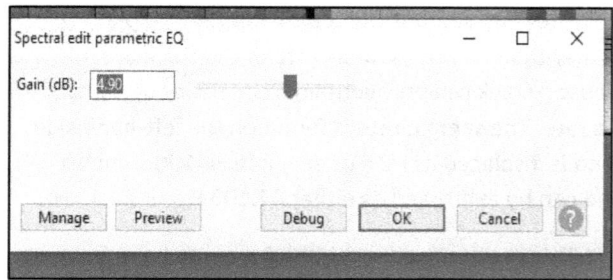

Fig 2-61 Spectral metric EQ effect box

Depending on how the track is displayed and what spectral selection has been made, this effect will do one of the following: If the track is not in Spectrogram View with Spectral Selection enabled, an error message will be displayed

When the spectral selection has a center, upper and lower frequency this effect performs a band cut or band boost according to the value entered in the "Gain (dB)" control. The center frequency is defined by the center frequency of the spectral selection and the bandwidth is defined by the upper and lower frequencies of the spectral selection.

If either the upper or lower frequency boundary is undefined, an error message will be displayed to that effect. If the lower frequency boundary is 0 Hz there is no center frequency or bandwidth and an error message will state that the lower frequency must be above 0 Hz.   Note: Due to a limitation in Nyquist effects, the effect dialog will be displayed before any error message.

Manage gives a dropdown menu enabling you to manage presets for the tool and to see some detail about the tool. For details see Manage presets

Preview plays a short preview of what the audio would sound like if the effect is applied with the current settings, without making actual changes to the audio. The length of preview is determined by your setting in Edit > Preferences > Playback, the default setting is 6 seconds.

Debug applies the effect to the selected audio with the current effect settings, but unlike OK the effect runs in debug mode. This is primarily of use when writing or editing Nyquist plug-ins.

In addition to the normal plug-in behavior, a "debug window" opens to display error messages, normally the debug window will be empty. To close and keep the changes press okay to leave without keeping changes press cancel

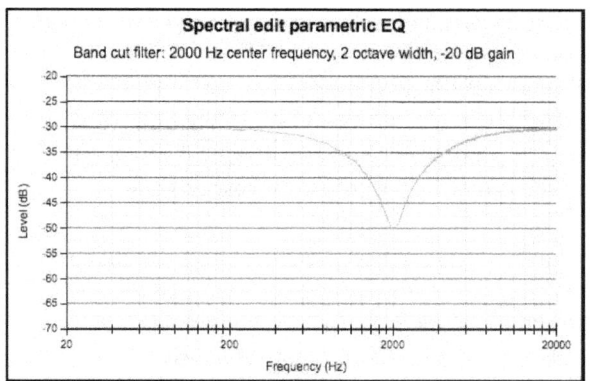

Fig 2-71 In the following example the spectral selection had a center frequency of 2,000 Hz and a bandwidth of 2 octaves. In the Spectral edit parametric EQ dialog, the Gain was set to -20 dB.

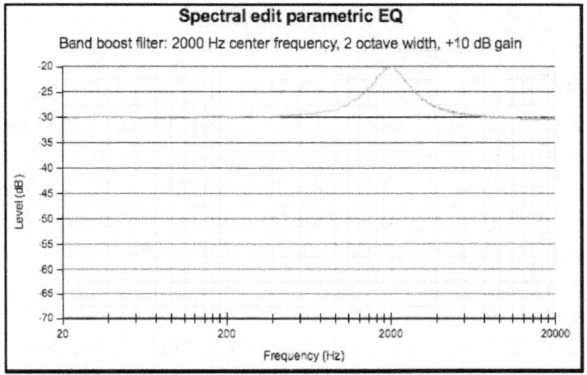

Fig 2-62 In the following example the spectral selection had a center frequency of 2,000 Hz and a bandwidth of 2 octaves. In the Spectral edit parametric EQ dialog, the Gain was set to +10 dB.

SPECTRAL EDIT SHELVES

The Spectral edit shelves effect is used with a Spectral Selection to apply either a low-shelving filter or a high-shelving filter to the selection, depending on the type of selection made.

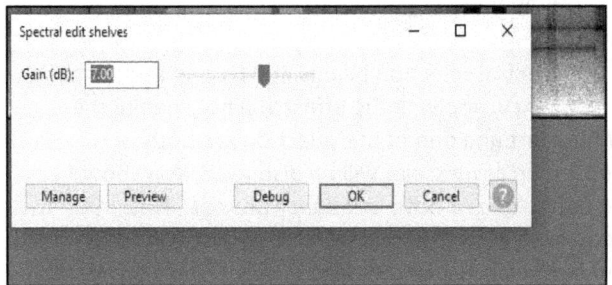

Fig 2-63 Spectral Edit shelve box

A shelf filter curve is flat at both ends rather than flat only at the frequencies being passed. Use these filters when you do not want to reduce the lowest bass or highest treble frequencies in the spectral selection as much as you would with a standard high pass or low pass filter, or if you want to boost either the low or high frequencies respectively.

Depending on how the track is displayed and what spectral selection has been made, this effect will do one of the following: When the track is not in Spectrogram View with Spectral Selection enabled, an error message will be displayed

If the spectral selection begins at 0 Hz or its lower bound is undefined, this effect applies a low frequency shelving filter with the half-gain frequency (the mid-point of the gain section of the curve) defined by the upper boundary of the spectral selection. The gain control sets the amount of low-frequency boost or cut. This is similar to adjusting the bass control on a stereo.

When the spectral selection ends at the Nyquist frequency of the track or its upper bound is undefined, this effect applies a high frequency shelving filter with the half-gain frequency defined by the lower frequency of the spectral selection. The gain control sets the amount of high-frequency boost or cut. This is like adjusting the treble control on a stereo.

If the spectral selection has a center frequency and upper and lower frequency boundaries this effect applies both low- and high-frequency shelving filters. In this case the half-gain frequency of the low shelving filter is defined by the lower frequency boundary of the spectral selection and the half-gain frequency of the high shelving filter is defined by the upper frequency boundary of the spectral selection. The gain control sets the amount of boost or cut between the two frequency boundaries.

When the spectral selection begins at 0 Hz and ends at the Nyquist frequency, applying the effect will not change the audio. If the start and end of the selection are both undefined, an error message will be displayed. You should go back and define one or both frequency bounds. Note: Due to a limitation in Nyquist effects, the effect dialog will be displayed before any error message.

Manage gives a dropdown menu enabling you to manage presets for the tool and to see some detail about the tool. For details see Manage presets

Preview plays a short preview of what the audio would sound like if the effect is applied with the current settings, without making actual changes to the audio. The length of preview is determined by your setting in Edit > Preferences > Playback, the default setting is 6 seconds.

Debug applies the effect to the selected audio with the current effect settings, but unlike OK the effect runs in debug mode. This is primarily of use when writing or editing Nyquist plug-ins. In addition to the normal plug-in behavior, a "debug window" opens to display error messages, normally the debug window will be empty

Click *OK* if you want to apply the effect to the selected audio with the current effect settings and closes the dialog box. Press *Cancel* if you want to close the box without the selected effects.

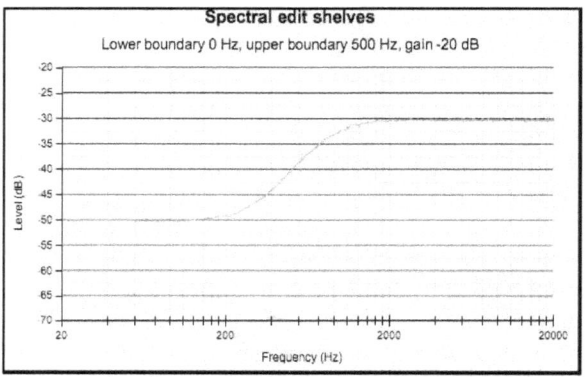

Fig 2-64 In the above example the spectral selection had a lower boundary of 0 Hz and an upper boundary of 500 Hz. In the Spectral edit shelves dialog, the Gain was set to -20 dB.

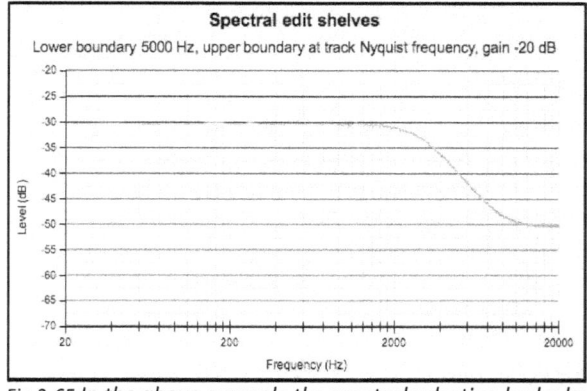

Fig 2-65 In the above example the spectral selection had a lower boundary of 5,000 Hz and an upper boundary of the Nyquist frequency of the track. In the Spectral edit shelves dialog, the Gain was set to -20 dB.

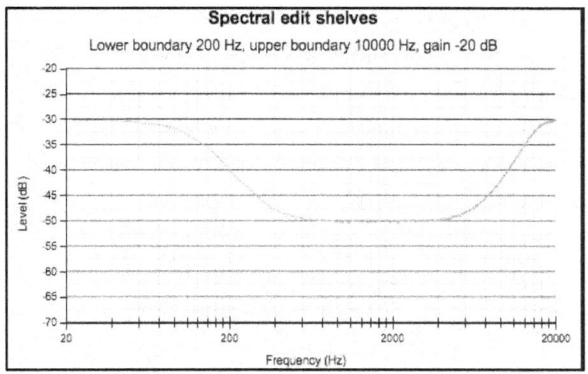

Fig 2-66 *In the following example the spectral selection had a lower boundary of 200 Hz and an upper boundary of 10,000 Hz. In the Spectral edit shelves dialog, the Gain was set to -20 dB.*

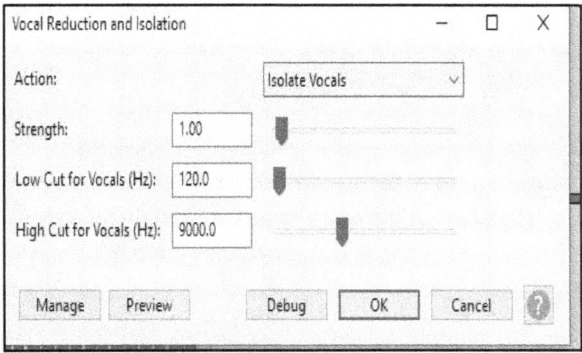

Fig 2-67 *Vocal reduction and isolation box*

STUDIO FADE OUT

What is it?: Want that sound of the record fading out you hear on albums and the radio. Or for your pod cast you hear on the talk shows. This is the effect that will do it. However, if you cut out to late or too soon it will sound strange.   For more on this see the See the Mastering section

TREMOLO

What is it? This effect is often thought of being with guitar and then later the Rhodes and Wurlitzer electric pianos. Here however it is often mislabeled as a vibrato effect. Proof? Strike and note and produce the effect on a Fender Stratocaster. Does the sound double? No, it vibrates. In recording terms *tremolo* effect cyclically changes the volume, with preset wave forms. It does this by varying the signal up and down. Vibrato varies the pitch up and down.

TOOLS

Waveform Type: Determines the "shape" of each tremolo (how it progresses between the lowest and highest volume as determined by the wetness level). Choice of sine, triangle, sawtooth, inverse sawtooth, square. The best way to understand this is just to try them out.

Starting Phase (Degrees): Sets where to start the tremolo in the waveform cycle. The default (zero) starts the tremolo at the start of the cycle (as the waveform starts to rise from the lowest point). It goes from -180 to +180.

Wet Level (percent): Sets the depth of tremolo. 0% is no tremolo, 100% sweeps between zero and maximum volume based on the original amplitude level. The more the slider is pushed to the right the more the effect can be heard.

Frequency (Hz): Controls the speed of the oscillation; use higher frequencies for faster oscillation. The scale goes from 0-1000

VOCAL REDUCTION AND ISOLATION

What is it? Really misnamed as it does not hunt for only vocals. It attempts to remove or isolate center-panned audio from a stereo track-which is usually vocals.

TOOLS

Remove Vocals: to mono: If the audio is center-panned, removes the vocal range defined by the *Low Cut and High Cut* sliders, and returns it as a dual-channel mono track. Audio is said to be "center-panned" if it is common to both left and right channels-meaning they *hard panned* to each channel.

Remove Vocals: If the audio is center-panned, removes the vocal range defined by the Low Cut and High Cut sliders, and returns it as a stereo track.

Isolate Vocals: If the audio is center-panned, extracts the slider-defined vocal range and returns it as a (dual) mono track.

Isolate Vocals and Invert: If the audio is center-panned, extracts the slider-defined vocal range and returns it as an inverted (dual) mono track.

VOCODER

What is it? Vocoder... synthesizes a modulator (usually a voice) in the left channel of a stereo track with a carrier wave in the right channel to produce a modified version of the left channel. Vocoding a normal voice with white noise as provided in the effect will produce a robot-like voice for special effects. Other carriers can be used for subtly different voices, such as a sawtooth tone, a musical tone or a synthesized string chord. Fig 2-68

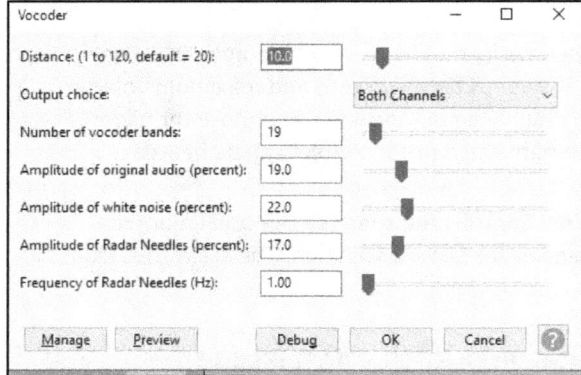

Fig 2-68 Vocoder effect box.

TOOLS

Distance: Defines the distance between the center frequency of the vocoder band to the cutoff frequency of the respective envelope low pass filter. With the default distance of 20.0 the envelope signals (generated from the modulator band-pass filters) are twenty times slower than the center frequency of the band-pass filters of the respective vocoder band. The distance controls the "responsiveness" of the Vocoder to changes in the modulator signal. The higher the distance, the slower the response. The smaller the distance, the more of the original modulator signal can be heard in the output signal.

Output choice: Both channels: The modulated vocoder output signal is duplicated into both stereo channels. This is most convenient when fine adjusting the vocoder output using headphones.

Right only: The modulated vocoder output signal appears only in the right channel, while the left channel still contains the unmodified modulator signal. This is useful when applying a mono modulator to a stereo carrier since the modulator can be reused when processing the right channel of the carrier.

Number of Vocoder Bands: Defines the frequency resolution of the Vocoder. This behaves similarly to a multiband equalizer. The more bands, the finer the different frequencies that can be manipulated and modulated. The default setting is 40. Increasing the number of Vocoder bands slows down the processing time.

Amplitude of Original audio (percent): Defines how much of the original audio signal shall be contained in the carrier signal; the default setting is 100%.

Amplitude of white noise (percent): The amount of white noise that is added to the right channel before applying the vocoder; the default setting is 0%.

Amplitude of Radar Needles (percent) The amplitude of "radar needles" that are added to the right channel before applying the vocoder. The default setting is 0%.

Radar needles" are a series of very short pulses (clicks), also known as "pulse train" in speech synthesizers. They have a pulse width of only one sample and a spectrum ranging from the frequency specified by the Frequency slider (below) up to much greater than 20 kHz.

Frequency of Radar Needles (Hz; The number of "radar needles" per second where only one sample per period has a non-zero value. This is the most-broadband signal possible, even more broadband than white noise. The default setting is 30.0 Hz. See also Wikipedia Dirac Comb for a detailed description.

Best results may be obtained if you first mix the radar needles with another sound, then apply Vocoder.

Chapter 3 Analyze and Tools

DRAW TOOL

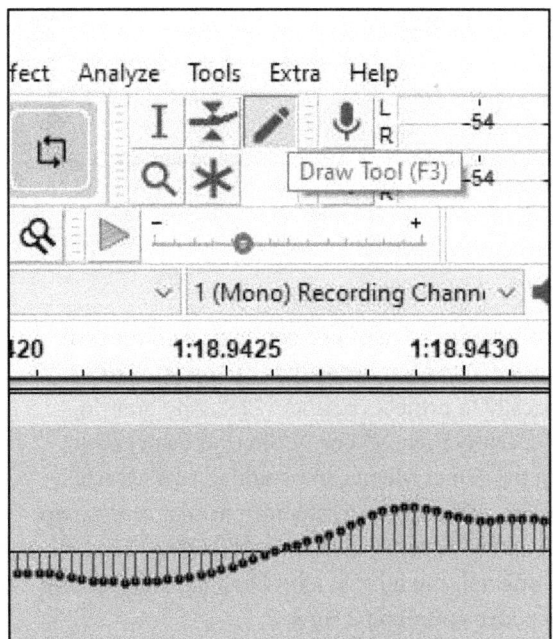

Fig 3-1 Zoom in using the zoom tool (the magnifying glass symbol at the bottom left). Then click on the drawing tool.

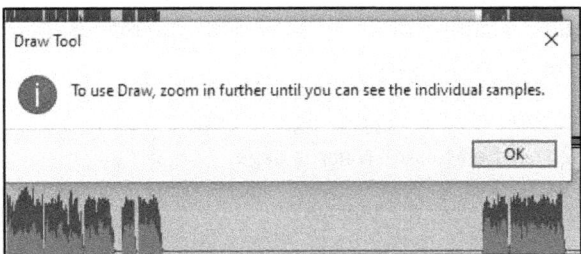

Fig 3-2 If you try to use the draw tool before zooming in you will get this error.

Draw Tool enables you to redraw the waveform; it can thus be used to make volume changes to individual samples or effect repairs to clicks/noise. If the draw tool is not selected it is not available. So, click on the tool and then zoom in until you see dots in the wave form. Fig 3-t0 3-2

When zoomed in close to maximum level, the Draw Tool enables you to adjust the volume level of individual audio samples. The closer the sample is to the horizontal line through the center of the track, the quieter the sample will be. The Draw Tool

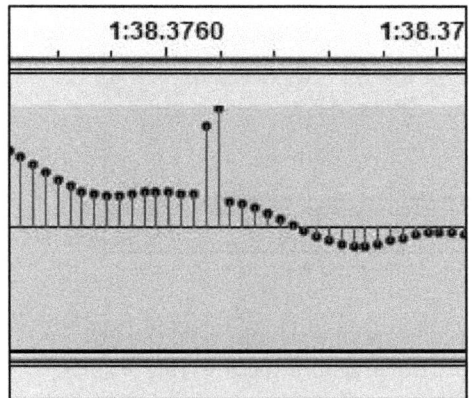

Fig 3-3 Clicking, and holding the mouse you can move the dots up and down.

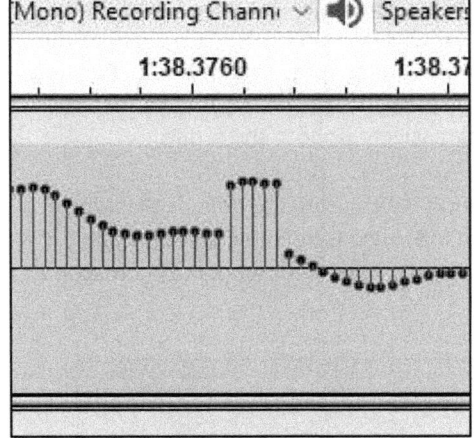

Fig 3-4 Click and hold the mouse and move left or right and dots will be added to the wave.

button can be used to eliminate narrow clicks and pops in audio by smoothing out the contour of the samples, so that one sample is not at a very different vertical position to its neighbors. Fig 3-3 to 3-4

Click above or below a single dot sample then while still holding the mouse key move up or down sample to move it to that vertical position. You can keep holding the mouse and drag it to the left or right and it will add samples to the wave.

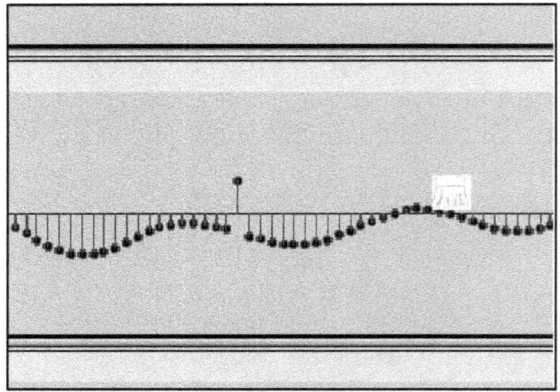

Fig 3-5 Holding down Alt. the draw tool will turn into a brush.

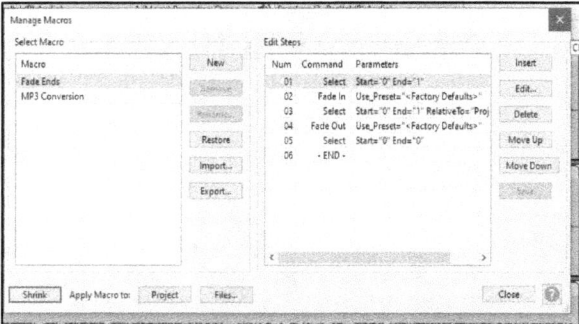

Fig 3-7 Marcos

If you only want to move one sample, hold the Ctrl button the keyboard down *before* clicking. This ensures that no other samples are affected, even if you drag slightly left or right by accident. Fig 3-5

Smooth the vertical disparity in a group of samples by holding down Alt (or Ctrl + Alt on Linux). This changes the mouse pointer to a brush (or spray can on Linux). Position the pointer halfway along the group of samples then click repeatedly to progressively smooth the group.

Draw Tool only works when using the default Waveform view or Waveform (dB) view (selectable on the Audio Track Dropdown Menu). It does not work in Spectrogram view.

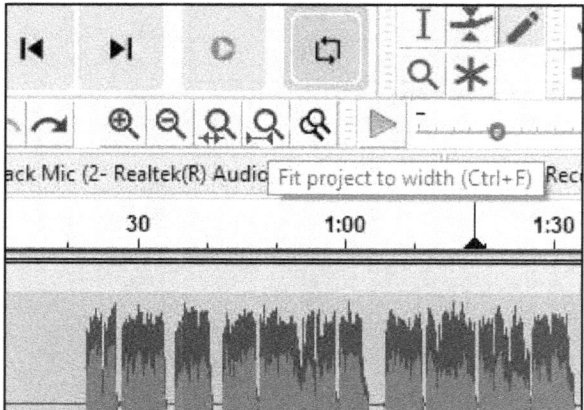

Fig 3-6 To return to original wave click the symbol or Ctrl and F.

MACROS

A Macro is a sequence of pre-configured commands (mainly effects) in a set order that can be applied automatically to projects or audio files. Any built-in, LADSPA, LV2, Nyquist, VST or Audio Unit (Mac) effect shown in the Effect Menu can be added to a Macro. You can also add plug-ins in any format that are shown in the Generate or Analyze Menus (including Vamp analysis effects), the built-in Find Clipping analyzer and several export commands. Fig 3-7

Macros follow a fixed sequence of instructions. If you want more flexibility than that, you may want to look at Python Scripting which uses the same commands and the Python language.

For further details on creating and editing Macros please see the Manage Macros page.

What are the uses for Macros?

The three main uses of Macros are: Batch processing: where many audio files are processed unattended with one or more effects then exported to a new file.

To use batch processing use the Apply Macro to: Files button in the Macros Palette or the Manage Macros dialog.

Effects automation: where the selected audio in the track or tracks in the current project is subjected to the same prescribed sequence of effects, and optionally, a file exported from the entire audio.

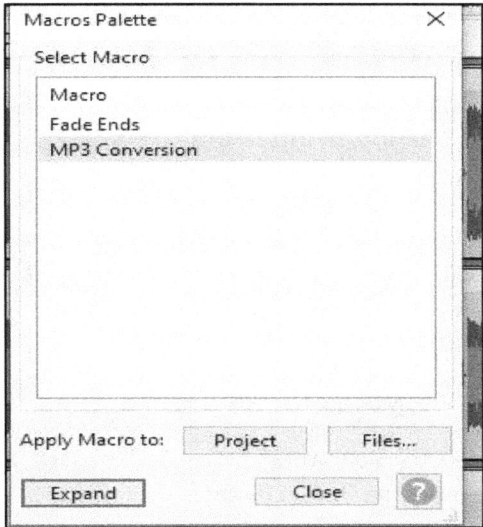

Fig 3-8 Use the Shrink button to show a reduced Macros Palette dialog with a simple list of the existing Macros. Click expand and it will return to the above menu.

Note that Macros can contain Select commands to make their own selections as the Macro runs.

Effect presets: where selected, commonly used, effects are stored with your preferred settings for quick re-use.

Apply Macro to: contains two buttons: *Project* applies the selected Macro to the current project and *Files* which applies the selected Macro to selected external audio files that are in a single directory. Note do not process more than 500 files at one time.

Click Delete and it will remove the selected area in the Marco. Click *Move Up* and the line will move up one. Note if it is at the top line, it will not move. Click *Move Down* and the line will move down one if at the end it will not move. Click *Save* and it will save your changes to the Marco.

Clicking *Close* will close the box it will alert you to save or not save the changes. Warning be sure if you don't want to save the changes click *No,* as this can't be undone by clicking Control Z or undo.

Where Macros are Stored

Each Macro is automatically saved as a separate text file with TXT extension in the "Macros" folder in Audacity's folder for application data:

Windows: Users\<username>\AppData\Roaming\audacity\Macros

Mac: ~/Library/Application Support/audacity/Macros

Linux: ~/.audacity-data/Macros

Note in order to see the Macros folder on Windows, macOS or GNU/Linux, you must show hidden files and folders or type the folder location into your file manager's address bar.

Windows: In the tree on the left of Explorer, double-click "Users" then double-click your username, then on the right, double-click the AppData or Application Data folder and navigate through that. If necessary, show hidden files and folders on Windows or type *%appdata%\audacity\Macros* or *shell:appdata\audacity\Macros* into the Explorer address bar then press Enter on your keyboard.

macOS: Open Finder, use the Go menu, choose Go to Folder and *type ~/Library/Application Support/audacity/Macros*, or set Finder to show your User Library folder.

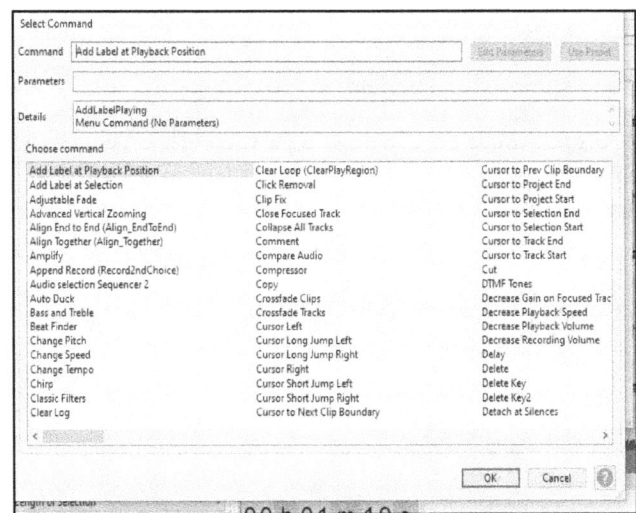

Fig 3-8 Click Insert and this box appears

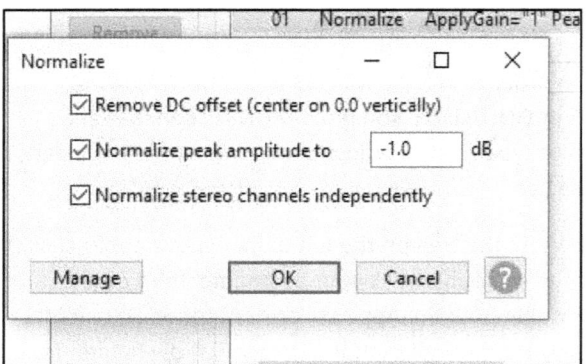

Fig 3-9 Click edit and the Normalize box pops up.

Examples Of Marcos

Loud MP3

A batch processing Macro to compress and normalize WAV files then convert them to MP3: Insert Compressor to reduce the dynamic range of each WAV, also normalizing them to maximum amplitude of 0 dB Fig 3-10

Insert Export as MP3 to convert them to MP3 format

Click "Apply Macro to:" Files to select the files on which to run the Macro. Click OK to close the "Manage Macros" window

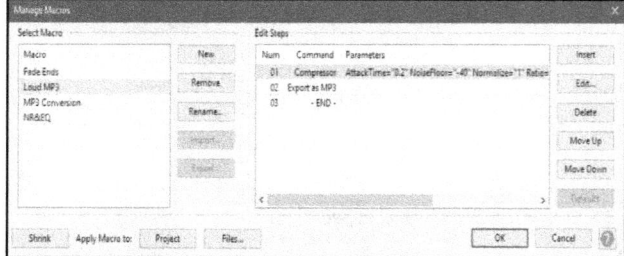

Fig 3-10 Example of the Marco menu with Loud MP3 Audacity

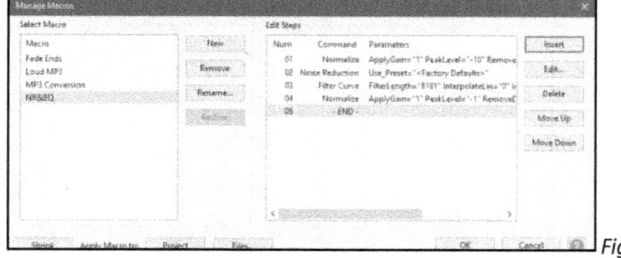

Fig 3-11 Noise reduction and EQ. Audacity

To create a Marco that applies noise reduction and equalization: Fig 3-11 Do this:

Insert Normalize with settings of: Remove any DC offset -10 dB (to allow for boosting frequencies later in the Macro without clipping).

Insert Noise Reduction: Insert Filter Curve EQ (to perform the frequency adjustment). Insert another Normalize at different settings (without offset removal, setting a final amplitude of -1 dB)

Click OK to close the "Manage Macros" window

When later needed in your workflow, choose Tools > Apply Macro..., select the "NR&EQ" Macro then click "Apply Macro to:" Project to apply the Macro to the selected track(s) in the current project window.

Note if a Noise Profile exists, that Noise Profile will be used. It is often best to capture a suitable Noise Profile before running a Macro. If a Noise Profile does not exist and the Macro is applied to the current project, the current selection is used to create the Noise Profile. Therefore, other effect commands in the Macro will also only apply to that selection. If an export command is added, the entire file will be exported.

If the Macro is applied to files, the first file (all of it) is used to create the Noise Profile. It may be useful to prepare a file containing a suitable Noise Profile and name it so that it is alphabetically the first file of those to be run in the Macro.

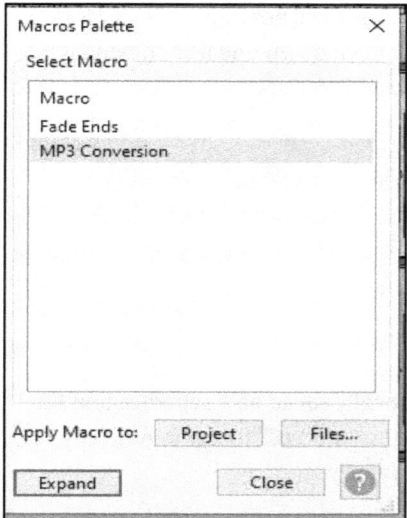

Fig 3-12 *Click Marco Palette and this box pops up*

Useful Commands

Command	Description
"Select: RelativeTo=Selection Start=-1 End=1"	This command expands a selection by two seconds:
"Select: RelativeTo=Selection Start=1 End=-1"	This command contracts a selection by two seconds:
"Select: RelativeTo=Selection Start=1 End=1"	This command moves a selection right by one second:
"SelTrackStartToEnd"	This command (from Select>Region>Track Strat to End) Selects all audio in all selected tracks.
"SelNextClip" "SelPrevClip"	These commands are useful with Clips

RESET CONFIGURATION

What is this! Be careful do not click on this out curiosity. It resets your Audacity configuration (preferences, export settings and toolbars) to default settings. **Warning: this command acts immediately with no dialog and no choice of actions or chance to abort. Undo is NOT available for this command.**

It accessed by clicking Tools > Reset Configuration. Using Reset Configuration will reset all your Audacity Preferences settings to their default "factory settings". The exception is the setting for "Check for updates" in Application Preferences, which remains unaltered with the use of this command.

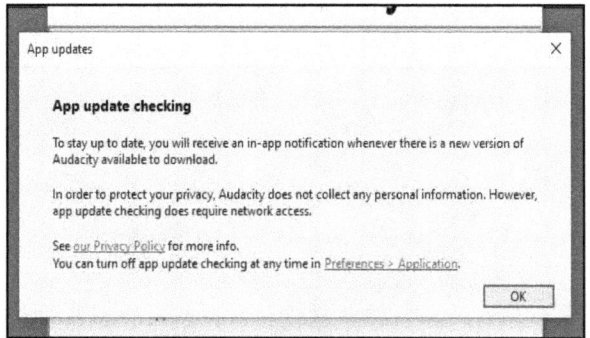

Fig 3-13 -Example of app checking box.

Note rest will not erase your files, especially if you have stored them in a different file. Which is always a good idea. But when you click open, it will automatically go to the audacity file, even if you had another file open. But click open recent files and you will see your recent files. To get back to your other file folder click open and find your file and then open it.

What is Not Reset

Settings in Preferences Update Checking: the setting you make in Application Preferences for update checking is not changed by Reset Configuration.

Settings in Effects Generators and Analyzers

User Presets that you have saved for any Effect, Generator or Analyzer will not be removed by Reset Configuration.

Importantly this includes equalization settings you may have made in Filter Curve EQ and Graphic EQ.

Last-used parameter settings that you may have used in any Effect, Generator or Analyzer are not reset to default values.

If you need or want to reset these to Factory default values for any particular effect, Generator or Analyzer please use the Manage button and choose Factory Presets.

Font setting for Label tracks

The global Font setting made in any label track's drop-down menu is not changed by Reset Configuration.

Plug-ins: Any plug-ins that you have added will not be removed. Also, Macros that you have created will not be removed or altered by using this command. In most cases you will never need this tool.

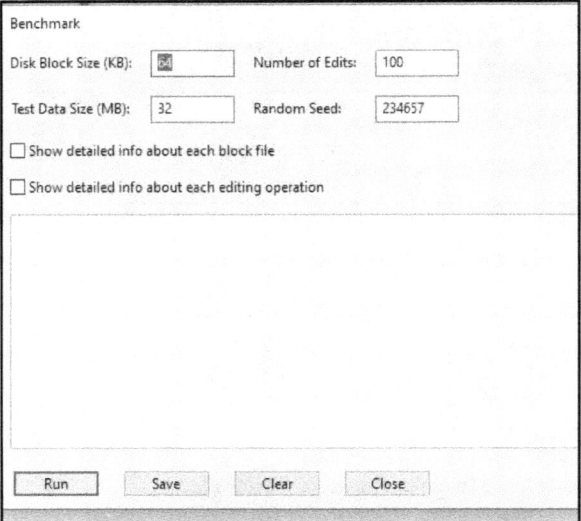

Fig 3-15 Has nothing to do with recording, mixing or mastering. It is to run a test to see if your computer and run the program.

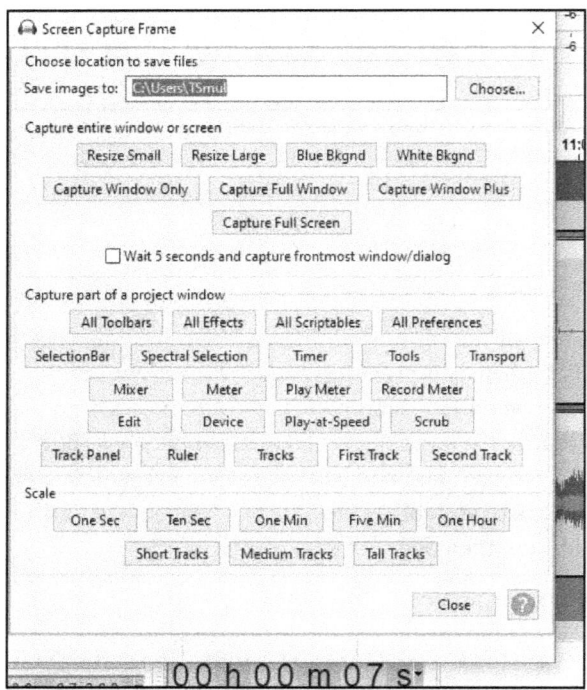

Fig 3-14 Access by clicking Tools> Screenshot. When you click on one of the boxes it will create a png photo in your file

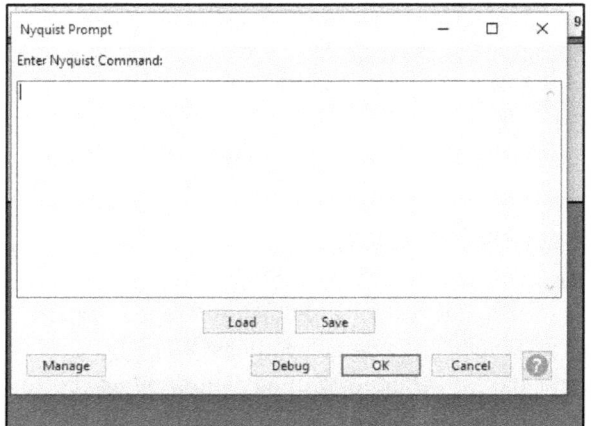

Fig 3-16 Click Nyquist Prompt and you get this box.

NYQUIST PROMPT

This lets you run and debug code snippets for your own plug-ins created using the Nyquist programming language. See the Manual's Nyquist page for more information about writing Nyquist code. See also the Audacity wiki page on Nyquist. Fig 3-16, To process audio with Nyquist commands, first select some audio. Then click *Tools > Nyquist Prompt...*

Enter Nyquist Command

Type the command as required. Enter on the keyboard moves the cursor to a new line. The last entered code is stored in the *pluginsettings.cfg* file in Audacity's folder for application data so is retained after exiting Audacity.

Plugin GUI can be tested if you include complete Nyquist Plug-in Headers. The Nyquist Prompt interprets header comments to produce a plug-in of the defined type on the fly. By default, the plug-in is a process type, though other type may be created by including the appropriate header.

Load: will load a Nyquist plugin or script file saved with .ny extension. Click Save to save the current contents of the editor window it will be saved as an .ny file.

There are no presets, but you can save the ones you create, and they will appear here. By clicking *Manage then click save preset.* Name the file and click *OK*.

Debug: Clicking this button redirects error messages from Audacity's error log to a non-editable "Debug" window. An empty debug windows indicates that no errors were detected. Click OK to close the debug window or using the keyboard, hold Ctrl on Windows (or ⌘ on Mac) then press Enter.

OK Applies the code to the waveform selection without debug output. Your entered code will be retained next time you open Nyquist Prompt in the Audacity session. Using the keyboard hold Ctrl on Windows (or ⌘ on Mac) then press Enter. Using the keyboard on Linux, hold down Alt and press O. to exit and not save any changes click *Cancel*.

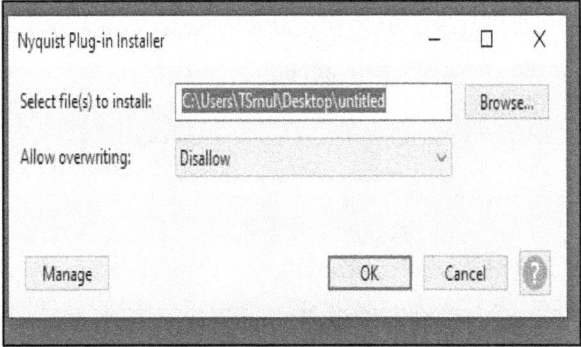

Fig 3-17 Click Tools>Nyquist Plug-in installer and you get this box

NYQUIST PLUG-IN INSTALLER

The Nyquist Plug-in Installer is itself a Nyquist plug-in that simplifies the installation of other Nyquist plug-ins. All Nyquist plug-ins are plain text files that have the filename extension '.NY'. This plug-in installer provides a file browser for selecting the plug-in '.NY' file, and then copies the file to the correct location. Once the plug-in has been installed, it may be enabled in the Plug-in Manager. Fig 3-17

The Nyquist Plug-in Installer installs one or more selected plug-ins for the current user, by copying the file(s) to the appropriate plug-ins folder.

After installation, plug-ins must be enabled in the Plug-in Manager.

To Install a Nyquist plug-in:

Click the 'File Browser' button and select the plug-in file. Click the 'OK' button to install, or 'Cancel'. Carefully review the output message.

Use the Plug-in Manager to enable the installed plug-in. Allow overwriting This is off by default, preventing you from accidentally overwriting an existing Nyquist plug-in of the same name. If you do wish to overwrite an existing Nyquist plug-in, change that to "Allow".

Note: In Windows / Linux: If you are unable to locate a plug-in that you have downloaded, this may be due to your web browser adding '.TXT' to the file name. In this case, you can change the file type filter in the file browser to show text files, or to show all files. The Nyquist Plug-in Installer can automatically correct the file name if '.TXT' has been erroneously added.

Marcos: When downloading a Nyquist plug-in from the Internet, the web browser may add '.TXT' to the file name. Nyquist Plug-in Installer can correct this error automatically. If the filename extension is anything other than '.NY' or '.NY.TXT', then it is not a valid Nyquist plug-in and installation will fail.

.ZIP files: If the plug-in file name ends with '.ZIP', then it is an archive file. The plug-in file(s) inside the '.ZIP' files must be extracted first before they can be installed.

On successful installation: The Nyquist Plug-in Installer will display the name of the installed plug-in, and the full location of where it has been installed. Note that the installed plug-in will not be available in the Audacity menus until it has been enabled in the 'Plug-in Manager'.

You may end up with some Error messages:

<file name> not found or cannot be read. Check that you have selected the correct file.

<file name> is not a supported plug-in. The selected file is not a Nyquist plug-in, or is malformed., it may be a valid plug-in, but is not fully compliant with Nyquist plug-in standards.

<file name> is not a valid Nyquist plug-in. This error occurs if the file does not have the correct file extension (NY) and the Nyquist Plug-in Installer is unable to correct it.

<file name> cannot be written. The plug-in cannot be written to the default installation location. Ensure that you are logged in with a full user account-not a 'guest' account.

<file name> is already installed. To avoid accidentally overwriting other plug-ins, if a plug-in with the same file name exists, the Nyquist Plug-in Installer will not overwrite it. If you want to update an older version of the plug-in, you will need to enable the Allow overwriting option.

If you are sure that the conflicting plug-in is a totally different plug-in that happens to have the same file name, then you could try renaming the new plug-in. In this case you must ensure that the new name retains the '.NY' filename extension.

Advanced Usage: Although currently rare, some plug-ins may include additional files in TXT, HTML or LSP formats. TXT / HTML files may be used by plug-ins to display a user manual for the plug-in.

Plug-ins developers that wish to include help files should refer to this documentation in the Audacity wiki files on the internet. LSP files may be used by a plug-in to provide additional code that is, or can be used by multiple plug-ins.

To install other supported file types (TXT, HTML, LSP), select the appropriate file type filter in the file browser. Note that the only file type for a Nyquist plug-in is .NY. The other supported file types are copied to the user's plug-in folder so that the associated plug-in can access them, but do not need to be enabled in the Plug-In Manager, and do not appear in the Plug-In Manager.

Plug-in Developer Note:

If a help file is included with a plug-in, it should be named in a manner to clearly show that it belongs with the plug-in. For example, if the plug-in is named "my-plug-in.ny", then the associated help file may be called "my-plug-in.html" or "my-plug-in-help.html".

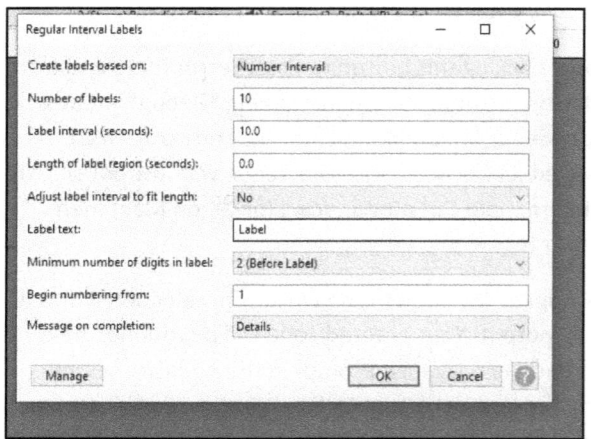

Fig 3-18 Click on Tools> Regular interval labels and this box pops up.

REGULAR INTERVAL LABELS

This tool places labels in a label track so as to divide the associated audio into smaller, equally-sized segments. This can be useful for distributing a large file on the Internet or ensuring that all exported files are the same size. Fig 3-18

You can specify the number of labels and the interval between them, or fit labels to the current audio selection. Each label produced can contain specified label text and the labels can be given sequential numbers before or after the text.

This effect requires an audio selection, even if the selection is not used. So, select the track first then click *Tools > Regular Interval Labels...*

Note Regular Interval Labels" may be used to divide a long recording into sections, which may then be exported in one process using File > Export > Export Multiple...

If the selection includes one or more label tracks, the new labels generated by this effect will be merged into the first selected label track. To generate labels into a new label track, ensure that no labels tracks are included in the selection.

Create Labels Based on

This enables you to choose the label placement method: This includes Number of Labels; Number of Intervals or Label Interval.

To place labels within the selection a chosen distance apart, select Label Interval menu dropdown from the dropdown then enter that distance in Label interval (seconds).

If you selected Number & Interval menu dropdown (the default) then the specified number of labels will be created at the specified intervals. The number of labels may be between 1 and 1000 (default: 10 labels). The interval may be between 0.001 3600 seconds (default: 10 seconds). The selection is ignored by this labeling method.

If you selected Number of Labels menu dropdown, then your specified number of labels (default is 10) will be created to fit the selected region. The number can be changed by typing in the input box, the allowed range is between 1 and 1000 labels.

When you selected Label Interval menu dropdown then the labels will be placed at your specified interval to fit the selected region. The default interval is 10.0 seconds. The allowed range is between 0.001 and 3600 seconds.

If set to zero, point labels are generated. When set greater than zero, region labels are generated, each with the duration specified by this control. The allowed range is 0 to 3600 seconds.

Note to create region labels that meet end to end, use either the Number & Interval menu dropdown or Label Interval menu dropdown option, and set the Length of label region to the same duration as the Label interval setting. If Label Interval menu dropdown is selected, ensure that "Adjust label interval to fit length" is set to No menu dropdown.

Adjust label interval to fit length: The default setting for this control is No menu dropdown. This setting only applies when you create labels based on Number of Labels menu dropdown

If you select Yes menu dropdown from the dropdown for this control, it adjusts your chosen label interval if necessary to make all the segments of equal length, including the final segment between the last label and the end of the selection.

Point labels: (Length of label region = 0) "Segments" are defined as the time between one label and the next (or the final label and the end of the selection). In other words, segments are the same as the label intervals.

Region labels: (Length of label region greater than 0) "Segments" are defined as the time from the start of the label to the end of the label. In other words, the segments are the same as the label regions.

When set to No menu dropdown, the interval between labels will be exactly the length specified in the Label interval control, but the final segment from the last label to the end of the selection may be different (depending on whether the selection length is exactly divisible by the specified interval duration.

If number & Interval menu dropdown is selected, the label interval will always be the length specified by the Label interval. If Number of Labels menu dropdown is selected, the labels will always be placed evenly to fit the selection.

For point labels, the interval will always be the length of the selection divided by the number of labels. For region labels, the end of the final region will always be at the end of the selection.

Label Text: The text that will be included in each label. The default setting is Label, but this can be replaced by any text (or no text) by using the input box.

The label text may include spaces and/or punctuation characters but note that if you intend to use the labels with Export Multiple, some characters may not be valid for file names. These will include those same ones that are not included with other flies like / and among other symbols.

Minimum Number of Digits in Label

Choose the minimum number of number of digits in the label numbers and whether the number is placed before or after the label text. The default setting is 2(before label) menu dropdown. With that setting, if you had 10 labels with "Label" as the label text, the first label would be "01Label", the next "02Label" and the last would be "10Label". If you select None - text only menu dropdown, then no numbering will be applied to the labels. If you choose this and set no label text, then you will produce a set of empty labels.

Begin Numbering From

If a minimum number of digits has been chosen in the control above, enter the number from which the sequential numbering will start. The default value of 1 can be changed by typing in the input box. You can enter any whole number equal or greater than 0.

The number of digits that are produced in the label is determined by your choice in Minimum number of digits in label above. For example, if you type "10" in Begin numbering from and your minimum number of digits is 3, then the first label will be numbered from "010".

Message on Completion

This setting determines what messages are displayed when the effect completes. Note if you wish to use this effect in a macro for batch processing, it can be useful to disable message reports.

Details Menu dropdown (default) Displays a message with the number of labels generated, and the interval between them. Details. Warnings only or none are selected from a drop-down menu.

This tool as the standard type buttons: *Manage* gives a dropdown menu enabling you to manage and create presets for the tool.

OK applies the effect to the selected audio with the current effect settings and closes box. To return to the project page without any changes click *Cancel*.

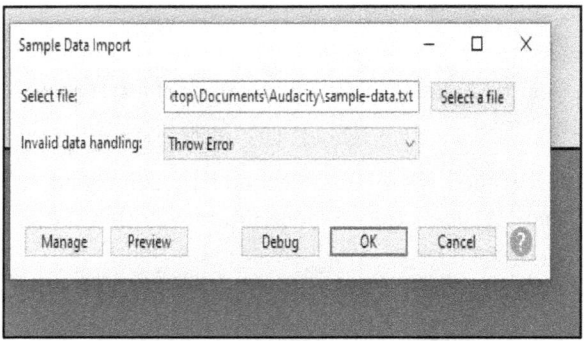

Fig 3-19 Sample the importing file the file MUST be plain ASCII text, and values should be separated by spaces, tabs or line-breaks. The file name must have a '.txt' file extension.

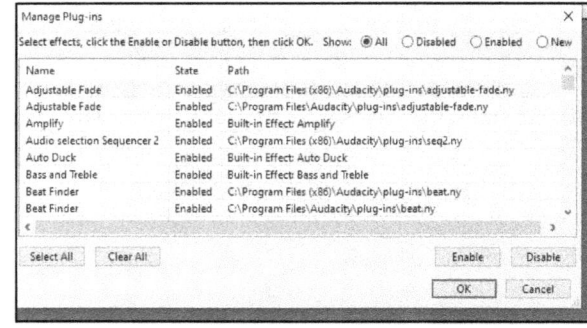

Fig 3-20 Click Tools Manage plug -ins and this box opens up. To control the plug ins just click enable or disable. This is also found under Analyze> Manage plug is.

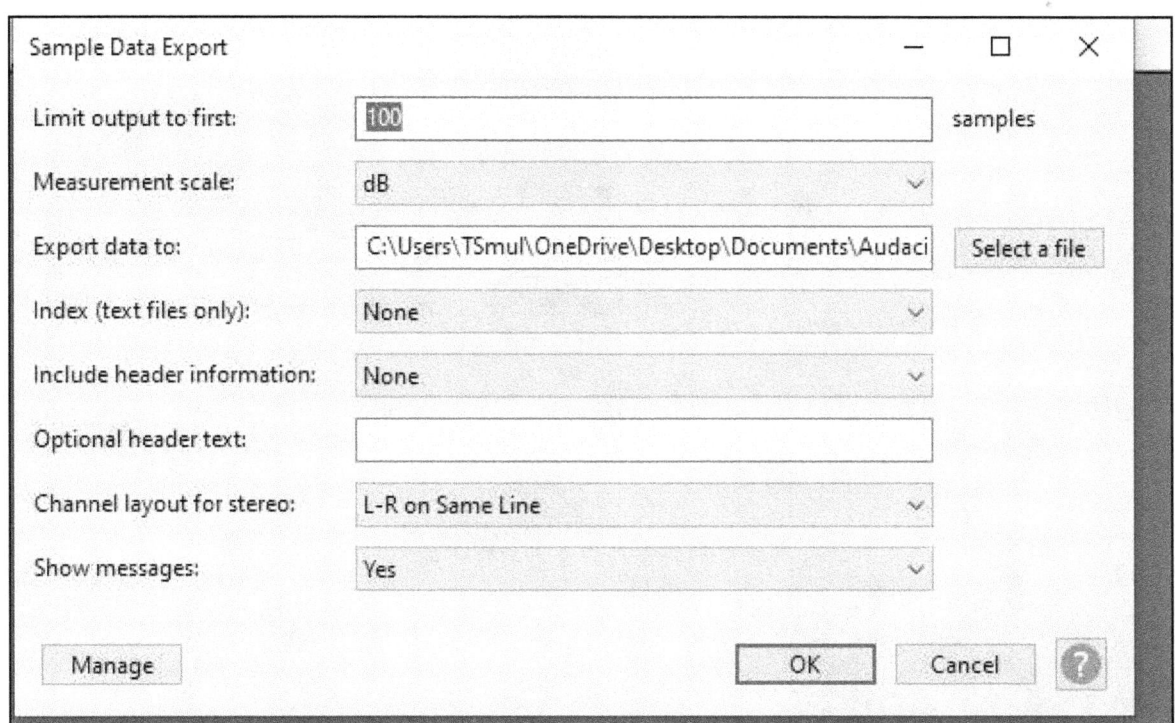

Fig 3-21 Sample Data Export reads the values of successive samples from the selected audio and prints this data to a plain text, CSV or HTML file. Further information may be added as a "header" at the top of the file.

CONTRAST

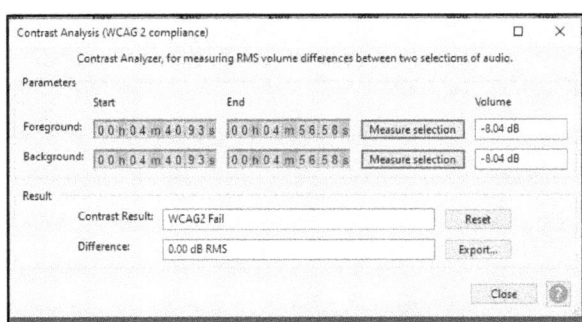

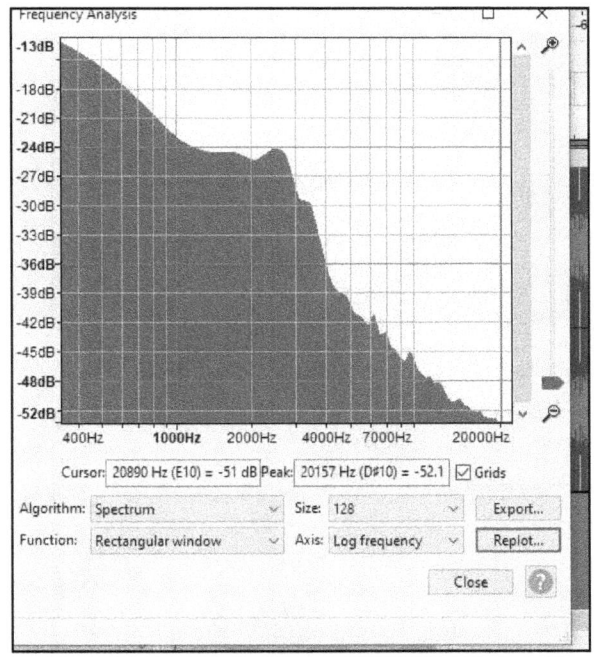

Fig 3-22 Contrast is comparing the fore ground sound to the background sound. It is not much use in recording music. But can be helpful in a pod cast for a voice with background music. It can only do one single track of audio at a time. Or one single stereo tack. It uses the WCAG2 pass or fail. If there is a difference of pass is given if the difference is 20 dB or more. If there is no difference as seen in the example it seen as fail.

Fig 3-23 Click Analyze >Plot Spectrum and this is the default box. It has meaning different views. It is just best to go through them and see how the same selected piece of audio looks at the different choices. It is great for finding the hidden sounds and removing them.

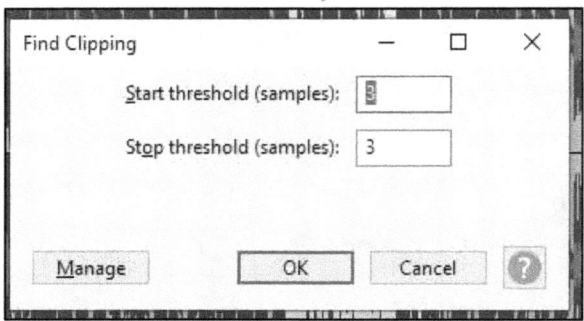

Fig 3-24 Click Analyze> Find Clipping and this box will appear.

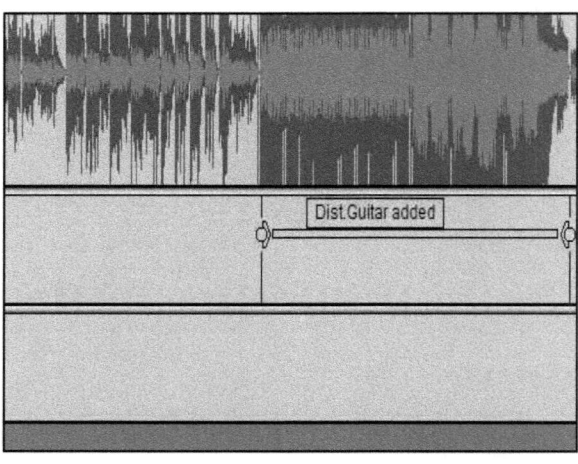

Fig 3-27 When you add to Label Sounds it automatically adds a label track for each label.

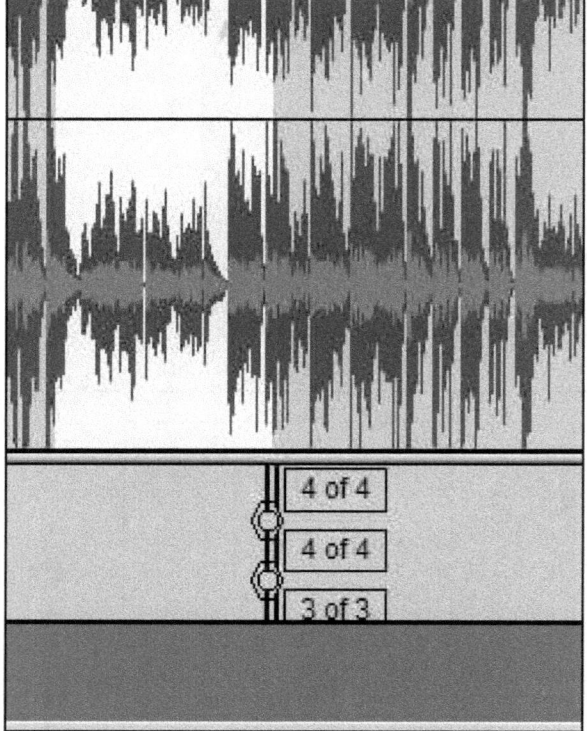

Fig 3-25 Click OK in the box above and the clipping will be found.

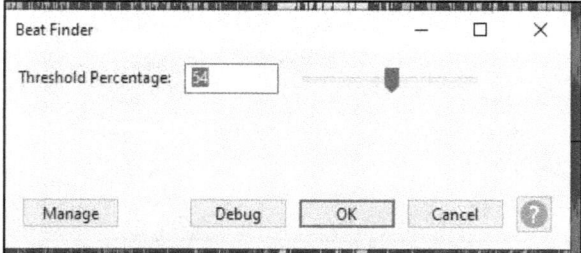

Fig 3-26 Beat Finder attempts to place labels at beats which are much louder than the surrounding audio. It's a fairly rough and ready tool and will not necessarily work well on a typical modern pop music track with compressed dynamic range.

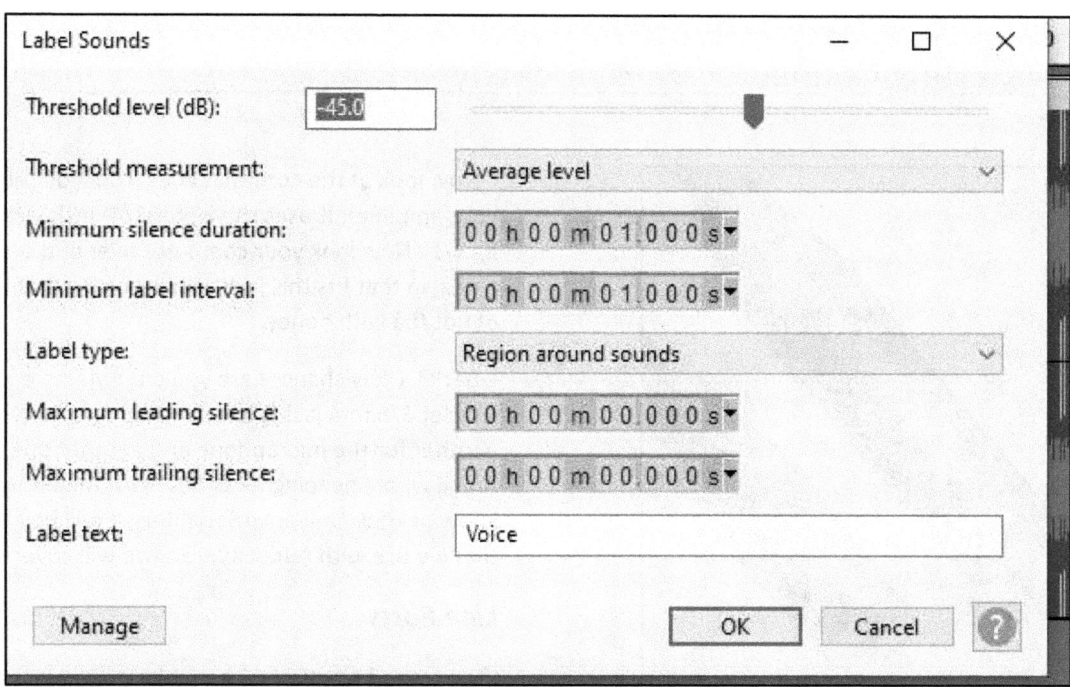

Fig 3-28 Label Sounds is a tool which can be useful to label the different songs or sections (or silences) in a long recording, such as the tracks from an LP or cassette

CHAPTER 4   Getting Connected with Audacity

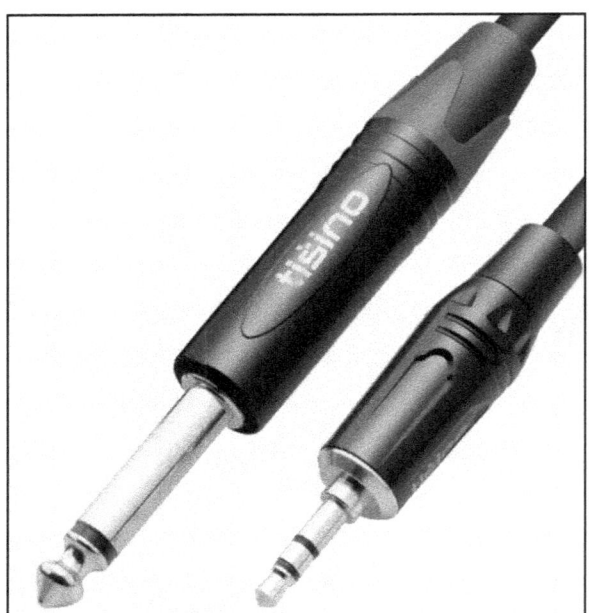

Fig 4-1: The big problem most instruments and microphones use a ¼ inch jack (left) and most computers use a 1/8 (3.5 mm) jack.

CONNECTING UP

First, your computer must have a sound card installed for Audacity to operate. Fortunately, most do. If you have listened to music or played games and heard sound on your computer, then it has a sound card.

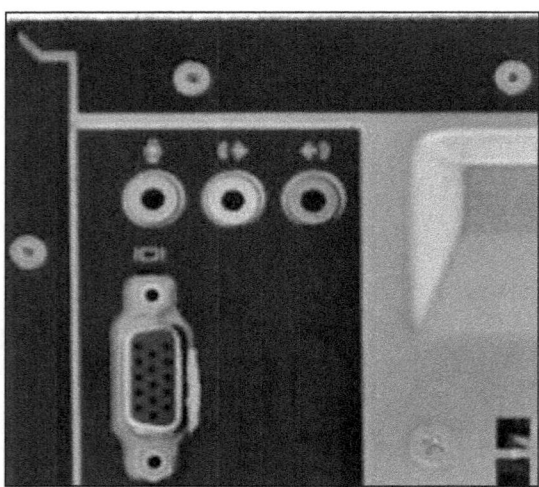

Fig.4-2 Speaker, line, and microphone ports on back of computer

Now look at the cord that goes from your electric guitar to your amplifier. It uses the larger 1/4- inch jack that is seen in fig 4-1. Now look your computer over and see if you can find a plug in that fits this jack. While you do that I will get a cup of hot tea with honey.

Back? Okay chances are you did not. Instead ,you found the smaller 3/5 mm jacks, one for output (speakers/headphones) another for the microphone and another one for line input. And a whole heaping lot of little rectangular shaped slots know as USB- Universal Serial Bus, it will be all these ports that we use with Audacity.   So, we will cover each one.

Line Ports

The rear of a typical PC has color-coded jacks fig 4-2 on the sound card. The pink port is normally the microphone input and is usually mono but might be stereo. The light blue port is normally the line input port and is usually stereo. The green port is normally the headphone/speaker output port, also usually stereo. Check your computer manual to be sure.

PC laptops vary widely in the types of sound input and output ports they provide, where they are on the laptop, and how they are labeled. Many modern laptops do not have a line input at all or a microphone port as microphone is built. This type of set up is not suitable for recording, so opt for one that has the required ports, and a built-in microphone is not suitable for recording. If you try you will not be pleased with the results.

These ports include:

Mic In: Generally, the Mic In port on a computer is only meant to have a small computer microphone plugged into it. If you have a microphone with an 1/8" (3.5mm) 3-conductor jack plug, it will probably work if plugged into this port.

Fig 4-3 Macs Computers do not generally have a microphone input port. Usually only one for the headphones and the line ports.

Line In: The Line In port is the highest quality input available on most sound cards (like the one pictured above). It expects to have a Line level signal plugged into it; this is the same level used by most consumer-oriented audio equipment. Equipment such as tape decks, record players, MiniDisc players, Video Game Systems and so on should be plugged into this port. This port can be used with some piano keyboards.

USB PORTS

PC usually have several USB ports these are the ports that the printer, computer keyboard, mouse and plug into. So, to run Audacity you are going to have a free USB port.

USB cables come in three different sizes: *Standard* this like the one that runs from the computer to the printer fig 4-4. *Mini:* This usually runs to another device like a recorder fig 4-5. And *Micro:* Which used to charge your phone fig 4-6.

Fig 4-4 Standard USB cable

Fig 4-5 *Mini USB cable*

Fig 4-6 *Micro USB cable*

USB CABLES SPEED

Cable	Speed Megabits per Second
1.1	12
2.0	480 (Best overall for recording)
3x	5Gbps
C	Over 100 Gbps (Has special end) Used on high data devices like digital recorders

Fig 4-7 The fast downloading USB is the C-cable which has a special end, and now other cable will fit, these are used with items like multiple track digital recorders, due to the vast data. A standard cable would take hours, while the C-cable can do it in a couple of minutes.

Fig 4-9 RC Cables on the left vs the 3.5 mm standard small jack cable that is as line input cables.

Fig 4-10 A front view of an interface by Behringer. The instrument 2 port is used to pug in a ¼ inch plug from and instrument

INTERFACE

As you can see there no way to shove a 1/4-inch jack into the 3.5 mm jack or the USB port. To accomplish this, you need an interface. An interface is a device that allows you to attach guitars, microphones to it and then attach the interface to the computer with a USB cable. See fig 4.8 for USB ports.

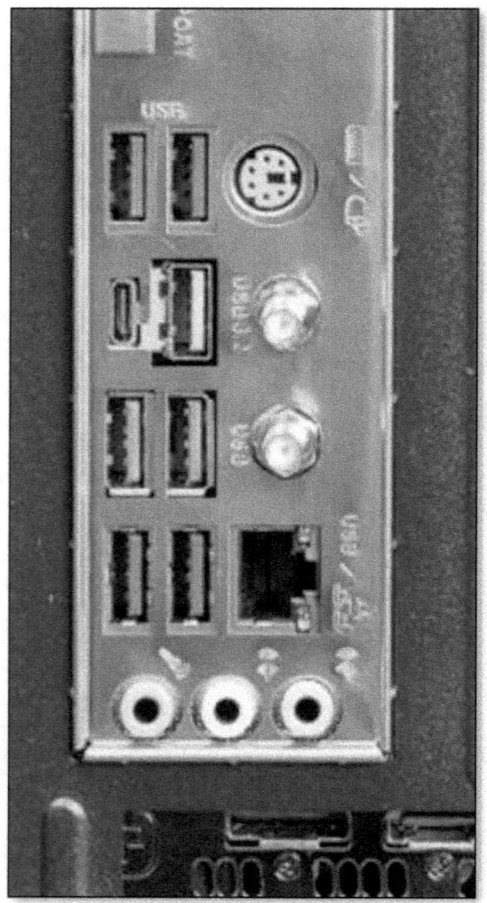

Fig 4.8 USB ports can be found on the front and the back of the PC.

Fig 4-11 Back of the Behringer interface. See the USB port this is where you will attach a cable, then the other end to a USB port on the computer. We will cover how to use this later in the recording section.

Fig 4-13 You will also a good set of monitors.

OUTPUT

If you want to hear what you have recorded, then you must need a pair of headphones fig 4-12 and a set of good *studio monitors fig 4-13*. Notice we did not saw speakers. The common little, small discount store speakers cannot handle the output of recorded music. And what might sound good on them, might sound horrible on quality playback systems. Be sure to use both headphones and monitors. I once mixed a whole album with just headphones and it sounded great, but when played back on monitors it was horrible. So had to go back and remix.

The difference between monitors and speakers is that monitor have a one that is active and one that is passive. The active monitor has a built-in amp, and usually is located on the left, and is connected to the computer (fig 4-14) much heavier than the passive monitor on the right. They connected to the active monitor a twin wire fig 4-15 and 4-16). While speakers have usually one speaker, Monitors have multiple speakers one for the bass and another for the treble. Make sure your headphones can handle these different sounds also.

Fig 4-12 A good set of headphones are required to listened to the recordings you make.

Monitors can cost a few hundred dollars, but sometimes you can find them on sale for musical outlets like Sweetwater® and Guitar Center® Be sure to take care of them cover them when not in use, as dust can be an enemy, and be sure to turn them off when not in use. **Monitor's attach to the** computer, while headphones can attach to the computer through the headphone port, or in the interface.

Fig 4-14 Back of active monitor RCA wires that are used to attached to the computer. Always follow the instruction of your monitors

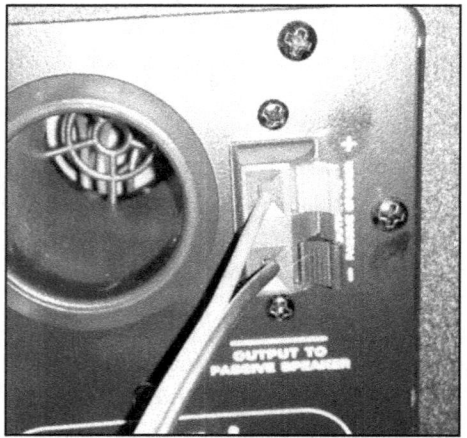

Fig 4-15 Wire from active monitor to passive speaker.

IMPORTING SOUND

You can import sound/music from either a file on the computer or another device-as log as it an convert the file to a file recognizable by Audacity Audacity can import only standard PCM (Pulse-Code Modulation or compression formats (e.g., .wav, .aiff, .mp3), it will not import formats like Microsoft's Windows Media format (.wma). Nor will it support Ogg Vorbis, Speex, or FLAC formats. If you need to import a file of these types into Audacity, you will first need to export it in one of the standard formats mainly a .wav file.

Fig 4-16 Back of the passive monitor.

To import from the computer simply click File>Import>Audio then file the file you want to import (fig 4-17) -it is best you know where this file is located before trying to find it in Audacity-then click on the file and it will import into Audacity.

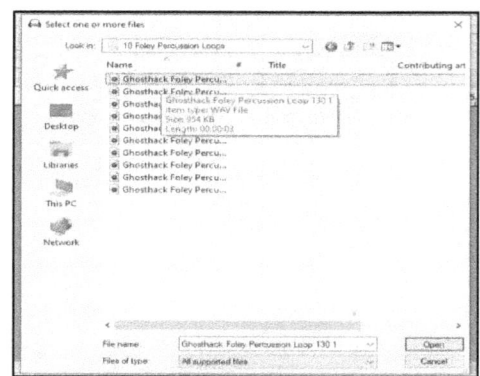

Fig 4-17 Click on the file then click open to import the file.

78

Fig 4-18 You will have to connect the device that you will import from to the computer, usually with a USB cable. But follow the instructions for the device.

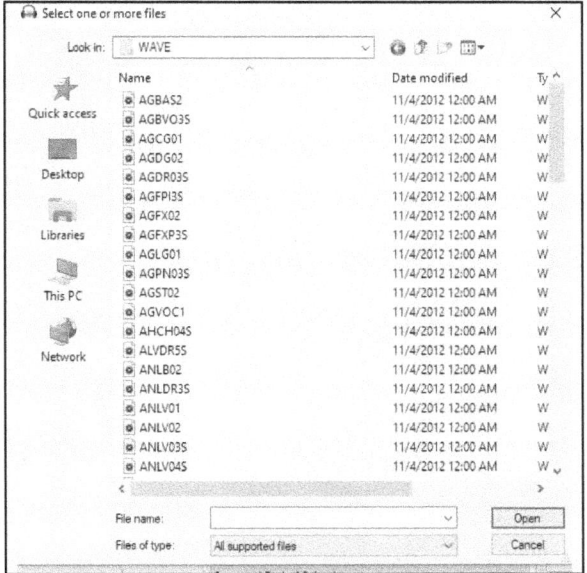

Fig 4-20 A list of wave files on the device. Click on the ones you want to import and click open. These files will be imported.

Now you know how Audacity works, and how to get connected. In the next section we are going discuss how to set up a recording studio and the equipment that goes in it. How and where to buy and set a recording desk. If you want you can take a little break, we will still be here. When you get back.

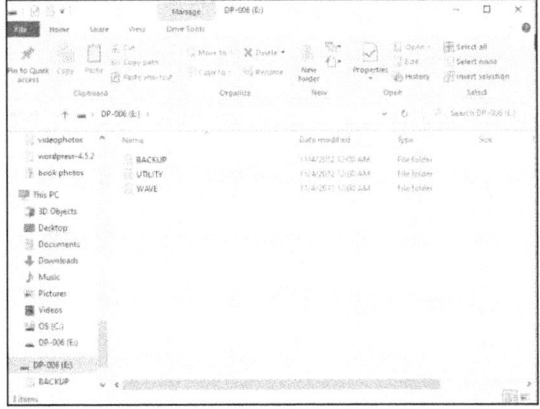

Fig 4-19 A box that contain the files on the device will pop up. Kick on the WAVE file. If it does not pop-up hunt for the device on your PC.

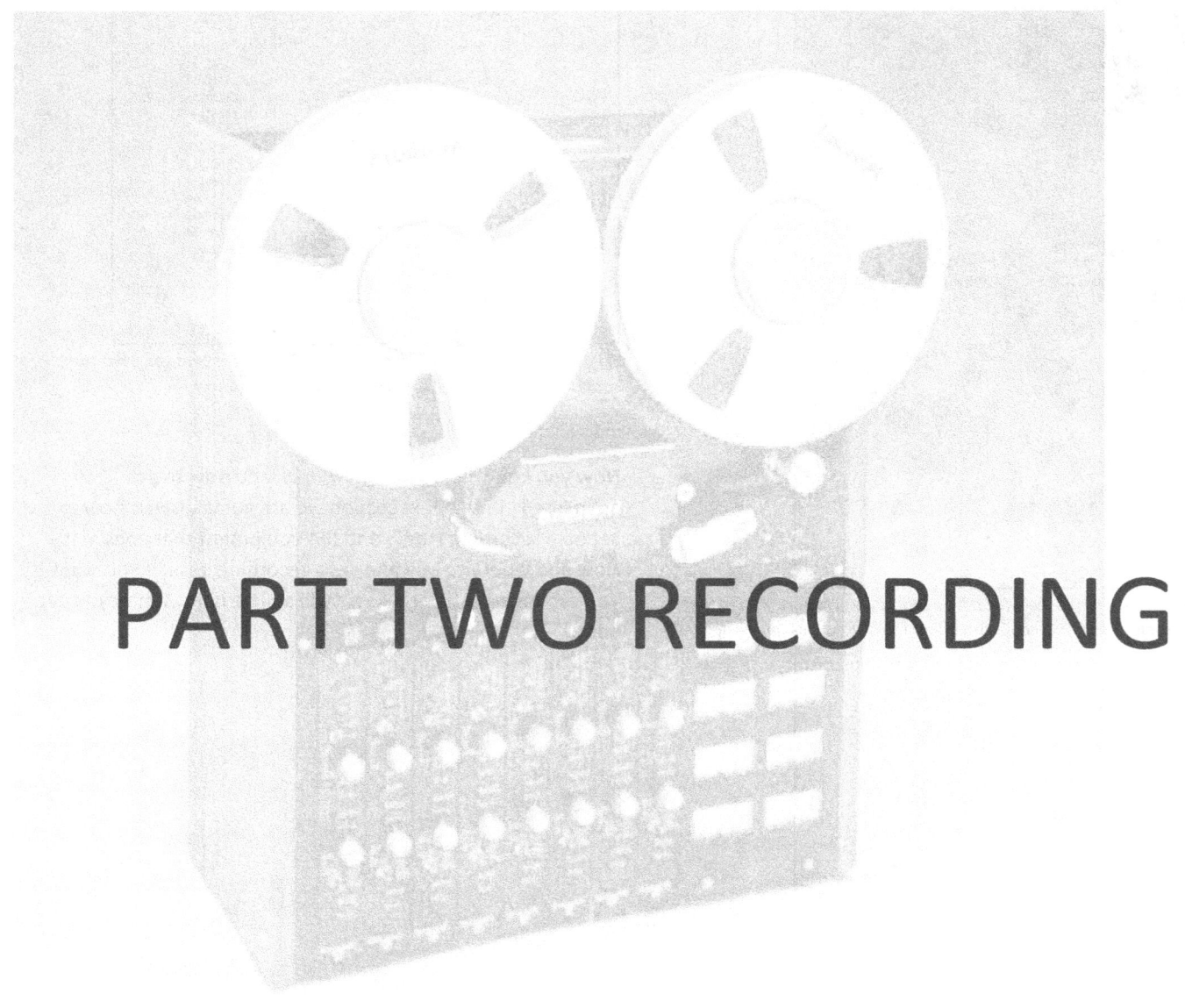

PART TWO RECORDING

CHAPTER 5   Setting up a Recording Studio

Rested? Good. Told you we would still be here. Although it is not covered in the instructions from Audacity® if you set up a proper place to record you will get more favorable results. If you record in a bathroom you are going to get a different sound than if you record in closet. Likewise, you will get a different sound if you record in large living room with hardwood floors then you would if you were outside.

This due to the acoustics of each environment. Each one has it's own. Test each area go sing. "Yeah!, yeah *bab--y I love youuu sooo!*' in each room of your house and then outside. Back? I knew it took you little while trying to explain to the neighbors what you were doing when you were outside. Did you notice the differences?

How the voice bounced off the hard tile walls of the bathroom and returned quickly. Outside the return carried away, may be bouncing off the sides of the house, taking longer to return. But when in the closet it sounds muffled and there was no *'reverb.'* This what short echo is called in recording. Reverb can make everything sound better, but there are times it can make it worse. So, you want to be able to control this.

Ideally it would be if you have a room you can convert to a studio alone then you could put sound absorbing material on the walls and create vocal isolation booth and make the room acoustically acceptable.

How big should this room be? The only answer is... it depends! Depends on how many people will be in the studio at one time. Depends on how much space do you have? How big is your budget? Do have a room you can convert to full time studio, or will it be part time?

How Many?

How are you going to record? One person at a time or a whole band? Is this going to be only for you, or are you going to have others come over?

If you are the only one that is going to use it, and you are only going to record one thing at a time then you can by with a large walk-in closet. And it won't cost you much to turn it into small studio, the bigger the closet the better. Note when you're in there with all the equipment it is going to feel cramped. Make sure you take the equipment and instruments into account when selecting a room.

But the saying goes bigger is better, a spare bedroom, or garage, another choice is a storage building. Note this will be costly as you will have the price of the building and the modifications which will be many to transform it and hook electricity to it. Think and plan things out before you act.

Budget

Even a small studio is going to cost you several hundred dollars, this due to making the room soundproof. So, sound does not go out and more importantly sound (unwanted sound) doe not come in. To fully isolate a room will require double drywall and MLV (mass loaded vinyl) Fig 5-1, along with acoustic foam on the walls to stop the sound from reverbing. Plus, ways to seal over door and windows, controlling sounds from air conditioning and heaters and the list goes on.

Full Time vs Part Time

A full-time recording studio is wonderful dream come true. For most readers all of this is impractical, and we can only have a temporary studio that doubles as another room in the home like a bedroom.

Luckily, we are going to tell you how you can do this with temporary items that help with the sound quality of the room. However, there are some things you need to watch for when you select the room you will use.

Finding a Temporary Studio

Choose a room with not a lot of windows, and doors that can seal the room off and preferably NO PHONE in or near it. The last thing you need is someone coming in or the phone ringing just when you are just in the middle of laying down a track. Been there and done that, it will not make your day.

The room should ideally have hardwood floors, or vinyl floor covering, carpeting should be the last choice. It does not mean you can't have a room with it, and in many cases carpet will be on the floor. You can get around this.

Use heavy drapes or moving blankets to cover the windows, sounds can reverberate off the glass, it can also make the glass vibrate. Ever had a loud clap of thunder and hear the glass shake? Or a car drives down the street with a loud bass and the whole house shakes. A loud bass or drum set can do the same thing, and it will ruin your recording.

Shape, and ideal shape would be one that has angled in some of the corners. But any shape can work.

You need a large desk or table that you can set up for a computer. And a play back system. Laptops can work, if they are powerful enough, but a desktop model is preferable along with a very large monitor, like a 32-inch TV screen. When it comes to editing the tracks, it will be hard to see them on a small screen.

Another thing to make is a sign **that says 'Recording in Process. Do Not Disturb"** fig 5-3 in larger red letters and enter on the other. Hang it outside the door, and when recording be sure the sign is turn so no one will interrupt you.

Whichever room you select, even a closet. take some time to just sit in quietly listening to the sounds around and in it. Can you hear outside traffic going by on the street, trains going through town, the central heat kicking on, a noisy window a/c unit in the next room, people talking outside of the room, walking upstairs, a hum of lights etc. All these things must be weight into the decision, as a good microphone is going to pick these things up in the recording.

Noises from outside in the hall can be contained by placing heavy drapes in front of the door on a rod or a strong piece of cable anchor to two walls. You have seen recording studios with the ribbed foam on the walls, be these are not used to control sounds from entering but to control the sound on the inside. If you are converting a room to a full-time recording studio you should put a second wall. That is a layer of drywall, with a sound absorbing material like MLV *Mass Loaded Vinyl* fig 5-1 Plus foam panels that can be attached to the wall fig 5-2.

Fig 5-1 Mass Loaded Vinyl sound absorbing roll from Xtrm Ply. It is expensive and is 52 or 54 feet wide and comes on roll from 10 foot to 50 foot rolls it can be hung overdoors and wall using grommets.

Fig 5-2 Ribbed foam can be attached to the walls to help control noise. Or attached to paneling and a with wire to the wall for a temporary solution. We will show you how to make these later in the chapter.

Or if you want you can buy a recording light, Fig 5-4 which can be as simple as a lamp on the wall with a red blub, and a sign that reads "Recording DO NOT ENTER When Red Light is on."

If you are having only a part-time studio you can attach heavy-duty gourmets in the MLV and hang in on the wall with heavy-duty cup hooks. Note if you rent this may not be possible unless you are allowed to attach things to the wall. So, ask the landlord first. This product is made to be glued to the wall to accurately work and stop noise. But it can cut some noise, even just hanging. Note it is expensive, so another idea is to hang up heavy drapes or moving blankets along the walls.

There are desks made specially for a home recording studio but all you need is a table or desk that is large enough to hold the computer, monitor, keyboard and mouse and large payback speakers. Or you can opt to mount the speakers on the walls or stands away from the table, this will also give you better sound quality during the master session. If you are using a lot of keyboards in recording, then it is wise that the table be also big enough to hold the keyboard in front of the computer. Fig 5-5

Fig 5-3 A simple sign you can make and put on the door

Fig 5-4 If you have some extra money, you can buy one of the battery or ac power lights that will really get attention

With instruments like an electric guitar, bass or keyboard you can plug the instrument directly into an Interface and get the sound to the computer. But with vocals, and acoustic instrument this will require a microphone, we will discuss the different type in the next chapter. This where the acoustics of a room become involved.

We all have seen the walls that were lined with ribbed foam. This can quickly go over the edge, and you can end up in a '*dead zone*' this is an area where sound will not have any depth or feeling. In some cases that can be okay, other it will not.

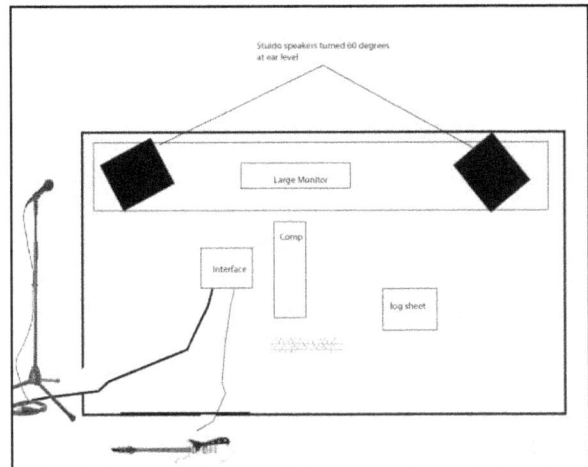

Fig 5-5 Typical recording studio table layout. Be sure to turn the speakers at a 60-degree angle.

Something like a 12-string guitar you may want the room sound for the instruments, while for voice you need major control. So, **you don't want to cover every wall with this stuff, even if you have a permanent -studio.** You only need to attack the acoustical high points.

Finding the Acoustics of a Room

If you ask your room to sing, chances are you are not going to get a response. If you do an answer back, then you have bigger problems than acoustics and is way out of the range this book can cover.

Instead, you find these spots with two things - your ears and a mirror. Play a bass heavy laden song in the middle of the room now walk around the room listening, notice how the bass seems increase in the corners of the room? This is normal and to combat against this you need to install *Bass traps*. We will show you how to make these and Acoustic panels also.

Bass traps are heavier and thicker than acoustic panels, they are placed on the walls. However, **you don't need to line** the entire walls with these. Just find the right spots. This is done with a mirror and pencil or piece of tape.

Place a chair, guitar or have someone stand in the spot in the room you plan to be when recording. This could be in the center of the room or at the desk, it depends on your tastes. I like to record away from the desk and sitting on a stool or standing; depending on if I am playing or singing.

Place a hand mirror flat against the wall fig 5-6 and 5-7, at eye level. Slowly slide it over the walls at the same level. Anything you can see the item you placed mark this spot with the pencil or a small piece of tape. Continue until you have gone around the entire room, including windows and doors.

You will be surprised at the places you cannot see the reflection. These points it would be wasteful to put up baffles as it will not absorb or reflect the sound here. Now we know where we can muffle reverb if it is needed.

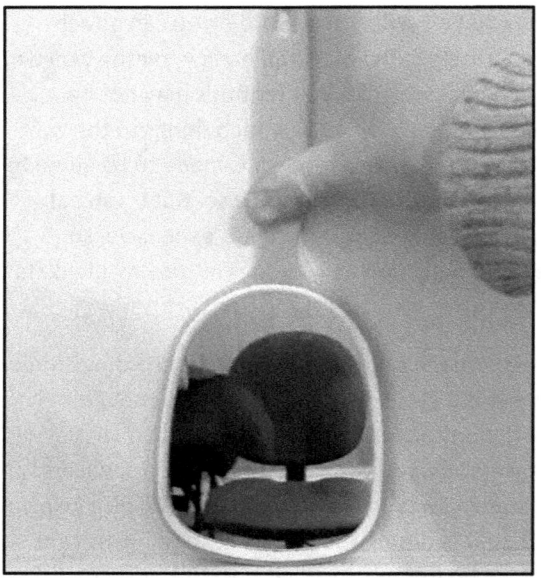

Fig 5-6 Finding acoustic points with a mirror on the walls it will be here we will place acoustic panels

Fig 5-7 Be sure to test the doors and windows also. Here we will place heavy drapes lined with sound panels.

MAKE TEMPORARY SOUND BAFFLES

Now we have all seen the photos of studios with the wall covered with ribbed foam panels, there is no need to do this except in an isolation booth-which we will cover later in this chapter.

Some acoustic panels have a peel off backing with an adhesive back, this is stuck on the wall, these have a habit of the glue letting go and the pad will fall off the wall. So, if you do put them up put them up with additional glue. However, when you do this, you set the room to one set value acoustically a better way is to make these temporary.

Beside if you are using a room from something else and part time recording studio you can attach the panels permanently to the wall, and if you do you might be transforming the doghouse to your studio.

Materials Needed for One Sound Baffle

Qty.	Material	Size
4	Foam, Acoustic Panel	12x12 in
1	Wood panel scrap	12x48 in
1 can	Spray Adhesive	
1	Scrap of cloth	
1	Picture frame hanger	

Instead of the wall the panel is glued to a piece of thin wood paneling. No need to buy this new, hunt around for architecture salvage yard and find a used sheet, or you may have some tucked away in the attic or basement. It doesn't matter the color or gain as you are going to cover it anyway. Order some acoustic foam panels, they are available from many places including Sweetwater even Walmart ® online. We will be using these also in bass traps, and an isolation vocal booth so order lots of them.

Cut the paneling to the desired dimension which can be any size you in our example we are using four panels 12x12 panels in a line. So, we have a 12x48 inch piece of paneling.

Lightly sand the surface of the paneling to provide the glue a better grip. Now wipe the paneling down with a soft cloth.

Next turn the paneling over and check the fitting of the foam pads and their layout. Decide with you are placing them in same direction or alternate them, once they are glued in place you cannot remove them. Now spray the paneling and the back of the foam panels and replace in the order you selected.

The cloth on the back has nothing to do with sound it is to protect the wall and the foam. It can be found at places like *Joann Fabric*, this is just to protect the wall so look in the 'remnant section'. This is left over fabric that there only a little amount left, and you can get it at a huge discount. It must be at least three- inches longer and wider then then the panel so that it will wrap around the panel, this will keep you from getting splinters in your hand. We know you put blood, sweat and tears into your music but you don't want to do it this way. A cheap cloth is a twin sheet, it has enough fabric to completely cover the panel, and inexpensive.

Carefully lay the cloth down, then place the panel with the foam upside down. Now pull the cloth up and around snuggly over the back and staple into place. And making sure the cloth has and overlap appearing along the edges of the paneling

Now carefully and tightly pull the edges of the cloth up and round the edges of the paneling. Press down firmly after working out the wrinkles. And staple into place.

Attach a picture hanger to the back and attach it a nail that is at one of the acoustical points you marked. Note you can use two picture frame holders on the side amount the panel sideway.

Fig 5-8 Layout the foam in the pattern you want.

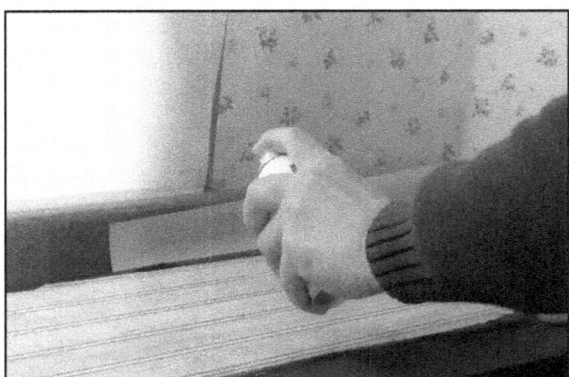

Fig 5-9 Spray the paneling and back side of foam with spray adhesive. Press the foam into place.

Fig 5-10 with the foam glued into place turn the panel over with the foam facing down over the cloth.

Fig 5-10 Pull the cloth up snugly and over the back and staple into place.

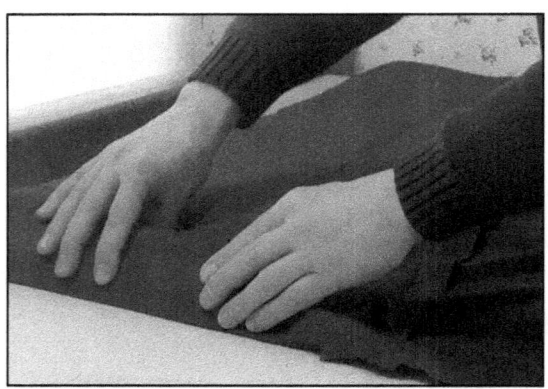

Fig 5-11 Tuck the ends down and then staple into place.

VOCAL ISOLATION BOOTH

Dead, dead, dead that is what you need for vocals. We are not talking about going a killing spree but making the environment that way. The best way would be to build a small separate room out of wood padding and thick glass, that is a way out of nearly every hobbyist there is.

Most of us just cannot give up that space, even if we have a separate full time recording studio, for this. Luckily, we can build a temporary booth out of PVC, moving blankets and acoustic frame.

Build a Temporary Vocal Isolation Booth

There are somethings you just cannot directly input in a recorder. Anything that requires a microphone input. When your record with a microphone, you are going to pick up the room, position, and distance of the microphone from the sound source will determine how much of the room is picked up, sometimes this is wanted and sometimes it is not. One of those case is with vocals, ideally you want vocals acoustically dead as you can. If you have the room and money, you can build separate room in a room for this, but most of us do not have a luxury. Fortunately, you can build temporary structure that can be used only when it is needed, for a portion of the cost. It will NOT work as well the permeant structure, but it will work effectively. It is made from PVC pipe, moving blankets, cardboard, and acoustic foam. Good thing is you can build it any size you want.

The frame is key to this and will be the biggest cost. Our booth is going to be three-foot square. Which is just enough room for one singer and a microphone. And occasionally a musician, acoustic guitar, and microphone. And we added battery powered light for illumination inside the booth.

We choose 3/4-inch PVC pipe with 480 psi rating, do not use the 200-psi rating as it too flexible and will not support the heavy blankets. You can go up to one inch PVC pipe, but we found the 3/4-inch diameter 480 psi rated pipe works well and it is less expensive than the one inch. Our design took ten 10-foot sections of pipes and is 3x3 foot. We started by saw the all the pipes into three-foot pieces.

First lay out the basic floor plan, using 3/4-in x 3/4-in x 3/4-in diameter 90-Degree Side Outlet Elbow PVC Fittings, these fittings allow three pipes to fit going at 90-degree angles of each other allowing you to make a square and a pipe that goes straight up that will form the walls. Since we need to make this stronger, we will place an extra pipe that will form the wall in the center. This will require T- fitting. We will cut the pipe in two separates 18-inch section and join them with the T-fitting. Make sure the opening for the T-fitting and the one for the upper right pipe on the 90 elbows both faces upwards. Repeat this for the next side.

At the front is our doorway. We choose a two-foot doorway, where no pipe will be in case, we would like to roll a stool or such into the booth and it would not have to be lifted over the pipe. Remember we cut the ten-foot pipe into three 3-foot sections this left over one foot. We will use this as our front wall. At the end we will used a simple elbow joint to allow the one-foot section of pipe to end in an upwards pattern for another three-foot section of pipe.

The back will a three-foot section of pipe but cut at the one-foot mark and joined together with a section fitting, this will provide a place for another upward pipe and will give the structure more strength, with the base on the front.

Push the pipe into the fittings, they should fit snugly and not easily twist out of shape. If you want a stronger and permeant structure glue the pieces together with PVC glues, if you want it portable do not use glue, or glue to main sections, floor to, wall together as separate structures, this will still allow you to store it flat. Even if you want it permanent do NOT use glue until you have the entire structure built, for you may have to make changes.

Fig 5-12 PVC cut into 3-foot sections, except for one and be sure to retain the left over 1-foot sections we will need those later on.

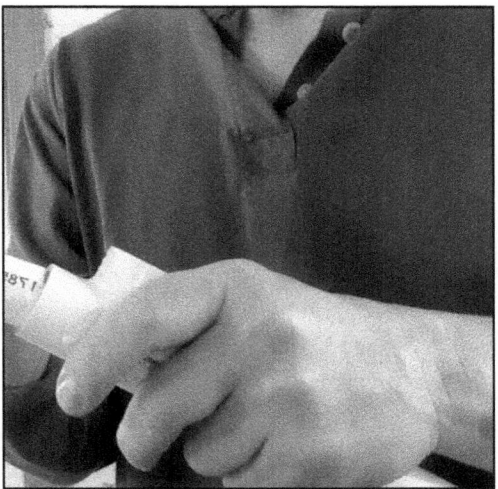

Fig 5-13 Push the pipe into the fitting it should fit snuggly.

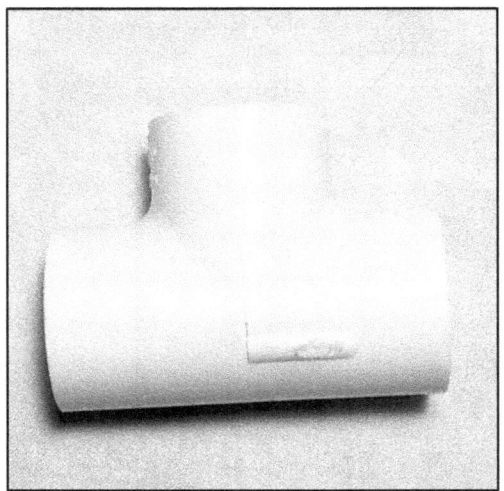

Fig 5-14 T-fitting Marked T in plans

Fig 5-15 90-degree elbow PVC fitting are used at the corners of the booth. Marked E1 in plans.

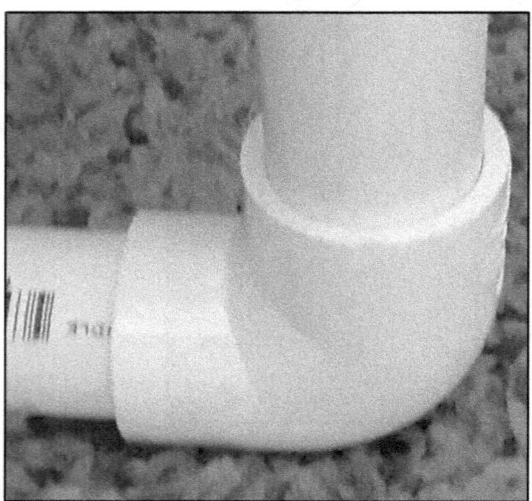

Fig 5-16 Simple Elbow joint marked as E2 in plans.

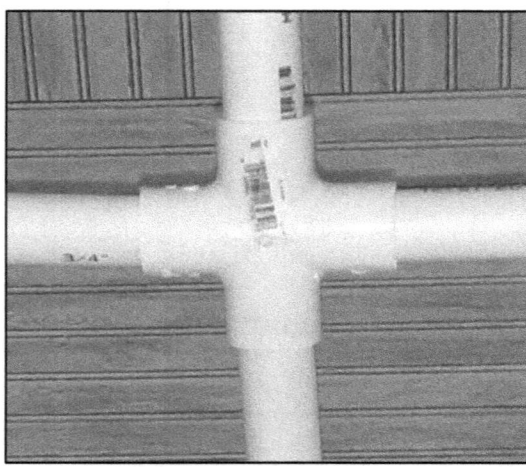

Fig 5-17 Example of a 4-way connector, this allows four pipes to be connected and give extra strength.

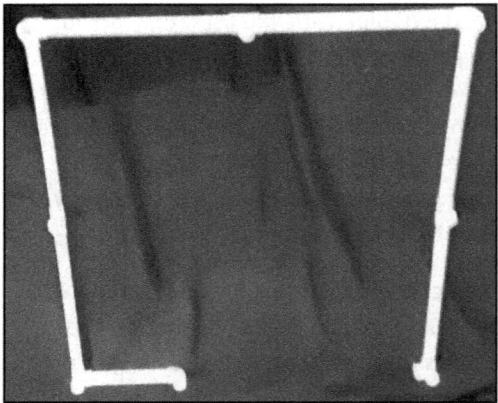

Fig 5-18 Basic floor layout

Now with the floor built we are ready to start building the walls. Place a three-foot section of pipe in the fittings. Use T fitting on the outsides of the pipe and a four-way cross fitting in the middle and attach it to the top. The cross will allow you to attach pipe in a four-way pattern, providing the necessary strength for the frame. The front will not require a four-way cross. Instead brace it with a pair of T- fittings and a another piece of the left over 1 foot sections.

Continue building up the walls adding more three-foot pipes. Now we are ready for the ceiling. The ceiling is going to hold all the weight of this project, so it needs to enforced well. With extra pipe that crisscross using 4-way fittings. Follow the photos for instructions.

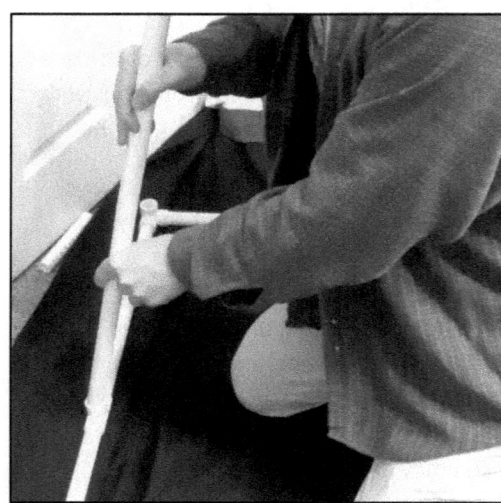

Fig 5-19 Build up the lower wall

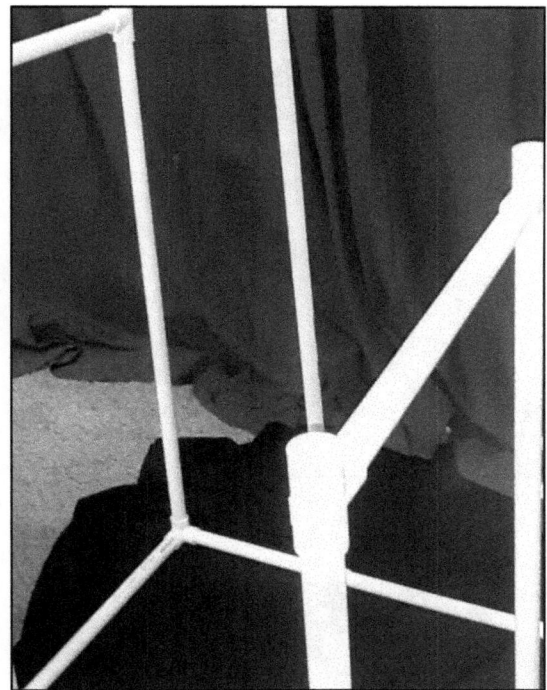
Fig 5-20 With the lower wall built, build the upper half.

Now that the frame is build, we need curtains that can be hung over it The curtains are heavy-duty moving blankets. With grommets installed and hung with simple shower curtain rings. Then use spray adhesive to glue the acoustic foam to the side of the blanket that will face the insides of the booth.

The top is a large piece of carboard that is sturdy enough to hold more acoustic foam and it is laid on tap and secured with tape. To provide illumination inside the booth use battery powered lights.

A tip number the parts, so that it easier to reassembly when you need them. Use a permanent a marker. If you glue them into individual components i.e., floor, top back wall, front wall etc.

PVC Pipes and the fittings can obtain from a plumbing supply or build supply outlet like Home Depot or Lowes. Moving blankets can be found at many locations including discount stores. Acoustic foam can be found online.

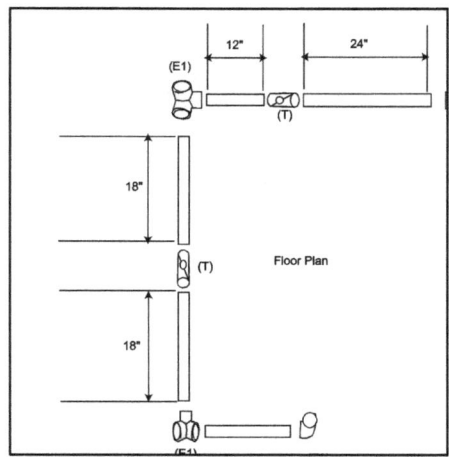
Fig 5-21 The blueprints for the floor.

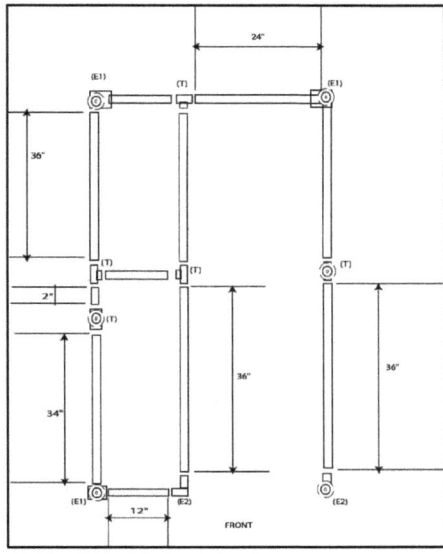
Fig 5-22 The blueprints for the front.

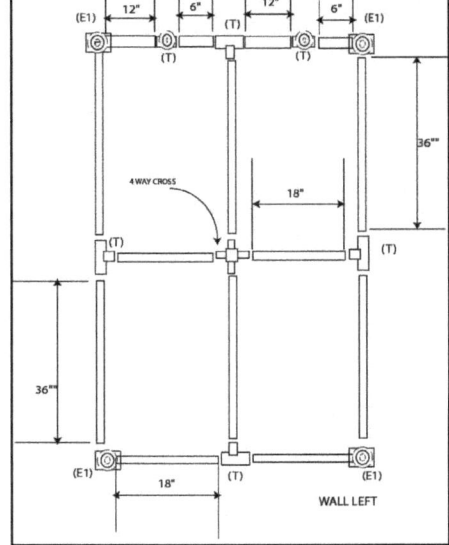
Fig 5-23 The blueprints for the left wall.

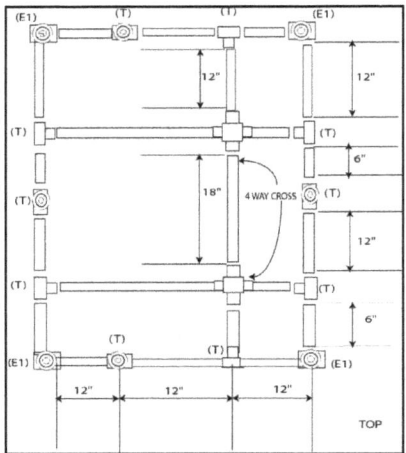

Fig 5-24 The blueprints for the Top notice the extra bracing.

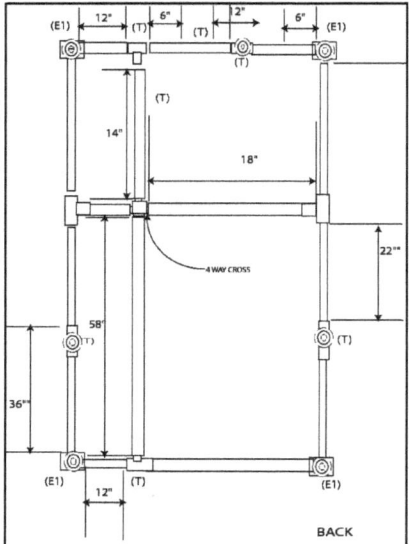

ig 5-25 The blueprints for the back

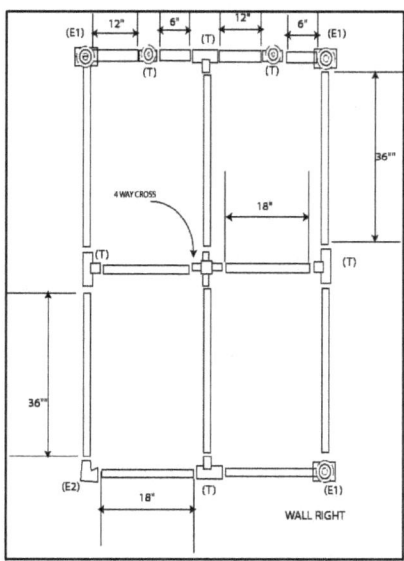

Fig 5-26 The blueprints for the right wall

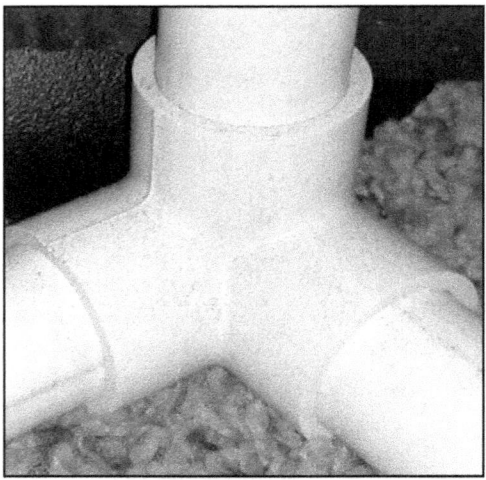

Fig 5-27 the E-2 elbow in use.

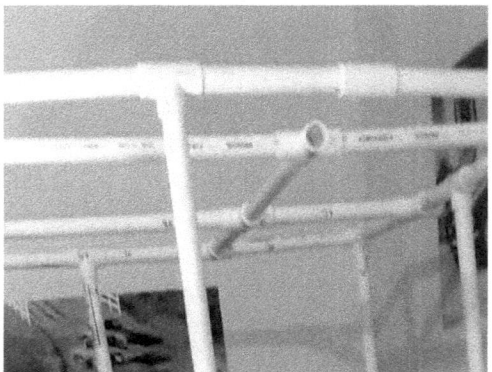

Fig 5-28 Start with the outer pipes on the top and work in the inner pipes.

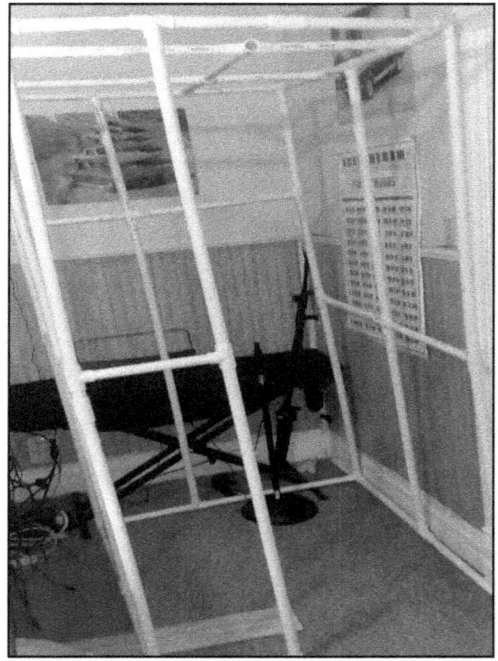

Fig 5-29 Basic framework.

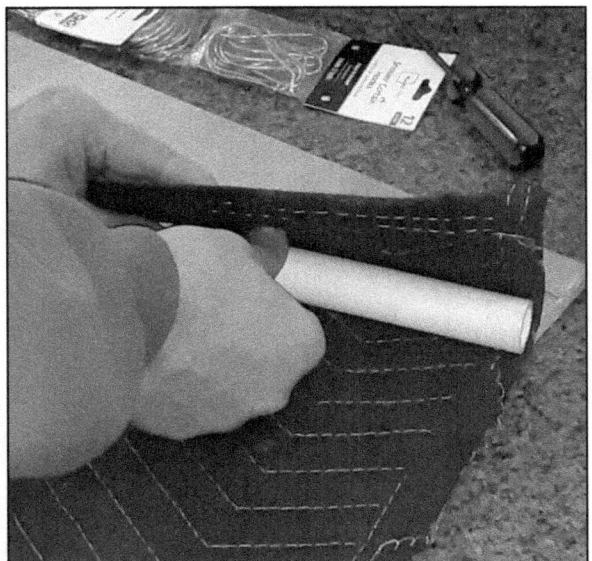

Fig 5-30 Our curtains are heavy moving blanket. Hold them up to the frame to find the proper layout and will fit the booth frame. Then create an overlap using a piece of PVC pipe as a guide.

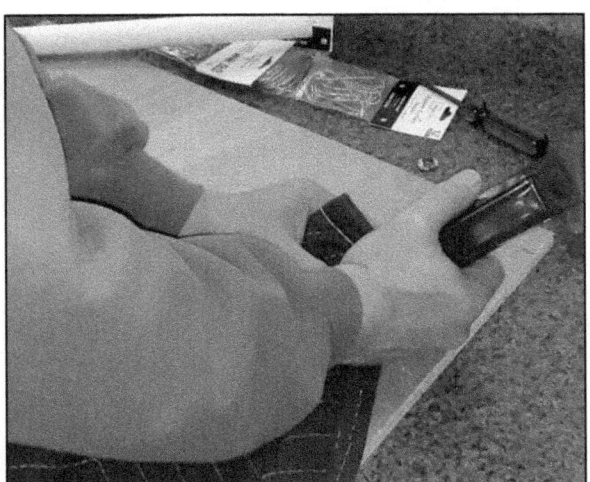

Fig 5-31 After creating the hem at the top, remove the PVC pipe and the use a heavy-duty stapler to attach the hem together. Attach one end, and then other Making sure it is straight then attach the points in between about six inches apart.

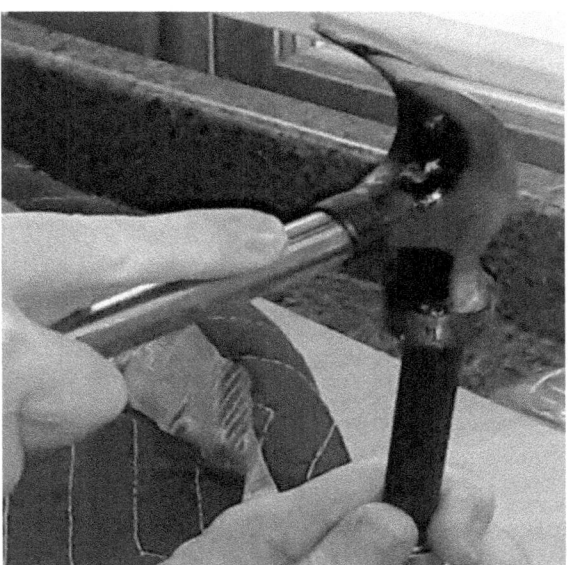

Fig 5-32 Use the cutter tool to cut out a hole in the cloth

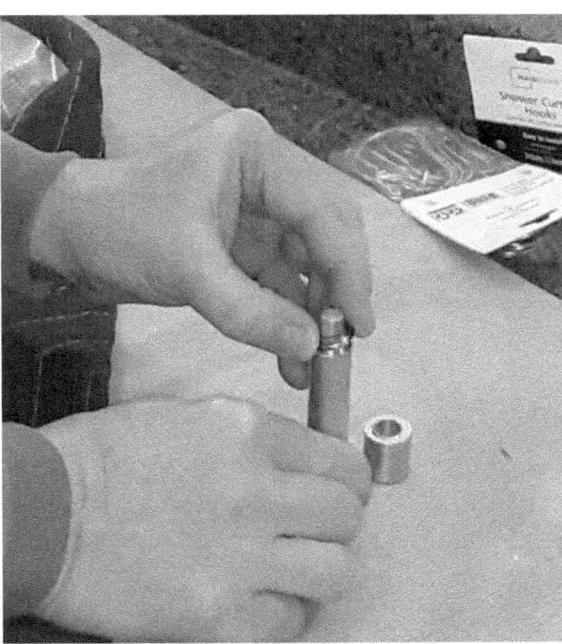

Fig 5-33 Place the larger gourmet ring on one side and the smaller one on the other side. To the right shows a ring that is installed. A strip of clear duct tape will protect against the staples from pushing out.

Fig 5-34 Hammer the two rings together

Fig 5-35 Use shower curtain rings to hang the curtains. See the number in the background. Numbering helps when putting it back together again.

Fig 5-36 the top is a larger piece of cardboard. Place it on top and then mark the location for the pipes.

Fig 5-37 Place the foam panels in place using the marks for the PVC pipes as guides Leave a blank space at the front for the lights at the front of the boot.

Fig 5-38 Trim the foam panels with a sharp single edge razor blade

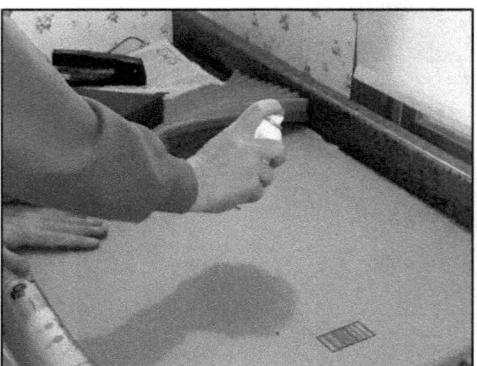
Fig 5-39 Use spray adhesive on the cardboard and the back of the foam. Then press the foam into place.

Fig 5-40 Use the gourmets a the edge of the cardboard and use a Shower curtain ring to attach it to the pipes.

CHAPTER 6 Microphones and Mixing Boards

MICROPHONES

There are several different types of microphones and four different types of connectors. For connecting there is the 1/4- inch jack, XLR plug, the mini plug and the USB plug. The mini plug and the USB plug can be plug directly into the computer and you are ready to go, providing you have these ports available. With the ¼- inch jack and the XLR plug you will have to use an interface or mixing board if you are using more than one microphone at a time.

If you use a microphone with a 3.5 mm all you must do is plug in the 'microphone' port on the back of the computer. DO NOT plug it into the 'line in' port. The volume will be way too low (the line input port does not apply the needed amplification to boost the very quiet signal from the microphone). You will not break anything, but you will be very frustrated with the results. This will also happen when you try to use a ¼ inch jack microphone with a USB adapter. Again, the volume will be too low.

What do you use if there is no microphone port on your computer? Then you can use an interface or use a USB microphone. The USB microphone is gaining popularity. They have a built-in preamp so all you must do is plug it into a USB port. That said they are really on good only for podcasts, they are just not that good for music or singing vocals.

Types of Microphones

You have heard said, "*it not what is on the outside that matters it is what is on the inside that matters*", and with microphones that is certainly true. Microphones can come in a variety of shapes and sizes, and two microphones can look exactly alike and but are totally different. Fig 6-1

Fig 6-1 Various shapes of microphones

Fig 6-2 Insides of a dynamic microphone

Fig 6-3 A true workhorse the Dynamic microphone.

Fig 6-5 Typical Ribbon microphone use d from the 1930's to the 1960's

They use a (fig 6-2) moving coil inside of a magnet to transmit sound. They are tough microphones and are not sensitive to temperature or humidity changes. They also not need a pre-amp to operate. Their disadvantage is they do not do well at frequency beyond 10kHz. This is a must have in any recording studio.

Ribbon Microphone

This microphone operates like the Dynamic mic, but has a corrugated ribbon instead of a coil, (fig 6-4) and is placed in between to magnets. It also does not need a pre-amp to operate. They were popular during the 1930's to the 1960's. Seen old shots of performers in WW II that is (fig 6-5) ribbon mic. How about the *King-Elvis Presley* twist about holding that mic- is a ribbon microphone.

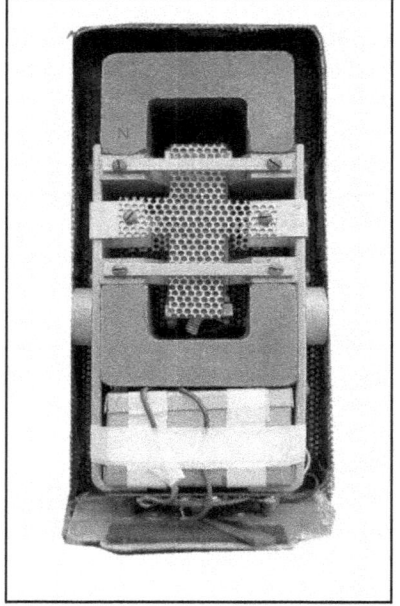

Fig 6-4 The insides of fragile ribbon microphone

Dynamic Microphone

This is the workhorses of the microphone family; they range from fairly inexpensive to moderately expensive. They can withstand harsh treatment, like live shows. Chances are if you have ever spoke into a microphone, it was this type. They can handle lots of volume which is known as SPL or *sound pressure level* in the industry. This makes them great for vocals for rock songs plus drums, and amplifiers.

Ribbon microphones give a smooth sound, that crooner sound- like *Frank Sinatra,* or *Frankie Avalon.* As they roll off high frequencies and some of the low, so that are not good for hard rock singers. The drawback is they expensive the cheapest is around a grand, and they are easily damaged. A sudden gust of wind can damage the ribbon.

Condenser Microphone

Uses two electrically charged plates; one that moves which called a diaphragm and the other is fixed called a backing plate, which is a condenser with positively and negatively charged electrode and air space in between. As your sounds enters it pushes down the diaphragm causing a change in the distance in between the two plates. To boost the signal a PET transistor is used as an amplifier. This why some sort of power must be required to use the microphone.

Cost wise they range from cheap to very expensive. But they have high excellent high frequency and low frequency response. Disadvantages are that temperature and humidity affect their performance.

Condenser mics (fig 6-6) must be kept in a case when not in use, as dirt can get inside and harm the diaphragm. Also, if you are going to leave it set up overnight cover it with a soft cloth or a plastic zip lock bag.

Fig 6-6 Condenser microphone is sensitive to dust, and changes in humidity.

There are two things that happen on TV shows that really make me roll my eyes. One is the use of a 'silencer' on a gun and the shot makes no sound. That does not happen. The other is where someone blows into a microphone to test it. This simple thing can damage a microphone. In a condenser microphone the sound it can cause the plates to stick. If this happens; turn of the mic and disconnect it form, its power source and it may reset. To test the microphone simply say 'test, test' into it. This word is not just simply used, it is perfect because of all the 't' and 's' sounds which test a microphone. If one sounds good when saying test, it should sound good with other sounds.

A condenser microphone uses an extremely thin strip of metal or Mylar that sense the sound. It is suspended in front of a metal backing plate. Polarizing voltage is applied to both the thin strip and the backing back, creating a charge in between the two strips. When the thin strip picks up sound it vibrates into area between the two, this produces a signal.

Prices wise they are moderately expensive and can be purchased for $100 to $500.00. And they come in two different types small and large diaphragms.

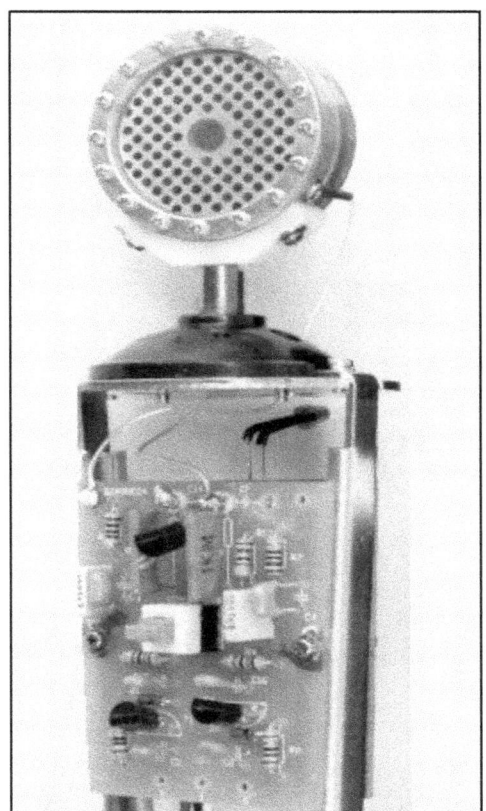

Fig 6-7 Inside of a condenser microphone. With large diaphragm

They also come in tube or solid-state style. Which do you use? Depends on what sound you are after. If you want a warm overall tone with less high-end, then the tube mic is the way to go. For clearer sound go with solid state. As for the size the larger diaphragm style is more popular-in studio language they are known as *LDC -Large Diaphragm Condenser (fig 6-7)*. The LDC's **produce better bottom end** tones and have lower feedback that is created by microphones.

However, the *SDC's (Fig 6-8)* have a more balanced frequency response and are better at picking up an instrument sound.

Boundary Microphone

Basically, inside it is SDC fig 6-9 in a special that allows it to pick up sound from multiple sources including reverberation of the room. It is great for interviewing several people in the room without using multiple microphones. It is also good for recording live shows, a conference or for church broadcasts, for picking up the crowd when the sing along. They are also useful on piano, and instruments **that don't have low pitch** because they do not respond well to low tones.

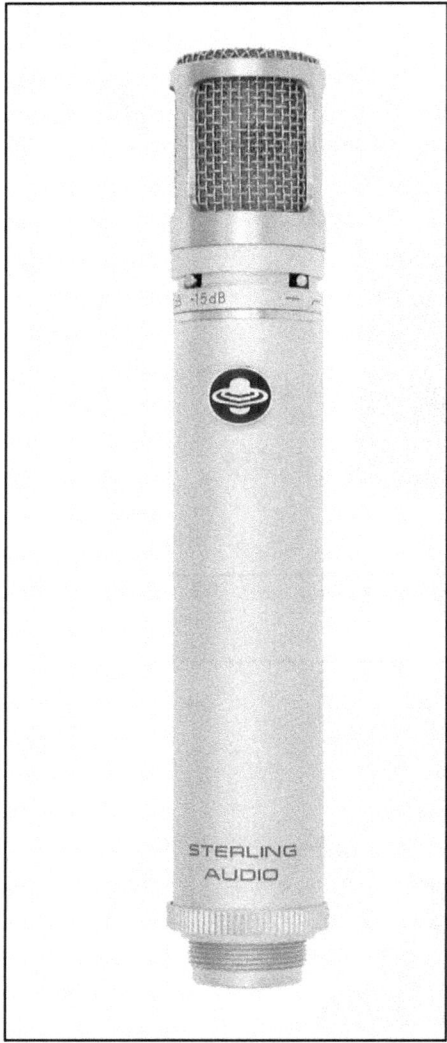

*Fig 6-8 **Condenser microphone with small diaphragm***

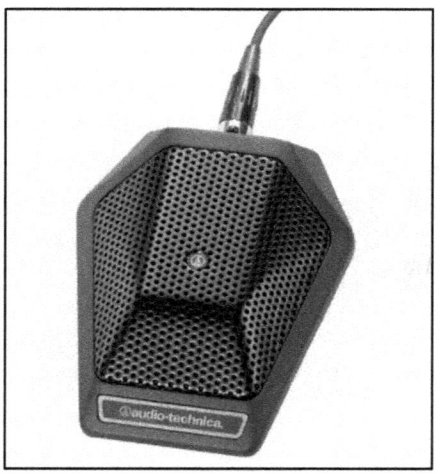

Fig 6-9 A boundary microphone is basically a small diagram condenser microphone with omni direction.

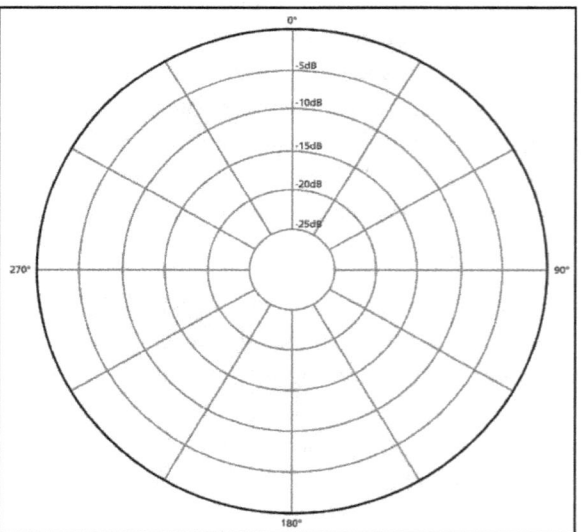

Fig 6-10 The omnidirectional microphone picks up from all sounds around it. Thus, it is good to record multiple singers or instruments with.

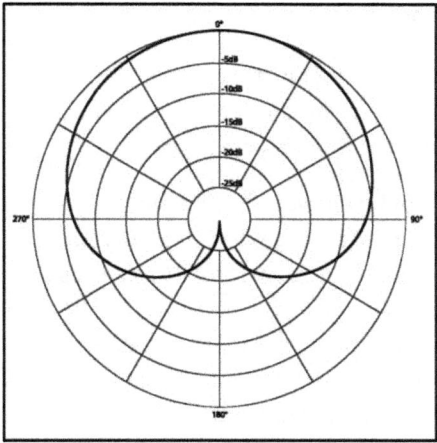

Fig 6-11 Cardioid directional microphone pattern. Also called a Unidirectibna mic, a sit picks on sounds in front of it. They are good for solo singers and micing single instruments.

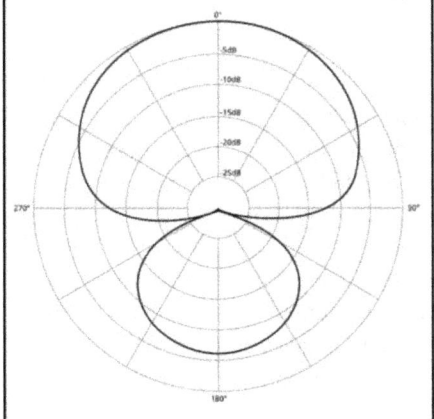

Fig 6-12 Hyper Cardioid pattern

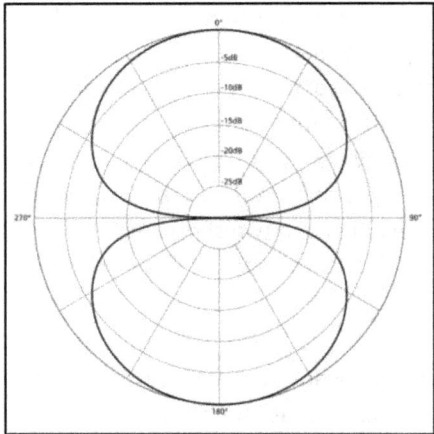

Fig 6-13 Figure 8 or bidirectional polar pattern.

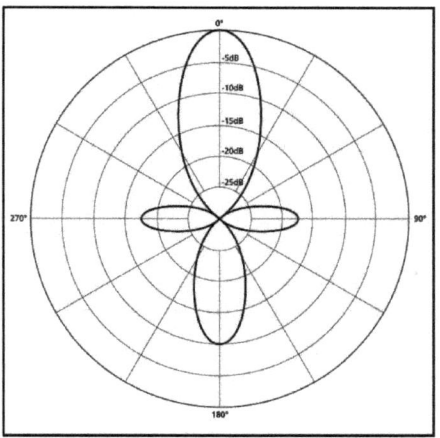

Fig 6-14 Shotgun mic pattern, These are great for recording hit-hats

Polarity Patterns

Microphones pick up sounds in different patterns. It is the patterns that are important to what type you use when recording. This is represented on a chart that comes with the microphone, and is called a *polarograph*, we have included example of each type. Figs 6-10 to 6-14.

Omnidirectional: Pick up sounds from all around the microphone.

Cardioid: Also known as a unidirectional that mostly picks up sounds in front of them.

Figure 8: Also known as a bidirectional. Mostly picks up sound in front and back of the microphone.

Shotgun: Picks up sound only directly in front of them.

Omnidirectional

For general microphone that picks both the room and the sound, they are so good for recording a group of acoustic instruments like a string ensemble but also useful in pairs as drum overhead mics. They are not good for *"close miking"*- that is under a foot away from the object being recorded- because they will catch background noise in the room.

Cardioid

So called because of the shape of sound it captures looks like a heart. This is the type of mic to use during live sets, because you can easily control the sounds. They are also good for recording a true drum se, where they will pick up one drum type-like tom-toms and not the others.

Their drawback is what is known as the *proximity effect* which adds more bass, when they are placed in close miking. The better mics have switch that can controls that. It is also good for lead vocals.

Figure 8

Commonly called a bidirectional it picks up sounds on two different sides. It is good when trying to record two different instruments at the same time. Or two different singers like background vocals.

Shotgun

These are commonly seen in recording studio as they pick up the sound directly in front it. They can be used for vocals but are most commonly seen on drums and other instruments when you want to isolate them.

Fig 6-15 An example of a multiple pattern microphone. Which has switched those controls what type of pattern it uses. Even though you can change the types, they do not sound the same as same as the single use type.

WHAT KIND OF MICROPHONE(S) DO I NEED?

"Grasshopper, you traveled many miles across many galaxies to find the answer to this question, and the answer is…depends on what you want to do with them."

Some questions cannot be answered with a simple answer. As the mics for a simple podcast is going to be different than if you want to record songs that you wrote. Which will also be different if you are only recording your voice and an instrument or are your own one-person band, and you will record all the instruments one at a time, or if you have a band and will record the entire band at one time. The type of music will also determine what type of microphones you will use.

If you are doing a podcast one simple omni- directional microphone will work if you interview anyone, and a shotgun if it only going to be you.

Recording most music, dynamic mics are the best as the rugged and inexpensive, the disadvantages do not mater with most music, the exception would be classic string section, which would suffer and should have a condenser mic, the pattern would be determined by what sound you would want.

Another thing is what instruments are you going to record. Recording an over driven guitar, bass or live drums would destroy a ribbon mic. Where a Dynamic mic would survive.

How Many Mics Should Get?

Your budget will likely be the answer to this question. But also, what are you going to record? If you are recording one instrument at a time and using a drum machine or electronic drums, then a couple of microphones one dynamic and one condenser should get you by-try a cardioid pattern. But if are recording a live drum set, you need at least four for it another for vocals. Two omnidirectional and two shotguns, for backing vocals a figure 8 should be added to the mix.

Large or Small Diaphragm?

Well…depends on what you want to do with and with who. No pun intended. LDC's works great for vocals or with drums as overhead mics. While SDC's are good for acoustic guitars, and other stringed instruments.

For vocals a mic is a personal thing, just putting on a pair boots may the perfect fit for one person, but a pair of slip-on loafers is better for another. There is no set rule, if you are the singer try many different mics and see which works for you. I personally like a dynamic unidirectional made by *Audio-technica,* because my voice is loud and powerful and mostly hard rock. The dynamic mic can with stand that without distorting.

What are the Best Microphones?

That question is like which cut of stake do you like better. It depends on one's budget and one's taste. Why tell you prime rib is the best if your budget is that of ground chuck? Microphones are the same way.

The best way you can find the right one is to try it them. You may be surprised that multiple thousand-dollar job, does not suit your needs, instead a cheap-o mic does. For example, the Audio-technica mic we use is not that expensive, but I like better than the more expensive ones. Now someone else will huff this idea, but some turn their nose up over a hamburger and rather have chopped up raw steak-to each is their own. Where to get microphones, they are everywhere, but one place we recommend for good prices, with great service is Sweetwater Music. www.sweetwater.com they have every supply you need including microphones.

Best Inexpensive Microphones For Studio

MIC	USES
Shure SM57	Great for amps
MXL R144 HE Heritage Edition Ribbon Microphone	Nice warm sound. Not good for hard rock vocals.
Audio-Technica AT2020	Good for vocals and instruments
Samson CO2 Pencil	Great for drums
SE Electronics SE7 SDC	Great for instruments, no so well for vocals
Shure SM57-LC	Studio for instruments

Microphone Cords

Big thing about microphone cords is the length, type of connector and price, price, and price. Maybe well-trained ears can tell the difference between a $25.00 and $200.00 cord, but I never could. That said, those super cheap cord you get at discount stores will not withstand use. The connection will break easily, and you end up with a cable that you must jiggle around to work. Believe us, you don't want this to happen when laying down a track.

How long do cables have to be? Depends on how far you are going to be a way from the computer. Microphones for drums may have to further away and will require longer cables, then say with a podcast, where you are right in front of the computer.

Microphones cables come in different type of connectors. The cheap ones are attached to microphone and usually end with 3.5 mm jack. Others will end with a 1/4-inch jack, Fig 6-16 but the better microphones will detach from the cable and have a XLT connector. This is a special three-point connector (fig 6-17) that can only connect to a special mixing board it will not fit to a computer. Some XLT cables will end in a ¼ plug, (fig 6-18) which is good for placing in mixers, amplifiers, and recorders.

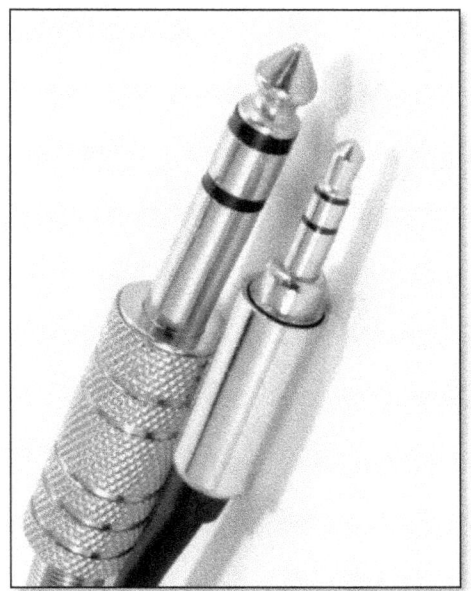

Fig 6-16 Comparing a ¼ jack to the smaller 3.5 mm jack. Note the two stripes on the plugs this indicates they are for stereo. Mono will have only one band.

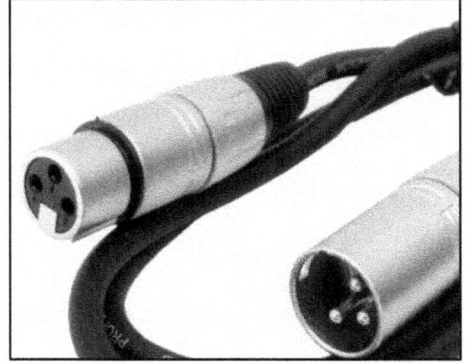

Fig 6-17 XLT cable will not fit to a computer without an adapter.

Fig 6-18 There are XLT to ¼ inch jack cables that make it easy to connect to an interface.

Fig 6-20 A typical windscreen.

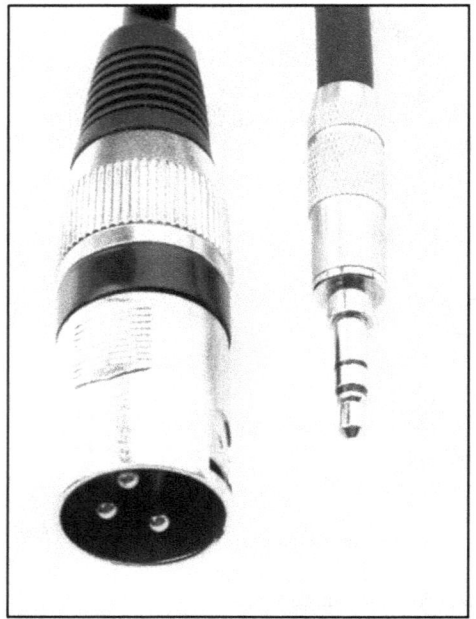

Fig 6-19 There also cables that convert a XLT microphone to a 3.5 mm jack that connect to the computer, providing what type of microphone you have you may need a preamp.

Other Items to Have

A wind screen (Fig 6-20) is good item to have to combat against breaths and a pop filter (fig 6-21) is must when recording vocals this will lessen the *sibilance* in vocals. That happens with words that contain the letters 's' 't' and 'c' if it they make at snake sound-hiss. **Try singing** "Cindy surely loves Sammy so much. And there, there he is." **And you will hear the hiss of the words and the pop of the T-words. They are inexpensive and worth it as no matter what effects, you have available you still can't get rid of it, but a pop filter will make it more manageable.**

Another item that is must have is a 'shock mount' (Fig 6-22) this keep the microphone from picking up wanted vibrations. Say you are recording an acoustic guitar riff that is slow and easy at first then tears into a hard driving one. You are hammering away ending a drive solo down the neck then when you play it back you hear an unwanted sound as the vibrations that you were making were picked up by the microphone stand and transferred to the microphone. The bad news is that great take is not useable.

Fig 6-21 A pop filter is a must have when using a microphone with vocals.

Fig 6-23 Two different types of microphones stand. On the left is sturdy unit with a round base that holds well up to a heavy microphone. The unit on the right contain a telescoping boom which is good for different positions. However, the tripod design is a little unstable with heavy microphones, especially the cheaper stands. Get some steel bars and tape them to the legs when this happens. Just make sure it is on the legs that are the opposite of the microphone.

Fig 6-22 Shock mount

The draw back to this type of shock mount is that it will not fit all types of microphones. A small pillow under the legs of the stand will also work. **That brings us to...**

Another must is a microphone stand. Avoid cheap light weight stands as they cannot hold up a heavy microphone, like the DB125. However, you **don't need** the most expensive either. Try to find one that is adjustable and comes sturdy base. Is there a connection that can hold a boom this is useful in placing microphones for drums, pianos, and other instruments. A small tripod stand is great for recording from amplifiers. If the stand will not hold the microphone tape metal bars to the outside leg to help with the balance.

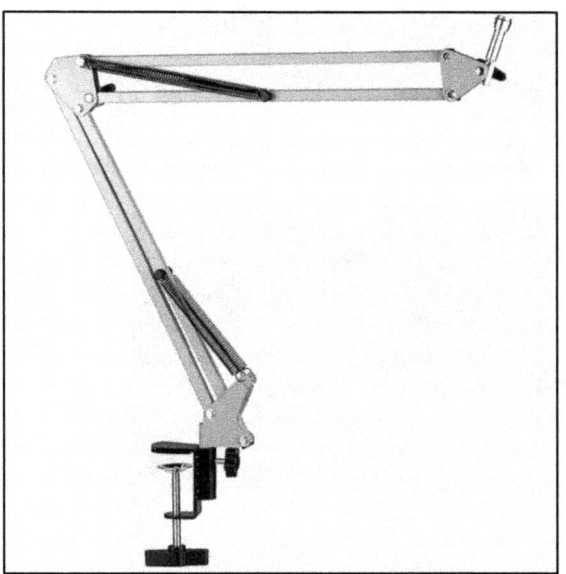

Fig 6-24 a good stand for a podcaster is a clamp on type this puts the microphone up over your head providing for a better voice track.

MIXING BOARDS

A mixing board is essential if you are going to use more than one microphone to record, such as in recording an acoustic drum set. There are many on the market but one that is affordable and easy to use is those from Alesis® corporation. They come in either a 4 channel or 8 channel versions and can be bought for a few hundred dollars.

Fig 6-27 The MULTIMIX 8 uses phantom power to power a condenser microphone.

Fig 6-25 A eight channel mixer for Alesis is great for mixing down drums.

Fig 6-26 The input section of the MULTIMIX 8 USB FX by Alesis. Microphones or instrument cables are plugged in here.

Fig 6-28 *Controls on the mixing board these are used to mix down the sound and send it to the computer with a USB cable.*

Fig 6-29 *The USB port on the back of the mixer.*

MICROPHONE PREAMP

If you plug a microphone directly into the computer or a recording device, you are going to get a weak signal. A microphone preamplifier will boost this signal that is coming into the recorder, or other device like an PA or amplifier. Any preamp will have at least one microphone input and one line level output. That will get the job done. However, you may want more function out of your mic preamp. Some mic preamps have a hi-Z Direct Input (DI) on them. This is beatifical in recording guitar, bass, and other electric instruments directly — look for this input if you record electric instruments often- even if you usually just mic up an amplifier.

Some mic preamps have more than one output — it's not uncommon to see an XLR output and a 1/4" TRS output on t he same mic preamp to give you more connectivity options, for instance. Mic preamps with multiple outputs will sometimes allow you to use the preamp as a signal splitter: so, can run one line-level output to your recording interface and another to a compressor or EQ for processing before recording. Depending on how you prefer to run your sessions, having a mic preamp with multiple outputs may be a huge help.

A word about recording to digital including Audacity. You need to look for a built-in A/D converter, which allows you to run a digital signal out of the mic preamp directly to your recording device. If you don't have this and use only and analog device, you can put up more noise. Preamps come in two different styles.

There are two type the tube type which creates a warm lush, euphonical sound that tube saturation can provide, or the crisp punch and clarity of a good solid-state design. Only you can decide, what you need, but if you can afford try one of each. There is also the hybrid type which contains both a tube path and a solid-state circuit, with the option of selecting either — or even a combination of the two. This is a good choice if your recording content is equally divided, between vocals and instruments, or between guitars and k eyboards.

Question how many channels do you need? Answer how many microphones do you record with at one time? And with Audacity that is one. However, you may be recording with record with more than mixing it down to send to the computer. So however, many microphones you use at one time is the number of channels you will need. So, if you are a one-person band and you record one track at a time, and only use one mic, you could get by with one single channel. But think ahead you might at least want two or more channel preamps.

That all said most Audio Interfaces have built-in preamps, so **you won't really NEED a preamp. However, getting an** external- and higher quality one should help you achieve an overall better signal and, therefore, a better sound as well. **But just starting out you won't need one.**

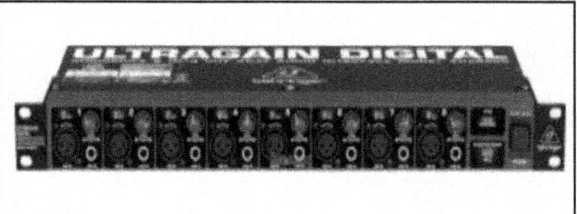

Fig 6-30 This preamp converts from analog to digital.

Fig 6-31 some mixers also come with preamps. This shows a close- up of one with 8 preamps.

Chapter 7 Connecting Instruments and Microphone Placement

There are only two ways to connect an instrument and record in Audacity. One is connecting the instrument to the computer itself, or by a microphone. The other is through an interface. An interface is device that converts the signal from an instrument to a *wav* pattern that the computer and Audacity can read. There are many different brands and models out there. They can range from a few bucks to a couple of hundred. An interface is a must have in digital recording. We use one from *Behringer* ® but any brand is good. Follow the instructions for your interface as how it works and hooks up. Most interfaces have room for one or two instruments at a time. However, there are mixer/interface available like the *Pyle PMX466 fig 7-1* that have multiple instrument or microphone capabilities. This is good when recording items like an entire band or drums.

Some instruments can be connected directly to the computer like electronic drums, USB guitars, and electric keyboards. While microphones will be needed to record piano, acoustic guitar, drums, brass, or woodwind instrument. We will each instrument discuss each of these separately and how to place the microphones.

Fig 7.1 The *Pyle PMX466 interface mixer. Has provision for six different channels that will be mixed down to one stereo channel that can be sent to Audacity.*

GUITAR

If you have a "USB Guitar" then hook up is simple just hook the USB cable from the guitar to the computer.

Generally, the output level from an electric guitar (or electrical pickup in an acoustic guitar) is sufficient to drive the line input port on a computer. You just need away to connect to 1/4 inch cable to the computer.

This can be done a few different ways. One with a USB interface fig 7-2. Another way is with a USB to Guitar cable. There can be easily found for under $30.00. See fig 7-3 and -7-4

When looking for a cable make sure that the cable is well covered and insulated and hopefully one that has a LED light to indicate that it is working. Cables that are thin can some something lead to buzzing in the recording.

Fig 7.2 Plug one end of the 1/4-inch guitar cable into the interface in the instrument slot. Most interface are powered by the USB cable.

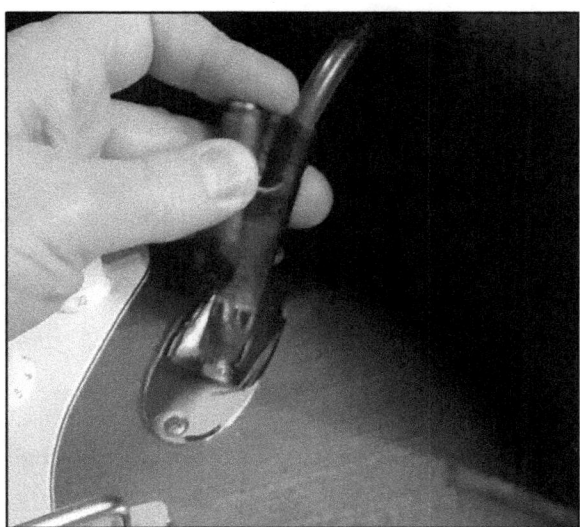

Fig 7.3 Plug the other end of the guitar cable into the electric guitar, shown is a guitar to USB cable being inserted the USB end of this cable goes into an empty USB slot on the computer.

Fig 7.4 Plug the square end of a standard USB cable into the back of the interface.

Fig 7.5 The other end of the USB cable into an empty USB slot on the computer.

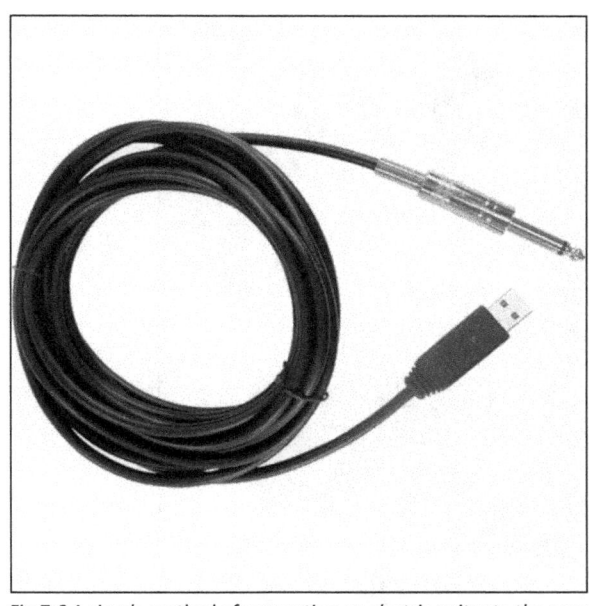

Fig 7:6 A simple method of connecting an electric guitar to the computers. A converter cable, it has a USB plug on one end and a stand ¼ jack on the other. Bread ties make a great item to control cables when not in use.

You can also use a cable that has a 1/4- inch jack on one end and a 3.5 mm on the other and this plugs into the line port of the computer, but we are not a big fan of this as sound seems to lack some, especially if an effect pedal is also place in the line between guitar and computer. The better choice is the 1/4 inch to USB cable or better the interface box.

You probably have a guitar cable for plugging the guitar into an amplifier, and you may be tempted to buy a 1/4 inch to 3.5 mm adapter instead, plug it into the computer line input then connect the guitar to the adapter using the cable – DO NOT do this! This creates a heavy, stiff cable hanging off the back of your computer - the slightest tug in the wrong direction could damage your sound card!

Most effect pedals fig 7-7 are designed to deliver about the same volume to the amplifier as the unaffected guitar sound (the volume you get when the effect is bypassed). Thus, you can connect your guitar to a pedal and then connect the pedal to the computer. Connect the 1/4 -inch cable to the input port of the pedal, and then the USB to Guitar cable to the out port of the box. Warning if the volume is too high, drop the volume on the effect box and if that does not help drop the volume some on the guitar.

Have the Audacity

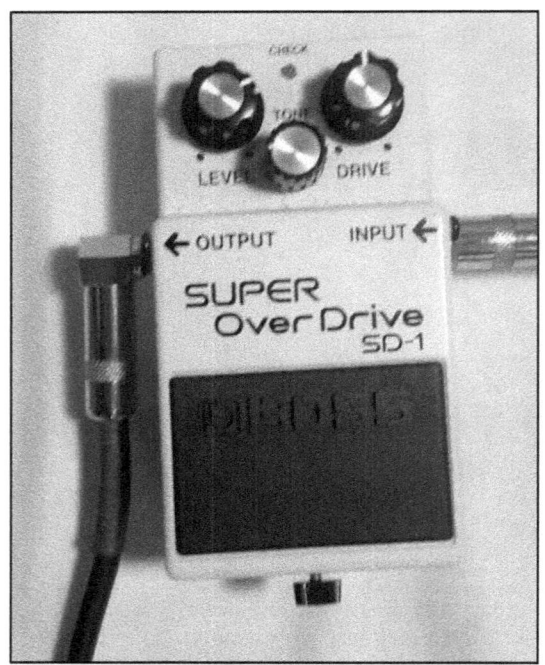

Fig 7-7 An effect pedal can be used in between the guitar and the interface. It requires two cables from the guitar to the effect box and the other from the effect output to the interface, or if using a guitar to USB cable to an empty USB slot on the computer. If volume become too high try turning down at the effect box first, then the guitar.

If you have a standard acoustic guitar, you will have to record it with a microphone, instructions on this are later in the chapter. Acoustic guitar with electric pickups is recorded the same as a standard electrical guitar, as is an electric bass.

KEYBOARD

If the keyboard has RCA jacks on the back, then the best way to connect it is with a dual RCA to stereo mini-plug cable as shown below, fig 7-8 plugged from the RCA output jacks (fig 7-9) on the back of the keyboard to the line input port of the computer.

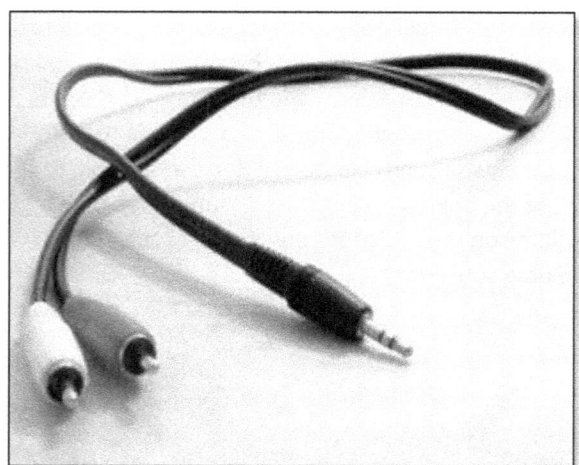

Fig 7-8 RCA cables to mini plug.

Fig 7-9 Some keyboards my RCA out jacks these are the best way to record on Audacity.

Fig 7-10 If a keyboard does not have RCA out jacks, it will not work try the USB to Host slot.

If the keyboard as a USB plug, (fig 7-10) you can run a cable from this port to the computer and record directly from here.

If the keyboard does not have either of these but does have a provision for headphone you can plug a cable here and use a 1/4 to 3/5 mm converter to the line input port of the computer or to the interface. You will lose the ability to listen directly to the keyboard using headphones, and any internal speakers will probably be muted. You can get around this using a headphone splitter cable. Or listen at the interface, which there is less delay.

However, on some keyboards this will not work on. In this case you will have to use an additional recorder like those from TASCAM to attach the headphone jack to the recorded then import the track from the recorder.

ELECTRONIC DRUMS/DRUM MACHINE

First of all, follow the instructions of how to do this on your drum kit. If the unit has a port that connects to the computer through a high-speed USB port, Fig 7-12 this is the best way.

For drum machines (fig 7-11) the best way is using cable to the interface and then USB cable to the computer. ` another way is to use a 3.55 mm cable that will plug into the line port of your computer and then to the headphone jack of the drum set. If your drum set has 1/4-inch headphone jack, you can use a 1/8 to 1/4 inch adapter. Or a 1/8-to-1/4-inch cable. Note 1/8 is the same as 3.5 mm cable. Make sure you are plugging into the line port on the computer and the headphone jack of the drums.

Fig 7-11 A typical drum machine, best way to connect this is through the headphone jack to the interface. You can tap out a drum riff on the pads and create your own drum track.

Fig 7-12 The USB outport is one of the best ways to record an electronic drum set.

MICROPHONE CONNECTIONS

Microphone Placement

Many instruments do not have a USB out or a cable and to capture the sound you must use a microphone. You also might want to mic amplifiers to get the 'real sound' you want for a distorted guitar This also requires microphones. Proper placement to the instrument is the key to getting the best sound. Each instrument has its own special needs, and we will cover each one of them separately.

Accordion

Alright we can see your face drawing down and eyebrows lifting in puzzlement, it is a joke, right? No here is the joke.

A couple go to see a judge for a divorce. The judge asks the wife "What is the reason you want the divorce?"

"It is too awful I just can't tell you!" The wife said.

"Does he drink too much?"

"Yes, but that's not reason."

"Does drugs? Beats you? Poor provider?"

"Yes, yes! YES!" the wife sigh, "he beats me, he beats kids, he beats the dog. We live on stale bread and water, but that is not the reason."

"Then what is the reason!"

The wife drops her head and begins to cry as she sobs, "He plays the accordion."

"Divorce granted!"

Fig 7-13 If the mic is too close to the accordion, you will pick up to much key tapping noise and the air from the bellows.

It may not be the first choice of heavy rocker song, but it does have it place in music. The problem is unlike miking a guitar which is easy, an accordion is the second biggest nightmare in a studio (the first place will follow). The reason for this is:

- The sound comes from both sides of the instrument.
- The action of the bellows means that the instrument is always in motion, and this will cause noise.
- An accordion radiates a different timbre in every direction, and each accordion surface produces a distinct pitch.
- An accordion makes the sound of the keys being depressed, the wheezing sound of the bellows, along with the music all this must be consider when choosing a mic technique.

So here is how to do that. Use a single dynamic microphone placed about two to three feet from the bellows works best (fig 7-13). The dynamic mic will cut down on the button and air noise. You may have to move it back and forth from the instrument to get the proper sound.

Banjo

If the accordion is a bad dream to record, then the banjo is the nightmare. Of all the instruments to record it is a banjo that will drive the preamps and the recorder crazy. It will likely have to be calmed and the noise brought down in the mix. Because most are played with a metal thumb pick, this makes for lots of string brushing sounds.

Use a cardioid condenser mic and, try placing the **microphone away from the players' hand**, below the bridge or directly below the hand but at a distance of eight to ten inches. Again, this is not set value it may be closer or further depending on the player themselves.

Clarinet

If all possible used more than one microphone should be used. With one **pointing down at the small "A' Key with** the second mic at the bell. If you only mic at the top, the bottom notes are weak. Mic at the bell only and the top notes are lacking. This will require the mic be connected to a mixing board and then the computer to be on one single track on Audacity.

However, if you only have one microphone use an omnidirectional mic and place it about 2 feet away from the bell and two feet above the instrument.

Fig 7-14 One microphone on drums.

Drum Kit

The drum kit is the one instrument that gets the most attention and is the hardest to mic. And many think that you have to mic ever single drum and cymbal to get that big drum sound. But that is not true. In fact, you can use just one mic if you like and many hit records have just that. Ideally two to four is perfect.

Stop thinking of the drums as several different instruments and see it one single instrument. Know that it is going to take several tries and moving of the mics to get it right.

One Microphone

To truly record a drum set you need more than one microphone, but in case you only have one microphone. Place a single microphone (fig 7-14) on a stand and boom six to eight feet directly in front of the kit and four to six feet high. If you are getting too much from the cymbals. Place the microphone behind the kit over the drummer's head and angled at the kit. Another positioned behind and over the drummer's right shoulder and angled down into the center of the kit.

Fig 7-15: Two microphones on drums. See text for distance.

Two Microphones

Using more than one mic will require you to use a mixing board/interface. With two microphones (fig 7-15). Place a one microphone on the hi-hat side about 4-5 feet away. The second mic on the ride cymbal side. Blend the mix into a good mono sound.

Multiple Microphones

The key to using multiple mics is to keep the distance from the mic to the drums all the same, if you must adjust the distance on one mic you must increase or decrease the same amount with the other microphones. This does not mean that mics are all a certain distance away. It means if you move the mic for the kick drum back an inch and it was at four inches and now is five inches, you move the mic that is over snare that is at one inch away is now two inches. This will keep everything in balance.

Kick Drum

First mic should be 4-6 inches away and 1-2 feet off the ground in front of the kick drum. This should pick up the good bass drum sound but also the bottom of the tom-toms. Fig 7-17

Fig 7-17 Micing the kick drum.

Fig 7-18 Microphone peaking over the tom-tom and over the snare.

Snare Drum

Second microphone is placed where the drummer hits the snare (Fig 7-18) and so it is just peeking over the floor tom. Do not get the microphones to close to the drums as they can be hit by the drummer. But start with a few inches, and a just the microphones from there. If you want the true snare sound place another microphone under the drum. Remember you will have to have an empty channel for this, and this will have to be mixed down to send it to a single track in Audacity.

Overhead Microphones

Use the microphone placements at the kick and the snare plus the third and four microphones are overhead and with one mic on left and the other on the right. At distance of six to eight feet, angle the microphones down towards the kit. Hit hats usually loud enough to not have to be miked. This is like the two-mic set up fig 7-15 but they place behind the drummer.

Test and mix the sound in a mono sound that will be sent to the computer. Again, if one mic is moved all must be moved the same amount or it will be out of balance.

Fiddle or Violin

This one instrument that changes according to where you listen to it as the sound changes in a radial pattern and it is uneven. And each one and each player is different. The way you find the **'sweet spot'** is to have the musician play while you roam around the room (about six feet in front of the musician) with one finger in your ear that away from the sound and find the spot where it sounds the best. If anyone asks you what you are doing? Reply *this how you hear the magical fairy and if you find her; she will give you three wishes*. While they are trying to figure out that, you will find where it sounds best. Now squat down and slowly rise. If you hear the sound improve, note that spot. This will be the spot where you will place the microphone. To get the sound of the room and the instrument use an omnidirectional mic, to get only the instrument sound try a Condenser microphone in a cardioid pattern.

Flute

This one instrument that is easy to record. However, do record from the open end of the flute, as it does not right there. Instead pick the spot by listening by ear. Beware of placing the mic to close or you could pick up key clicking or mouth notices. A good starting point is several feet away on one side, make a test track and check the sound and move, if necessary, try one side and then the other side. With classic flute sound try four to six feet and with the jazz sound 6 to 8 inches to catch that breathy sound also.

Fig 7-19 Do not **'close mic'** near the sound hole of an acoustic guitar, sound will be unnatural. Move it back

Fig 7-20 For close microphone placement do it where the body and neck meet.

GUITAR

Acoustic Guitar

Most recommendations you will see that you should place the microphone near the sound hole. This will create an unnatural sound. So, push the microphone back a few feet, but be warned that this will pick up the room sound.

The better sound is achieved from placing the microphone near the bridge or at the point where the neck and body meet at a distance of eight to ten inches. If possible, a two-mic option is even better with one at the point where the body and neck meets, and another one over the guitarist shoulder aimed at the 12th fret. However, you must be careful of getting microphones out of synch.

You will get a full sound aiming the mic at the sound hole, if you do this pull the microphone back at least 3 feet away.

Electric Guitar

The electric guitar can be plugged directly into the computer using a guitar to USB cable or an interface. You an even place a distortion pedal in between them. However, if you want to 'amp sound' you will have to mic the amplifier. However, whatever you do NOT use the line out of an amplifier to connect to the computer as it could damage the sound card.

First thing is getting the amplifier up off the floor. Do NOT mic an amplifier on the floor, the results will be less than favorable. Place it on a chair or table or large wooden box. Even a small amp can be used to record with. Different sounds can be achieved by different angles and distance of the microphone. A good starting point is one inch away from the speaker, if the amp has more than one speaker choose the best sounding one. The mesh on the amp will vibrate during playing so be sure it does not touch the mic any time during the song. IF two mics are used place them at a 45-degree angle from each other. Use a Dynamic Cardioid microphones both and dual applications.

Fig 7-21 Single mic on guitar amplifier.

Fig 7-22 When using two mics place them at a 45-degree angle with one slightly higher than the other one.

Fig 7-23 for micing a Bass amp place a dynamic mic about 2-3 inches from the amp and then move accordingly.

Bass Guitar

The electric bass guitar can be plugged directly into the computer using a guitar to USB cable or an interface. You can even place a distortion pedal or other effect pedal or pedals in between them. However, if you want to 'amp sound' you will have to mic the amp. This differs from the electric guitar.

Unlike the lead and rhythm electric guitars, the bass sound will also be affected by the room and how it is played. There is a softer sound when it is played by fingertip then when the player uses a pick.

Place the microphone 2-3 inches (fig 7-23) from the amp. For that hard rock sound spilt the bass sound running one to the bass amp and another to a guitar amplifier. This is done with a Y-Spilt ¼ inch cable, (fig 7-24) like those available from Pig Hog. This allows you to attach other cables to it and not just plug into the amplifier. While you can add distortion to the amp live it seems to overwhelm the Audacity track, so it best to add this later to the mix, which we will cover later.

Brass (Trumpet, Trombone, Tuba)

For the *trumpet* place the mic 3-5 feet away, but above the bell and aim toward the mouthpiece.

For the *trombone*: If you want an aggressive sound that will cut through the mix. Place the mic 1-2 foot in front of the bell. For a more mellow sound place the mic 2-3 feet away and aim it at a 20–30-degree axis from the bell.

The *tuba* can quickly overpower a mix. To make it sit better in the mix place the mic over the top of the bell with a 15 degree off axis of center. If it is too much, aim the mic off axis more even up to 60-70 degrees.

To record a group, place the musicians in a circle and with a ribbon microphone in the center in the center hanging over the group at a height of about 4 feet. If you don't have a ribbon microphone, use an omnidirectional condenser microphone instead, but it may not have the warm tone that the ribbon has

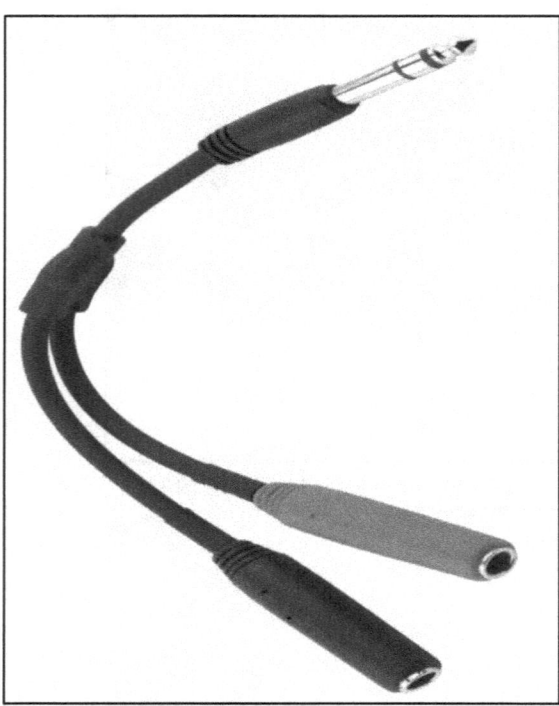

Fig 7-24 Use a Y-cable to split the bass to two different amplifiers.

Hand Claps

There two ways to do claps and one is in person. This requires a live large room as claps will quickly peg the meters. The microphone should be set back at least 8 feet. You can use hand claps, or you can clap your thighs, which gives you a fuller sound. But you may have to move the microphone in some and lower to get a good sound. It is good to have sound sort of backing behind the claps to avoid too much of an echo effect. An LDC condenser microphone works well.

The second way is with a drum machine if it has that provision on it. Just simply press, in time, the button to lay down the track and you can add effects later.

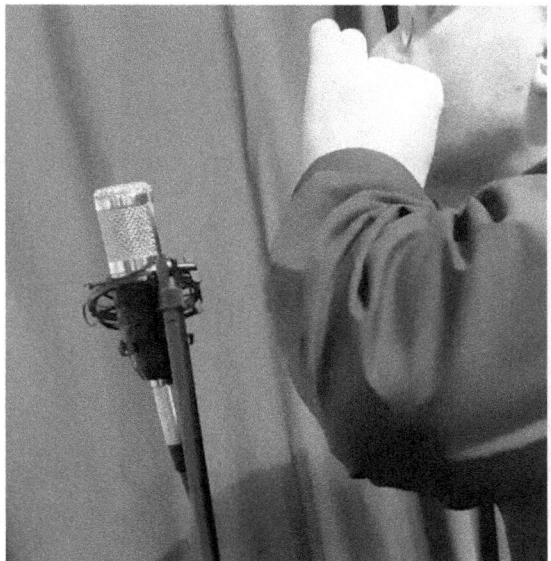

Fig 7-27 When recording the Harmonic **don't hold the microphone with** cupped hands.

Harmonica

Given this is a reed instrument powered by the human lungs, many of the techniques and approaches commonly applied to vocals and orchestral woodwind are transferable to the harmonica.

The microphone should not be set up though like for vocals it should be lower, at about chin height and six inches away. At this point the sound should be full and focused. Moving it back to 12 inches or more will give a more open, airy sound and capture more room noise, which may be more desirable for a bluesy sound.

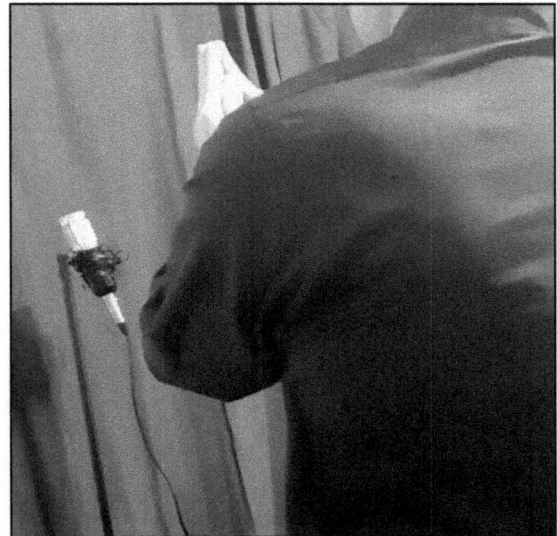

Fig 7-25 When recording hand claps stand back from the microphone and use a barrier like heavy drapes behind the microphone.

Piano

Microphone placement will have a lot to do with the sound. For a bright sound place the microphone inside of the piano. However, you will also pick up hammer and pedal sounds.

Placing it outside but near the opening looking in will take away the bright sound which can be good or bad depending on the song.

Miking away from the piano will record the piano and the **room. If the room sounds good, you won't need a close** sound. This is great when the piano sound does not sound right until you get a few feet away.

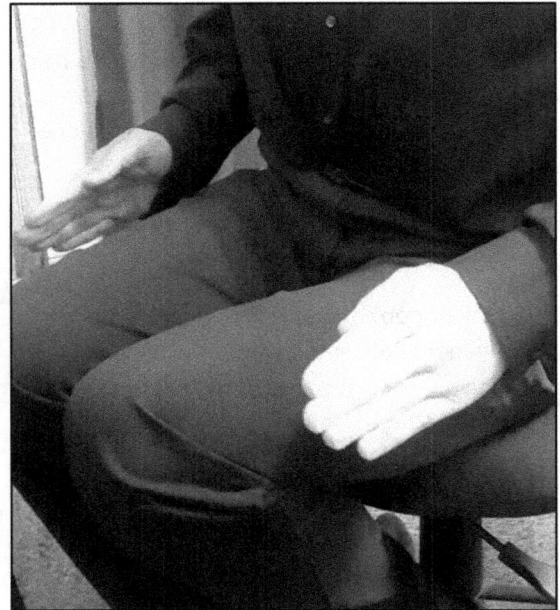

Fig 7-26 For fuller sounding clap sit on a stool and slap your thighs

Fig 7-28 qnd 29 Place one microphone near the front.(top). Of an open Grand Piano. And the other near rear. (bottom)

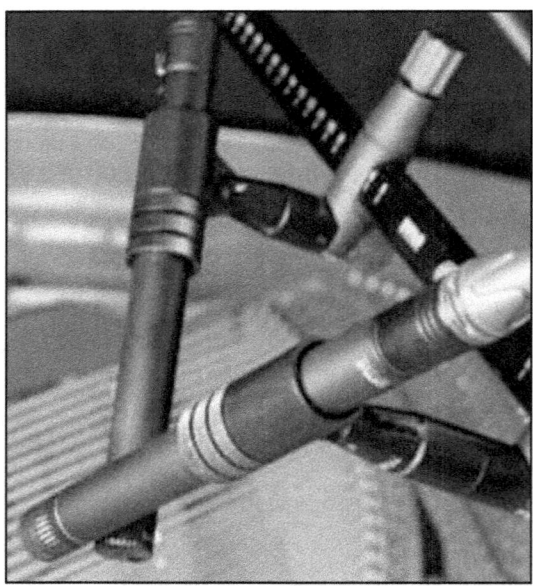

Fig 7-30 A great set up is the y-pattern

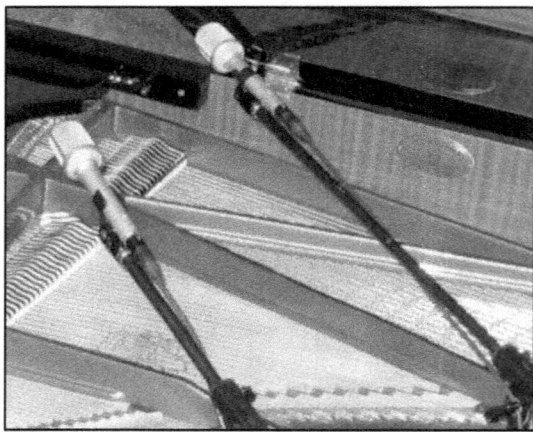

Fig 7-31 A common pattern with two mic is one over the low keys and the other the high keys. A common set when recording church performances.

Placing the microphone at the side of the instrument you will hear more of the high sounds, inside more of the middle notes will be heard. However, the main factor in placement will be the music style. Also note you can use more than one mic and mix them together or on to individual tracks.

For classic music or a piano solo on a grand piano, try a pair of mics placed in the middle of the part near, where it starts to curve at about 6 feet away. Place one mic pointing to one way and the other the way in a Y pattern see fig 7-30.

Another method is inside the piano place one mic over the upper strings and the other by the lower strings. Fig 7-31.

For the rock and roll or pop sound place two microphone in a Y pattern within two feet of center, where the high and low strings cross. If using only one mic place find the sweet spot and place the mic there.

All the above is for recording a grand piano not an upright. We have seen too many beginners open lid and drop a microphone inside. This is not good idea, as the sound is lacking, and you get more of the sound of hammers. We have seen other pull the face off the cover of the piano to expose the strings, this still lacks the warmness the upright delivers, which is the reason you would be using an upright for recording.

A better way is by pulling the piano away from the wall and place microphones in the sweet spot at the back of the instrument see fig 7-32. To find the sweet spot listen as someone plays the scales. With one ear towards the soundboard and the other ear plugged with your finger, move up and down and to the sides. When you find the spot where the music sounds the best place the mic there. It is a good idea when you find it mark it with a small piece of tape. Note you may find more than one sweet spot-especially with low and high keys. The best type of microphone to capture the upright piano sound is a LDC Condenser Microphone.

Fig 7-33 A small clip on microphone is useful in micing a saxophone and other instruments with a bell.

Saxophone

No other instrument has the **mood sound that a 'sax'** does. It can create the bright cheeriness of love, or darkness of heartbreak. This is because the sound does not come out of the bell but out of every hole in the instrument. So, in doing so if you only mic the bell you not going to capture the true 'sax' sound.

So, to really get that real sax sound you need at least two microphones. Place a large condenser mic about 1-2 foot away and aimed up that the player at the top of the neck of the instrument. Another position is between 1-2 feet at angle that points at the left hand of the sax player.

Tambourine

This should be recorded in a larger room. Oddly a cheap condenser mic works the best like. Place six feet way and elevate to about head high. Close miking does not work so keep back

Fig 7-32 Place mic at the sweet spot at the back of upright piano.

VOCALS

Note that the best and most expensive mic does not necessarily mean it works the best, it is the tried-and-true method of selecting the microphone, listen and select on the sound. We are not even going to give recommendations, as vocalist are different and one microphone that works for a female with a soft soprano voice will not work for a hard loud male rock vocalist. So, it is best you try out different microphones. Also note what may work on the stage may not be that great in the studio. What we are going to cover here is the position of the microphone.

Position of the microphone is the key thing. Most of the time **you don't want to be right next to** the microphone. The ideal distance is to spread your fingers with your thumb on your lip and your little finger should just touch the tip of the mic. The exception to this rule is when you want a low breathy sound-especially with female singers. In this case the voice is whispered with lots of breath. For this effect you need to be very close to the microphone.

In fact, distance and position of the microphone has a great effect on how the voice will sound. Moving closer to the mic will deepen the tone and moving back will rise the tone.

Everyone has seen the photos of a singer in the studio singing into a microphone turned upside down and hang up **above the singer's head. There is a reason for this:**

By having to tilt your head back (fig 7-33) and up it opens the air passageways, allowing you to get a full body voice and hold a note longer. It also helps prevent that nasty popping and breath blasts. That does not mean you forget the windscreen and pop filter though.

You can use a mic stand and boom to place the microphone so that the **windscreen is even with the singer's nose** (fig 7-34) and from 4-16 inches away. The distance will depend on **the singer's voice and the style of the song.** If you have a singer with a soft voice and it is a slow ballad, then you may have to move the mic close (fig 7-36). While if you have a loud singer doing a full out metal song with full screams then you might want to pull it back some. If you must place the stand up on a sturdy box to elevate it.

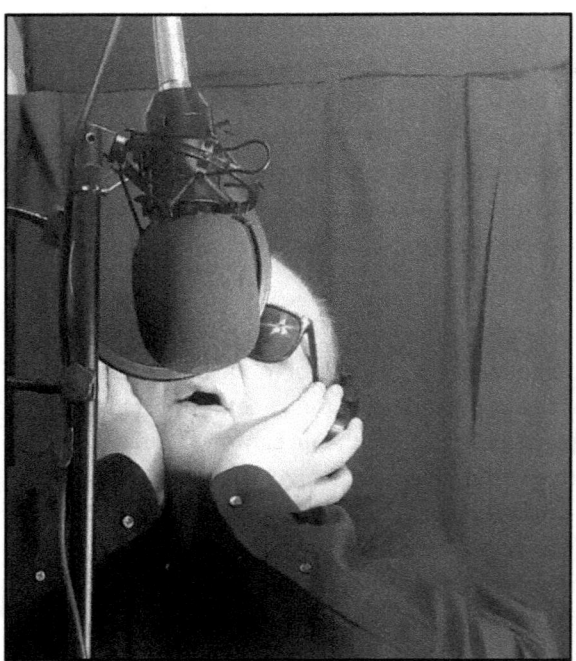

Fig 7-33 Placing the microphone up above the singer can help improve vocals.

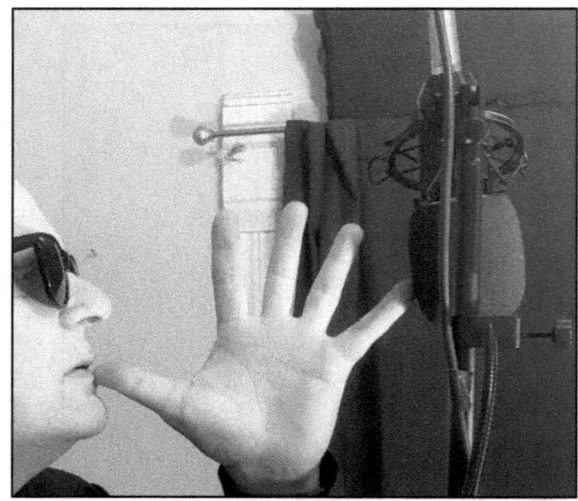

Fig 7-34 an ideal way to measure how far away from the microphone you should be.

Fig 7-35 Placing the microphone at chin level and off to one side of the singer can help with the **problem with the esss' sound.**

Fig 7-36 Moving in closer to the microphone or further away can change the sound.

Another method is to place the microphone at chin level (Fig 7-35) and them angle the microphone back *away* from the singer. Or place it off to the side of the singer and the angle the microphone *towards* the singer.

For background vocals it is better to have one microphone and have the back singers around it then having each one has their own microphone, which causes an uneven mix. Just make sure to use an Omni or figure 8 mic when group vocals are down. Or you can use two microphones place them in a X-Y pattern or sperate the two spaced microphones with a *Jecklin disk-* this is a round disk that is covered with foam that used between microphones to keep them from bleeding into one another.

You have likely seen that backup vocals will have photos of the backup singer with one of the head-phone cups off one of their ears, this is done so they can hear the other backup singers, because you cannot hear the mix while recording. See fig 7-37 Audacity allows you to become your own back up vocalist and we will cover this in a later chapter.

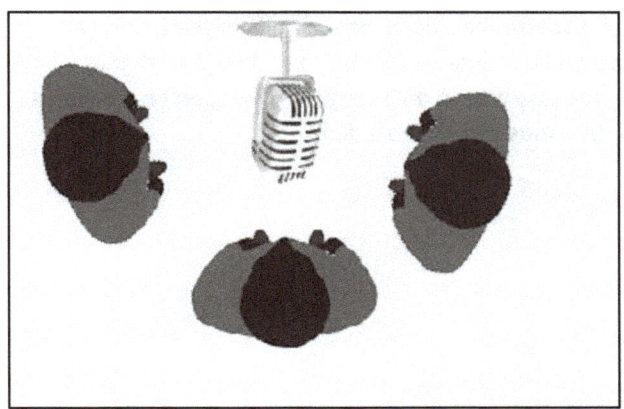

Fig 7-37 Group around an omnidirectional microphone for backup vocals.

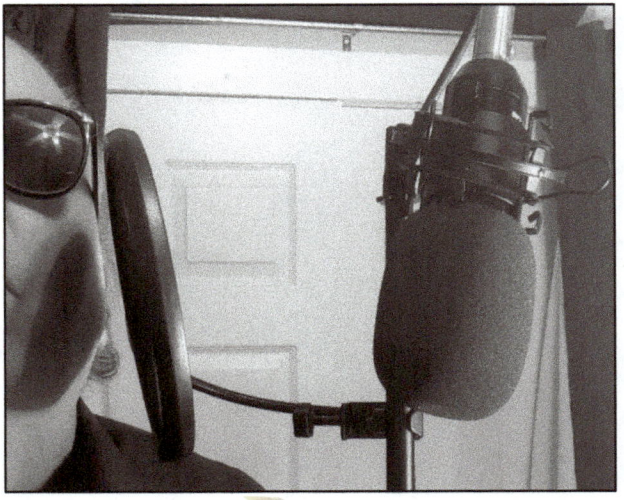

Fig 7-38 when recording whistles, humming, ooh and ahhs place the microphone off to one side and use the pop and windscreen filters

Whistling and Humming

These are two of the simplest sounds to make, nearly everyone can do it. And those oooh's and ahh's and included in this. Simple to make and are two of the hardest voices to record. Place the microphone in front of the singer and you will end up with an unpleasant sound the whistle will be mostly air, and the humming you will hear pops and breaths. So, it is better to place the microphone to the side and at a height for where the singers hears. And get ready this will take many takes to get right. And here you though that **sound was easy way to do a song that you didn't have words to.** Another music myth busted.

Xylophone

This is a percussion instrument and falls into that they way it should be set up for microphones. Use two condenser microphones that position 1-1-1/2 feet above it aimed down on to the instrument about 1-1-1/2 feet apart or angled sharply with the grilles of the microphones touching.

Chapter 8 Laying Down a Track

ALL TRACKS LEAD BACK HOME

There are many times in life that we are both excited and scared to death at the same time. This includes the first day at school when your parents drop you off and you are surrounded by people you have no idea of who they are.

That first date with someone, your hands are sweaty your heart is pounding, and you just know you are going to do something stupid.

Taking the driver's license test, you got it down you know it cold but that 'little demon' in your mind is telling you are going to blow it and your breath comes out in quiver when you turn the ignition on.

Laying down your first track is no different. You are in place where that first time **that you don't know what you are doing.** Your hands are cold and clammy as you move the mouse over to hit record and the timer starts ticking away and your breath quivers as your fingers start play or your lips utter out the lyrics. And sure, enough you hit the wrong note. You yell out a cuss word as you click the stop button. "**My life is ruined!**"

Don't panic!

Unlike many other things in life, when you mess up in recording it easily fixable with another take or use a *punch in/out* method to record the part you messed up on. More on this later.

Ideally what happened is you over thought it. You cannot **be thinking 'Okay I go from a E to D to back to E chord** then to the A chord.' **You can't be thinking about that the record is** running, you must let it come to naturally' just as in playing music, recording is the same way.

One **doesn't** have lock yourself away without food and absolutely not anything to drink. Believe it or not recording can be hot hard work. It is important to keep hydrated. Especially during vocals. **And during vocals I don't** recommend just water. Instead, hot tea with honey and lemon, **if you don't like tea, like it with hot water. Not hot enough that it can't be comfortably drank, but warm enough** the warmth of the liquid help rehydrate the throat muscles. The honey and lemon soothes and works excellent in keeping vocal cords in shape. The reason a voice will crack is because it is dry.

I would not recommend alcoholic drinks, not even wine. There is no moral reason, but the fact that alcohol dries your throat out. Just note that recording sessions can and will get long, it is easy to forget time. So have something to snack on, that provides energy-like trail mix. Just keep it away from the instruments and recording equipment. And remember it is unlikely you are going to get it right during the first take, even the *'gods of music'* themselves do not get right on the first take-usually. **So don't get frustrated when** it comes to take 34. Because al tracks lead by home, where you can jut re do it.

So, before you press down on record just take a few deep breaths and relax. Do not get concerned about the time that is ticking away. Instead, just wait and then begin, that blank space before can be removed during the mix. It also good for saying what they track is or the take. But now you ask?

WHAT INSTRUMENT DO YOU RECORD FIRST?

That is like asking which came first the chicken or the egg? Do we just assume it was the egg because to get a chicken you need an egg, but to get an egg you need a chicken to lay one. So, the old rule that you have heard from many 'start with the *rhythm section-drums and bass* is not always true.'

Rhythm Section

In most songs you will start with the rhythm such as drums or a bass and build on it. But let's say the guitars has a riff going and the song is built on this. Or you have a song that is dominated by say an acoustic guitar, such as the case of our song "*Dead Roses*." Where it starts out with a simple acoustic guitar and remains the main instrument through most of the song until a hard distorted guitar takes over with a hard drum section, having the drums being recorded first would not work well with this format. Thus, the first track laid down here is the acoustic guitar. *So how do you keep the rhythm?* By adding a click track.

Click Track

A click track is just what it sounds like, a track of click sounds that are at preset rate, that takes the place of the kick drum. Fortunately, Audacity allows you to add a simple click track that will provide a steady 'click' that will be used as the rhythm section to get the guitar and other instrument on time.

Tempo (bpm): The total number of beats, (clicks) per minute, default is 120.

Beats per bar: The first beat of each bar is always louder than the remaining beats in the bar. So, for example, three beats per bar will sound like a waltz in 3/4-time signature, and four beats per bar (the default) will sound like the 4/4 of a march or like most pop and rock songs.

Swing amount: When set to zero, each beat has the exact length specified by the Tempo (beats per minute). When set to a non-zero amount, alternate beats are delayed or advanced to give a swing feel. At maximum / minimum settings the rhythm plays with triplet timing.

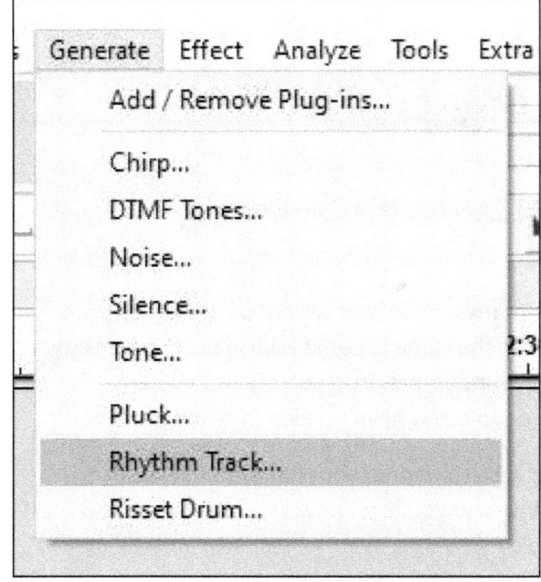

Fig 8-1 To add a click track click Generate> Rhythm track.

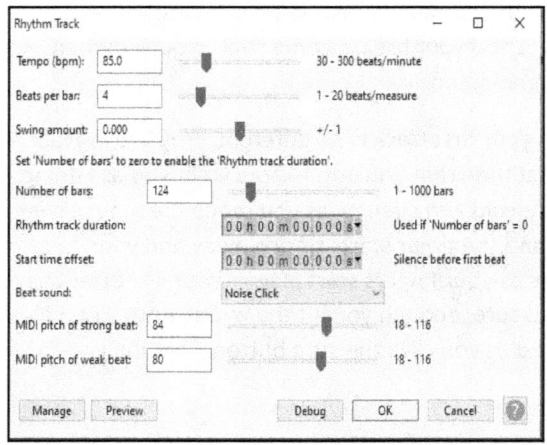

Fig 8-2 A new box will open. Set the values to want this song is. And set the sound to click.

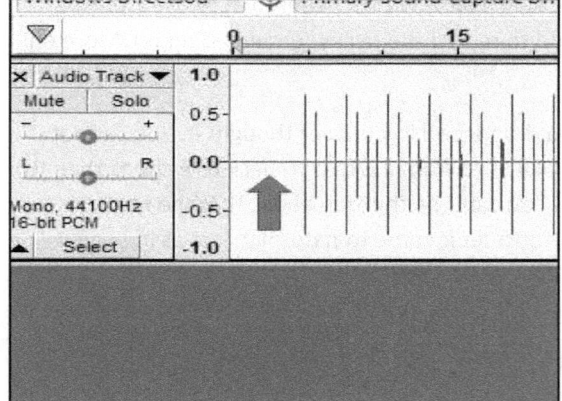

Fig 8-3 An example of a click track notice the delay at the beginning (arrow). You want at least a five second blank space even with a click track. So it gives you time to start playing after clicking the record button.

Number of bars: Beats per bar is repeated for the chosen number of bars. The default is 16 bars. The combination of tempo beats per bar and number of bars determines the length of the generated track unless the rhythm track duration is specified (see the next control).

Rhythm track duration: If you know the length of your song or rhythm section enter the value into this time control, the generated rhythm track will be at or slightly longer than this duration.

Start time offset: Makes the rhythm track start at a later point on the Timeline than the very beginning (zero seconds). The maximum is 30 seconds, and the default is zero. This is useful to have some silence at the start to allow you time to start playing after hitting record. Five seconds is a good time.

Beat sound: Choose which sound to use for the beats. The default is "Metronome tick".

MIDI pitch of strong beat: The pitch of the first beat in each bar. The MIDI values indicate what pitch to use. Examples: C-notes are 24, 36, 48, 60 (middle C), 72, 84, 96, 108 C# (C sharp) above middle C is 61 The default is 92 (G#).

MIDI pitch of weak beat: The pitch of the remaining beats in each bar. The default is 80 (G# an octave below the strong click).

Once created, the track can be edited (for example, its volume changed) like any audio track. It can also be deleted when it is no longer needed.

Create a Click Track

We will create a click track for our song '*Dead Roses*'. It starts out moderate beat with a 72 BPM then increases to 120 bpm then back to 72 bpm.

With Audacity open, click on *Generate>Rhythm Track* fig 8-1. A box will pop up fig 8-2. Fill in the amounts you need to create the track, this includes the bpm, number of beats per bar, this would be you timing. The number of bars it will create. Note if you are going to use the length of the song to set the track then set this to zero (0) to enable the length duration. Then set the duration length and the delay time that you want before the track starts. Choose the sound you want, this can be a choice many including a cowbell, that can add to the song. See fig 8-4. Then click okay, a track will automatically appear (fig 8-3).

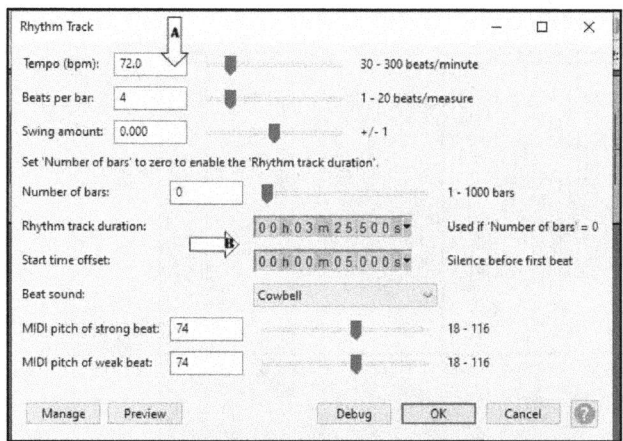

Fig 8-4 We set the BPM to 72 and beats per bar to 4. A Set the number of bars to 0 because we are using the length duration instead B. We set it to 3.25.5 seconds until the overdrive guitar takes over and BPM changes.

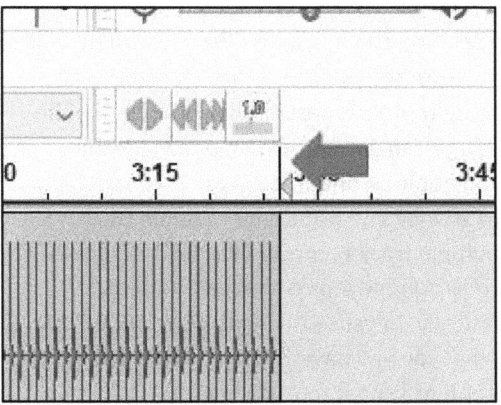

Fig 8-5 To change the BPM in a click track place the curse at the end of the track where the change is to take place.

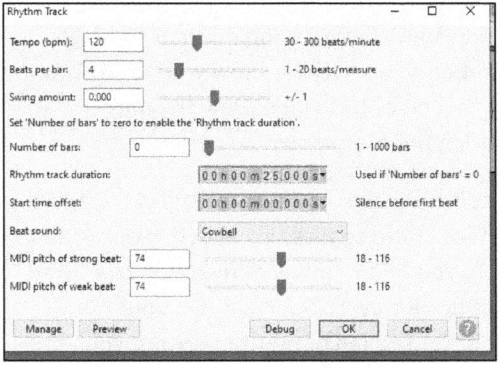

Fig 8-6 Click Generate>Rhythm Track again, and change the BPM and the timing, and the length that the change in tempo occurs, for us it is 25 seconds. Also making sure you have zero in the delay section. Click okay.

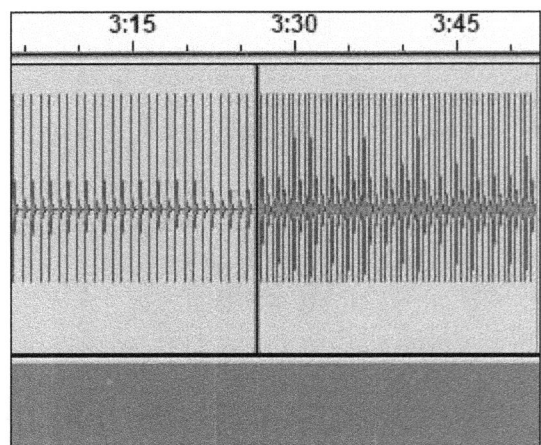

Fig 8-6 Notice the faster beats on the left. To slow it down again, we repeat the above using the 72 bpm.

Creating a Drum Track

If you have drum set, you can mic it and then record it. Or if you have electronic drum set you can attach the output to the computer with the methods described in chapter 7. The advantage of this is you can get it down on one track the drawback of this you get it on one track. Again, we stress that Audacity is not a true DAW and not a true multiple track recorder. A true multiple track recorder like TASCAM 24SD, which has several microphone inputs that can be sent to different tracks. Basically, because Audacity can only record one channel at a time, you will have to use a mixer that we described in Chapter 6 to send it to Audacity.

Since each drum gives a different wave pattern you can separate the wave pattern into different drum tracks, and this allows you to add special effects and mix it accordingly. Be warned this is not easy, but we will show you how this is done in the mixing section of this guide. How the main purpose here is getting the drum down on a track.

Having a drum set is nice, but they take up lots of room and many of us just cannot afford to lose that space in our studio. Plus, there is reason, you find so many of them for sale. They are noisy and it that noise travels. So, if you see your neighbor suddenly become a fan of mystery novels, you might want to lay off those late-night drum solos.

However, you can however add a drum track with a drum machine, by creating the track on the machine and then attaching the machine to the computer with a 1/4 to USB cable or an interface.

If you all you **don't have a drum** machine, or a drum set you can still add a drum track using only Audacity and a plug in along with drum samples that you can.

Now you will have to import drums, drums samples are found all over the internet. Many free or at a low cost. Such as www.ghosthack.de/free_sample_packs/

Once the drums are downloaded and opened place them in file you know where they are at. These are .wav files and can be read by Audacity. If you have friend with drums or is band teacher at school. You can make your own by miking and recording one single beat of each instrument. Converting them to .wav files and placing them into a computer file. And import them into Audacity.

Whether you record the sounds yourself or download them off the internet. You will have to build a drum track. This is not easy as you will have to place each drum on a separate track and move them around to create the rhythm and beat you want. The distance apart from each drumbeat will set the timing. Further apart will be a slow beat while closer together will set a faster beat. Use the click track to help with the timing.

To create a drum track you must have an idea of how drums work and what the drum track is going to sound like. For example, the basic drumbeat is kick drum lands on beats 1 and 3, snare drum on beats 2 and 4 while the high hats land on every 8th notes all the way through. There are many other patters like *four-on-the floor*-where the kick drum is hit on every beat, which is very common in rock, but it could be something totally different. We do recommend if you are going to create one this way make it simple and a short pattern that repeats over and over.

Create a Simple Drum Track

For example, here we will use our song *'Keep On Rockin'* which is drum and bass base with a simple rhythm that repeats.

With Audacity open. Click on *File> Import>Audio*. Select the file where your drum samples are. Then click on the sound of the drum sample you want, for example a kick drum. Fig 8-7 Now repeat with the other smaples; snare, and high-hats. This will create new tracks, now make them Mono tracks fig 8-8, and delete one track fig 8-9.

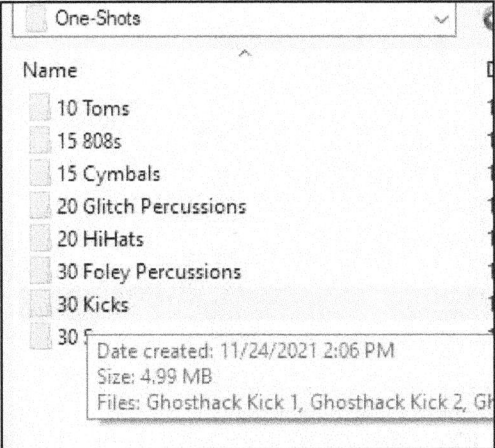

Fig 8-7 Find the file where you have the drum samples located at. Here our file is One Shots. Now we are going to click on Kick drums. Then click on the file you want to import and click OK.

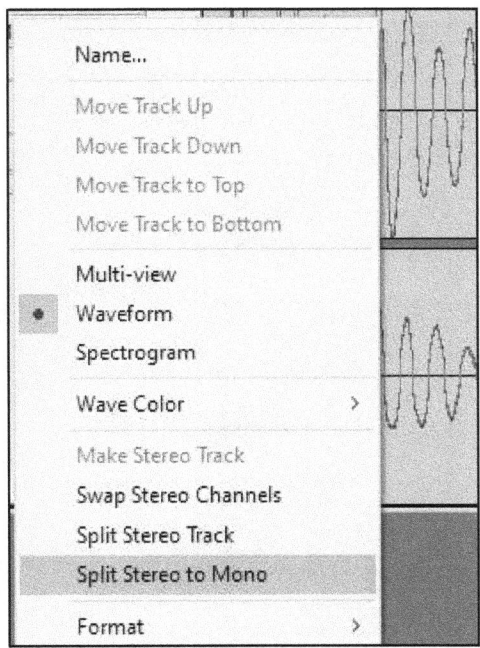

Fig 8-8 If it is stereo channel. 'Split Stereo to Mono'

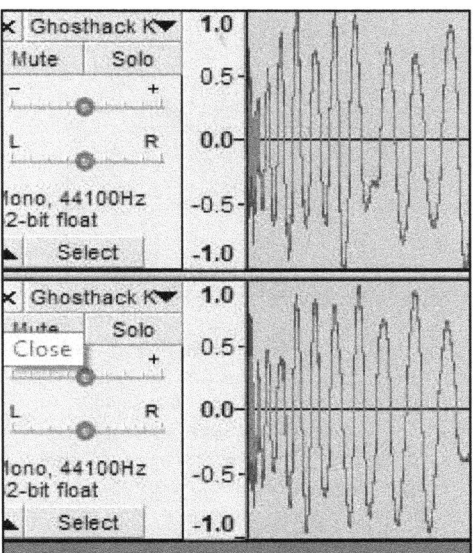

Fig 8-9 Delete one channel by clicking the X on the track.

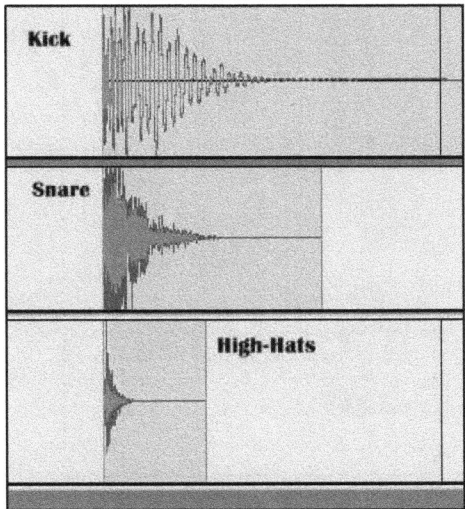

Fig 8-10 You end up with this track with all the drums happening at once.

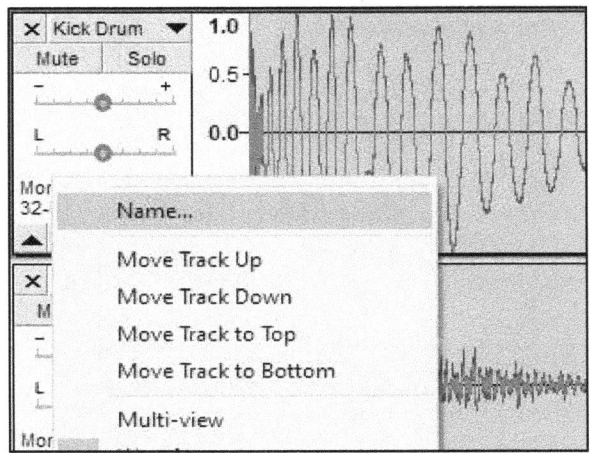

Fig 8-10 Name the tracks, by clicing on the down arrow on that track and then click on 'Name' and type in the track name i.e. Kick drum, Sanre drum.

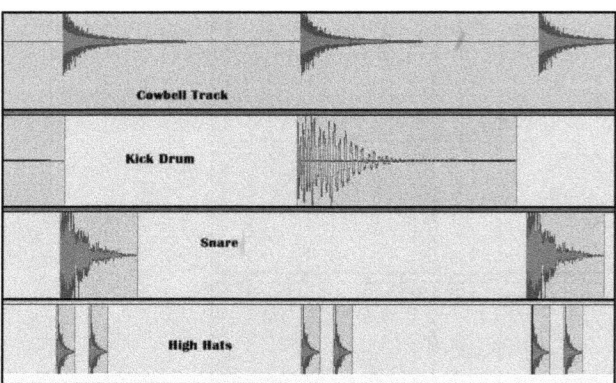

Fig 8-11 We have copied cut and pasted the drum, into a pattern, notice we had to duplicate the high-hats hits because they are struck on the 1/8 note. We use our Cowbell (click) track to set the timing. Placing each drum wave under it. If it is a little bit (ms) off on timing it will sound more human than if it is perfectly on time. Create two to four bars of this pattern., especially if you are going to add a cymbal to the mix.

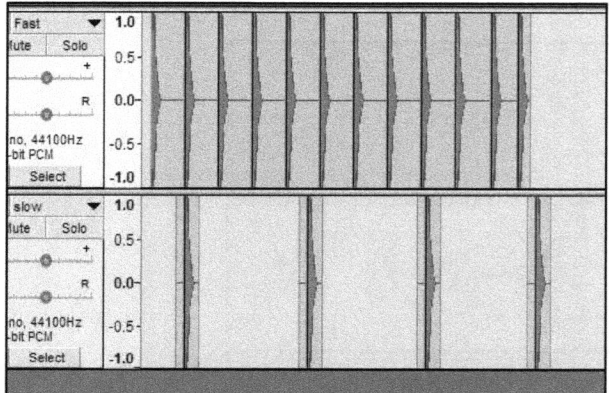

Fig 8-12 Example of how space creates the timing for the kick drum. Top the beat is tight tougher creating a fast beat while the bottom creates a slower beat.

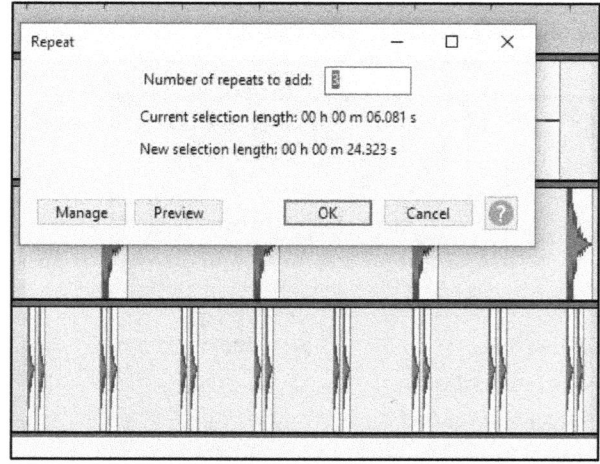

Fig 8-13 Select the drum track you want to repeat the click Effects>Repeat. Place in the number of repeats you want and click OK.

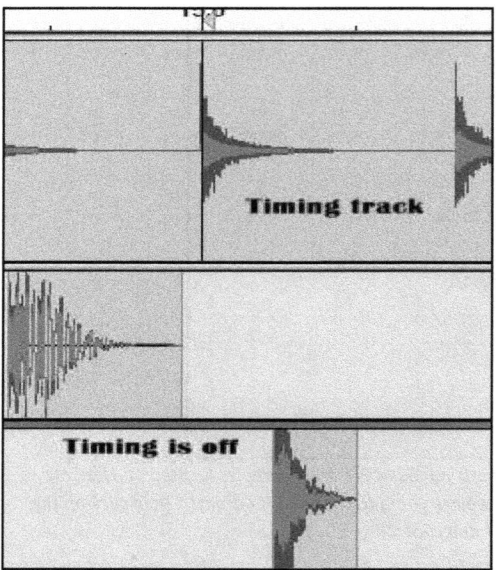

Fig 8-14 Notice the timing is off from the timing track at top.

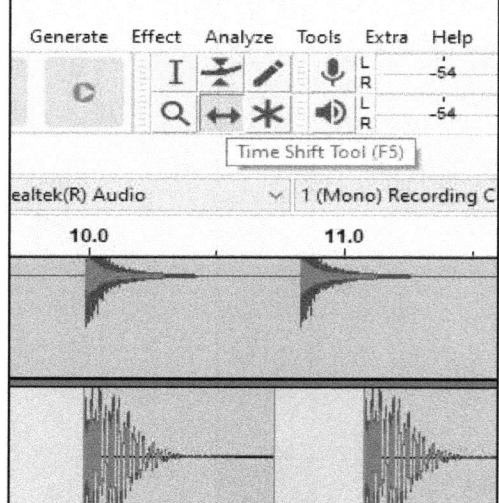

Fig 8-15 Click on the Tim shift tool at the top of the screen.

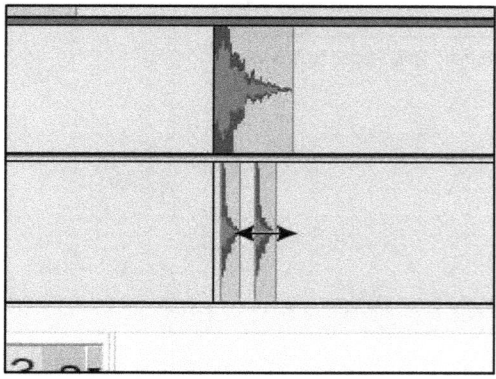

Fig 8-16 Place the time shift tool over the way you want to move and double arrow will appear. Click the left mouse key and drag it to the position you want it to be and the release the mouse key. On the newer addition of Audacity, there is no Time Shift tool just grab the wave by the handles and move it.

Now we can create the pattern for the chorus and another fill for the transition to the guitar solo and back to the verse, and outro. And you have a drum riff. It will take a while and you may have to tweak the tracks by adding or deleting and the rearranging the other tracks to fit. Once you're satisfied with the track save it and close Audacity. And move on to the next track.

Creating a Drum Machine Track

There are different ways you can create a drum pattern on a drum machine. One of the easiest is just to tap the keys to the time you want. We have found it easier to keep time using one finger. AAnddo.do. them one at a time, except the kick and snare which are done on one finger on each hand to keep the correct timing.

Set up the drum machine as we have described with an interface, press R to start recording. Then tap out the rhythm on the kick and snare drums. Listen to the track, and check to see if this the basic track you want. Tap *Shift R* to start recording on a new track (be sure to keep blank space at the beginning of each track so you are not hurried), now record the highs hats. Adding high hats (*fig. 8-20*) and cymbals are best done after the main rhythm of the kick and snare are laid down, as it is easier.

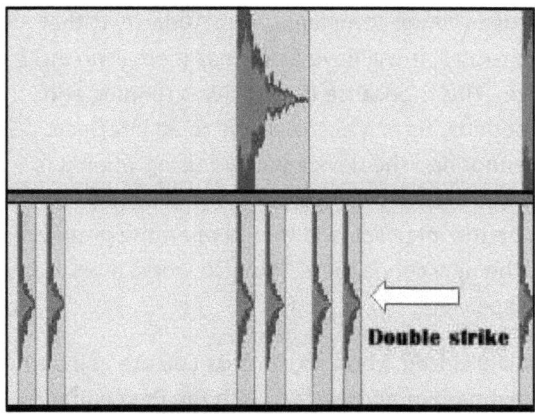

Fig 8-17: We have a double strike of the high hats. We need to remove this. Cut it and it will throw off the timing for the rest of the tracks.

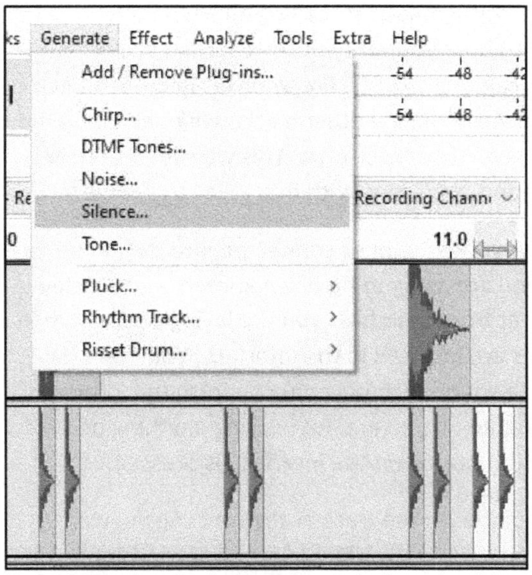

Fig 8-20 Laying down a high-hat track on a drum machine.

Fig 8-18 We select the double strike we don't need and then click Generate>Silence. And the double strike is removed without effecting the timing of the track.

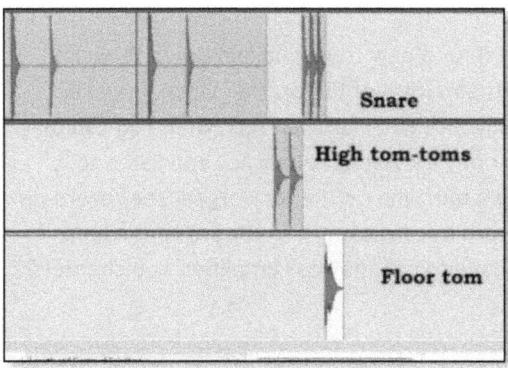

Fig 8-19 Now if you want to add tom-toms all you have to do is import them and place them in the proper place using different track. the tracks up to another to compare the timing. Note how we have grouped the snare drums together tightly to create a faster pattern. These are things you can do to change the drum sound and make it sound more human.

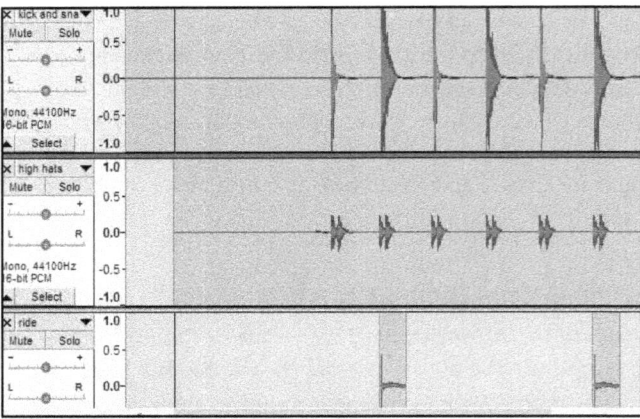

Fig 8-21 Drum tracks done with a drum machine.

Now you can add other drum sounds like tom-toms and cymbals to the mix. Just do it like you did the high-hats. If you, do it this way you create separate track for each type of drum which is useful when adding effects that are for each type, for example the is a different EQ used on the kick drum then there is the tom-tom. If they are all together on one track it makes it harder to apply these effects. But we will explain later how to break these tracks apart, then put them back together.

Creating a Bass Track

There are different ways to get a bass track. The most common is with a bass guitar. Which you just use a USB to guitar cable or an interface to connect it to the computer. Another is using a keyboard like a 'rock organ'. Many of the Door's epic songs were done with this as the bass and not a bass guitar including *'Light My Fire'*.

Another way is doing it like you did the drums and import bass sounds and add them one by one into a track.

The bass line is sometimes seen as and after thought in music. Everyone wants to be the lead singer, lead guitarist. How many times have you seen someone playing 'air bass'? But it is a good tight rhythm section thereby enabling the rest of the instrumentalists find their musical metaphors, and the bass is part of that.

Imagine if you will, a world where Queen's *Another One* bites the Dust without that opening bass line, or Rush-where one of the most know bassist- *Geddy Lee*. Not the world I would want to live in.

Note now you are going to see the benefits of multiple track recording, as we are going to lay a track down a bass track top of that drum track. And when played back they both will play at the same time.

One of the most common complaints with Audacity is that when you go to record, it will have error that there is no input or output device. This is because if Audacity is running and you switch something, form a micro-phone to an interface. The program cannot find the device you are using when it is running. You want to save your work, then shut down Audacity hook up the interface and then reopen the program, usually it finds the new connection. This also works if you add headphones or speakers.

So, with Audacity closed, hook up the bass you are going to use. Through keyboard or an interface with the Bass guitar. Now open Audacity and the file you just save with your drum tracks.

Press 'Shift R' this will start recording on a new track. You should be able to hear your previously recorded drum track(s). If you can't, click *EDIT. Preferences*, Record. Check to see if the box marked *Play other tracks while recording (overdub)* selected. If not click on it. This way you can hear the drum track and play along with it.

Do not have your headphones connected into the computer, or you are going to be disappointed with a delay that you will hear from your bass you are laying down. When the headphones are inserted in the interface, you don't have this delay, as the sound is coming directly form the interface and not the program. If you are not hearing anything be sure the Direct Monitor switch on the interface is pressed.

Position the pointer on the track at the zero. Again, we stress it is a good idea to have five to seven seconds of blank space at the beginning of each track this way you can be prepared after hitting record. Otherwise, we get hurried in trying to play, and this will undoubtedly cause us to make mistakes.

Now tap Shift R for a new track and laid down the bass track, following the rhythm of the drums. Once done click *stop* and then playback what you just recorded. You can play all track together or click solo on one track and listen to it alone. To create a bass line on the rock organ, see recording Keyboards for more information. If you want to the amp sound, you will have to mic the bass amplifier. See chapter 7 for details.

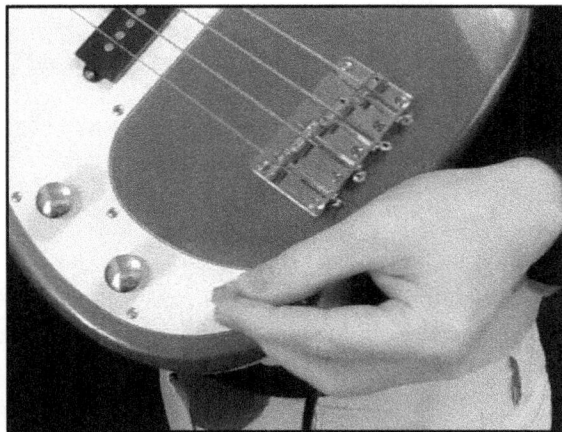

Fig 8-22 Using a ¼ inch cable plug in the bass guitar on one end and the interface on the other.

Fig 8-23 The style you use to play a bass will affect the sound. Using a pick will create a sharper sound, while using fingers will be softer.

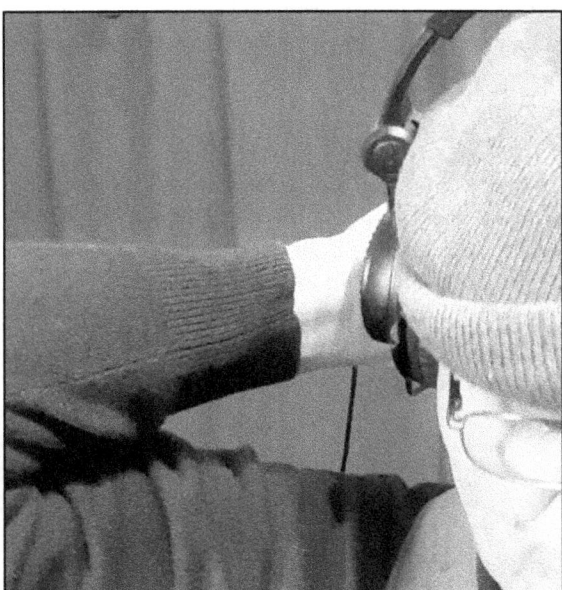

Fig 8-24 A tip with wearing headphones, run the cable down your back and tape the cord to the back of your shirt. That way it does not get in the way of playing.

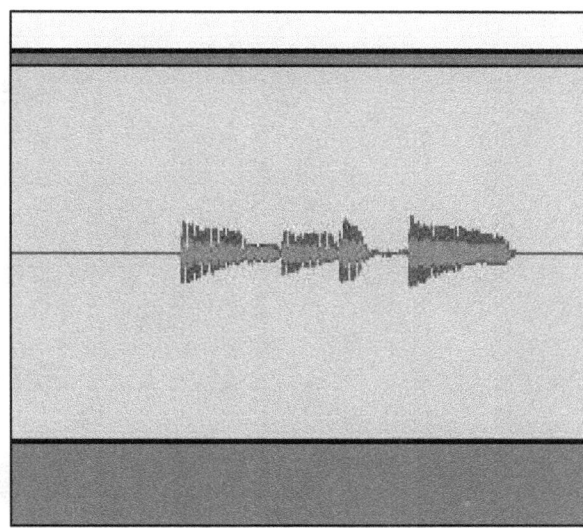

Fig 8-25 Basic Bass guitar wave, for 'Keep on Rockin' boom-boom-boom/boom-boom beat.

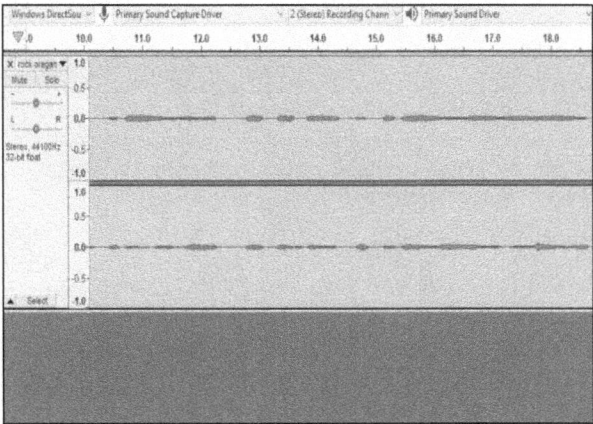

Fig 8-26 A bass line done with a rock Organ. Notice the difference is the wave sizes. We like the guitar line better so we will used that.

Creating a Guitar Track

We have the beginnings of a song down. The rhythm of the song. Now we are ready to add some of the life blood to the song, with the sound of the guitar.

There are basically two different types of tracks with guitar either the rhythm or the lead guitar, but there can be a combination of both. We also have the choice electric or acoustic. Or we can have both. In our example we are going to lay down a rhythm and a lead guitar. We are going to use our song *Dancing with the Devil* as it is guitar driven.

When doing both the rhythm and lead guitar, it is best to lay down the rhythm guitar first as it creates the sound of the song-if it is guitar based. While the lead adds a filler to the song. If the song were a cheeseburger, the rhythm guitar would be the meat, the lead guitar the cheese, and the bass and drum the bun-for it holds it all together.

Overdrive and Distortion

Distortion and overdrive are two words that are often used synonymously, but these two effects are actually very different from each other. Both distortion and overdrive have a completely unique impact on your overall tone and effect Audacity differently.

Overdrive was originally developed as a reaction of cranking a tube amp, as the true definition of the term 'overdrive' is what happens when you send too much power to a tube amp. The Jimi Hendrix sound is famous for this. When you feed too much power to the amp it makes the amplifier 'clip', the sound which is what makes the amplifier send out the overdriven tone.

Now with solid state amplifiers this is a big in effect with the amp or is done with a pedal like the *BOSS Super Overdrive SD-1* With overdrive you will notice that the over drive is affected by how you play. If you are playing slowly and softly there is not as much of an effect, as when you crank it up and start jamming.

Distortion is going to be a lot more aggressive than overdrive, as a distortion completely transforms your tone to create something brand new. There are different levels of this also the basic distorted sound and the heavy metal sound, as with the *Behringer Heavy Metal Pedal*, which creates sound is famous with the hard rock heavy metal scene in the 1980's. Unlike the overdrive sound distortion come in even when you are playing soft.

Of the two distortion is the one that will create the loudest and more power sound. So powerful it can overwhelm and push the VU meters into the red all the time which is not good for recording.

The good thing there are ways to go around this by adjusting the levels on the pedals or adding it after you record a clean sound. As Audacity contains a built-in distortion in it effects menu. (We will discuss effects in the mixing section). Granted it is not the same sound as with a pedal or amp, but it does give you a choice, and as with all music it all up to you to choose what you want.

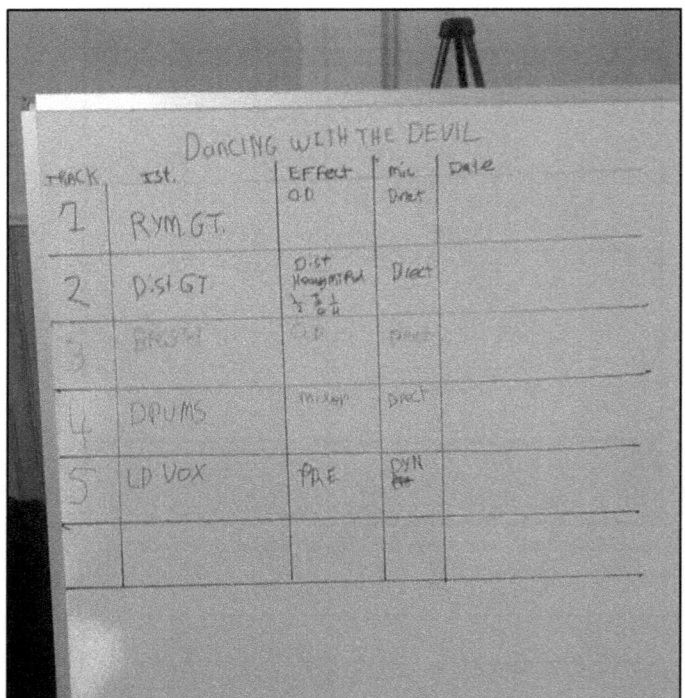

A way to keep on top of the tracks is use a white board and colored markers. Use different colors for the different instruments or you could color code them to the color tracks on Audacity. It can be placed on the wall or for a more temporary use, placed on an easel.

Go Dirty or Go Clean

With the electric guitar you have two choices. You can go clean (meaning no effects at all) or dirty (meaning) some sort of effect box between the guitar and the computer. Some amps also have built in effects. However, if you do use an amp mic-DO NOT RUN a cord form the amp out or headphones to the computer, it can damage the sound card.

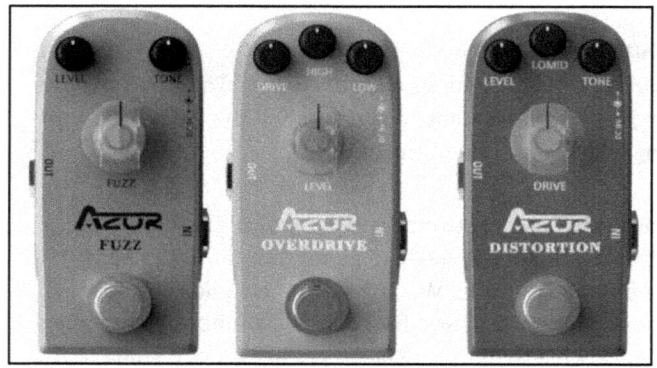

Fig 8-27 Azor effect pedals fuzz right Overdrive center and distortion right

Main decision will be what the song is, if you are going for a soft edge pop sound, then a heavy distorted guitar is not the choice. However, with you going full scale heavy rock and roll then a distorted or overdriven guitar at least is going to be a must. There are also other effects like 'fuzz'- that creates that warm tube amplifier sound of the 1960's

Electric Rhythm Guitar

Plug in your device, be it the USB to guitar cable, interface to the computer and the guitar. Do this before you open Audacity, this way the program can find the microphones. Most of the USB cable will light up to show they are working as will the interface. Do a sound check, especially if you are using effect pedals. Play a small part of the song while you check to VU meters on the program and make sure the screen on the amplifier is not moving and touching the screen of the microphone, adjust as necessary.

If you are using effect pedals (which we are in this case)be sure to place in in between the guitar and the interface unit. If using a cable to connect to the computer. Place a regular ¼ cable from the guitar to the box and the USB cable from the output on the box to the USB port on the cable.

We suggest you do a sound check with the softest and loudest parts of the sound. Once you get dialed in levels on the effect box and guitar write this down on your **"Studio Log"**. This is a sheet that list all the adjustments you make so that if it must be redone you will know what to do and not have to go through it all over again.

Fig 8 -28 our downloadable studio log. The back can be useful for microphone placement measurements.

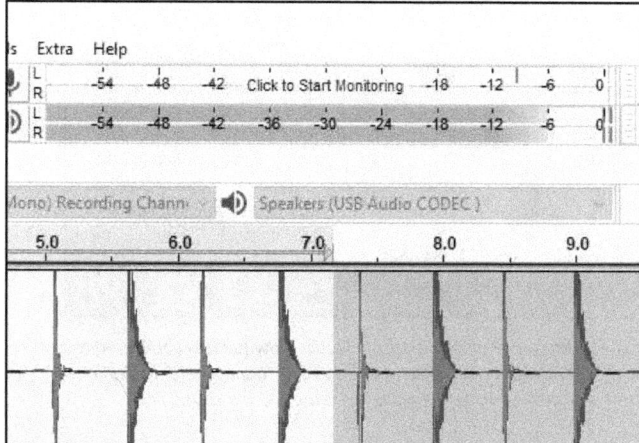

Fig 8-29 Monitor the VU meters. It is okay if they bounce into the red, as long it does not stay there. A bouncing meter is a good signal, if it stays in the green that is too week of signal.

Get ready to play. Tap shift R. Remember when you are recording to leave a few seconds before you start playing after hitting record. Now play. When done press stop and playback. It does help if you have someone to press the record and monitor the meters as you play. They can give you a cue with their hand when recording starts. They can also monitor the meters and if they are pushing too much into the red adjust the recording volume for such. This is done by simply using the mouse to move the slider next to the microphone symbol down, or if too low up. Fig 8-29 shows a good example of a VU bounce.

Once you are done playing press stop. However, take into consideration how the song is going to end as to how you stop playing. Is it a hard rocker with hard ending? Make sure **you don't press stop too quickly if the last notes are still decaying.** Or is it softer song and you want a fade out, then play on after you think it should end as you need a lot of leeway for this to happen and sound right.

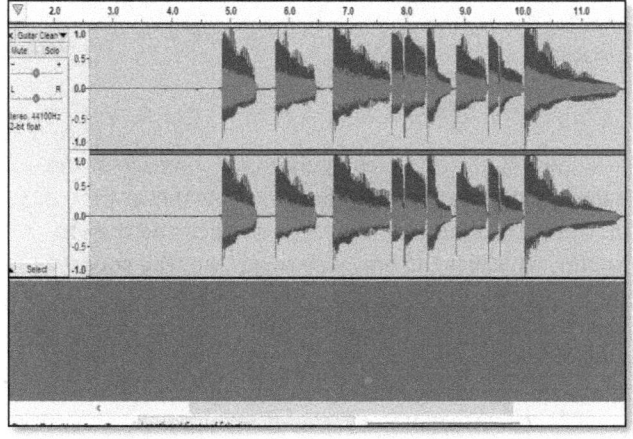

Fig 8-30 Sound waves with a clean guitar

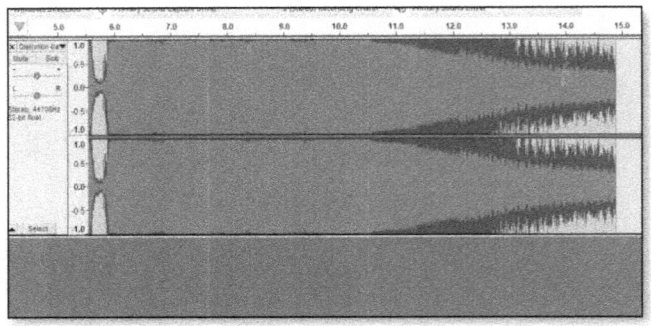

Fig 8-31 The guitar wave with distortion. Notice how full it is compared to the clean wave above. Also notice how at the end the sound was decaying but stop button was pushed to quickly and just chopped the sound off.

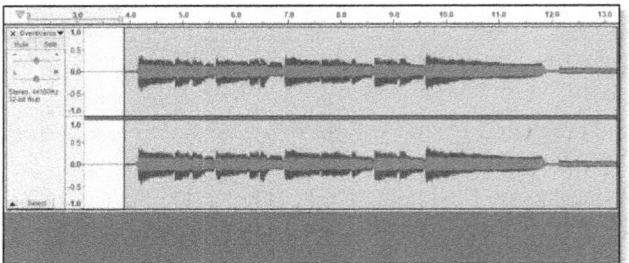

Fig 8-32 By dropping the Volume and the Tone down but keeping the Drive knob all the way up on the effect pedal we were able to record more usable wave.

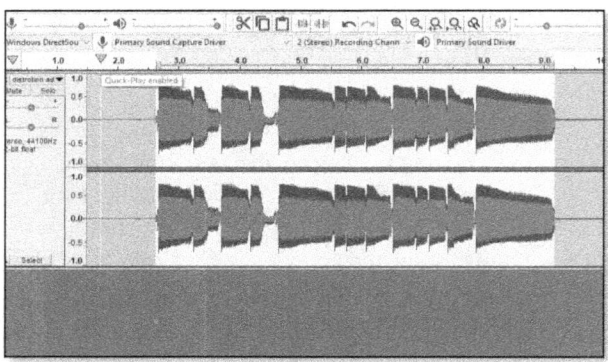

Fig 8-33 A clean wave with distortion added with the effect menu. As you can see it adds a good dirty sound to the guitar. That does not peg the VU meters creating clipping.

Electric Lead Guitar

With our heavily distorted lead guitar that comes in at the end of each line of the verse, we choose to mic this at the amp. Run the microphone cable to the interface and then to the computer. This was the only way to get the true sound we wanted.

The key to micing an amplifier, as we covered earlier, is to get it up off the floor. On chair or cabinet works excellent. Just as with the rhythm guitar run sound check, to see if it clips. This time do one low on the next and then high on the neck. Once it is dialed in note your knob locations on the pedal, amp and on Audacity itself.

Once ready on the file you have been creating press Shift R and it will record on a new track, you should be able to hear the other track you have just recorded. If the tracks are too loud, turn them down. This is not mixing the track you are just trying to lay down a new track. Likewise, if the lead is overpowering and you can't hear the other tracks you can turn them up.

Fig 8-34 You must get that amp up off the floor.

Fig 8-35 With a guitar to USB cable you can connect the guitar to directly to the computer.

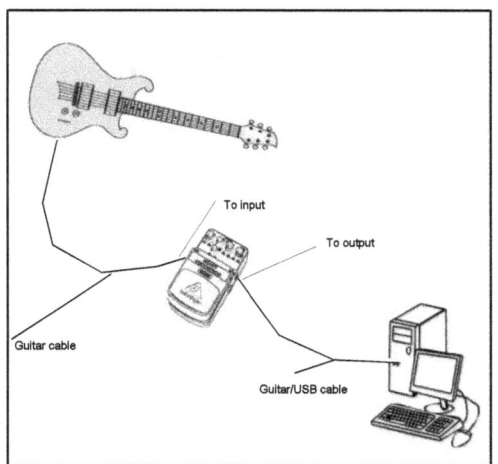

Fig 8-36 Connecting guitar effect pedal and Guitar to USB Cable.

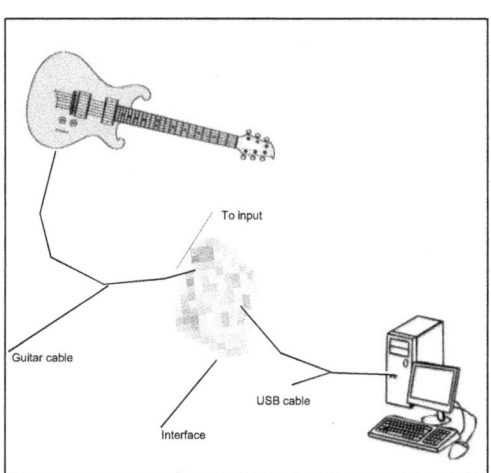

Fig 8-37 Using a n interface to connect a guitar

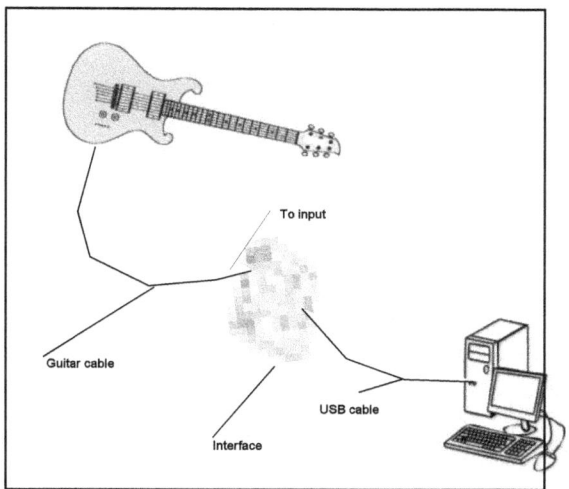

Fig 8-37 Attach effect box to interface.

Acoustic Guitar

Even if you are the hardest rocking band out here, there are times that you have to drop that sound down and get it slow mellow so the crowd can sway back and forth and hold up the lighters and a screaming distorted electric guitar is not going to work, you have to drag out the old acoustic six string, or maybe even the 12 string job for a real mellow sound.

Now some do have electrical pickups and you can just plug in using the USB to guitar cable or the interface. And record like a clean electric guitar. However, many do not. And it will have to use a microphone, using the techniques that we described in chapter before this one.

Just because it is acoustic does not mean you can't use any effects. If it has electric pickups, it is done the same as with the electric guitar. If a nonelectric guitar, then it is more complicated.

While you may not want to use a distortion pedal with an acoustic you might to want to use a *chorus pedal* for a fuller sound. To do this you will have to place the effect box in between the microphone and the interface. However, note that this will require a microphone with an 1/4- inch plug. Using adapters that up a 1/8-inch jack to a 1/4-inch will not work and the effect pedal will not sense the microphone and will not work. You may also have to use a preamplifier to get a good signal or use the amplify effect in Audacity.

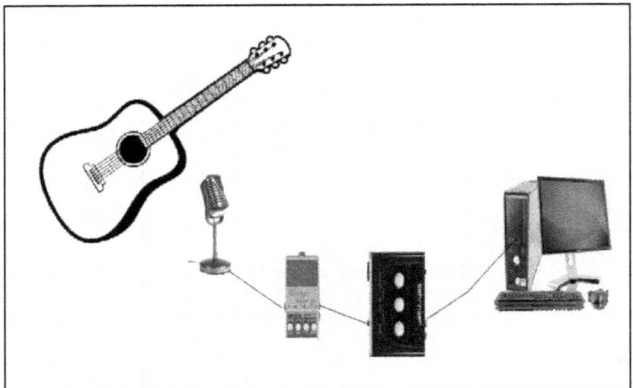

Fig 8-38 How to add an effects box with an acoustic guitar. Place the output in the Mono outlet of the effect box if it has both mono and stereo.

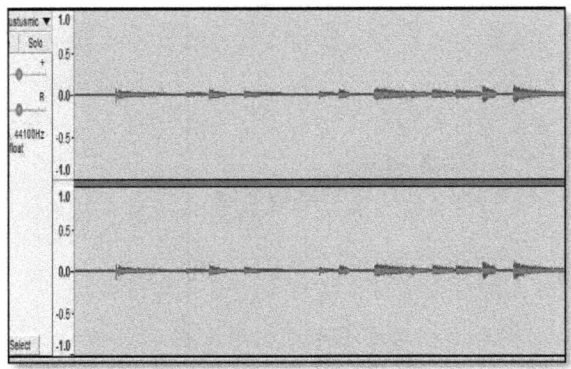

Fig 8-40 Typical acoustic guitar wave recorded with a USB Microphone. As you can see the wave is weak compared to electric guitar but can fix this with amplification which will be covered more in the effects chapter of this guide.

We used a chorus pedal on out song *Dead Roses,* as it begins with an acoustic guitar. The strings are strummed slowly and adding the chorus effect gave it the fuller sound we were wanting. That would carry through the song until the point that hard overdriven electric guitars takeover guitars take over, then ends with the acoustic guitar.

You may lay down an acoustic guitar track may compare to a direct in line signal. Thus, it will have to be boost. Fortunately, Audacity has this built in. Select the track or parts that you want to amplify. If you want to select the entire track, click on the side (fig 8-39) and it will select the entire track. Next click *Effects>Amplify*.

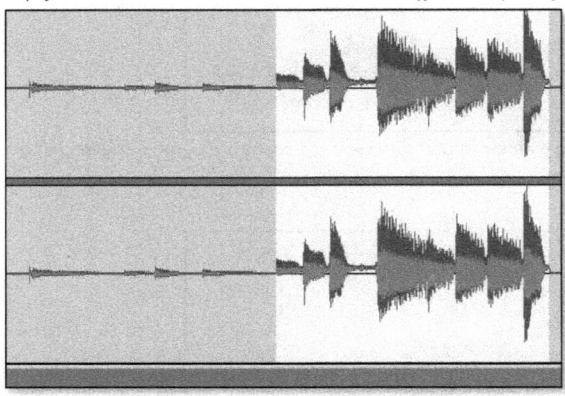

Fig 8-41 An example of how amplification can help a weak signal. On the left is without on the right with.

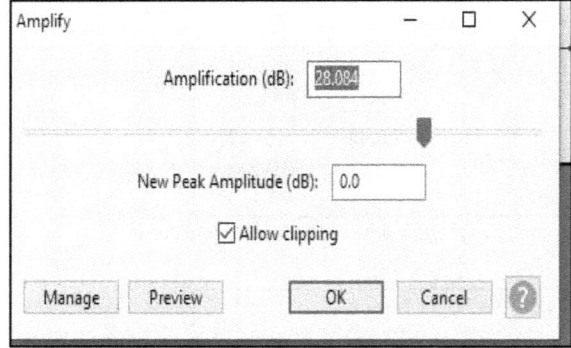

Fig 8-42 the amplification box

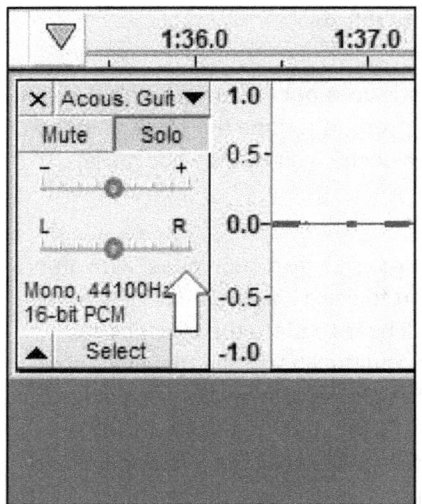

Fig 8-39 if you want to select the entire track click here.

The amplification box (fig 8-42) will pop up and it will show the need amplification to boost this signal. Preview will allow you to hear it. You increase of decrease as you like. In most cases all you do is just click ok. It will return to the project page, where you should listen to the changes with the other tracks to make sure it does not overpower the other tracks, or it still fades into the other tracks.

Keyboard, Piano and other Instruments

If the piano or keyboard drives the song more, it should be recorded quicker, possibly even before the drums. For our song *Another Love Song,* it is driven by an electric piano, and it was the first track that was laid down, and the other tracks built on top of it.

If the keyboard is filler, then it should go on after the other tracks. To make our hamburger comparison it would be onions and pickles, and percussion the mustard or the sesame seeds on the bun. Like the acoustic guitars these waves may need to be amplified, using the same method as the acoustic guitar.

You can hook up a keyboard by using a 1/4-inch cable from the headphone outlet on the keyboard to the instrument jack on the interface. Again, note that you may have to use amplification to boost the signal. (*Fig 8-43).*

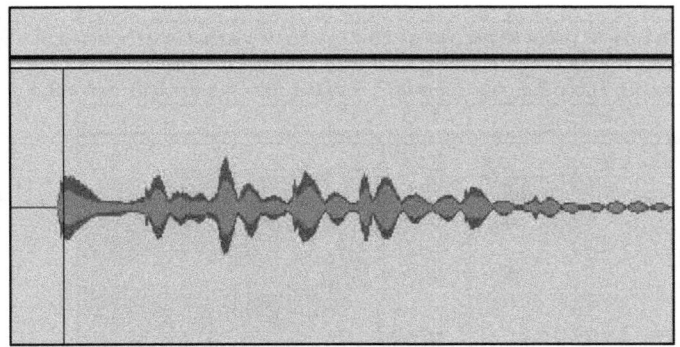

Fig 8-43 Typical keyboard wave after being amplified.

Creating a Voice Track

Of all the tracks it is the vocal track that is the most intimidating. We all can remember the first time we heard our voice that had been recorded. *"That's me*?" Goes through our mind. We all can sing in the car to our favorite song in the car, or in the shower, maybe even at church with everyone else. But to stand in front of a microphone alone! And everyone is going to hear it? That is the equivalent of standing in the mall buck naked on Black Friday.

So, what are vocals to a song if a song is like a cheeseburger? The tastebuds! The pure complete pure flavor. Ever have a cold so bad that you cannot taste anything? That is what a song is without vocals. There have been a few hits without a singer, but it makes it hard to sing along with when there are no words. Take Queen's *We Will Rock You.* Would it be the same if the crowd could not sing along? In fact, Brain May is quoted that '*it was written so the fans could sing along and clap their hands with the band.'* That could not be done without the words.

That said vocals will also be the most likely track you record that will take the most takes. So don't get freaked out and want to give up if or when you mess up. And you will. Just start another take.

In the previous chapters we had discussed on the positioning of the microphones and using windscreens and pop filters. So, we won't get over that again. What we will cover here are tips on helping get the best recording with your voice.

Don't Start Out Cold

You would not go out and run a 10K marathon without preparing for it. The first day you may not get around the block, then the next day a little more and little more the next day and so on until you are able to take on the 10k distance. Even if you are an experienced runner, you must exercise and stretch those muscles before the run.

Likewise, you should not come in and just lay down a hard high pitch vocal track without exercising your voice first it first. Believe it or not your vocals are like muscles, and instead of cramping the voice will crack or you could damage it that will require medical attention.

Start out by running through the scales, with low volume first and then building up. Have a cup of sweet hot tea with lemon and honey around to sip on to keep your vocal cords moist. Avoid lots of alcohol as it will dry out your vocal cords. Yes, we have mentioned this before, but it bears repeating.

Another exercise is to sing with mouth almost closed, where your finger will barely fit into your open mouth. Try to push up the volume and the tone higher than before. That restriction helps in building up power. Another thing is learning how to breathe. Okay you really don't need to learn this to survive. However, you do to sing. Breathe deeply use your diaphragm, your breaths should be deep and make your stomach move. Try to take a few deep breaths and get relaxed.

Next try a vocal test first trying a few bars of the chorus (or where the tempo and tone picks up) this will give you a reading to where you need to place the mic and adjust the input level in Audacity.

Just as before, make sure you plug the microphone into the computer before you open Audacity, so that the program can recognize the input device. It might be wise to just record a sample of the vocals on a separate new track, without any of the other tracks playing. It does not have to be long just a few lines. Then you can play it back and listen and make any adjustments that are needed. Now you can delete the sample track and began to lay down the real track.

Click *File>Open>(your song name)* and your ongoing project will open. Before you start to record take a sip of the honey/lemon tea and have a copy of the lyrics in front of you. You may know it cold, but when under pressure you may suddenly forget a line or a word.

Punch record, or Shift R. Recording will start and remember we have blank space at the beginning. If you like you can say name of song and the number of the take, (this can be removed later). Wait for the music to be begin. Now if you are using a vocal booth, make sure you have at least ten seconds of silence before music begins so that you can press record and have time to get into the booth and get ready. You might want to time it so that you know how long it takes. Then if you have to add time to the other tracks (see fig 8-44 to 8-47) or have someone **start the recording while you're in the booth**.

When you sing try to stay in the same position moving closer of further away from the mic will cause change in tone. It might be hard to do, but keep those feet firmly planted and **don't dance** around and keep your head in one place.

Ever see photos of singers holding on to the headphones? There is reason for this. Headphones can easily slide off your head during a recording, especially if the signer starts to get hot after the many takes. **You don't want the headphone** sliding off and causing noise. So, hang on to them.

Not everyone has a voice like Freddie Mercury or Adel but think there is also Mick Jaggers and Bob Dylan, among many **others that don't** out there. Just do your best and try to stay in tune. If after 15 or so takes, you feel your voice beginning to get weak even drinking the tea, just take some time to relax. Do not push it, this especially true with high pitched tones or severe damage to your voce could happen. Softer songs you can have more takes. But if you feel your throat stating fell sore that is a sign to stop and rest that voice.

For example, our song *Dancing With the Devil* begins with a pick being draw down the guitar strings and high pitch scream from the vocalist. And the rest of the song is power driven so after a few takes, my voice was beginning to grow weak, and had to wait until later to complete the song.

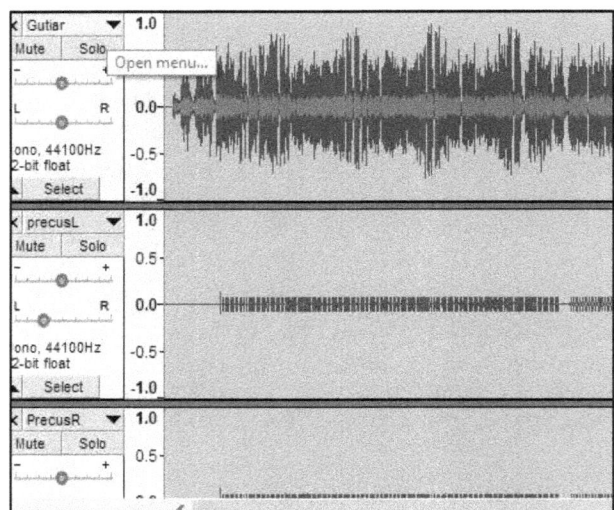

Fig 8-44 You want to add enough time to allow you to get into the isolation vocal box. And you are adding 10 seconds to the front of the vocal track. But you don't have that much time in front of the other already laid down tracks.

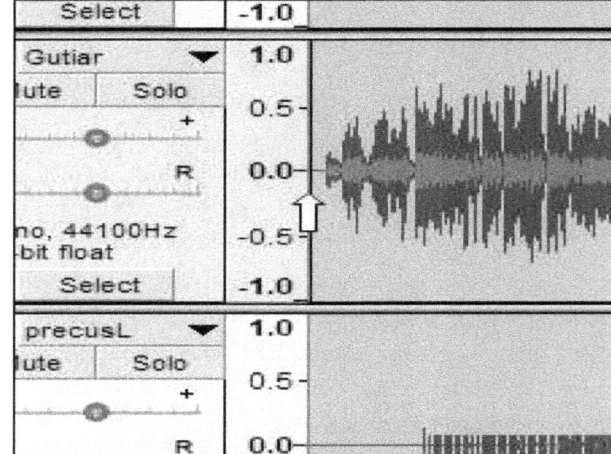

Fig 8-45 Click at the Zero mark of the track.

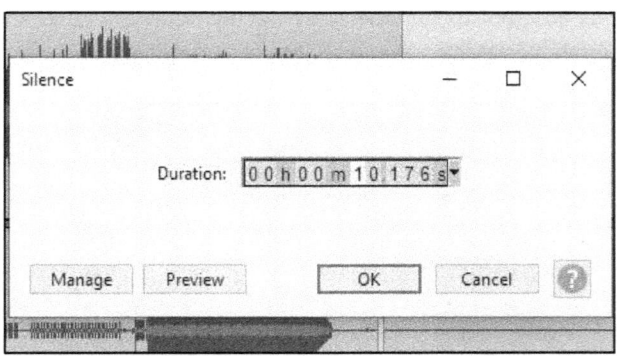

Fig 8-46 Click Generate>Silence. Type in the amount of space you want to add. Then click OK.

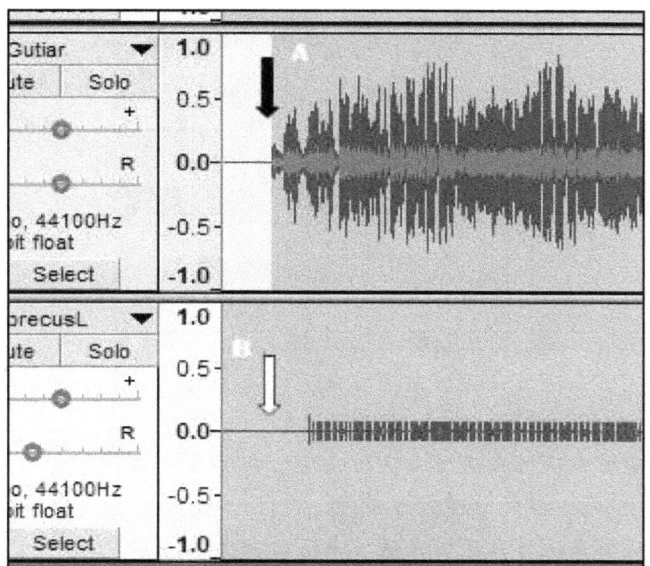

Fig 8-47 We have add that time to the front of the (A) guitar track. Now you must repeat this for every other laid down tack. Even though we have blank space before the percussion track, (B) the timing has been thrown off without adding the extra time at the front.

PUNCH IN PUNCH OUT

If you dug out the boxing gloves, put them back, and stop doing your Rocky imitation. *"Adrian! Adrian!"* This is referring to the method used to record just a part of the track and not have to rerecord the entire track. For example, you can get the first part and the last part right, but you've dropping the note on that one word in the first chorus. You don't have to go back and rerecord the whole thing again, and possibly mess up the ending. You just need to rerecord that one part.

First thing you must do is back up the tracks by saving as new file new name. Next select the track you want to correct and press Control D. This will duplicate the track you selected, and it will appear at the bottom of all the track. Select this track and the paste into a new file. the track and add a new track naming it Backup. Bring the new track up to where they are under the old one. Paste the track into the new track making sure you begin at the zero mark. The tracks should be identical to one another if the new is off, you didn't go clear to the zero-mark use Control Z to undo and paste again making sure you are at the zero mark.

Press on the track you want to change, find the spot to change by listening to it and noting its location. Or you can use the scrub and seek tool. Which will allow you to play the track by dragging the mouse over it, it can be played forward or backwards. Note click the zoom button to get the timeline down to seconds and note the section you want to correct.

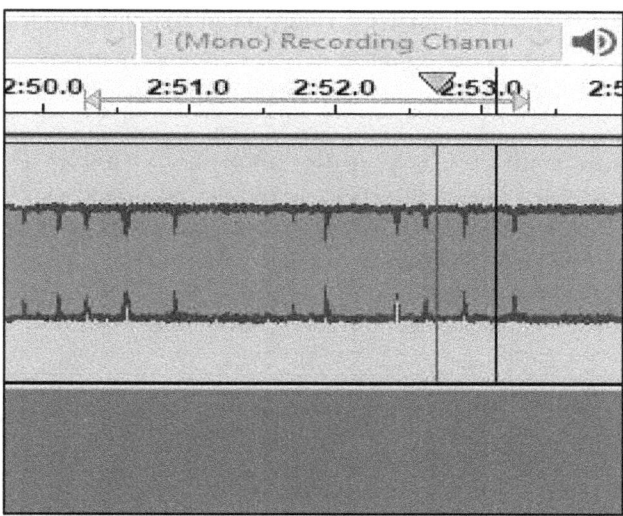

Fig 8-48 This is the section we are going to punch in. However, to make things smooth we need to start playing before and after this, so we will play from 2.46 to 2.55 seconds. Now select this part and silence it.

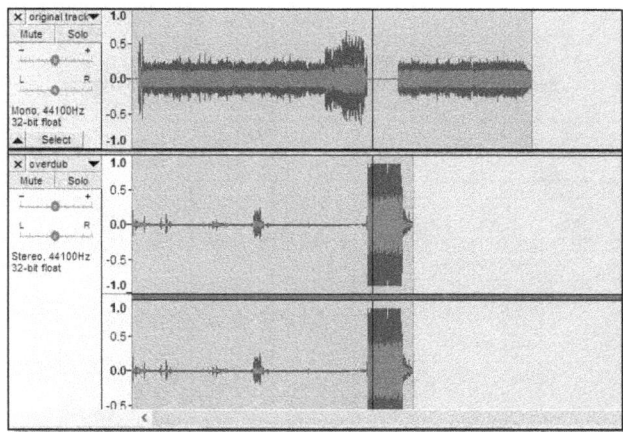

Fig 8-49 *The new drop in punch in is created on the track below. If you don't like it, you can press CONTROL Z and it will undo the record and start over. Or You record a new track by again doing the above steps. And choosing the best one. If you notice, there is noise from fingers pressing against the strings. This can be removed by selecting the area then pressing CONTROL L which will silence it. Do not delete it or it will throw the timing off.*

By using a new track, the "**punch-in**" a correction to a recorded track, we use a new track for each take. This allows us to hear a "lead in" and "lead out" (pre-roll / post roll) and, if necessary, to make multiple attempts at correcting, from which we can select and use the one that we like best.

Start recording on a new track by press Shift R. Listen to the copied track waiting to play and the spot that is selected, use the time bar to cue you, and be sure to start playing a few seconds before and after the spot to get a good punch in without a noticeable change. If the other track is throwing you off, you can turn it down.

Once you have completed the replacement track listen to it as a solo track. Now you can mute this track and do more and use the best take or if satisfied with this take use it.

Now play both tracks and see if it sounds okay. If it does select both tracks and mix; click Tracks>Mix> Mix Render to new track. (Fig 8-50). This will create a single track of the new mix, (fig 8-51). Now copy and paste this track in place of the original track, (fig 8-52).

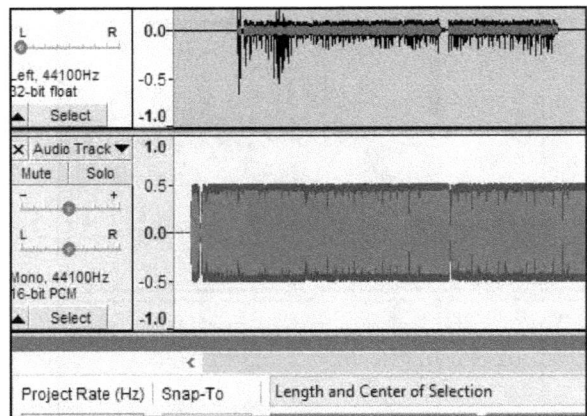

Fig 8-52 Paste this track into the original project and then delete the original track it replaces. Play it with all the other tracks. Sounds good save the project.

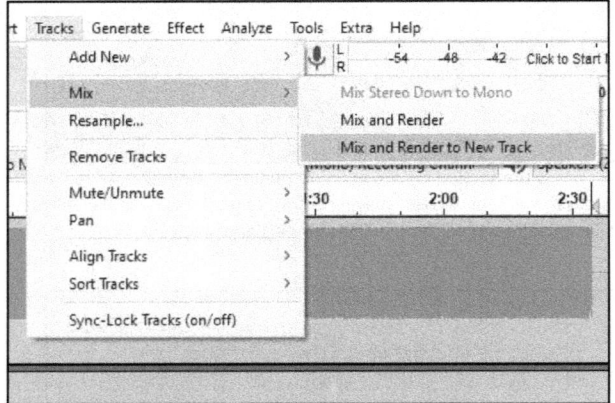

Fig 8-51 Select both tracks and then click Mix>Mix and render to new track.

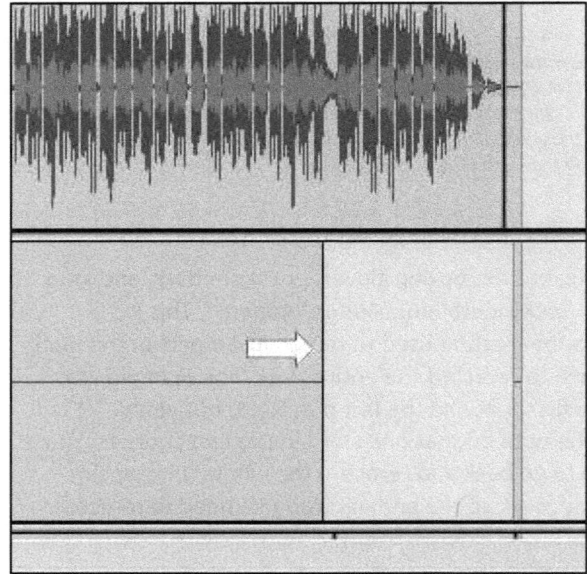

Fig 8-53 *We don't want to wait through the entire recording to play at the end and risk noise being picked up. So, we click on the new track, a little bit before where the recording was going to start to give a lead in.*

OVERDUB

An overdub is not the same a punch in or drop in. This is exact recording of another or additional sound that is laid over the **other tracks. For example. In** our song "*I am the Night,*" we wanted a screaming distorted guitar played high up on the neck to come in at the end of the song over the other distorted guitar that was playing low on the neck.

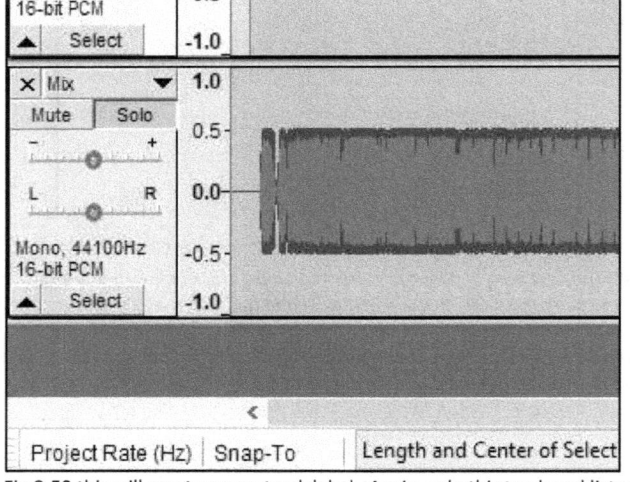

Fig 8-52 this will create a new track label. Again, solo this track and listen to it. Next select this track and copy (Control C)

So do this we record on a new track and position it under the track we want to over dub over. Then click a little bit before (fig 8-53) the place we want to start recording at this will give us a "lead in". **Now we punch 'R' record . If we punched Shift record it would take us to a new track and we don't want that.** The playback will start at the place we have selected, then we can lay down our screaming guitar tracks, watch in making sure it does not peg the meter. Since we plan on fading out this song, we play on longer than it when it should end. Then press stop. You should have a separate track below the one (fig 5-54) you are overdubbing.

   Play it back and see how it sounds, something wrong then tap control Z and it will undo the recording. Or you and click to undo button on the menu. IF you delete it by accident, click the redo button or Control Y and it will restore your delete.

One of the best ways to improve vocals or make a guitar bigger than life is to over dub them. This not the same as coping and paste as it does not have the same sound. You, just simple must duplicate the same track over again. As easy as this sounds, it hard to do, as the singing the same thing or playing the same thing will not be 100 % identical as it would be in just copying and pasting the tracks, therefore it sounds bigger when it is overdubbed and not just copied. It was through over dubbing that Queen created that choir sound in *Bohemian Rapsody.* It would not have the same sound if they were just copied.

PODCAST

Most of this book will be about recording music and creating your own album. However, Audacity is also excellent for creating a podcast also. A podcast ii is not just a talk show, while most are that they can also be a recording of a live show or church services. But basically, a podcast is like having your **own radio show, but you don't have to listen to it live, the** listener can listen to it on the internet at their choosing

If it is like a radio program, you need to think of it as a radio program. Complete with music and sound effects or just your voice. You want music to be your introduction then fade out as you come with the introduction of your pod cast to be followed by music that fades in as you finish up speaking about the introduction and then stop as your podcast begins. You cannot do this on one single track this it will require several tracks.

If you have guest or there is more than one person speaking, you need more than one microphone that will go into a mixer before going to the computer.

Recording is the same as with music, you plug in the microphone before opening Audacity. The hit record leaving blank space before you start recording. After you recorded your pod cast push stop. Listen to it. You do another take; however, podcasts are meant to sound like they are done live on the radio and getting it too perfect can make it sound too fake.

Make sure the project rate at the bottom of the page is set at 44100 Hz. Yes, the higher the rating the better quality of sound but this rating is the preferred setting it will give high quality sound with interfering with the sound itself.   Now just your **voice sounds okay but doesn't sound professional.** So, you want to add music. You can find free music on the internet and download it, or crat your own. Download any music file as a wav file. To import click on *File* then *Import,* and then *Audio* find the file you want.

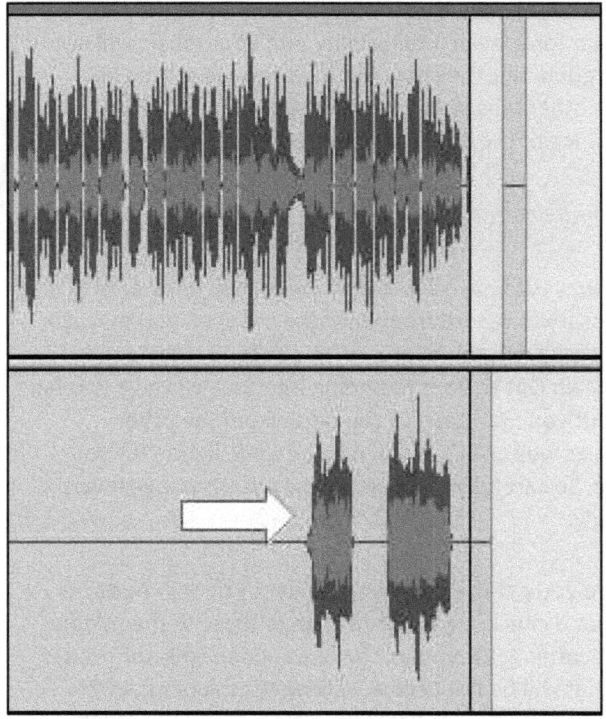

Fig 8-54 This is over-dub of the distorted guitar high up on the neck That is playing over the over one lower on the neck.

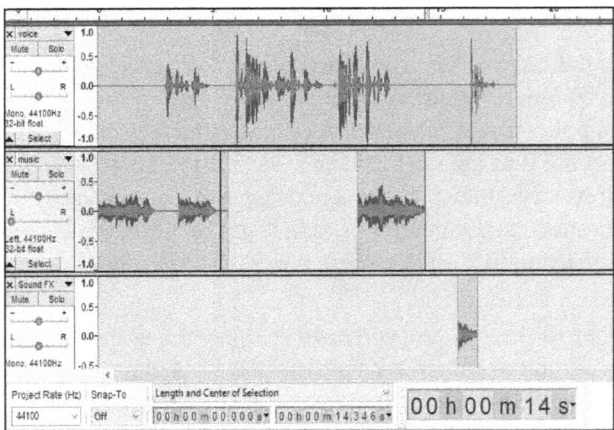

Fig 8-55 This is for a podcast about classic cars. Notice how it begins with music and includes the sound effect of a starter cranking. Also notice how the music overshadows the voice. We will correct this later in the mixing section of this guide.

Fig 88-56 Podcast of church services are becoming a common thing now, and Audacity can help

RECORDING CHURCH SERVICES

Audacity is an excellent way to capture the audio of your weekly service and make sermon MP3's or audio CD's. With a simple USB interface, and some knowledge about mixing consoles, your computer can be a recording station.

WARNING: *Before you record a worship service, make sure you have the rights to record the music. Check with Christian Copyright Licensing International (CCLI) for more information on how to legally record and distribute music. The preacher's sermon is OK to record because he/she is the copyright owner. But music is different, however many churches pay a fee so they can do this. This especially true if you play a CD with music.*

A Music Mix

You could record simply using the "Main Out" of the console. If recording a mix, this may give bad results, because any instruments that are not miked are not going to be in the recording, for example like drums or the organ.

Instead, use a pre-fade auxiliary send or a group send, with the output going to the recording interface. This allows you to have a separate mix for the recording. If you have a stereo auxiliary send, you can pan stuff around, and be as creative as you like. This can add to your appeal and make it sound more professional. Many USB interfaces have a monitor output, so that you can hear exactly what's going to be recorded. You may notice that some voices may sound distant and unnatural this can be changed using effects like reverb which can make speech sound more natural. If you want to hear the congregation in the recording, you will have to mic them. This is useful when they join the choir to sing.

Your congregation mic should NOT be sent to the main mix, only to the recording interface (and in-ear monitors). Remember there will be a slight delay on the audience mic. If your USB Interface has 2 or more channels, the audience mic can be sent to a separate channel, so that you can later use the Clip-handle drag-bars to fix the slight delay from the audience mic. We will cover this in a later chapter.

There will also be much less reverberation in the recording; this is great for speech intelligibility, but your music will not sound as good. But the choir and instruments should be miked. Another reason to use congregation mics to capture the ambiance of the room and environment.

Recording Sermons

The best way is to have a microphone for the minster only. If it is necessary to record from only one channel, you may use the direct out from the board, or an aux send. Connecting the console Main Out to your recording interface will give you fair results, but you may have all the noise from the other channels, as well as EQ, which may be undesirable for your recording. So carefully monitor playback and change levels accordingly.

Make sure you get the recording levels set right in Audacity during sound check, so as not to change these in the middle of your recording. Or you will have a sudden spike or drop in volume that will be noticeable. Having the proper gain structure is absolutely critical for getting good sound! Make sure you save your recording as a project when finished.

Editing and Distributing

Use Audacity's Compressor effect along with other effects can help improve the sound. We will discuss the in the effect chapter of this guide. But keep in mind just the right amount of sugar can make for a great tasting cake, too much can make for a very unpleasant surprise. The same can be said for effects.

You may want to export your recording to the size-compressed MP3 format for upload to a website or for use on a portable audio player. If so, retain your Audacity project (or export your recording as WAV using File > Export > Export as WAV) to save an original, uncompressed copy. This lets you fix any problems that you find later without audio losses. MP3 files cannot be edited and then re-encoded as another MP3 without significant loss in quality.

If burning to an Audio CD, so the service can be listened to in the car or the home stereo, export to WAV, not to MP3.

Checklist for Recording and Editing Sermons

Make sure the levels are proper, and not so loud that it could clip. In other words, if you are seeing the meter constantly in the red drop the recording input levels. Verify that the signal sounds good. Make sure your power-saving features are disabled.

Save your work in multiple locations for safety. Save in an uncompressed/lossless format so that you can edit later.

Listen to the recording, trim to begin/end at the right place, compress the audio, and fix any other problems. We will over this in another chapter.

When finished, use the Audacity Metadata Fig 8-57 Editor to create the MP3 ID3 Tags ID tags (you can add tags for other formats too, but they may not necessarily be supported by all player software or hardware)

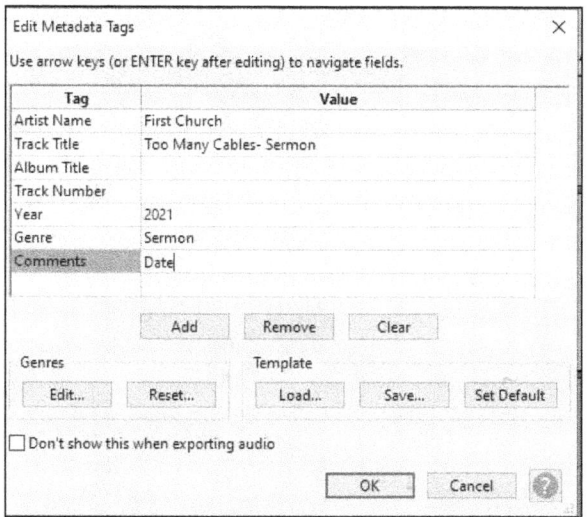

Fig 8-57 An example of a metatag. This box will come up when you try to export the file.

LABELING TRACKS

When you start getting several tracks on one project for example, lead vocal, backing vocals, rhythm guitar, keyboard, bass, drums, strings. This can get confusing trying to find the track you want to work on. Luckily Audacity allows you to label the tracks.

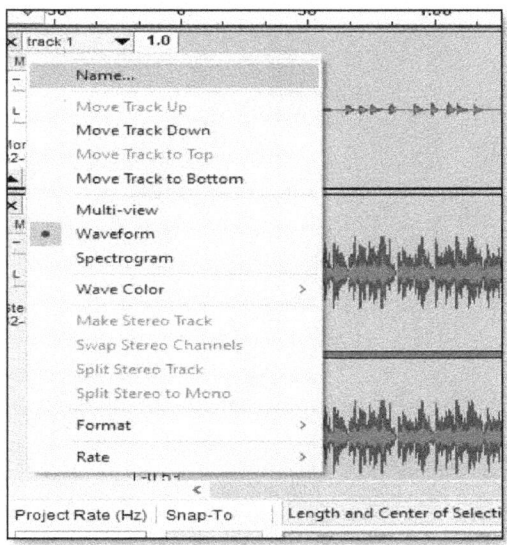

Fig 8-58 Click the down arrow on the track. Click Name. A box will appear. Type in the name of the track. Use simple terms like VOX-vocal. LD GTR-Lead Guitar BS-Bass, DRMs- Drums. You can make up anything but is wise to keep them all the same so you can easily recognize them.

Another useful trick is color code the tracks. The draw back to this is there are only 4 choices, and you cannot select your own color choices. The best way is to group these by basic instrument.

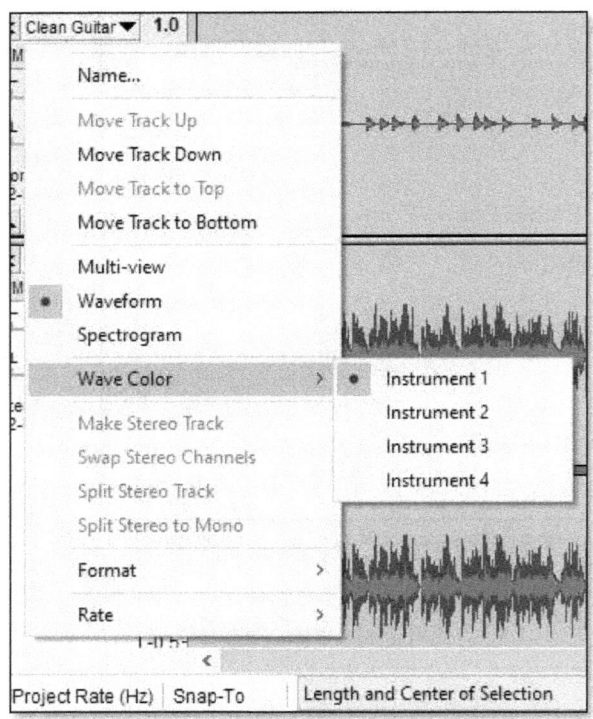

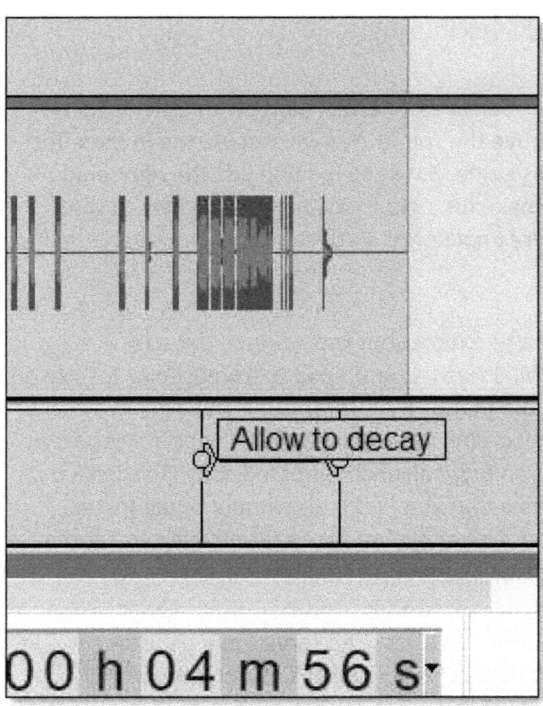

Fig 8-59 Choice a color pattern for basic tracks and keep it that way through all other projects. For example, all vocals (both lead and backing are Instrument 1) and Guitars and Instrument 2; Drums are Instrument 3 and Bass is instrument 4.

*Fig 8-60 You can also label tracks. This is useful when listening to it and you want to place a note on it for mixed down later. Click on **Edit** then **Label at Selection** this will create a Label track at the bottom of the project, you can use the move track up to place it under the track you want to label. If you had not selected anything on a track the pointer will appear on the track, but it can be positioned by dragging it with the mouse. At the right position just type the note. If you want to place another note, just click at that position in the label tack and begin typing.*

Wave Colors

Instrument 1	Blue
Instrument 2	Red
Instrument 3	Green
Instrument 4	Black

PROBLEMS WITH PLAYBACK WHILE RECORDING

You may have laid down a guitar track for a song and you try to play it back and you hear nothing. You can see a wave pattern, so you know it recorded the track. You save it and you try opening Audacity again, with the headphones and USB cable still plugged in, yet still there is no playback. In frustration you jerk out the USB cable and you hear your guitar track. *What is going on?*

Check to see what Audacity is trying to use for playback on the above menu. Try changing it from the *Primary Sound Driver* to one of the other choices in the menu and try again. The problem is when a microphone or a USB device is plugged in computers will sometimes try to return the signal cutting off the audio.

Now you are hear your guitar track you try to record your voice on top of it in another track. You hear the intro, and you begin to sing, you and hear the guitar track, but you can't hear yourself. *Again, what is going on?*

Make sure you have two things selected in Preferences under the Edit menu. Click *EDIT>Preferences* then click *Recording* make sure that the boxes for *Play other tracks while recording (overdub)* this will allow you to hear the other track while recording a new track. If you want to hear your self-playing or singing the new track, you will have to click *Software playthrough of input*.

However, this has one annoying big drawback there is a slight delay from what you hear to what it records. You are singing with the music track and your voice returns in a delay from where it should be. This can be very hard to get use to and can quickly throw you off.

Resetting the Latency

To correct this delay will depend on how you are connecting your sound source to the computer. If you are connecting a microphone directly to the computer, and the headphones to the computer then you connect a cable with 1/8 inch jacks (fig 8-61) at each end. One in the jack you use to record from and the other in the headphone jack.

Fig 8-61 Create a loop cable plug one end of the cable into the speaker jack and the other into the jack you use to plug your microphone in.

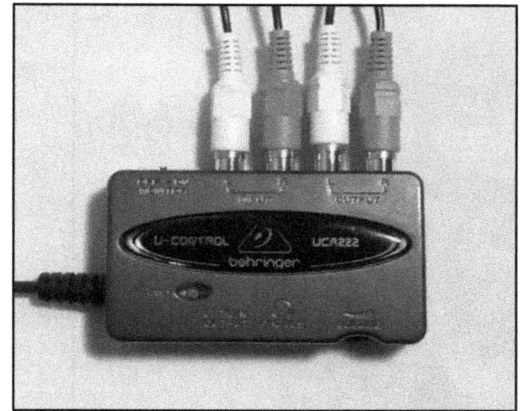

Fig 8-62 If you use an inface plug one end into the input and the other to the output. Then the USB cable to the computer.

If you are using an interface, (fig 8-62) then you will have to have a cable that runs from the input to the output the USB cable will be connected to the computer otherwise there is no power to this unit. Depending on your unit will determine what kind of cable to use.

If you are using a USB microphone to record overdubs, you'd better to look for another type of microphone. These microphones are great for podcasters who just want to record their voice and are not worried about syncing to music or another track but are not that good for recording music- once another track is involved. The problem with these microphones is that the only way you can hear yourself in your headphones is by turning *Software Playthrough On*. Software playthrough introduces its own delay (different from latency) which you will hear in your headphones.

In other words, Latency is the delay form when you sing or play until it is heard by Audacity and put on as a wave on the track in the program. This is what we are correcting. The delay from *Software Playthrough On* is from what you sing or play to what you hear in the headphones.

For example sing " *I am the night! I am the night..*" from when you sing the first "I am the night." You will hear it through the headphones when you start to sing the second one. This will throw anyone off their timing. And with USB microphones, this is what they do and there is no way to correct it. With a good microphone that can be plugged into an inface, (fig 8-69) and the headphones plugged into the interface NOT the computer this delay can be avoided.

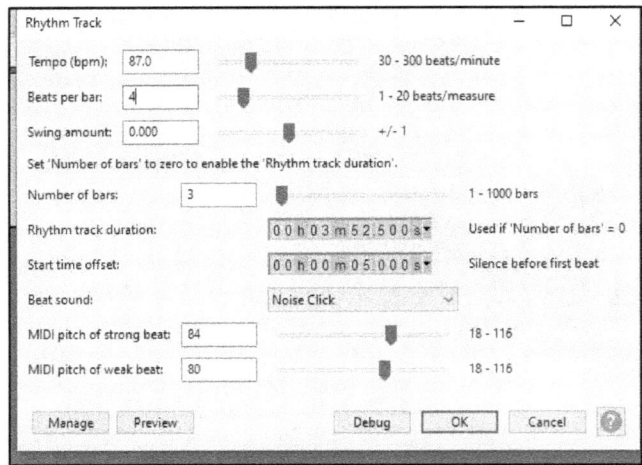

Fig 8-63 Creating a rhythm track.

Open Audacity. When a new program opens. Click *Generate> Rhythm Track*. A new box will open. (fig 8-63). In the box marked number of bars. **Put in the number '3"** Under *Beat Sound,* select *Noise Click*. Click *OK*.

A track of clicks will be generated. Now before pressing record, it is essential you balance the Latency Compensation, or you will not get an accurate reading. This is done by clicking on the *Edit* menu, selecting *preferences*. Now click on Device (on some versions this may be under the recording tab). In the box marked *Latency Compensation* put in the number 0. Click OK. (See fig 8-64)

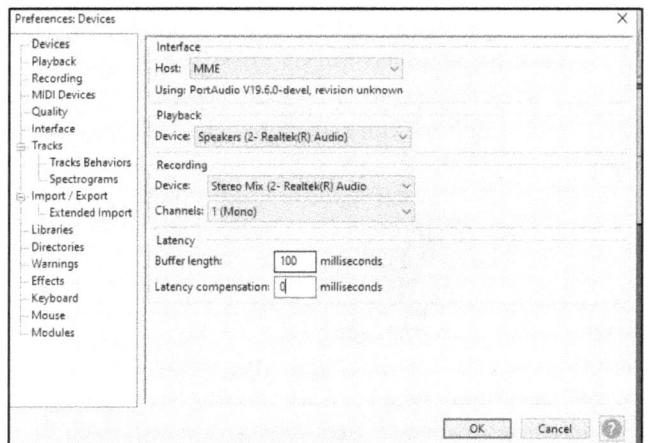

Fig 8-64 BEFORE YOU PUSH RECORD! Make sure 0 is placed in the Latency Compensation box, or it will not be balanced

Now click record. When the recording is done click stop. You will notice there is a gap between when the original track records and the second track this the is the delay, (fig 8-65) that we must compensate for.

To do this using the mouse drag a selection from the very beginning of the fist click in the top track (this should have begun immediately with no gap at the first) now drag the section over to where the first sound appears in the second track. It is best to you increase the image size by clicking on the zoom button in to tool bar.

Next click on the box just above the timer section at the bottom of the screen and select *start and Length of Selection*. Below this you will notice a time in the box. Write this down. (Fig 8-66)

Go back to Preferences under the edit menu and enter this in the box marked Latency Compensation (Fig 8-67) enter as a negative number by placing a minus sign in front of it. Now click Okay to save your selection. And try click recording again. The second track should right under the first one (Fig 8-68) if not, repeat the above steps.

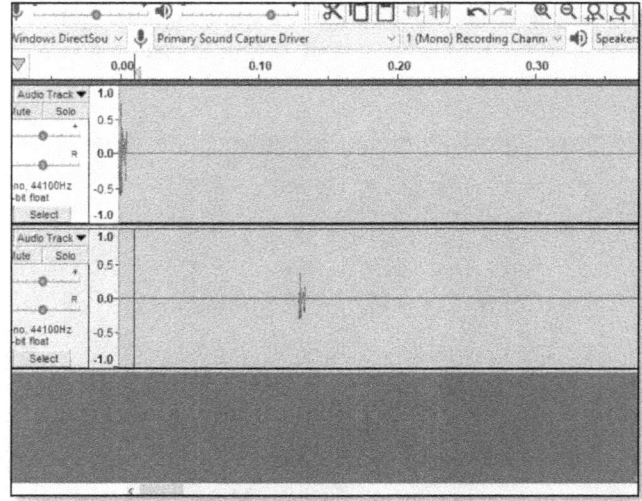

Fig 8-65 Generate click track and record it on a second track. Notice the gap between the two, this the Latency Compensation.

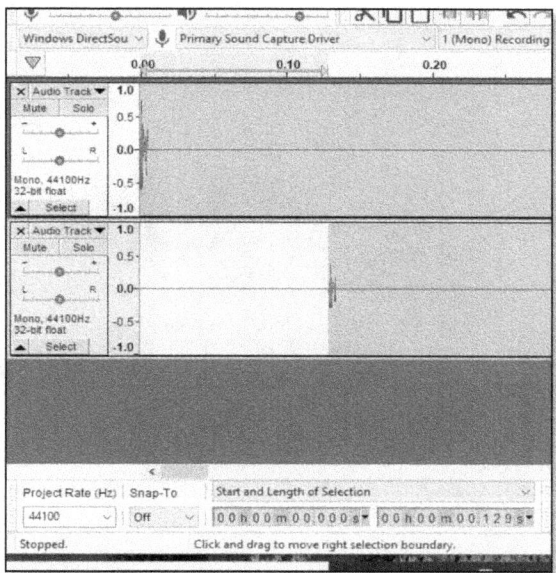

Fig 8-66 Select the space from the beginning of the first beat on the top track to the point where it begins on the second track. Note the amount on the timer. Make sure that snap to is turned off and that start, and length of selection is also showing.

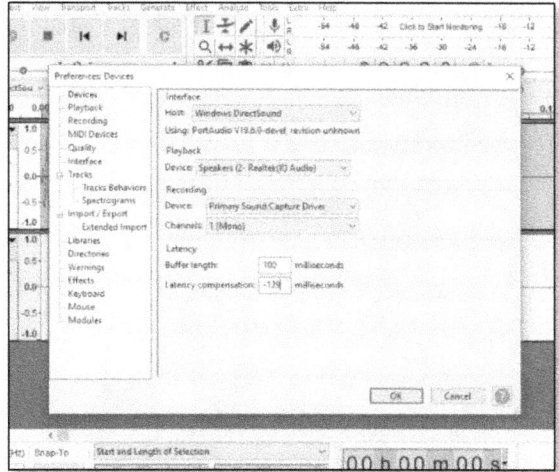

Fig 8-67 Enter the number from the counter in this box with a minus sign in front of it. Then click ok.

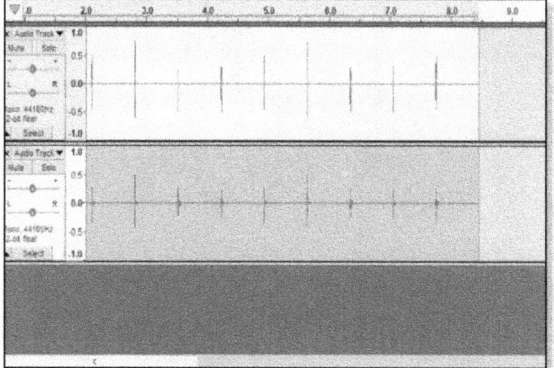

Fig 8-68 Notice how the gap is gone.

Fig 8-69 Be sure to plug the headphones into the interface device and not the computer in order not to have delay in hearing yourself.

Audacity Will Not Recognize Mic or Speakers

Another big problem with the program is if you insert headphones or a mic after you open you Audacity it may not recognize them. So, you must have the mic and headphones/speakers in place before opening up the program. If it still doesn't work shut Audacity down and reboot it again, this usually correct the problem. Note you may have to save your file and then reboot Audacity each time you change instruments.

Also do not place too much on a preamp that is going to Audacity as it will **overwhelm the program and it won't** recognize the equipment.

Audacity Will Only Record for a Short Time

If you push record and you only get a short sound then stops, make sure you have not selected part of another track this will be the only part that is recorded. Also make sure "*Sound Activated Recording*" is not enabled. This is found under the heading *Transport* in the menu bar at the top of the page.

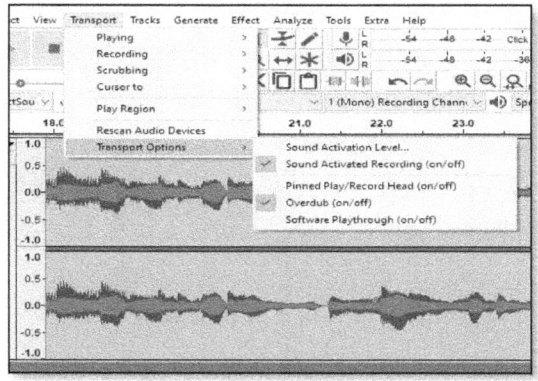

Fig 8-70 Make sure sound activate recording in not checked as it is it here.

TIPS FOR RECORDING WITH AUDACITY

1. Be sure to have blank space or even a count in the first track you record. "1-2-3-4" and use this as the starting point for the other tracks.
2. Make sure sound activate recording is not checked. Otherwise, if there is pause in the sound recording will stop and the timing will be off.
3. Always plug mic and speakers/headphones in before clicking on Audacity.
4. Before Recording more than one track reset the Resetting the Latency to make sure there is no delay in recording the new track.
5. There will be delay in hearing your new track that you are recording on top of tracks. If it bugs make sure Software play of input unchecked.
6. If you must hear yourself during playback when recording a new track, be sure to plug headphones into interface. If you are still having problems, use another recording device. Like a TASCAM and use Audacity as a mixer
7. Don't worry if everything sounds dull at first, most can be corrected with mixing and effects.

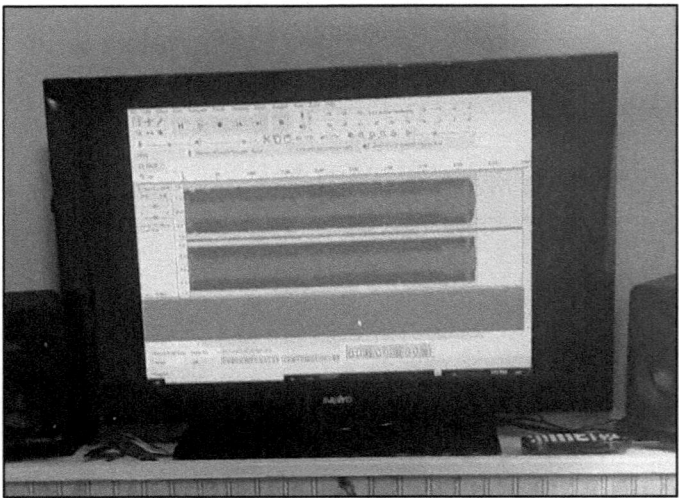

Fig 8-71 To better see the wave files it is better to use a flash screen TV as a monitor.

Okay we have drums, bass, Rhythm guitar, lead guitar, lead vocals backing vocals all laid down. You play back and it sounds like mess, each sound fighting it out with the rest, and they all seem to be blaring right at you. What to do? Next section Mixing,

PART 3 Mixing

Chapter 9 Getting Ready to Mix the Tracks

Okay for the past few chapters we have delved into some uninteresting information about how Audacity works. It reminds you of studying of test,-maybe your driver's test-to get the answers right so you can move on to the fun part- driving.

You have laid your tracks down and now you want to get into listening and mixing it. So, you can sound like your favorite band. Well two things. One no amount of mixing is going to make you sound like that like, there is only a certain amount of improvement that be had, the other you can't just jump into mixing. You must prepare for it. Again, using the driving comparison. You can't just jump into a car and take off-if someone else has been driving it- you must adjust the seats, mirrors and fasten the seat belts. So, get ready to fasten your seat belts and head out on the highway of mixing.

GETTING READY

Plug in your listening device this can be head-phones or speakers. Either one doesn't matter because you are going to end mixing it on both. Now open Audacity.

Now open the file up you want to mix. Before you listen to it. Save it as a new fille, so you can keep the original in case there is a problem. For example, you click save instead of cancelling and it was a change you did not want. A file name should be something you can quickly find. Examples of file names: *songname-mix-date or songname-mix1*, or any other one you want. (See fig 9-1)

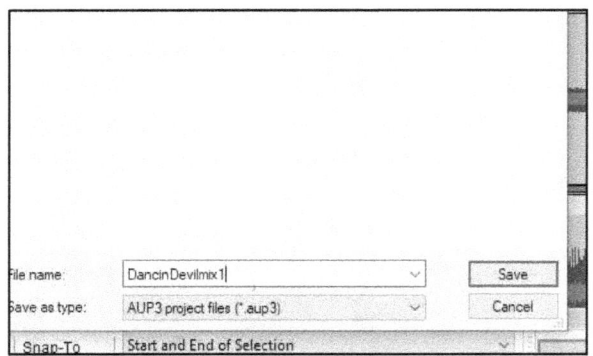

Fig 9-1 Click File> Save As to create a new file that you will work from. You can even shorten the song name. Like we did.

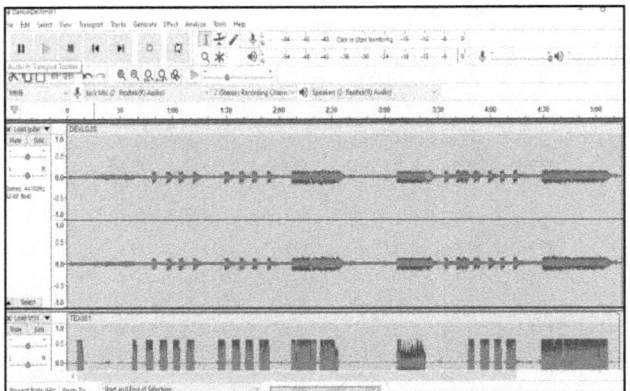

Fig 9-2 Here we have the raw recorded track for our song Dancing with the Devil. Shown is the Lead Guitar and lead VOX (vocal). Also here is a track for the Bass, Drums and Rhythm guitar. As seen below.

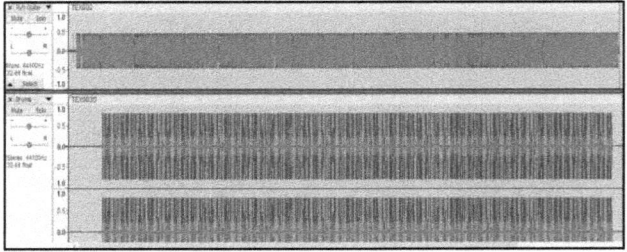

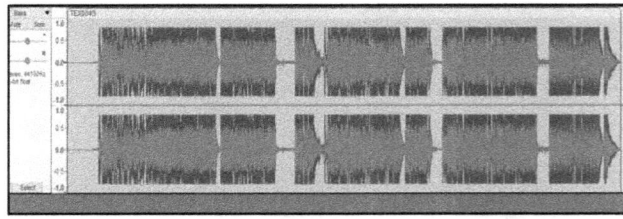

Fig 9-3 In its raw form we can see there is noise in these tracks the area between the waves.

In the above tracks you can see everything is out of order. To help you locate the track quicker create subgroups of the similar instrument. Let place the lead Guitar and Rhythm guitar together. And if we had them all the separate drum track together, plus if you have backing vocals place them all together. But keep the lead vocal separate as it is a special track. Move the track up or down to get them into place. (see fig 9-4 and 9-5)

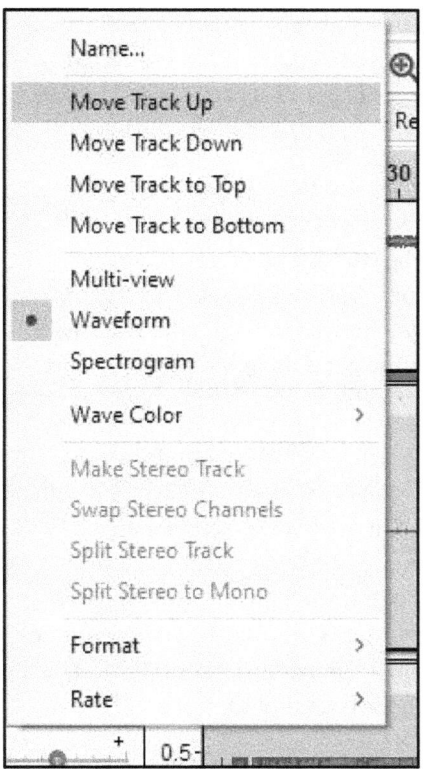

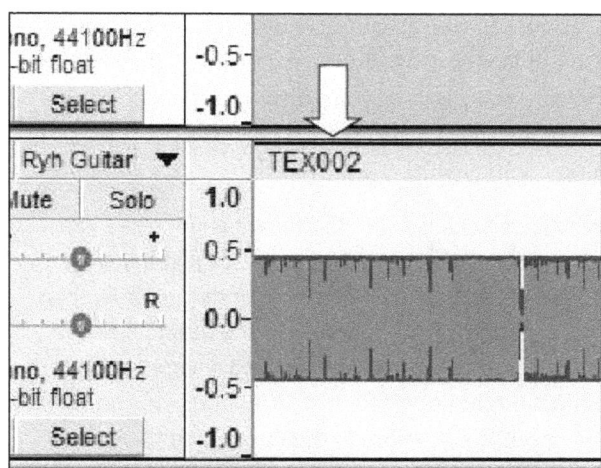

Fig 9-6 *We imported the tracks from another recorder and the track name that is on the Tascam Recorder is still being listed. To change this double, click on the white bar (at the arrow) delete the name and retype the name you want.*

One big drawback Audacity has is that they only have a limited color choice, and it would be nice if in the years to come they would add a way that you could create our own color schemes. We choose Red for guitars, Black for bass, green drums, and the default blue (instrument 1) for voices. You can create your own color key but keep it only one way. Now Save your changes.

Preparing Your Ears

When a gourmet chef creates a meal he gets everything ready before he makes the meal. Likewise, you should get ready. Copy our studio log sheet or create your own, You, will need a separate sheet for each track, and if you are creating separate stereo tracks you will need one for each channel. We find that it is best to place these on a clip board and use a pencil, not a pen so you can erase changes that do not work.

Before you start to listen give your ears a rest and a test. If you can go outside and listen...close your eyes...listen for the different sounds. Birds, traffic try to determine where they are coming from, how loud are they? Do some sounds overshadow the others? Does the trash truck rumbling along, make it to where you can't hear the songbird singing?

Fig 9-4 *Click on the down arrow on the track, then click on Move track up or down to move the track.*

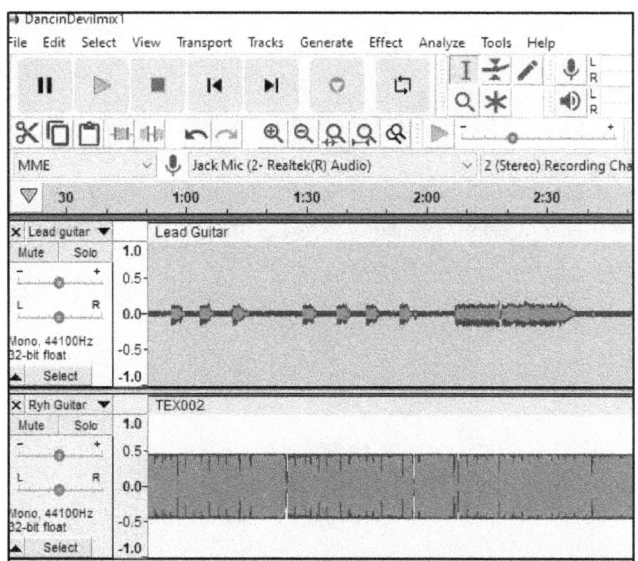

Fig 9-5 *Now we have the lead and the rhythm guitar next to each other. To further help identify them we have color coded the waves bright red by clicking the down arrow on the track, then click wave color, then select an instrument. You can use any color. But we advise whatever color you choose keep all other song and project the same. Here we choose Instrument 2 for guitars and the wave is red. Now do this with other colors for the other instruments.*

This may sound silly, but the number one instrument you are going to use in mixing are your ears. By doing these things you are trying to train your ears. To distinguish the different sounds-which ones need to bring down and which ones need to brough up.

Now back inside because **you don't want anyone see you doing what is next.** Smile, smile like you have just had your greatest dream come true. Now open your mouth as wide as you and move your jaw from one side to the other. Now tilt your head from side to the other, trying to lay your head on **your own shoulder, but don't force it.** You not trying to do damage only even the pressure in the Eustachian tubes in your ears. You when do all of this you may hear a popping sound in your ears (like we you descend a big hill). This the equaling pressure. You can also put your palms on your ears press down a few times then quickly release, this will even up pressure for you to listen better. It sounds crazy but it does work.

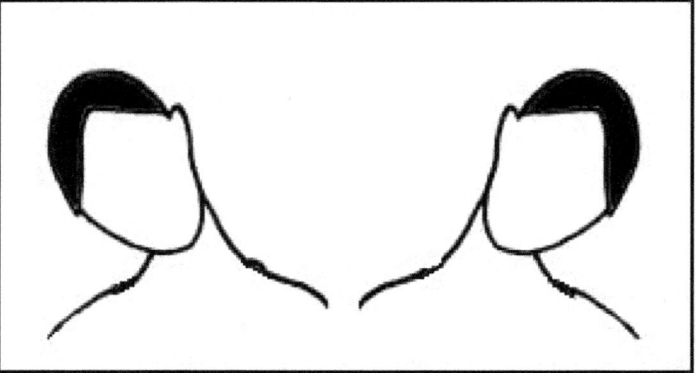

Fig 9-7 Tilt your head side to side to equal the pressure in your ears before listening.

Just as in recording it is best to keep hydrated. So, fix yourself a drink. Tea, water, soda your choice. We would **advise it to be in a sealed container so it can't be accidentally spilled.**

One last suggestion before you start to listen. Dress comfortably and get a good chair to sit in that will be comfortable, as you may be working on one song for the whole day. Also have a clock that you can see, so that you take regular breaks, you do not want to wait until your tired and trying to push yourself to get it done, this will only hurt your mix in the end.

While sitting in the chair listen for other sounds in the background. Listen for fans, TVs, or radios, especially if you are mixing with speakers. But even with headphones the noise of the computer running, or a nearby refrigerator running can be heard. And these will drive you crazy. This because they are not in the tracks themselves and cannot be removed like the hum from an amplifier. Therefore, you must learn to recognize the sounds and work around them and with them. This is especially true with the computer sounds. I know it from experience; I kept hearing this rattling sound, as if something was vibrating. I went through each track but **couldn't find it. It wasn't until I was sitting at the** computer with no sound, I realized it was the hard drive spinning.

Now take a sip of your drink and sit back you are ready to start mixing. Turn the faders all the way up on every track there. Have a pencil and paper (we found that the back of the log sheets works well. Now listen to the project. Marking the things down that are needed.

Chapter 10 What Is Mixing?

If a song is a cheeseburger, then the mixing is the French fries and soft drink that make it a meal. Another example, with cake mixes you can have the mix along with eggs, oil, and water. But they are not tasty until it is all mixed together-even unbaked. **Come on let's see the hands out there how many have tried to lick the bowl! Or maybe tasted raw cookie dough! Too much flour, or not enough sugar and that tasty cake is something the dog will not even eat. Same goes for music too much or too little of something can ruin an otherwise good track.**

Raw music does not have the same 'sweet' flavor that raw cookie dough has. In fact, with uncontrolled bass and drums booming and dead vocals it just sounds pretty sour. Mixing is where the sweetness is added, and an okay sound turns into a great sound. This done my controlling several different things. One position of the sound, the height and depth of the sound.

Before the days of stereo, yes believe it or not there was time when cars could be ordered with an AM radio with one (very poor) speaker that came out of the center of the dash. Every instrument every voice came out of that one speaker. To get an idea of what this would have sounded like. Take a small empty box, cut one two-inch diameter hole in the top. And cover the hole with two dish cloths. Put your phone inside and play music, shut the box, and listen to the music coming through the small hole from about a foot away. Depressing!

Unlike a recipe where you add this to that, stir well and bake, mixing is never the same for one song to the next. It is more like trying to create a gourmet meal with the ingredients in front of you, so you must keep accurate notes of what you do and add and how much you add, just in case you want to make it again. Take John Pemberton, the pharmacist who created the formula for Coco-Cola® or Harland Sanders with his famous chicken recipe. If they had not kept perfect notes, they could not have been able to duplicate it again. If you have a crash or save the wrong file, you need to a way to repeat this. So, **if you haven't done so download our log. There is also one at the back of this guide. That you are free to copy.**

In the 1960's stereo began taking over, with albums like The Beatles *Sergeant Pepper's Lonely Hearts Club Band.* Listen to this album with headphones on and you will truly hear what the stereo range is of this album is.

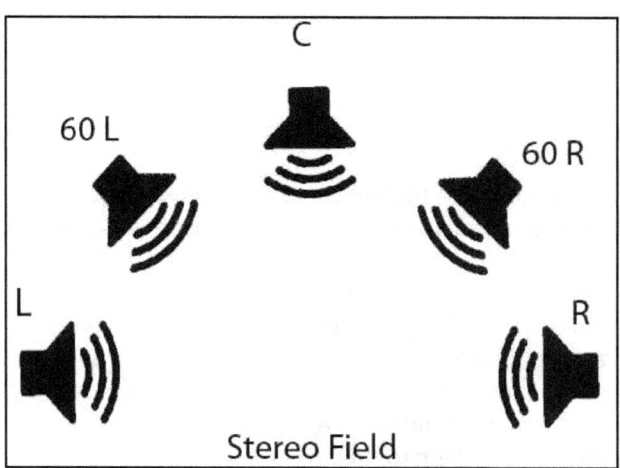

Fig 10--1 The stereo field. Where you place sounds will have a big impact on the sound.

THE BASICS OF MIXING

Position

Question how many positions does stereo have? Trick question it has two left and right. No, there is also as dead center, mostly right and mostly left.

The stereo field (fig 10-1) is where you place the instrument. This is called *panning*. *Pan Hard Left* means the fader is set to the far left as far as it will go. While *Pan Hard Right* is to the right as far as it goes. *Pan Center* is that each one is at 50 degrees and when played back with to speakers, sound as if it is coming from an imaginary speaker in the middle. If you place one at 60 % to one side it will sound like it mostly from that side but also from the other, but to a lesser degree. You can also pan one say 30 degrees and the other 60% that will make it sound as it is coming mostly from the 60% side. In other words, there are many different positions in stereo field.

Position of Instruments

So where is the magical map that places the instruments? There isn't one. There is no set formula- there are suggestive places, but it is all up to you and where you think they should be. Just make sure that your choice helps the overall feeling of the song. In other words, you mix a hard rocker differently than you would soft ballad.

The key to all of this is you don't want everything in one position, or it will start sounding like that horrible 1950's car speaker. We will list some suggestions that can be your starting point.

LEAD VOCALS

The vocals are the thing that drives a song so the lead vocal in usually place dead center. If you pan to one side or the other, you will take away to focus from the vocals, and you don't want to do that. There is one time you might do this and that is with a duet. Where you have singers, sort of telling a story, panning one to the left and the other to the right or 60% to the sides. And then when they join in vocals bring them to the center. This can be done in Audacity, but it requires copying and pasting that we will show a little later. But this can get really silly so be sure to listen with critical ears. Maybe you can could switch sides when the second verse starts, bring back together slowly as they sing together with the chorus being in dead center with both vocals.

Fig 10-2: By placing backup singers on the right and left you can hear them over the lead singers.

Fig 10-3 what happens when you send to many signals to one position, they get over shadowed and you can't hear them all. There is a lot of rom spread it out.

BACKING VOCALS

If you place the backing vocals in the center, it will get real crowded and they will be lost over the lead vocals. Most backing vocals are recorded in stereo, and they are panned hard left and right. These are two different tracks, and they will sound similar but slightly different. If you only have a mono track of backup vocals. You can select it tap *control D* and duplicate the track. It will be at the very bottom. Click the down arrow and click *move track up,* until it is just under the one you copied from. Move it back just a small amount (fig 10-4) so there is a slight delay (we are talking milliseconds here). This will give the track a slightly different sound, to make them two sperate soundtracks.

And if you really want to add depth to the backing vocals place a third track in the center, (fig 10-5) and have it off a few milliseconds the other way then the other one. For example, if you pushed it back 3 milliseconds, push the track forward that much.

BASS

A clean dry bass guitar is usually in the center, but those that are wet (with effects) have two tracks and one panned right and one panned left with the wet on one side and the dry track (no effects) on the other. This gives the bass more depth and feeling.

PIANO AND KEYBOARDS

These are usually placed just off center at the 80/20 that is 80 % percent to one side and 20% the other. If you have a rhythm guitar, they are usually place on opposite sides of each other with this same percentage. If the mix does not sound right. Then decrease one side and increase the other of one or both the piano/keyboard and the guitar until it sounds right.

HORNS AND STRINGS

Horns and strings sound at home on the sides, if you have both strings and horns, place the on opposite sides. This also works when you have both low and high frequencies in these. Place the high on one side and the low on the other, or mostly to one side. Beware of the other instruments that may be there that might hide them. Remember the more instruments you have then the smaller the part for each instrument must be.

PERCUSSION

They are best placed just off center to one side. If it is used throughout the song tag it to the high-hats. With the high-hats to one side and the percussion instrument to the other side.

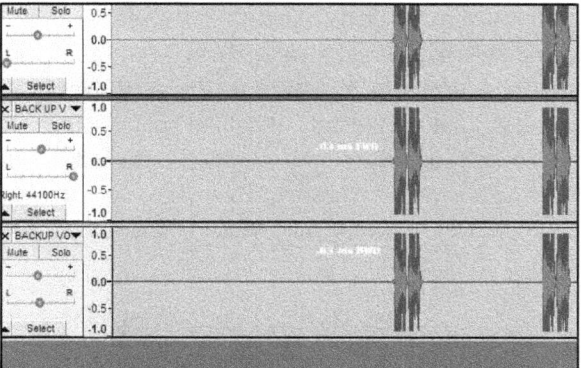

Fig 10-4 to move track forward a few microseconds, zoom in until you see the microseconds scale at the top of the timeline. Select a few microseconds at the beginning of the track and the click delete. If you want to put the tack back, do the delete at the end of the track. Now play to make sure your cut sounds right. If it *doesn't* click undone or Control Z and the cut will disappear, and you can add or subtract to the amount of cut you want.

Fig 10-5 We have removed 3 ms form the front and back of the track it is so little it unnoticeable to eye in standard track view, but it to the ear. Notice the Pan Settings. This will give the back vocals a full sound which is what we wanted for the song Dead Roses.

GUITARS

Rhythm guitar is usually carried to 60-75% one side, the side does not matter. But beware of the other instruments that have to go into the mix, and you don't want to over crowd the sound field. And if you have something like keyboard or piano on the one side then place the rhythm guitar on the other. Or mostly on the other. If you have two rhythm guitars pan each hard to each side.

Lead guitar is usually in the center or off to one side, this especially true when it comes to hard driving rock music. But if you want to added effects like compression or reverb to it. Have two tracks one sent hard left and the other sent to the hard right. One is *dry* (no effects) the other *wet* (with effects)- this makes for a unique sound.

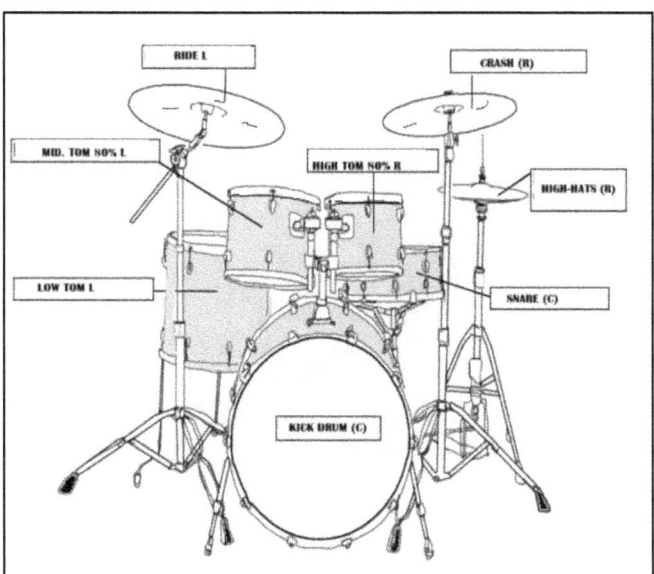

Fig 10-6 typical drum set up in mixing locations.

HARMONICA AND WOODWINDS

They are best placed just off center to one side. If you are using different types, try placing them on different sides.

DRUMS

Drums usually should be panned as they appear on stage, but again this all up to you. The main drums (snare and kick) are placed in the center the lower tom to the left and the how toms slightly to the right. The high-hats go slightly to the right of center about a 80-90/20-10 mix. Ride cymbals use this but to the left and crash cymbals to slightly to the right.

Fig 10-7 typical Mix layout

Fig 10-8 An example of how reverb adds distance to sound. The man at the far end of the hall will have lots of echo or reverb to his voice.

THE DEPTH OF SOUND

Relax, we are not getting into the philosophy of if a tree falls and there is no one to hear it does it a make a sound. No, we are speaking of how close and far the sound is to you by its sound. This can be best summed with picture a woman and two suitors in a long hallway fig 10-8. Suitor A is only 15 inches from her while suitor B is down at the end of the hand. She has her eyes closed and cannot see where they are. Both ask her to 'marry me' at the same time. She will first hear suitor A and before she hears suitor B, and he will sound as if he is miles away.

This effect is done in recording by the distance the microphone is away from the sound. Thus, the further back you place a microphone the further the instrument will sound away from the listener.

So, what does this have to do with mixing? That part of the room you hear is called reverberation or reverb for short. By adding reverb, you can make an instrument sound further away, and further back in the mix. This gives depth to the sound. And can make the instrument sound bigger. This is the reason your voice sounds so much better; this is the secret to sing along machine. Simple to remember any effect that is added like reverb will make it sound further away.

THE HEIGHT OF SOUND

The height of slide is controlled by volume of that individual track, this sets the mood of song. For example, you have a love ballad with the feeling of broken hearts and sorrow, or of broken hearts and anger! The song contains tracks of vocals, overdriven guitar, drum, bass, and a piano.

Now boost the volume up on the piano and down on the guitar and add softness to the vocals and it is a more feeling of heart break and tears. Boost the guitar up and the piano down, and make the vocals gritty and hard, and it is more of how dare you break my heart!" Same song but different feelings. So always take what the emotion of the song is when undertaking a mixing. Adding volume also creates the depth of instruments.

STARTING A MIX

Now take the musician hat off and put on your producer hat. Ever have a fight between yourself? If not, you are about to have one. Two creative sides are about to meet and that have very little to do with each other. In fact, you may get so mad with yourself that you may slam the door and walk on yourself.

Because the musician part of yourself is all about the sound and the music. And that 15-minute guitar solo is the a must have. But the producer part of you says we must cut it for time and push the guitar way back in the mix. Mute the drums down and get rid of the distorted guitar all together.

"You don't know about a damn thing about MY music. I give up!" SLAM. Music is free to the soul and is about the heart of the song. But don't make the mistake of letting emotions carry you away. Especially if you are going to put this out for sale, it must be similar to others out there. There is just so much time that a vinyl record can hold, and your recording should be aware of this. Note you will see this happen in the Mastering section of this guide, when songs must be cut, and this was not done intentionally.

If you have just finished recording the song do not go ahead and mix. In fact, when you have finished recording take some time away from it. Read a book, watch a movie, just let your ears, and mind rest from this then after a week or so, then go back and start to listen with new ears. You might find you want to rerecord that track that you loved so much a few weeks ago.

When you are ready to listen do not worry about **the mix, don't touch anything yet. Next in Audacity** turn all the volume faders up on each channel all the way up but turn the master volume down some so that it will not harm your ears. All tracks should be neutral and have no position yet. Fig 10-9 and 10-10.

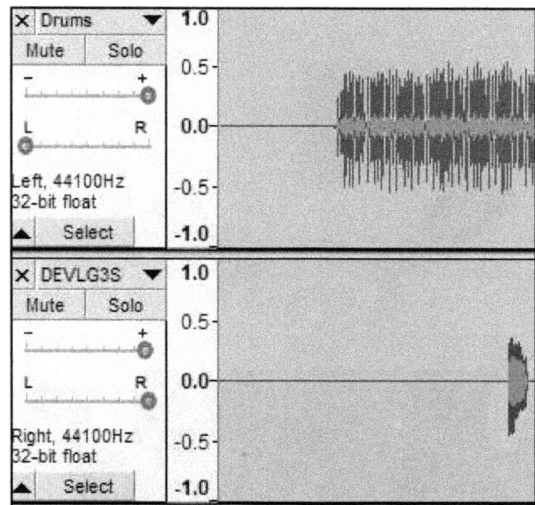

Fig 10-9 Push the volume faders on each track to far **right**.

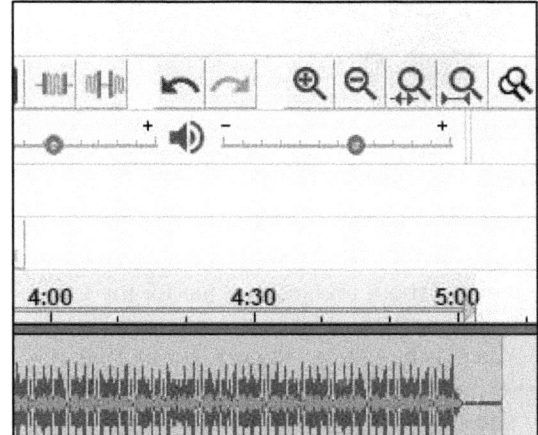

Fig 10-10 Turn the master volume down some.

Use the back of the log sheet or a separate piece of paper. Listen with critical ears. Are the drums too loud, guitar overpowering the voice, or does it need to come up some? Does something need to be pushed back in the mix or brought forward? Jot all this down. Now listen to each track separately and jot down things need, as to where you want it in the mix.

Fig 10-11 Do NOT add effects to the tracks until you have the mix sounding right.

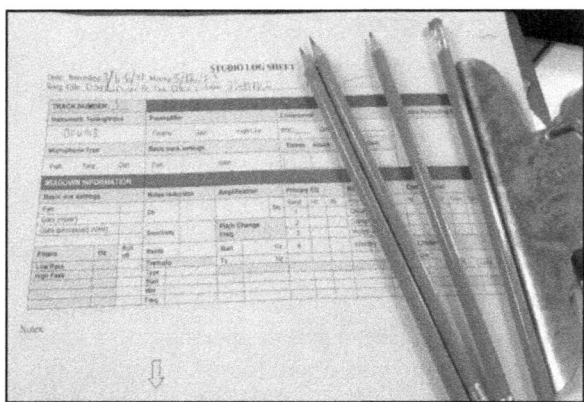

Fig 7-10 Studio log sheet and have lots of pencils handy, pencils are better than pens as you make changes.

Taste Before You Serve!

Are you one of those that just reaches for the salt and starts shaking it on, even before you taste it? (Guilty). You may be salting salt pork. For those that have never had this; it looks like bacon but is tougher and very salty due to it is cured in salt. Adding salt to it would make it where you could not eat it or find it not as appealing.

Music can be the same way to may beginners will sit down and start slapping on effect compression, Reverb EQ. PLEASE DO NOT do this. Instead adjust by the position of the tracks, the loudness of the tracks-and we are not even talking about adding amplification yet. Get the track sounding as good as you can WITHOUT any effects.

Where Oh Where Do I Start?

I like to start in the rhythm section with the drums.   Now listen to it again, once with sound up and then with sound down. What may sound great loud, won't sound good when the volume is lowered. Also listen to in stereo and then in mono. Did the sound change? Make sure it sounds good in both. Now we are ready to add effects. They will be covered in the next two chapters.

What About a Podcast?

"The only instrument I played was a Tonette ® that was in grade school. I now have a podcast on how to retire. How is this going help me? "

But you can still use mixing to help your podcast sound more professional. Having just a voice sounds like you did it in your basement but added music to the opening and end it will sound as if it was done in a studio.

Professionalism is what makes your podcast different than then the many, many others out there. Have music down to where parts of it come from the right speaker, and the rest from the left while your voice comes from the center can set you apart. Say you have a bit that is about "the person on the street" but it is all done in the studio. You could add traffic sounds, very low but coming from one channel, giving the sound that it really took place on the street. Plus adding effects can add depth and feeling. So yes, mixing can benefit the podcaster.

 Okay before we get into the nuts and bolts of mixing tracks. Go get your something to eat, drink and go to the bathroom, for this is going to take some time…Don't worry I will wait right here for you. Oh, and when you come back bring back a couple of soft cloths (microfiber) and spray bottle of plain water -first thing we are going to do is clean up that track.

Chapter 11 Mix it Up and Mix Well Part 1

CLEAN UP THAT TRACK

Okay back now? Time to clean up that dirty track. Hope you got that cloth and spray bottle. *Thought I was kidding huh?* This the first step in cleaning a dirty track. You must clean your screen; dirt specks on your screen can look like noise. So, spray the cloth just to make it damp and carefully wipe the residue from your screen. Use another to dry it. Do not use glass cleaner or alcohol to clean your screen or spray water on the screen. A tip to this is using a huge screen-like a TV screen it is easier to see the waves if they are large.

Now it does not matter what microphones you are using or if you have a room solely for your studio, or it is just in the corner of your bedroom there is one thing you are going to have-Noise.

It can be from the hum of an amplifier or effects pedal, (fig 11-2) it can also be from the crackle of paper of lyrics, a shuffle of feet or a breath of air. As we are human, we breath in and we exhale, and after letting a high-pitched sustained note and the microphone catches this. You may not hear it when it covered up by other instruments. But when you solo the track, it can be heard. The problem is when the track is compressed or other effects are added it could become more noticeable, especially in the final mix where there is no way to remove it. So, we will remove these noises now.

Solo one track, by clicking the 'solo' button Fig 11-1 all other tracks will be dimmed out and only the selected track will play. If you visibly hear the noise not the location. Next Use the zoom tool and zoom in until you see the small wave that is the noise.

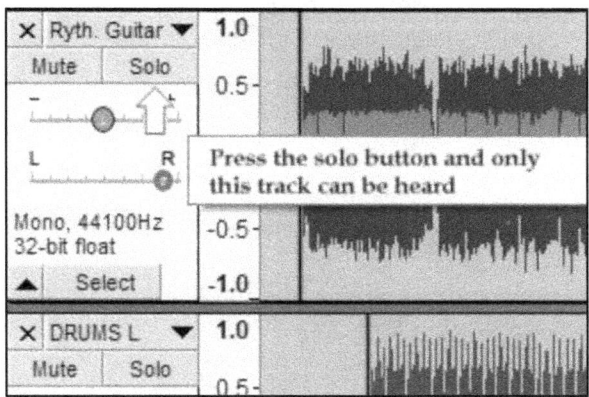

Fig 11-1 Use the solo button to listen to only a single track.

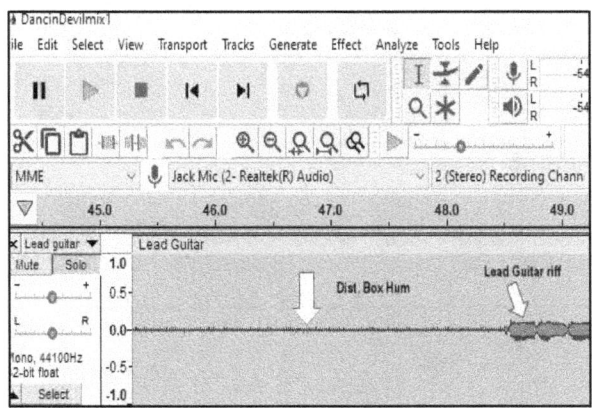

Fig 11-2 An example of the noise (hum) that a distortion effect box leaves behind.

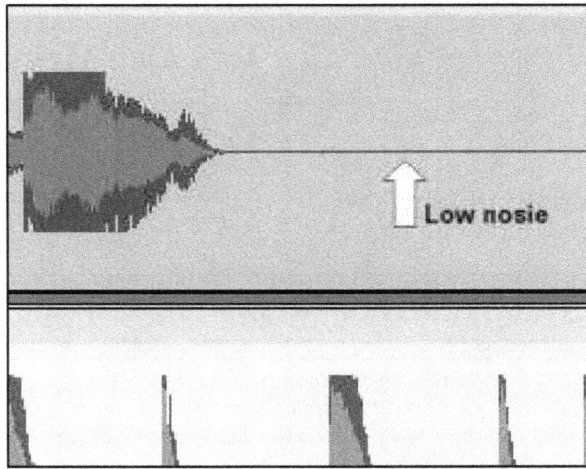

Fig 11-3 If the track you have selected has lots noise as in our above example take a noise sample from another track that low or no noise before running Nosie Reduction.

Select a portion of the track that shows no or low noise (fig 11-3) then run Noise Reduction. **Effect>Nosie Reduction.** Click 'Get Nosie Profile.' Then OK. Now select the entire track. Again, click Effect> Noise Reduction>OK. It will apply the reduction to the track.

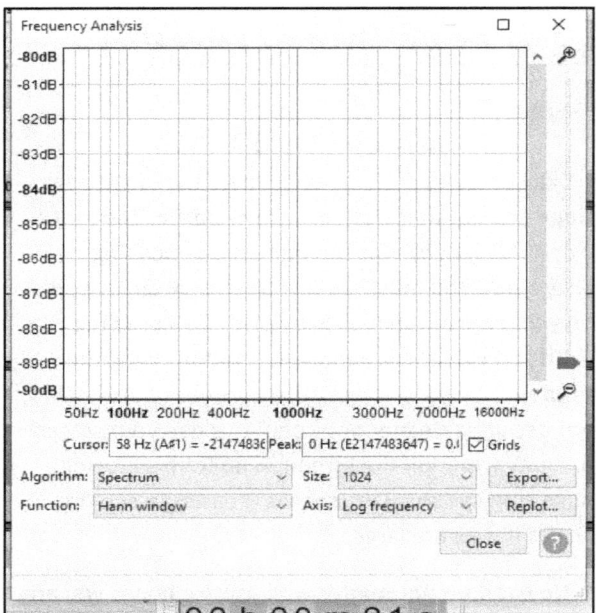

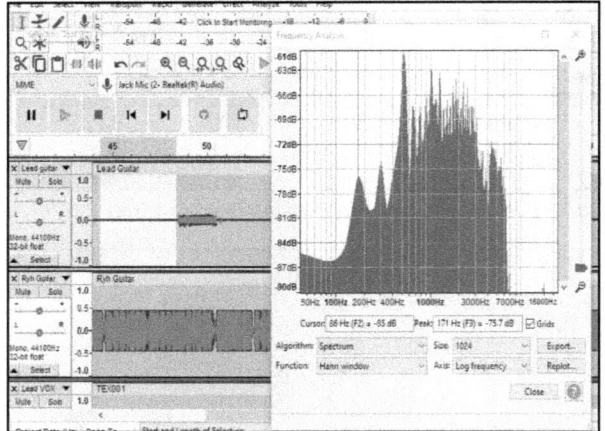

Fig 11-4 *Now select the area of noise on the track again. Click Analyze>Plot Spectrum, and we can see there is still noise on the track.*

Fig 11-6 *To prove it is clean; with the area still selected. Click Analyze> Plot Spectrum, it should look like this photo.*

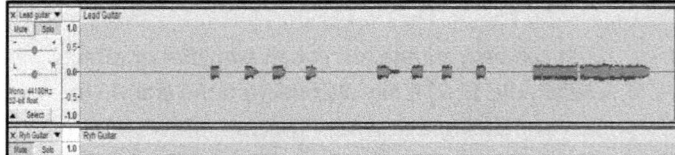

Fig 11-6 b *Our cleaned-up track.*

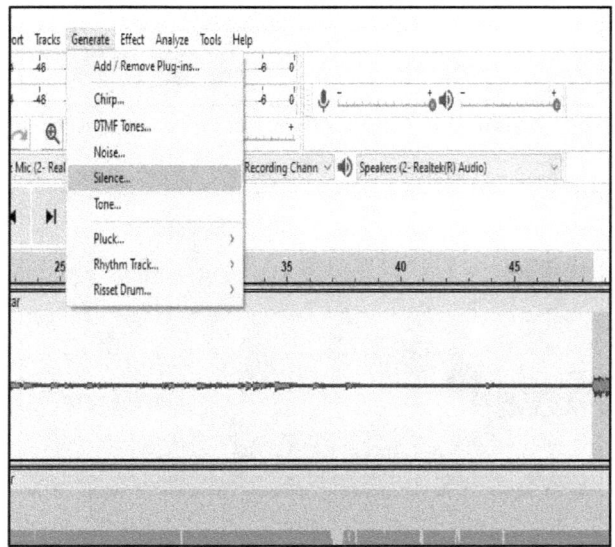

Fig 11-5 *Select the noise (only the noise) yet one more time.* **Being careful you don't cut any of the sound you want to keep.** *If you have to zoom in more. Click Generate>Silence>OK. This will remove all the sound.*

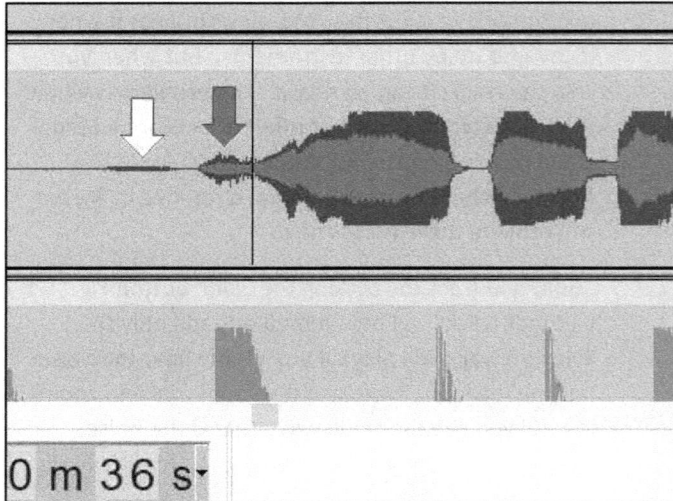

Fig 11-7 *Is it a voice or is it noise. The above photo is from a lead vocal track the Dark arrow is where the voice begins the white arrow is a breath. A place to look for breaths is at the end of a line where another one begins. In this example this is the beginning of the chorus.*

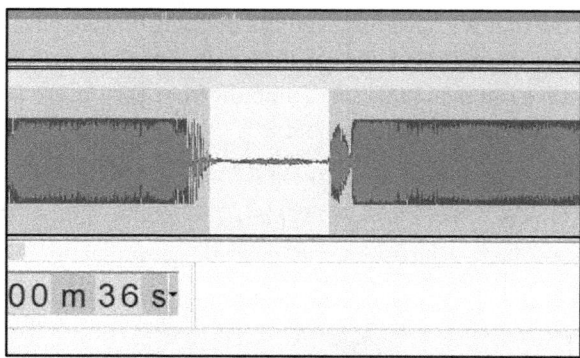

Fig 11-8 How to spot a breath, usually it will have a lower FQ wave then the vocals. Another way is to select just that area and paly only that portion of the track. If you find a breath, you can leave it or remove it by clicking Generate>Silence>OK. If the song is emotional and sound in a breathy tone removing the breath could harm the song.

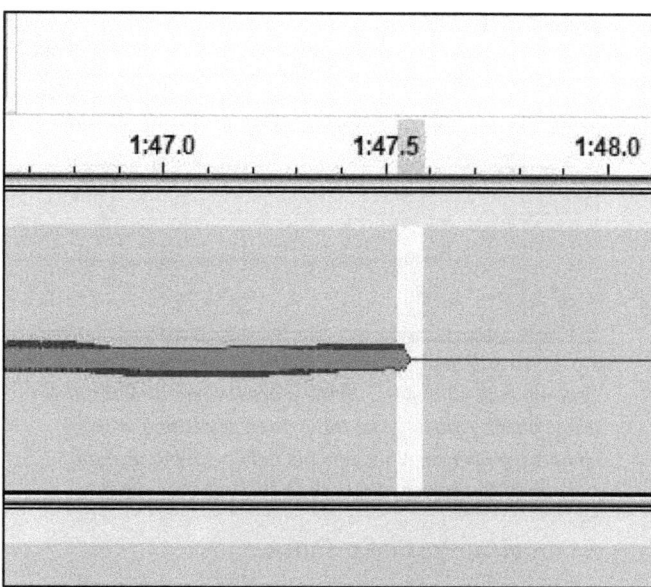

Fig 11-10 To ease the clicking sound select a few micro-seconds at the beginning and click Effect>Fade In. At the end of the wave select a few micro-seconds of the wave and click Effect>Fade Out. This will make the waves flow easily without the click.

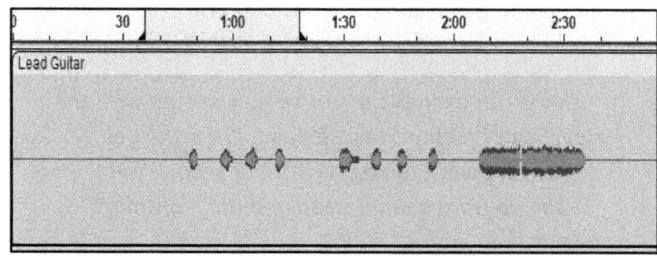

Fig 11-11 Our track with the fade in and fade out effects applied. If you have many waves to apply the effect to, do one side at a time. Example. Select the first microseconds of the first wave, then click Effect>Fade In. Next click the first micro-seconds of the next wave and type Ctrl R. This will repeat the last effect you used. Then move on to the next wave and so on. When you are done then you can start at the end and do the Fade out and move back to the beginning. This saves a lot of time.

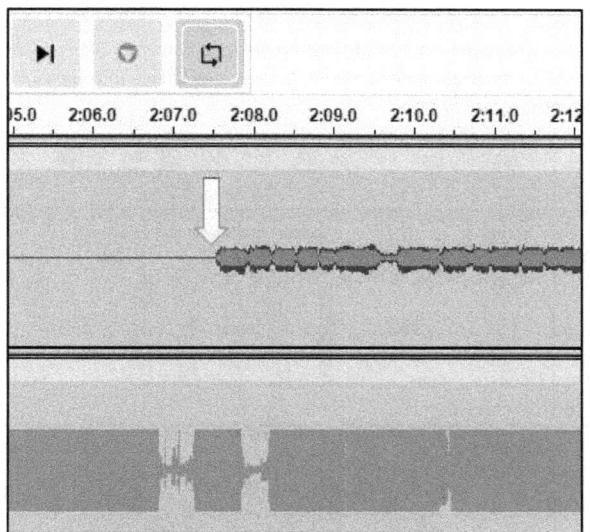

Fig 11-9 Now that we have removed the noise you will notice that there is a sharp beginning and ending to some sound wave and when played back, it creates a click sound.

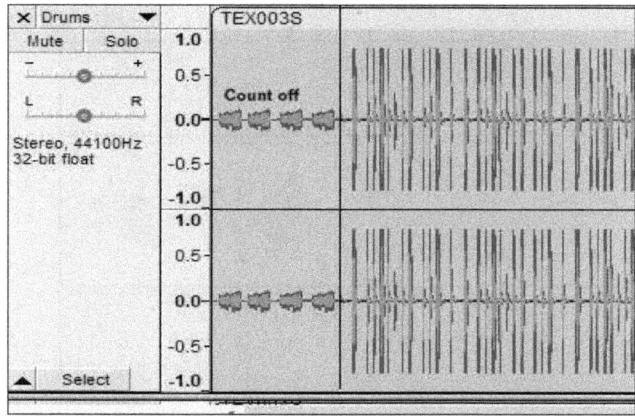

Fig 11-12 A count off is a useful item to place the beginning of a track or when there is major change. But now we want to remove them. Select the area and then click Generate> Silence. Do Not delete them or you will throw off the alignment of the track. If you have a click track the X delete it.

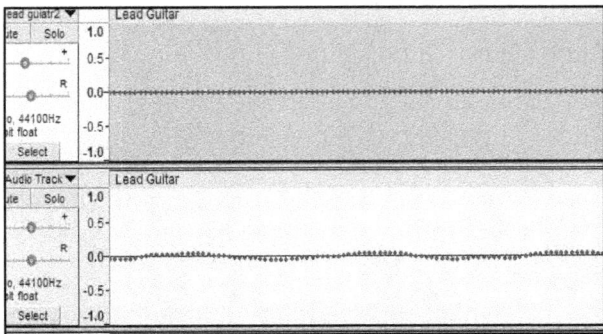

Fig 11-13 Still hearing noise? Zoom in until the tracks become individual dots. In the places where an instrument is not playing looking like this? Then select and click Generate> Silence. Note you will only be doing a small portion of the sound at a time so this will take a while.

Removing Part of a Track

Say you want to remove a part of a track, such as the mic was still on at the end of a podcast, and it overhears you talking to the guest. You don't want this on the final master for the podcast. Or you have a beginning of a song of lyrics that you don't want to use.

This is our example in our song *'Dancing with the Devil'* Our first line was *'Sleeping like an angel'* instead we want to begin with our second line. *"Wake up from a dead sleep and the nightmare begins.'*

Use the zoom tool until the waves become individual waves. Then select the wave and play it back to find the line you want to remove. Click Generate> Silence. The line is removed. However, before you remove it note the location at where the cut will begin and end. And write it down.

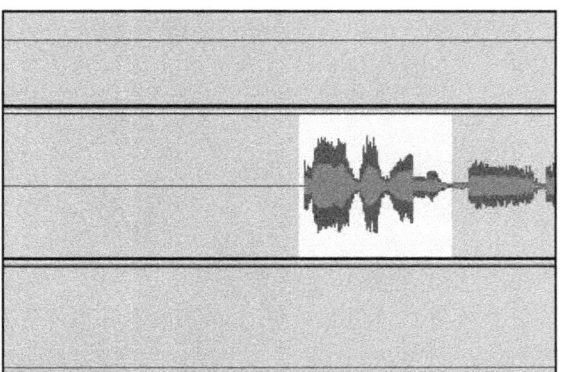

Fig 11-4 We select the line we want to remove. The click Control X. Note this will throw off the timing and you will have to cut the other tracks the same amount. Or you can just do the vocal and have a longer music introduction, by silencing this part of the vocal track.

Now that we have removed the opening line we have a longer introduction, we can either keep it removed which will involve removing this same amount from each track. Do this by following the below photos.

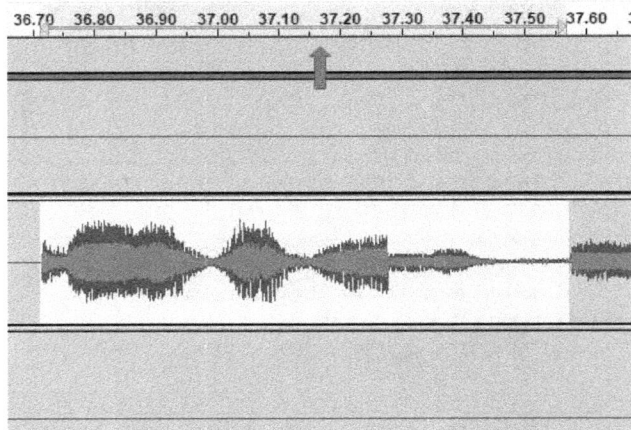

Fig 8-15 Note the timeline of the area before it deletes it Then use this to cut the other tracks the same amount. Note you may have to zoom in more to get an accurate timeline.

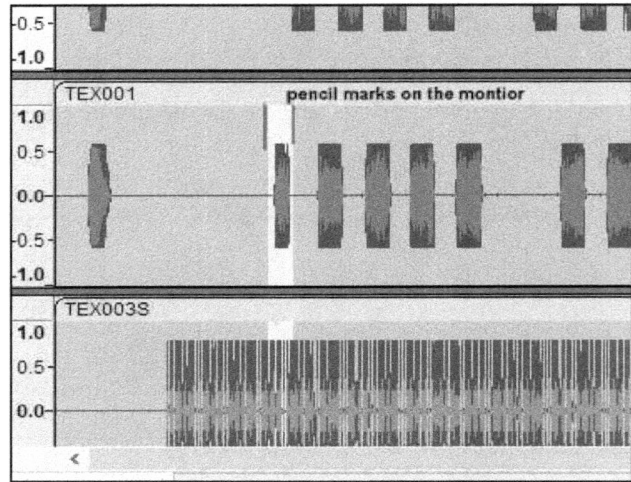

Fig 11-16 Another way is the use a pencil NOT A PEN. And lightly trace the area of the track you are cutting and use these marks as guides for cutting the other tracks. After you are done clean your monitor again.

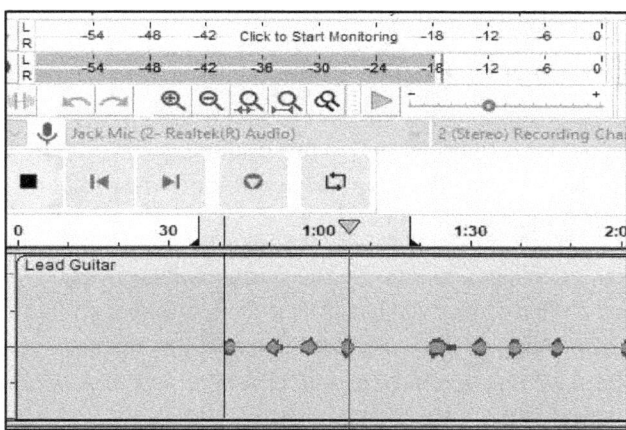

Fig 11-16 Also note tracks that are not getting even into the yellow. These tracks will sound weak compared to other track at are pushing past this point. Out lead guitar track here is weak and overshadowed by the powerful rhythm guitar.

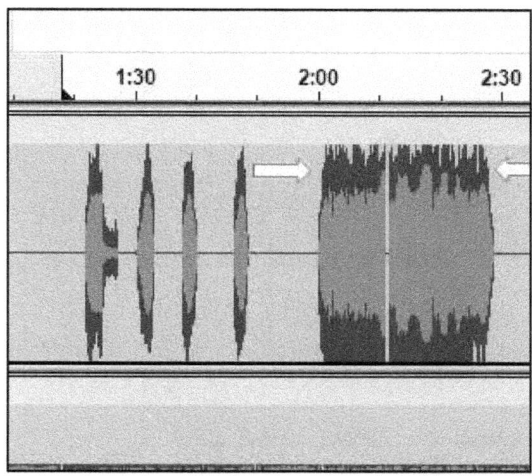

Fig 11-18 It is only a few notes after each line, but now our lead guitar pops out of the mix. However, we have a new problem The riff in the chorus and bridge now overshadows the vocals.

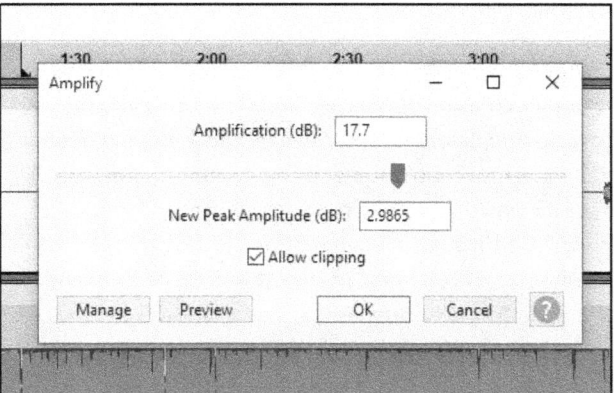

Fig 11-17 To make this track louder. We select the entire track (note be sure you start your selection right next to the first part of the sound, otherwise the preview may not work. Click Effect> Amplify. Then inset amplification. Click preview to hear it. Make the changes you need and click okay.

Check Each Track for Clarity and Sound

Play each track by themselves note the amount on the VU meter, that is burying into the red and staying there. Bouncing into the red and then out is okay. In fact, it is what you want. But you don't want tracks that hammered into the red all the time. You can remove this by reducing volume on the track that is doing it. If that does not do it select it and click Effect >Clip Fix apply the information and click okay. This will reduce the selected clip.

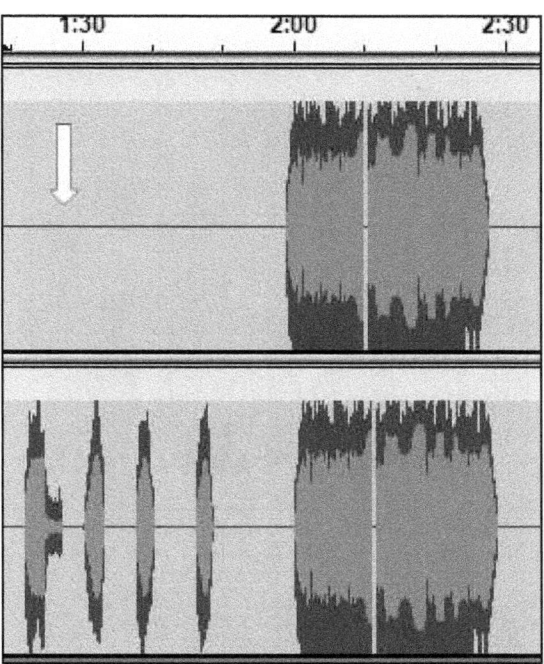

Fig 11-19 Audacity does not allow you to change volume in different location in a single track. So we added a track, then selected copied the whole lead guitar track then silenced the part(arrow) we **don't want to change.**

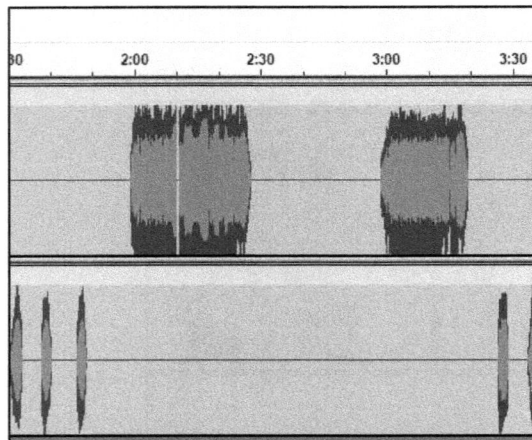

Fig 11-20 Now we silence the part we want to change in the original track.

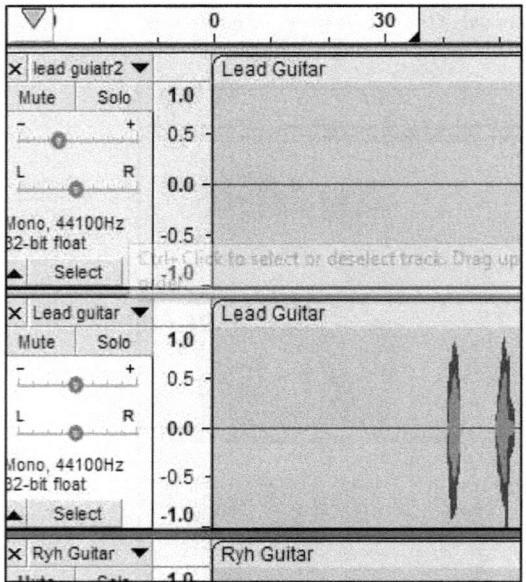

Fig 11-21 Now we drop the sound level down on the duplicated track And when played back. The sound is not over whelming.

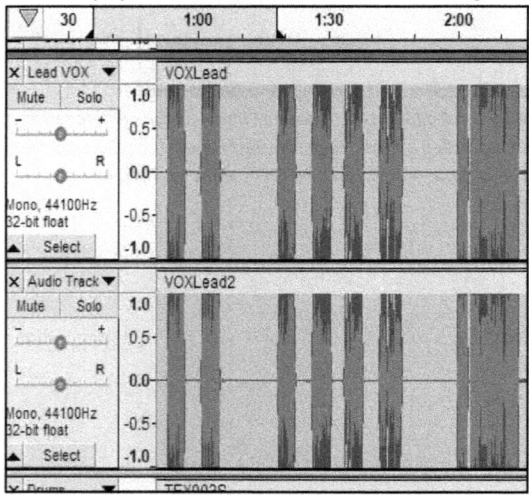

Fig 11-22 Another way of increasing the sound is to double a track. By copying and pasting it into another track. Works well with vocals. Also, can be useful to apply second voice trick, that we will cover later in this guide.

EQ...EQ...BRING IN THE EQ

The equalizer is the chief tool to make sound, sound better, brighter, bigger than life. However, it cannot change what is not there, it must work with what it has.

Earlier we told you to listen to the tracks all the way up, now you need a comfortable level. Not too low where you could miss things, or too loud it can be masked by the ear itself. Both will cause you to remember overcompensate-so the Goldilocks Rule-it has too just right.

The Golden Rule of EQ is cut first, add later. Cut narrowly, added broadly. Do one track at a time, then see how it plays with the other tracks, by the time you get to the last track you are mixing it all that have EQ.

First thing to determine is how does the track sound, and what do you need to do. Solo the single track by clicking solo on that track. And listen. Is it muddy sounding, does it need to be made brighter? Do you need to add more boom to the bass or cut it? Do you add more crunch to the guitar or take some away? Go through the whole track jotting things down that need change. If **you want to click the** '*loop button*' and listen to it over and over until you are sure there are no more changes that are needed.

We have given you some stating points for the sound below, and the magical 'sweet spot' according to instruments and voices. Other questions to ask are how do you want the track to sound is it to jump out or blend in?

If you want a track to jump out, you roll off the bottom; if you want it blend in then roll off the top. Beware of when soloing an instrument and making it sound good may make it awful when played with the other tracks. So, with each change you make compare it with the other tracks. If it does not work, you can undo it, and then make other changes.

Note if you are using EQ in stereo, you can add EQ only to one channel and leave the other alone to create a unique sound. However, you will have to click on the down arrow key on the track and then split the stereo track to do this. If you **leave it as standard** '*Stereo Track*' the same EQ will be applied to each track. Or you can use two Mono tracks and pan one hard to the right the other to left.

Remember whatever you change write it down on your studio log sheet. If you need more room, you can write on the back of the sheet.

EQ STARTING POINTS TO CUT OR ADD

Sounds	Starting Point
Boom	Cut/Add at 125 Hz
Muddy	Cut at 250 Hz
Boxy	350-450 Hz
Honky	Cut at 500 Hz
Body	Add at 750-850 Hz
Crunch	Cut/Add 1-2 kHz
Stand Out	2-5kHz
Edge	Cut/Add 8kHZ
Air	Cut/Add 16KHz

Drum and Percussion EQ SETTINGS		
Frequency	**Adjustment**	**Reaction**
KICK DRUM		
80-150 Hz	+1-2	Add depth
400-600 Hz	-3-4	Reduces boxy sound
2.5-5 kHz	+1-2	Increases Attack
SNARE DRUM		
100-150 Hz	+1-2	Adds warm tones
250-300 Hz	+1-2	Add Depth
800-1000Hz	-2-3	Reduces boxy sound
3-5kHz	+1-3	Increase Attack
8-10kHz	+1-3	Add crisp tones
UPPER TOMS		
100-300 Hz	+1-2	Adds Depth
600-1000Hz	-2-3	Reduces boxy sound
3-5kHz	+1-2	Increase Attack
5-8 kHz	+1-2	Sticks out in tracks
LOWER TOMS and Kettle drums		
40-150 Hz	+1-2	Add depth
400-800 Hz	-2-3	Reduces boxy sound
2.5-6K	+2-3	Increase Attack
CYMBALS		
HI-HATS		
200-300 Hz	+1-2	More clang to closed hi-hats
10- up kHz	+3-4	Adds brightness
RIDE and CRASH		
150-250 Hz	-1-2	Reducing shimmering sound
1-2 kHz	-3-4	Reduces clanging sound
10-14kHz	+3-4	Add brightness
PERCUSSION		
80-250Hz	-3-5	Reduces Mussy sound
250-500 Hz	-5-10	Reduces Boxy sound
8-10 Hz	+2-3	Increases Brightness

Guitar EQ SETTINGS

Frequency	Adjustment	Reaction
ACOUSTIC GUITAR		
20-70 Hz	-2-3	Reduces boomy sound
150-200 Hz	-2-3	Reduces Muddiness
250-400 Hz	+2-3	More weight
500 to 1000 Hz	+2-3	Add Warmth
1.5 – 2.5 kHz	+2-3	Increase Clarity
5-10 kHz	+1-3	Brighter
ELECTRIC GUITAR		
50-63 Hz	-1-4	Reduces Hum
100 Hz	-2-3	Reduce muddy sound
150-250 Hz	+2-3	Increase Warmth
2.5-4 kHz	+2-3	Increase Attack
5 kHz	-2-3	Soften a thin Guitar
6-7 kHz	+2-3	Increase bite
BASS		
50-100Hz	-1-2	Removes boomy sound
80-125Hz	+1-3	Increases Bass sound
200-220 Hz	-3-7	Reduces Muddy sound
500-1000 Hz	+2-3	Adds Punch
2.5-5kHz	+2-5	Removes string noise

VOICE EQ SETTINGS

Frequency	Adjustment in Db	Reaction
SPEAKING		
80-150 Hz	-1-4	Cuts bass proximity
80-250 Hz	+1-4	Improves general speech
200 -350 Hz.	+1-4	Improve thin female voice
350 to 2000 Hz	+1-4	Improve vowel sounds
1,500- 4 kHz.	+1-4	Improve consonants
1-3 kHz	+2-3	Improves booming male voice
5-7 kHz	-2-4	Cuts sibilance
SINGING		
0-125Hz	-7-10	Improves basic vocals
250 -315 Hz	-6-12	Reduces Boomy sound
400 -500 Hz	-6-12	Reduces Boxy sound
1-2.5 kHz	-6-10	Reduces Nasal sound
5kHz	+1-3	Bring vocals forward
7.5-10 Hz	-1-4	Cuts sibilance

PIANO AND KEYBOARD EQ SETTINGS

Frequency	Adjustment in Db	Reaction
PIANO		
40-50 Hz	-2-6	Improve headroom
80 – 120 Hz	+1-4	Increase warm sound
150-250 Hz	-1-4	Reduces Muddy sound
2 -3 kHz	-1-2	Reduces Conflict with vocals
3-5kHz	+2-5	Increases Brightness
7-9 kHz	+1-4	Increases breath of piano
10-11 kHz	-1-4	Sounds Darker
10-11 kHz	+1-4	Sharper
10-13 kHz	-1-4	Reduce hammer sounds
KEYBOARD		
100-250 Hz	-1-5	Reduces Muddy sound
15-25 kHz	+1-5	Make it stand out

VOICE EQ
Speaking Voice

Whether for voiceover for an ad or your podcast, EQ for a speaking voice aims to maximize clarity. Thus, make sure the voice is clear and easily understand-able.

Generally, the basic speech band is between 80 and 250 Hz, so this ban should be brought. However, if you find that you are having troubles hearing vowel sound increase the 350 to 2000 Hz range. While consonants are improved between 1500 and 4000 Hz. Note that some microphones exaggerate low frequencies especially if the speaker leans into the microphone, is known as *bass proximity*. To bring this under control using cut the ranges under 125 Hz.

Sex also has effect on where to use EQ. If the speaker is male and has a booming voice. Boost frequencies between 1,000 and 3,000 Hz. With a female with a thin voice add EQ in the range around 200 to 350 Hz. For voices with lots of sibilance, the "hiss" that accompanies strong "s" sounds in a voice, look to cut the ranges between 5,000 and 7,000 Hz.

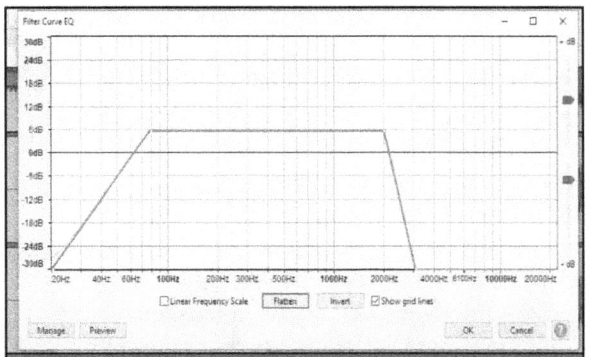

Fig 11-23 *A typical EQ band for the spoken word. Each voice is different so be sure to click preview with every change.*

Singing Voice

Many of the principles applying to speaking voices carry over to singers as well, but because the vocal is competing to be heard over instruments, there are a few extra points to consider when selecting the right EQ range to increase or decrease.

In most cases you can remove frequencies below 125 Hz, or the first 9 sliders on the left in Graphic EQ, as vocal content at these frequencies is usually hidden by other instruments. If **the singer still sounds 'boomy'** after reducing the low-frequency content, try a reduction of 6 dB using 250 or 315 Hz.

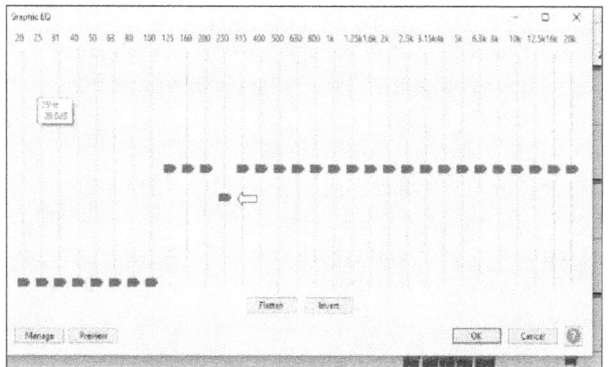

Fig 11-24 *For a booming voice cut the 250 or 315 Hz range by -6dB. When you place the mouse on the slider a box will show how much the dB rating is. Notice the first six slider and fully cut this is where voices are hidden by other tracks*

When it sounds as though the singer is in a box, low midrange frequencies are usually the culprit. Cut back on the 400 and 500 Hz ranges. A good place to start, is with a 6 dB reduction.

Nasal-sounding vocals may benefit from reductions between 1,000 and 2,500 Hz. Try reducing this range which are sliders 18 to 22 by 6 dB, one at a time, until the unwanted sound is removed. Once you find the frequency closest to the center, adjust the sliders on both sides for further improvement of the sound. To bring a vocal track forward in the mix add 1-2 Db at 5kHz. To cut the *hiss* sound of those words with **the letter 'S' you can** use a De-sser, but Audacity does not come with this. There are plugs in out there for this that will work on Audacity. Or you can cut at 7.5-10 Hz

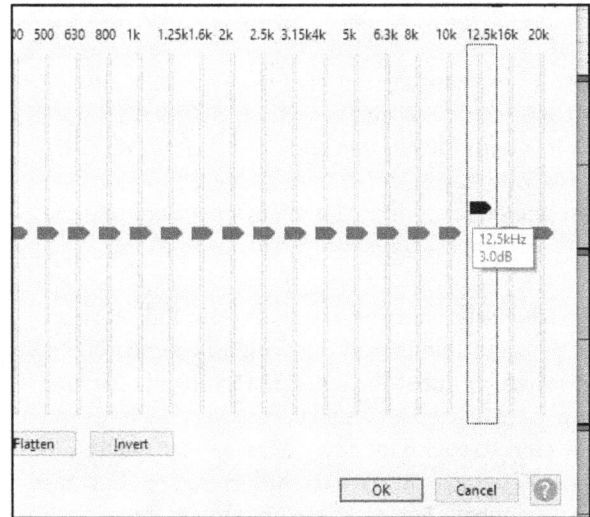

Fig 11-25 *To increase a scene of space and lightness to the vocal Adding about 3 dB at 12,500 Hz.*

To make vocals sound more *"chesty"* boost the 125 to 250 Hz range by 3 to 6 dB. If the vocal is lacking an important sounding range boost the 250 to 315 Hz until you get the sound, you want.

For an out of tun vocal decrease at the 3kHz range. To brighten vocals, increase the 10 kHz range by at least 3 dB. To increase a breathy sound, increase the 16.6kHz range do this by small Db increase of no more than 3dB at a time, tilly you find the sweet spot.

INSTRUMENTS

Drums

Kick/Bass: Boost the 63-8Hz range for the deep boom sound. If you want more punch out of the kick drum increase the 8-10kHz range. For all overall kick drum sound boost the 4kHz and cut the 200-400 Hz range, then boost in the 60 100 Hz range. For a heavy rock kick drum boost the 3kHz range.

If your drums are from a drum machine. Make sure that the kick does not mask any other sound, such as a sine-wave bass. Boost 2-3 dB within 50-60 Hz range with a low Q setting **if more energy is needed, but don't overdo it. Be sure to keep an eye on the meters as boosts in this range increase levels quickly. If needed use output slider for gain compensation when needed and reduce the sound level.**

Snare: Boost the 200-250Hz range for body and the 1.6-2kHz by 5-6 dB for more of a crack sound. This may take some fine tuning to get eh snare to jump out. To get rid of the ringing or hallow sound search the 25—600Hz range it. Then cut it.

Tom-Toms: To increase the boom of the Tom-tom's **increase the 100 to 300 Hz this will add body to it. Start with 3-dB increase if it sounds '*boxy*' keep adding to it until you find that drums sound 'too *boomy*'. Then go back down one step.** To increase the attack tones from the drumstick hitting the head of the drum itself. Boost the 3-4 kHz range.

Cymbals: Reduce stick notice by reducing the 100-250 Hz range. Increase the shimmer of the cymbals by boosting the 6.3-10kHz range. By boost the 200-300 Hz range you added more clang to the closed hit hats. Do this very slightly more it will quickly start to sound muddy. To lessen this sound, reduce the 200 Hz rage. Reduce the 400 Hz rage to decrease ambience on cymbals. For hardness on cymbals increase the 10KHz rage. And to brighten them increase the 12.-16kHz range.

Drum Machine

You recorded the drum track with a pattern that was on the drum machine and want to add these separate EQ's to each drum sound how do you do that? Let you know it can be done, but it is going to take a lot of work.

If you notice, there are different Frequencies used for the different drums but when using a drum machine. It only produces one track. However, if you zoom in on the track you will see that the track is made up of individual waves that represents the different types of sound that are included on the track. See the below photo for more information.

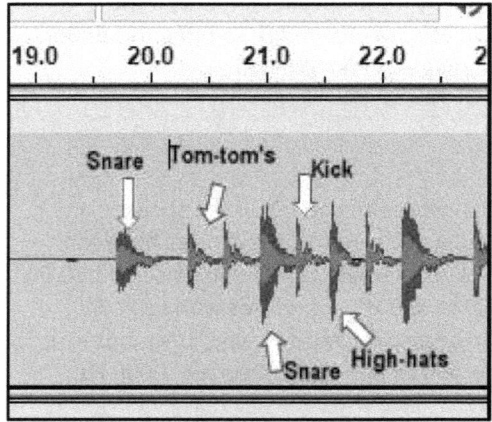

Fig 11-26 A drum machine track is made up of individual drum sounds.

To find out what wave are which sound select a single wave and click the space bar. Listen, is it a kick drum or snare? Note **it's shape and position.** Now you can go and change each individual wave (if you do this change all one type of wave then move to the next it will save time). Or you can copy the entire drum. open a new project. Add paste the track into the new project. Paste a track for each different drum patters you. If you have a track with Kick, snare, hi-hats you would need three different tracks. Label each of the tracks with that type of drums Kick Snare and so on. Fig 11-27.

Start with a single track, i.e. Kick drum and select and SILENCE fig 11-28 all the other drum sounds until you have entire track of nothing but kick drum sounds. Now move on to the next track i.e. Snare and do the same there Silencing the kick drum and tom-toms and Cymbals. Then do the next track and the next track until you have each track with only that type of drum sound. Fig 11-27. Now you add the proper EQ to each drum type. Before you start adding the EQ bands, play all track together to see if it plays right. If not check to see where you may have missed a drum or silenced the wrong one. Do not use delete to remove the drums or you will throw off the timing.

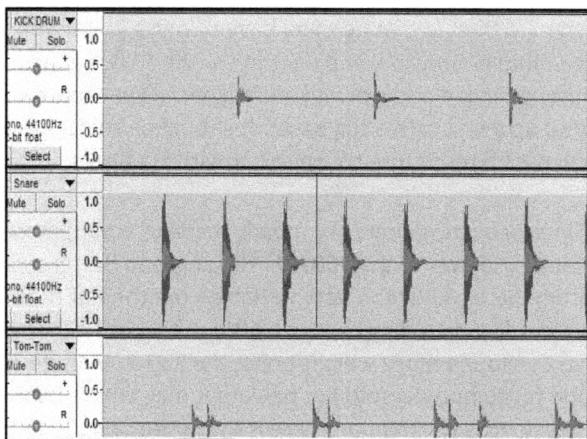

Fig 11-27 An example of the different drum part separates on to different track for a drum machine. Now you can apply the different EQ bands to each track

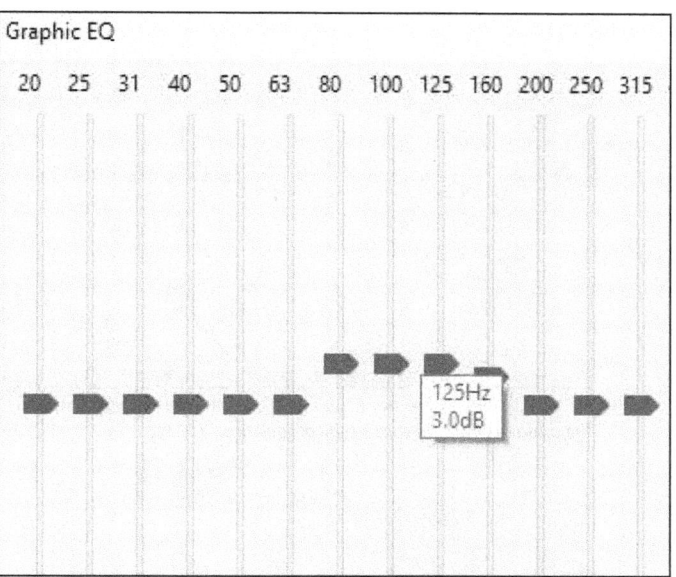

Fig 11-29 To use Graphic EQ, select the track or portion you wish to improve. Click Effects. Graphic EQ, move the sliders of that frequency you want to change. Up to increase down to decrease. Use the charts and text to get starting points. Here is the setting for the kick drum to make it sound deeper.

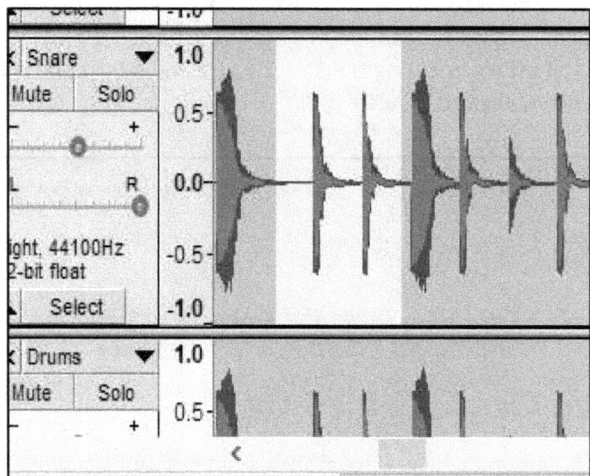

Fig 11-28 Here we select the drum we want o silence. I this case is all but the snare drum. We select a single wave then click Generate>Silence. Then move on to the next wave and repeat.

After applying the EQ to each specific drum type play the tracks back and check the sound and make any changes that are needed. Now copy all the track and past back into the original project (your song) and delete the original drum track. We will add more specific drum effects and it can be useful if they are on separate drum track. This same method could also be done with a drum record on one track.

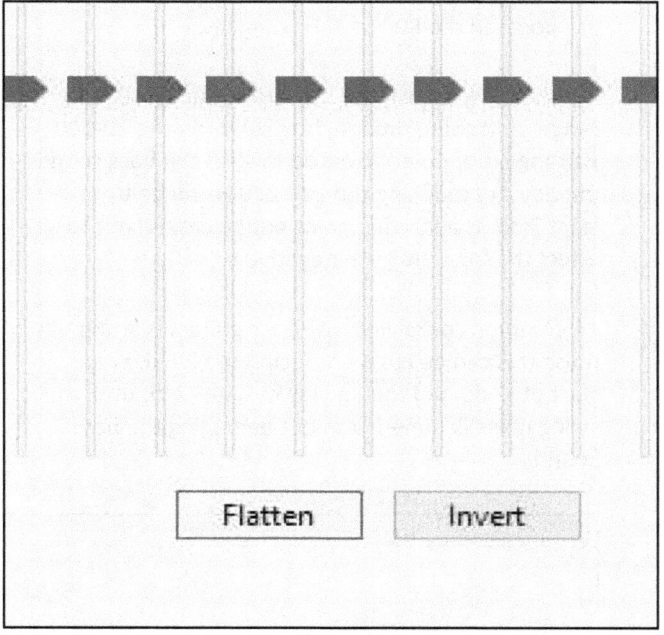

Fig 11-30 Be sure to click flatten when you go to the next portion or track, to get rid of the changes you made before. This brings the entire line to zero.

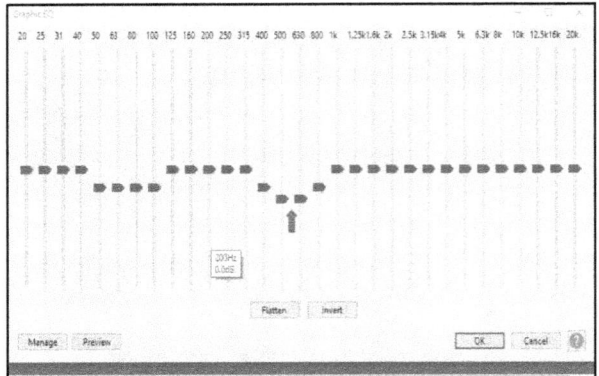

Fig 11-31 You can you the Graphic EQ also. Notice the dip (arrow) the already cut band this is typical rock bass line EQ.

Guitars

Bass Guitar: Reduce the 50-100Hz range then cut then dip between the 400 and 800 Hz range. This will decrease the "boom" of the bass and increase overtones and the recognition of a bassline in the mix. This is most often used in loud basslines in rock music. Enhance the deepness of the bass by increasing the 80-125Hz rage. While plucking sounds are boosted the 800 to 1kHz range.

With Hip Hop push the bass up in the 30-60 Hz range. And some time slightly higher in the 70-100 Hz range, but do not over do this. If the bass sounds *'muddy'* try reducing the 200-220 Hz range by at least 3 dB as a starting point but be careful not to affect the low-mid girth negatively.

A common complaint with bass guitars is string noise this can be cut by reducing the 2-5kHz rage start at -2 dB and then go lower with -3 dB until the string noise is tamed with out damaging the bass sound.

Acoustic Guitar: When you have to mic a guitar you will often find boomy low end note in the 20-70 Hz range. Although it can add warmth and fullness, it will more often cloud up a mix with a full band. It should be removed with a high pass filter before trying to cut with EQ filters.

Since acoustic guitars are mostly made of wood, most of their sound lives in the 200-400 Hz range. So be careful when cutting here as it is too easy to flatten the tone. If the track is **too 'muddy' sounding reduce a little at the 200 HZ range.** To give the sound more weight boost the 250-400 range. This is good for to boost a solo but beware it may create conflicts in a dense mix, so attenuate here if that's the case.

As previously stated, boost the middle to high end can add warmth and fullness to the acoustic guitar. To do this increase the 500 to 1kHz range. To give it clarity increase the 1.5 – 2.5 kHz range. Do this by a step-by-step process and if you boost it too far it can make guitar sound aggressive and harsh. To make it sound brighter boost the 5-10 kHz range. If is still off try boosting the 10-12.5 kHz and 12kHz spots to achieve desired result.

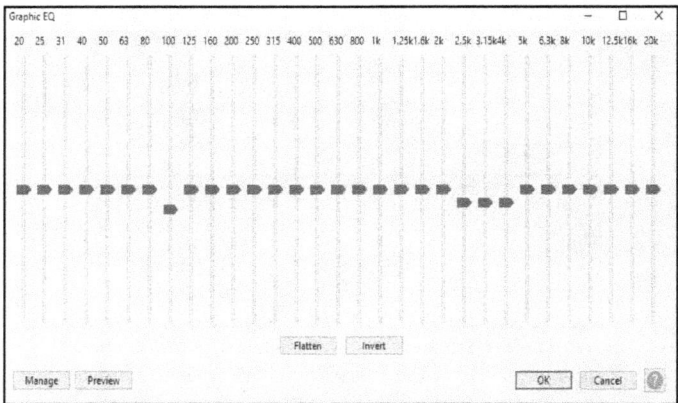

Fig 11-33 An EQ for electric guitar to cut the muddy sound and give some extra punch on the high end.

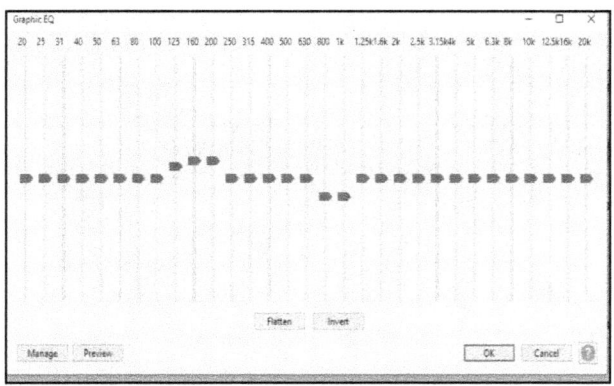

Fig 11-32 An EQ Setting for a warm sounding Acoustic guitar.

Electric Guitar: If there was scepter for the Rock and Roll Gods it would have to be in the shape of an electrical guitar. No other instrument dominates music like it does. And adding the right EQ and make the scepter glow brightly.

If recorded from an amp the hum can be reduced with reducing the 50-63Hz range, this can also be used to reduce the hum from an effect like a distortion box that is plug directly into the computer. To boost fullness sound with a boost at the 250 Hz slider and just a little bump 3db at the most around 2.5 kHz. Reduce to remove boom on guitars and increase clarity reduce at 100 Hz. Reduce at 2.5KHz to remove dullness of guitars. Reduce at 3kHz to disguise out of tune guitar. Reduce at 5kHz to soften a thin guitar. To add sharpness, increase at the 7kHz range.

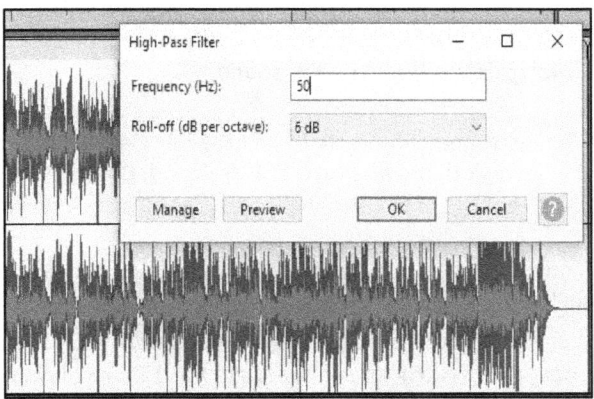

Fig 11-33 Our song "Another Love Song" is more Electric piano based, so the first thing we do even before apply EQ was roll off 50Hz on a high pass filter. this will give us more head room in the mix to use other instruments. This is done by selecting the track clicking Effect> High Pass Filter, and type in the Frequency you want to roll off and select the amount. In this case 6 dB.

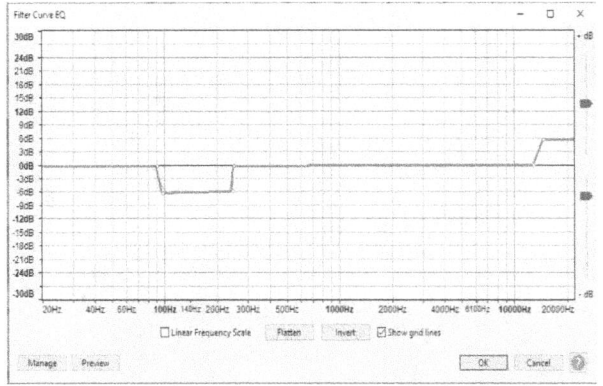

Fig 11-34 Frequencies can be cut or increase with the Filter EQ tool, this is a little harder to use, then the graphic EQ.but there are two different types of cut a narrow and wide cut.

Keyboards

Piano: Run the piano through a high pass filter to get rid of the 40-50 Hz range and save headroom.
This is an important setting if you mix bass heavy music.
 If the piano is sounding muddy boost 150-250 Hz slightly, and this should give the instrument a warmer feel. To added fullness if you want to warm the instrument up. Boost around 80 – 120 Hz for fullness. Try narrow cuts at 2 kHz or 3 kHz to keep a piano from conflicting with the vocal and guitar tracks.

 Boosting in the 3-5kHz range will brighten the instrument up and add presence. Beware of the string damper noises that occupy this range will increase also, but you may need this for creative reasons. To increase the clarity of the piano along with breath increase the 7-9 kHz. +Boost the 10-11 kHz frequency range to add sharpness, cut it to make the piano sound darker. Reduce 14-15 kHz to soften excess sharpness and make it sound warmer. If you are hearing the piano's hammer noise it can be cut by cutting the 10-13 kHz range Check 10-12.5 kHz

Electric Keyboard: While it might sound a little like a piano there is a difference especially if is in the Electric piano sound format. Use a high pass filter to cut the low end of the 40-50 Hz. Electric piano can quickly sound muddy this rest in the 100-250 Hz range. To make the electric piano stand out increase the 15-25 kHz range.

Synthesizer: Use a high pass filter and good judgement to get rid of the low end 80-160 Hz to taste and use good sound design judgement.

 Many synths become muddy in the 250-400 Hz range and can directly affect the quality of the tone and sound – especially if multiple synthesizers are layered. So be sure to check for muddiness within this range, if need cut to reduce the muddy sound.

 To make the synth stand out lift the frequencies within 1-2kHz range. By decreasing it can make it hide. Increasing the 2-kHz range will add more presence and to help the instrument cut through the mix.
 Just like the guitars and vocals, you can find the exciting, airy tonal characteristics by boosting the 3-4kHz range. Just like the others, too much can lead to being unpleasant. If you boost the 7-9 kHz frequency range, you to add more sharpness and clarity to the instrument in the mix.

Harmonica:

Be all that it is the harmonic a is reed instrument and takes some of its Eq rating from other reed instruments. Most sounds for the Harmonicas live I the 200 Hz and 7kHz block: a little boost here is useful. Set 800 Hz at 0. If you want it to cut through the mix better boost the 1.6 kHz range. Remove a little from the 3.15k Hz range. At the 6.3khz remove 5db to 10db. **This instrument doesn't usually use the frequencies.** From 8-10kHz you attack the shrilling of the instrument by reducing to cut it back or increase it to make it come forward.

ORCHESTRAL INSTRUMENTS

Use a high pass filter to eliminate the 40-50 Hz to get rid of unnecessary low end. Boosting the 80-100Hz range will deliver more sound while boosting the 100-300 Hz will add more warmth. The muddy sound happens in the 200-500 Hz, if it is occurring cut back on this range. Try boosting 400-600 Hz to add more roundness and fullness. To add more attack to the track, boost the 500-1 kHz to soften it, reduce this range.

String noise are always a problem with any stringed instrument here you will need to tweak the 2-5 kHz range for bringing string **noises more to the front if that's the desired** effect, or back to eliminate them.

High shelf boosting of the 7-10 kHz band brings more creak of the bows while 8-12 kHz will bring more sparkle and extra air to a string section.

Woodwinds

Bassoons: Use a high pass filter from 50-60Hz upwards to get rid of unnecessary low end. Carefully cut mud within the 60-250 Hz range.

Clarinet: Again, use a High Pass filter set for 120-140 Hz range to clean up the low end. Muddiness will appear in the 200-300 Hz range for muddiness. Cut with narrow Q factor.

Flute: Use a high-pass filter to cut 200-250 Hz. Muddiness will be heard at the 250-400 Hz range for mud. If there cut carefully with a narrow Q factor. Softness will occur between 2-4 kHz if it is there reduced it. To brighten it up boost the 10-12 kHz range with high curve.

Saxophone: No other instrument has the great appeal in all types of music as the this sext sounding woodwind. Yes, it is a woodwind, even though it is made of brass as it uses a wooden reed for the sound. The use of high pass filter set at the upper limit of 100 Hz can lessen the lower tones.

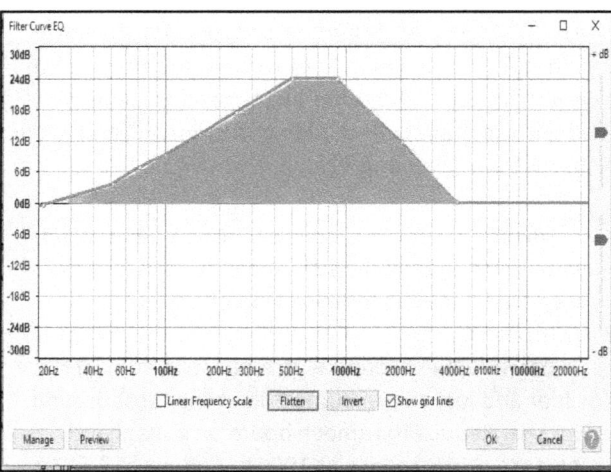

Fig 11-35 An Example of a wide Q- band increase

Some saxophones like a baritone sax, the low-mid frequencies may be found in the 120-400 Hz range. The deeper the instrument, the lower the range point becomes. Muddiness is usually founded in the 240-400 Hz band, carefully cut her to reduce the muddy sound. Boost 120-240 Hz range if you want a fuller sound.

All instruments have that one drawback and for the sax it the squawk that comes in a 1-2 kHz band. Cutting here can remove some of the shrillness and painful attack tones.

All woodwind instruments also can have reed noise. Where the reed vibrates, this tone is usually found around the 6 kHz range. To reduce the reed noise with a narrow Q factor. To boost the breathy tone, increase in the 12.5 kHz range. To less overblow cut in this same range.

Fig 11-36 An example of allow or narrow Q curve cut.

BRASS SECTION

Use a high-pass filter to cut up to 125 Hz to get rid of unnecessary low end and mud. But don't overdo, or the sound may be thinned out. Muddiness will appear in 200500 Hz range for mud, to bring out fullness boost 300-400 Hz with a moderate Q - curve. Boosting around the 800-1 kHz spot will add roundness. You can also try boosting at 5 Hz to add a brighter tone.

Dark sounding horns can be brightened up by increasing the 5- 10 kHz range. Manage this band of frequencies carefully. Too much can also destroy a mix with shrill and harsh high end. High curve boost around 5-8 kHz will add definition.

Tuba: A tuba has a deep low sound so be careful with low ends below 80hz and cut only when needed. To add fullness boost slightly at around 80 Hz to give the track a fuller, or "warmer" sound. Muddiness appears between the k 150250 Hz range for mud, cut with narrow Q factor. Reverberations can occur at the 500 Hz range if needed, cut with narrow Q factor.

Trombone: Like other brass instrument the use of high pass filter set at the upper limit of 100 Hz can help get rid of the low-end tones. However, with proceed carefully with a bass trombone, as you may cut out too much.

Boosting the 100-200 Hz frequency range to add fullness. Reduce at this range if it overlaps with more important low mid range instruments. For a brighter sound increase the EQ in the 4-8 kHz to add brightness and tweak in the 8-10 kHz to lessen the overblow.

Trumpet: Like other brass instrument the use of high pass filter set at the upper limit of 200 Hz can reduce to end sounds. Muddiness occurs in the 240-500 Hz range and can be reduced. However, doing this could reduce the full sound. To increase the fullness sound, boost slightly in the 160 to 500 Hz band. You lessen over bright with piercing tones by reducing the EQ in the 4- 5 kHz band.

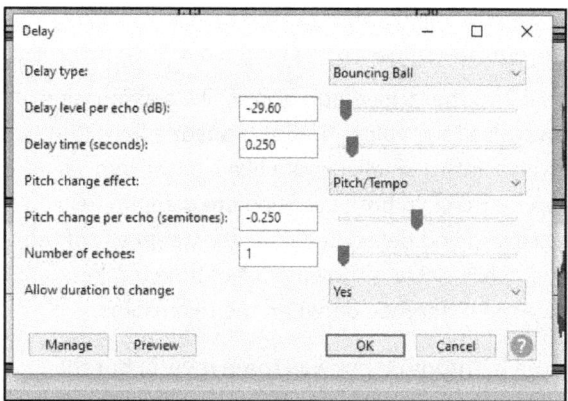

Fig 11-37 A great sound can be taking two identical channels and adding two different delays on each. Here we take a lead guitar. And place .25 ms on one side and .50 on the other. When listening with headphones, you will notice how the sound circles beginning one side then dying down in the other channel.

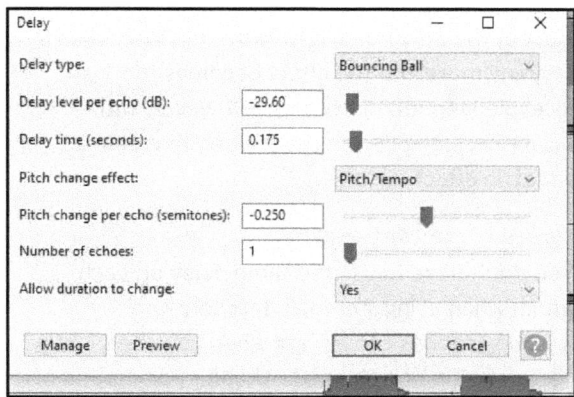

Fig 11-38 Applying little delay to a vocal track from .125-.200 can add some flavor to vocals, making them sound fuller. If you have two or more VOX track add the same amount of delay to each track, otherwise timing may be off. Note you may have to adjust other tracks the same amount to make sure it all sounds right.

DELAY OR REVERB

Walk into the large empty room, like a gymnasium and say in a loud voice, "Hello! Is anyone here?" Now walk into a smaller room like a bathroom say the same thing. In both case you are going to hear both reverb and delay. Reverb is the deepness of the sound, while delay is the amount of time it takes. Notice the difference between the two rooms.

In the bathroom there was some reverb, but the echo returned almost immediately, while in the gym the sound was deeper, but the echo took longer to return. Now yell this at the Grand Canyon, the delay will take even longer to return. Thus, reverb and Delay can work alone, or together.

Most of the time you will only use microseconds in delay, any more and the effect becomes too noticeable, and too distracting. However, with special effect long delays could work, to create a great echo effect.

Typical Delay Setups

You don't have to use the same delay on each channel when using stereo, in fact some on interesting sounds can be had when you use slightly longer delay on one channel. That big rock sound of the 1980's guitars can be created by placing a .025 ms delay on one channel and .050 or .075 ms on the other.

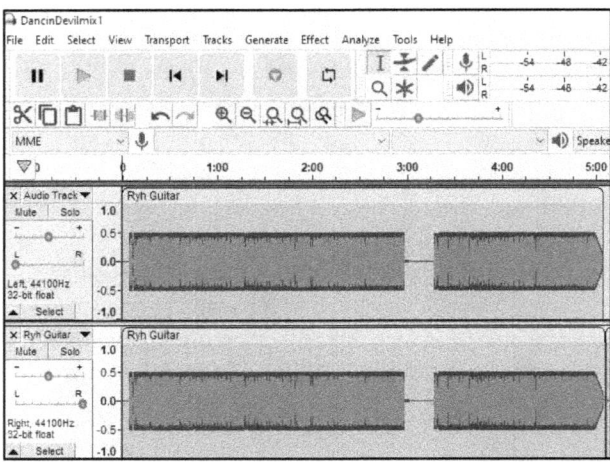

Fig 11-40 For that big two guitar playing at once sound. Set delay at .012 ms and hard pan each track.

To make a guitar sound larger than life use a delay of between .01 and .099 ms and use it only on one side. Pan the effect hard to one side and leave other side alone. Another way is to use a mono track with .010-.012 ms delay. Copy and paste into another track. Pan each of them hard to each side. It can sound like two guitarists playing the same thing. Another way is to pan the tracks to the middle and increase the delay to .025-.035 ms and the guitar will sound bigger.

Vocals are also great place to use delay. Using .175 to .200 ms on vocals can improve the sound and gives some depth. You can also change the pitch to a backing voice especially it I the same as the lead vocal to get more depth and feeling. Even change the type of echo effect. Say you have regular on the lead VOX have a bouncing ball effect for the backing vocals, this is especially true on OOOH and AHHH's.

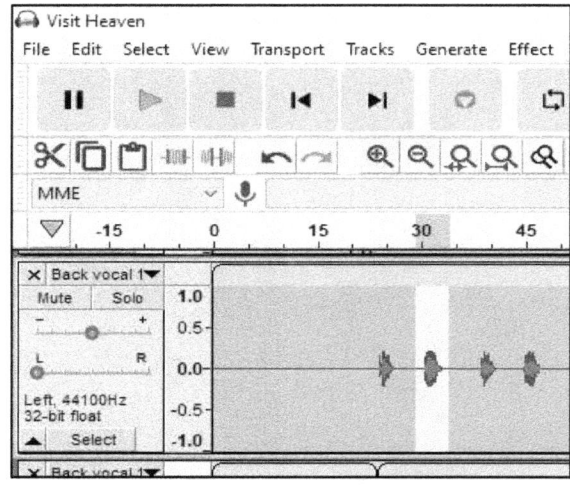

Fig 11-39 Using different delay and changing the pitch a little can bring backing vocal into their own.

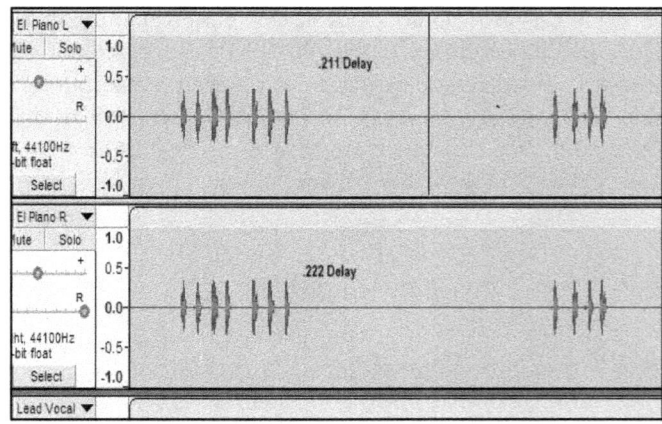

Fig 11-41 To add some flavor to a keyboard that plugged directly into Audacity then add .211 delay to one channel and .222 to the other.

For our song *'Visit Heaven'* which has a softer tone with Acoustic guitar we choose to palace a .175 ms delay on the lead VOX and a .125 ms delay with a .33 pitch change and bouncing ball effect for the backing OOOH's. This helped the backing vocals stand out a little more.

Have a dry sounding vocal, use delay to make it sound out. Use only a small amount of delay, and different amounts on the different channels. Start with .012ms on the left and .014 ms on the right. If still is not right bring up the delay by .01 ms until you can hear it in the mix, then back off one.

Setting up Reverb

Reverb can be used with or without delay effect. The biggest factors that will effect sound is the room size and the pre-delay.

Many professional audio engineers set their reverb according to the tempo of the song they are working on, thus a slower song will have longer pre-delay times. While a faster upbeat song will have faster pre-delay times. The formula for determining the Pre-delay is 60K/BPM. Thus, if you have a beat of 127 bpm It would be 60,000 divided by 472.44 or 472 rounded. Meaning .427 this is based on a quarter note, so we dived by 2 to make or for eighth notes and it comes down to .236 ms . Divide it again by two now for sixteenth notes it .118 ms, you can keep dividing in half until you reach a pre-delay that will work. Another way is to search for Delay & Reverb Time Calculator online. This will give you the set for your project.

This is not a set-in stone must that you use these number, it just a starting point and you can go up or down. If you want to avoid all that use the presets that Audacity has on the Manage>Factory Presets. This will give you a starting point and you can go up or down with the pre-delay times.

Even though the beat is the same the reverb and the amount used is different with each track. For example, with the Low dB band instruments-like the Kick Drum and Bass-you want to keep these 100 % dry in the mix. Too wet and the sound will shrink to nothing, no pun intended.

Use more reverb on the Tom-toms and cymbals than you do the snare drum. Use only enough reverb on guitars to push them behind the vocals. For vocals think of using salt, if you sprinkle a little on your veggies it brings out the flavor but sprinkle it on beef jerky or last pork and it will be leaving gasping for water. Just the right amount of reverb on vocals will flavor up the mix, while dousing the entire track with lots of reverb will ruin it.

You don't have to use the same amount of reverb for the whole track. You can use more in a verse and then less in the chorus. For remember the more reverb you use the further it sounds. So, it important that you keep the vocals up front.

You also apply reverb to one track and leave the other one alone, if you do this it is important to push the track to the middle otherwise you will have a split in sound. You can also send several tracks to a Bus Bar and added reverb to all there. We will cove this later on in the guide.

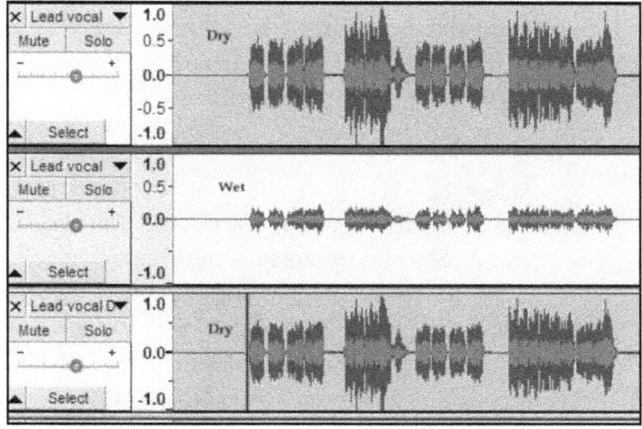

Fig 11-42 *You can added a Reverb as a single effect and place it in between two tracks that are dry then push it all to the center. This will give you over more control as to how much of the reverb is used.*

Typical Reverb Tips:

Audacity's **preset values are excellent stating points** and you leave there or tweak a little. However not keep the Dry and wet gain at zero or below this will keep it from growing in volume and prevent clipping. The amount of Reverb is controlled by the Reverberance slide to the left les and to the right more is added.

Vocal I and Vocal 2 are great presets for vocals with Vocal 2 have more reverb. Bathroom is great starting point for guitars especially an acoustic guitar. If you need a little more sound move up to Small Room. Bright has a more balanced tone, while dark set the low tone to max and the high tones to zero. Medium room is good for drums. Large room is good for pianos. Church is good for the organ and Cathedral works for orchestra instruments-especially when there are lots of them.

You may have noticed that you don't like the sound of when the add reverb to track or that it pegs the meters. You need to record only the reverb. How do you do that? Using on the wet. You may have clicked the box listened to it and though "Yuck!" Well, this is like eating a cake mix without the wet ingredients- you will choke on it-so don't try it. But when you mix the wet and the dry ingredients together-don't tell me you haven't licked the bowl. Same thing here when you mix the wet (the reverb) and the dry (the track without reverb) together. You come with a sweet sound. Also doing this way you independently control the levels of both the dry and the reverb.

Now select the track a click Edit>Duplicate Track or control D. A new track will duplicate at the bottom of all your other tracks. Now select this track. Click Edit>Reverb. Make you changes and preview. Now click the Wet Only check box. Click Okay. You will return to the project page. Now play the two tracks together, by soloing one and unclicking the mute button on the other, now you will hear the reverb on one channel only. Make sure you have both in the center or at the same place. Try placing them each at 30 degrees, a nice warm sound.

COMPRESSION

Of all the tools and effects use in recording this one that create a great mix, and at the same the one most likely to ruin a good mix. You will use it now, and in the mastering section. Do NOT use compression on a single instrument track if it is in stereo. Compression on stereo track should only be done in the mastering mix.

Audio compression is the reduction of the dynamic range of an audio track by attenuating the loudest parts and raising the volume of the quietest parts of the audio signal. The main use is to smooth out instruments that are too loud or too soft. In other words when you play the track back some burring the meter into the red and other are not even getting out of the green, and when played back with the other tracks can't even be heard.

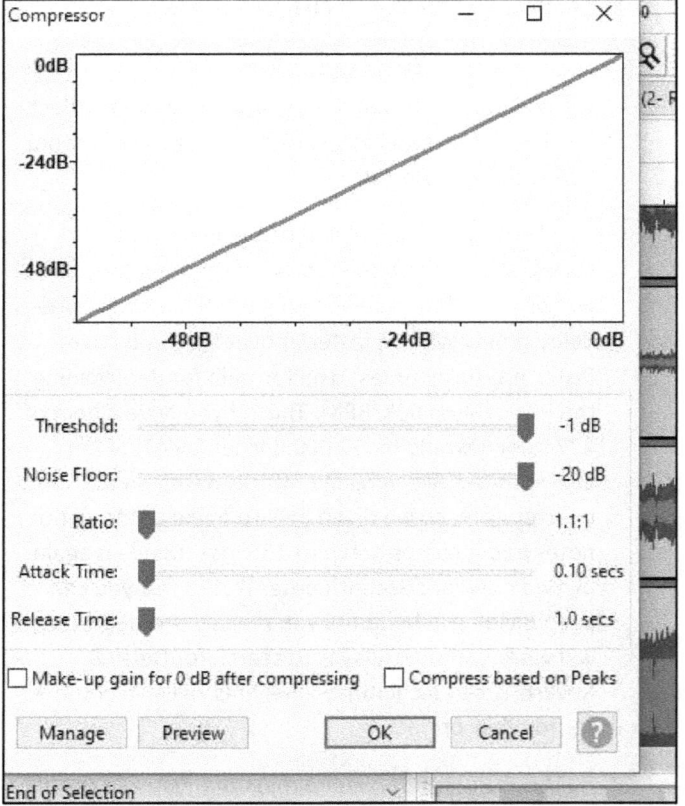
Fig 11-43 the Audacity compressor.

BASIC COMPRESSION SETTINGS

Again, as in most cases there are no set-in stone rules of that you use certain numbers with the compressor with certain tracks. Each one is going to be different, and you just have to play around with the setting to find what you like. What we are going to give you are just some basic settings that you can start with and work up or down from there.

Some instruments can be over loud, bass, drums and even the singer. There are parts of the song that are sung softly, then in comes the chorus and suddenly it gets loud. Compression can control all of that.

If you don't get it right the first time and you likely won't. Click Ctrl Z or the Undo button. Don't go back and redo the compression, adding more or reducing from the point you just heard, not the original track. The best way is to add a little or reduce a little check it by playing it solo, watching the meters at the top of the page. Then with the other tracks until you get it right. Then go on to another track if there are more tracks to compress.

Just like with Reverb, you don't have to add compression to every track, just the ones that need fixing. Note that when you change one track it will likely affect the others. And when you change another, it may affect the one you just did. So you may have to go back and readjust each type you make a change.

Do Not apply compression as a fit all bandage. What works for one song may not work for another. So be sure to keep record of your changes on your studio log sheet. If you want to apply a chorus effect, it would be best that you apply it before doing compression. This effect does not come with Audacity there is a few plug-ins available for it on the internet. Plus, in another chapter we will show up how to duplicate a chorus effect on Audacity using the tools it has. This is found in Chapter xxx page xxx. Remember to add the effects, before you apply compression.

Since most compressor setting you will find are for the classic 1773 compressor and do not use the same tools that the compressor that Audacity uses, we have included some recommendations and starting points. Since compression effects the tracks that you have already done, we will work backwards from the way mixed, starting with vocals and working back to the base rhythm section.

VOCALS

Backing Vocals: Just as the name implies, they should remain in the background, you don't want a lot of compression, but at the same time you don't want them hidden. They must have a presence but never overshadow the lead vocalist. They need just enough compression to bring them out.

Backing Vocals Recommended Settings
Threshold	-4 dB-6dB
Ratio	2:1-3:1
Attack	.10 seconds
Release	.35 -.40 seconds

Lead Vocals: Seems everyone recommends that some compression be use on all lead vocals to smooth them out and bring them forward in the mix. It can at the same time bring up the soft tones and tame those screams that create distortion. With vocals you should not hear the compressor working. A good setting should have a fast attack and quick release, to long of these and it will change the singer's sound- and not for the better-you just want it to come on quickly and smooth the sound. The type of music and sex of singer will have some effect on the settings. Female vocals need less compression than a male vocal, and rock and rap vocals need more than pop vocals.

Male Lead Vocals Recommended Settings
Threshold	-3-6 dB
Ratio	2:1 -4:1
Attack	.10
Release	.35-.40

Female Lead Vocals Recommended Settings
Threshold	-6-8 dB
Ratio	1:5-3:1
Attack	.10
Release	.35-.40

Rock and Rap Lead Vocals Recommended Settings

Threshold	-5-8 dB
Ratio	4:1--6:1
Attack	.10
Release	.35-.40

Instruments

Guitars

Electric:

In most causes you won't need a compressor on an electric guitar track, with one exception-a clean guitar, and you want to bring it out in the track. A slow attack is the key to bring it forward. If it brings it out too much you can short the attack time. Warning you and quickly cause a clean guitar that has no distinct sound.

Electric Guitar Recommended Settings

Threshold	-1-3 dB
Ratio	2:1-3:1
Attack	.25-30 seconds
Release	1-2 seconds

Acoustic Instruments: You don't need a lot of compression on stringed instruments that are plunked. The time to use it is when it is the main instrument and you want to keep it that way, up front in the mix. We used compression on the guitar for our "Dead Roses". This kept it and the vocals up front and keep the sustain. If you don't want the sustain, cut back ratio and the attack and release times

Acoustic Guitar Recommended Settings (Sustain)

Threshold	-4—6dB
Ratio	3:1-4:1
Attack	1.50 seconds
Release	2-4 seconds

Acoustic Guitar Recommended Settings (NO Sustain)

Threshold	-4—6dB
Ratio	2:5.1-3:1
Attack	.40-.75 seconds
Release	1-2 seconds

Bass: Bass guitars recorded through an amplifier or distorted can get muddy sounding quickly and compression can help with this. The key to this to have a medium to long attack time.

Bass Guitar Recommended Settings

Threshold	-4—6dB
Ratio	2:5.1-3:1
Attack	.40-.80 seconds
Release	1-2 seconds

Drums: Kick Drums: Kick drums respond well to compression and can tame the 'boom' sound. Us a medium attack time and a slow release.

Snare Drums: If you want a tight, punchy sound from the snare then compression is a must. They are many different settings but a common one is shown below.

Kick Drum Recommended Settings

Threshold	-5-8 dB
Ratio	4:1--8:1
Attack	.40-.75 seconds
Release	2-3 seconds

Snare Drum Recommended Settings

Threshold	-4-6 dB
Ratio	4:1--6:1
Attack	.10-.25 seconds
Release	1.25-1.75 seconds

Tom-Tom Drum Recommended Settings

Threshold	-5-8 dB
Ratio	4:1--8:1
Attack	.40-.75 seconds
Release	2-3 seconds

Listen each track after you applied compression alone, and then with other tracks, especially how the newest compression track sounds with those that you have already compressed. You may have to go back and redo. It is wise to make a backup before applying compression. As compression is one that can really mess up the sound. So, it is good to have a backup without any compression applied.

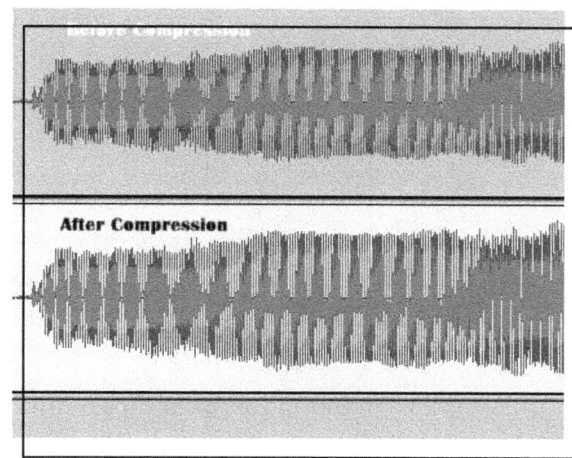

Fig 11-44 Shown the effects of applying compression.

LIMITER

If compression had a cousin, it would be the limiter. The difference is the setting of the ratio and application. Anytime a compressor is set at 10:1 or higher that result is considered a limiter. However, like where there is no speed sign you might claim you didn't know the speed limit. The limiter on the other hand is billboard size sign flashing in bright colors what the speed limit is, and right behind you is a cop car. You are not going to go over the speed limit. Thus, once a limit is set, it will not go over that amount. It is mainly for speaker protection and not used much in mixing. It is good for creating headroom creating a maximum level of the track. And it is good in mastering.

EQ AGAIN

Now that you have run some effects it is time run the EQ again as they seem to mess up the EQ bands. This is also where we can combat the sibilance. By reducing and cutting at the 4- 12K range. And run it through a low pass filter at the are the sibilance occurs. Listen carefully to the track noting where this occurs, it helps to have a copy of the lyrics nearby to refer to.

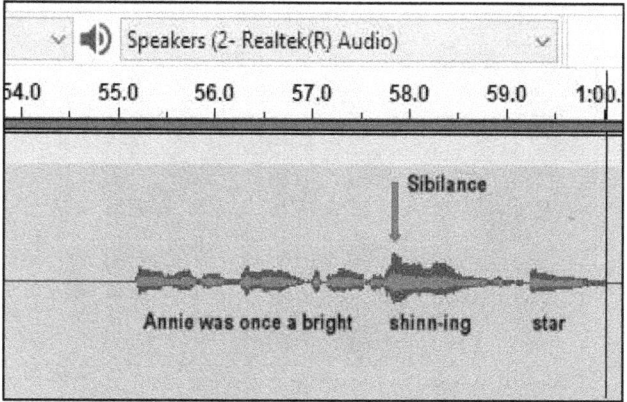

Fig 11-45 It is a wave with the lyrics of our song "Dead Roses" under it. Notice that not ever 'S-word' triggers it. The word 'star' did not while the word shinning push it up.

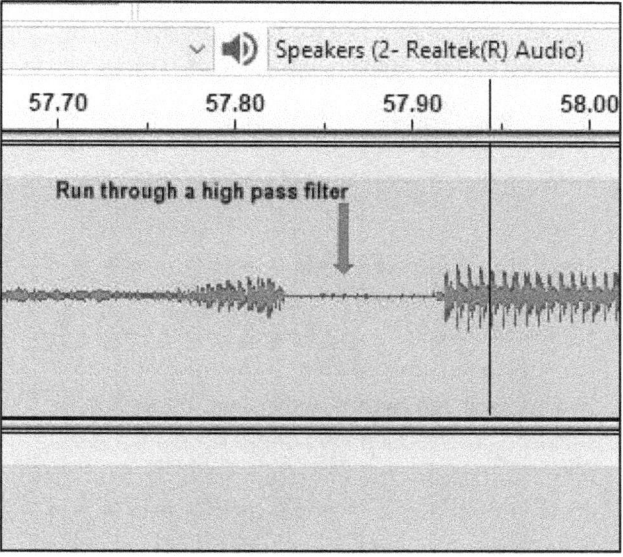

Fig 11-46 Now we will use this point of say 10- up with a high pass filter. Check how it sounds, if necessary, cut again. Or click Ctrl Z to undo the changes. There are no set values. But most sibilance occurs at 3-10K. Notice the above photo and how it has been cut. Don not cut the whole track, it will not sound good, only the point where sibilance occurs. Also be sure to fade in and fade out the beginning and endings of the filter area, include the un effected track it makes for a smooth transition.

SPITFISH

Fig 11-47 *Spitfish is available from the website in the photo for a free download.*

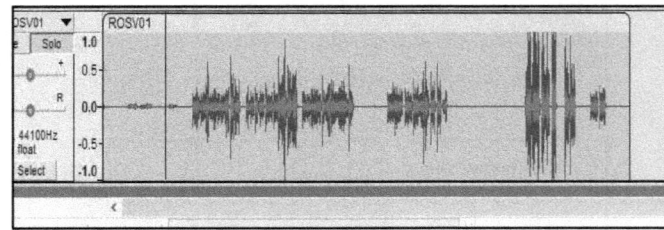

Fig 11-48 *The raw voice track for Dead Roses.*

Fig 11-49 *The same track cleaned up, and ran through EQ, Compressor and Spitfish.*

Spitfish is an aftermarket plug-in that works with Audacity providing you have the 32 bit system, at the time of this writing it will not work with 64 bit system. It is one of the simplest plugs and De-esser to use. Once you install it, it available by clicking on effects and then Spitfish. The above photo will show up.

Now click listen...**you likely won't hear anything.** To hear increase the Sense knob by clicking on it and slowly turn the knob to the right, until there is something to sense. Then turn the tune knob by clicking on it and twist it to the right, until hear the sibilance. Now click on the depth knob and twisting it over to the right to hear it removed. To hear how it sounds without the changes click bypass. To achieve the maximum, make sure the soft button is unclicked. It will only take a small amount of depth to remove it. This is great to use with cymbals, which can also create sibilance.

If the change is too drastic, then click the soft button. This will switch it a slower mode and creates softer transition curve. Now you can use a little more depth. The thing is do not overdo it, as the human ear except some of this sound if you are singing a song telling a story about *"Sassy Sally and Silly Will Sam"*. Best thing is just using your ears, what sounds the best.

If you have stereo track, make sure to click the stereo button to let the unit know it is stereo tracks. Once you have it make sure **you don't have bypass** clicked and close it will apply the changes.

Chapter 12 Mix it Up and Mix Well Part 2

Last chapter we processed the music through all the processors to make sound better. This chapter we are going to mix the sounds so that they sound as if they belong together. We will show you how create the dimension of sound and how to create subgroups, so in the final mix you don't have so many tracks to work with. Also going to cover how to create your own background voices. And building up the sound with a double track- and that is where we are going to start.

DOUBLING A TRACK

If you have a weak track that seems to just be overshadowed by the others one of the best ways is to simply the double the track. Now you can go back and rerecord the track, which is the best and will provide the best sound. Or you can simply duplicate track by selecting it and then typing Ctrl D. the duplicated track will appear at the bottom. Note this will duplicate all the effect you applied to the track, if you want the original track, open your original project that you made the copy from select copy and then paste into the new project. Then close your original file, making sure you do not save the changes. When you add a new track, it is at the bottom, you may have to move the track up to be next to the others like it. Now you may have to clean up the pasted track and add any effects that you would want to use.

Creating Your Own Backup Singers

If you are lucky, you have others that can provide backup vocals, but many of us don't have that luxury. So, we must create our own choir and chorus effect.

Use a Chorus Pedal

One way if you have a chorus pedal for guitar, it can also be used for voice. You must place it between the microphone and the interface. This will require several trials and errors to get the sound just right, and when you do, write the adjustments of the pedal down. Now record the track again where the backup singers would be.

Note you don't need to record the whole track again, instead only the chorus of the song. You can then go back change the pedal effect slightly just to change the voice a little and record another track, now you have three vocal tracks. The lead and two backup vocals. But because the chorus pedal works by changing the timing and the pitch and creates a different sounding voice. Another benefit is the pedal acts as a preamp, and you don't need one. Now you change the settings a little and record a new track, add two or three and you have created your own back up group with your own group.

Fig 12-1 A Chorus pedal (like this one from Boss) can be used to change the voice and create your own backup singers.

Create Your Own Chorus Effect

What if you don't have a Chorus pedal? You can create your own by recording a new track then tweaking it a little. *Why not just duplicate the track?* Duplicating the track, just causes the lead voice to be upped in power, they are the same exact wave file. But when you sing the exact same thing. It is not the same wave file, no matter how you try, and it gives a better sound.

Plug in your headphones and microphone. Open Audacity. Open the project, making sure it is at the beginning of the song. Now type SHIFT R. A new stereo track will appear at the bottom and will be recording. Listen to the tracks playing and then sing where you want to add the chorus effect. This is usually done in the chorus but can be anywhere. As in case with our song '*Gambling Woman*', when the lead singer mentions her, the back singers come in with '*ooo Gamblin Woman'*. When done, click stop and listen. Now you will likely have to clean up the track to get rid of the noise.

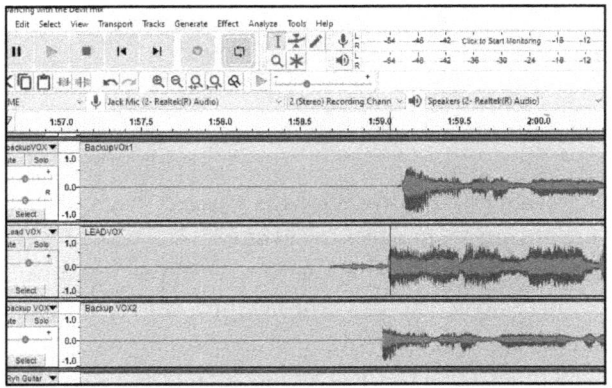

Fig 12-3 *Now zoom in grab the track with time shift tool, or the handles or the new version of Audacity and move one track slightly to the left and the other to the right. Play it back and see if you have the timing right, if It is too noticeable shrink the space, if not enough, add a little more.*

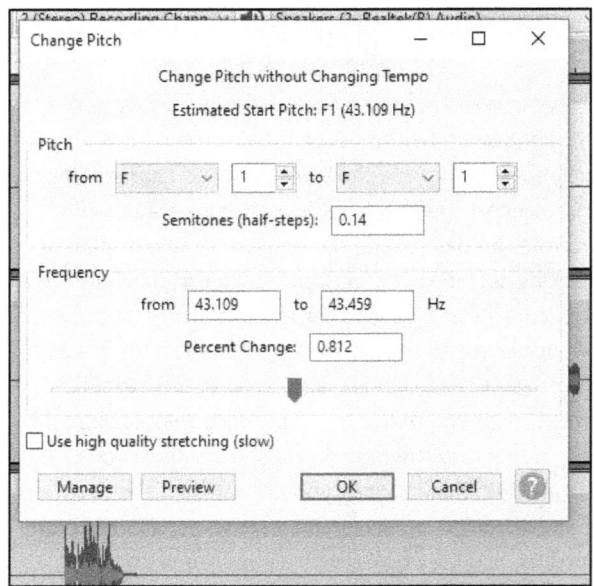

Fig 12-3 *Now select one track again, but not the lead vocal. Click Effects>Pitch change. Change the pitch by only 1 or 2 Semitones, Click Ok and see how it sounds. Now go to the other track and select it. Again, click Effect> Change Pitch and go up or down .1 or .2 semitones. Check to see how it sounds. You can go back a change the pitch again if want. Or add more voices.*

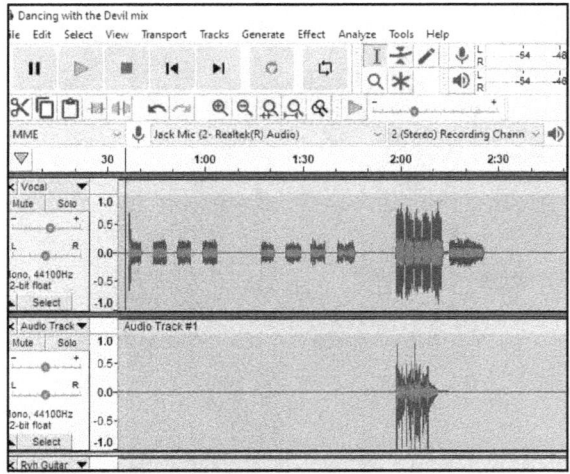

Fig 12-2 *Notice the difference between the lead vocal wave and the overdub.*

What would happen if you recorded a vocal say your cousin who is a great singer was visiting and recorded your song for your podcast but went back home thousands of miles away. But you want to add background vocals. You can duplicate the track, and then use the same method use above with pitch moving the tracks. It will not sound quite as good as the other method. But it will work. Just silence the parts you don't want to be effect by a chorus effect.

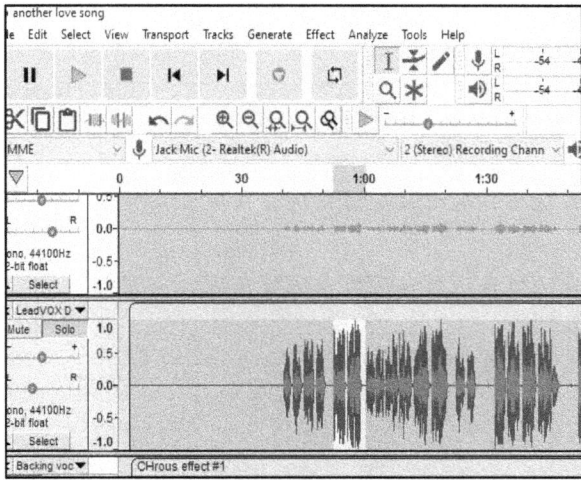

Fig 12-5 To add a harmony section. We selected pre-chorus of this song on only one channel of the lead vocal. The upped the octave +.1 in the pitch change. This created a building sound going towards the chorus, which is what you want.

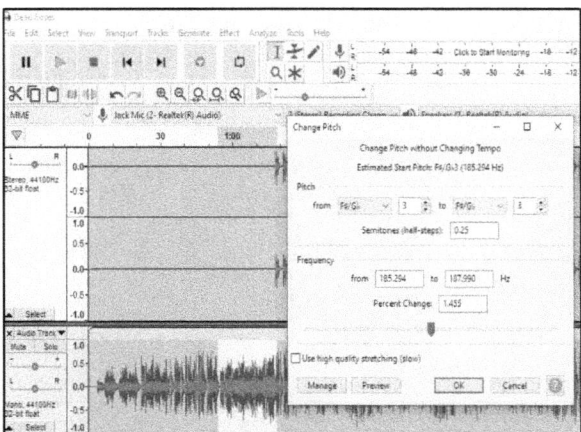

Fig 12- 6 The chorus effect and the harmony effect can also be used on instruments. Here out acoustic guitar is picking out single notes on the verses and we upped the octave a little to create a more harmonic sound. You may have to readjust the EQ band to make the two works together.

Creating a Bouncing Stereo Effect

With an outside mixer you could pull the slides back and forth as you were mixing panning them to each side. If you have stereo track each channel panned hard to the left and the right. You can move them to the right or to left. However, you are moving both channels. If you want more coming from the left channel and different amount coming from the right. You will have to split the stereo track.

Click to the downward arrow on the track and then click Split Stereo Track, this will give us two separate tracks. Again , each one will be hard panned 100%, but you can use 30% on left and 60% or whatever you want on the right. Do not make them back into a stereo track or you will lose the mix you have.

Another one is making the sound jump from one channel to the other. Again, spilt the stereo track. If it a mono track duplicate the track by clicking 'Shift D' if you need to move the track up next to the other where it is just below the original track. It is easier if they are side by side.

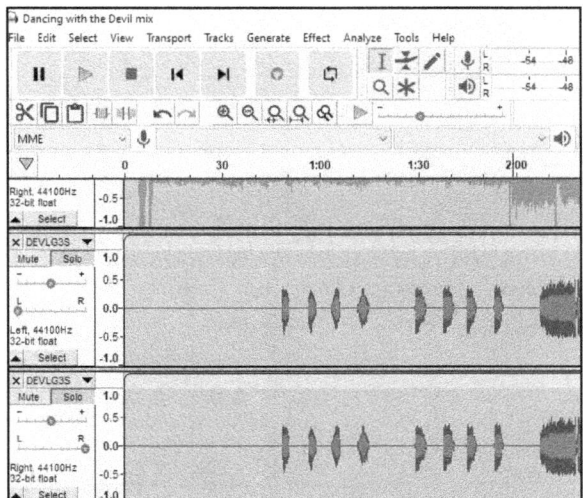

Fig 12-7 What we are going to do is make the guitar riff move. The first one will be on the right and the next on the left. The third one will be in the center and the fourth one will start on the right, and end on the left.

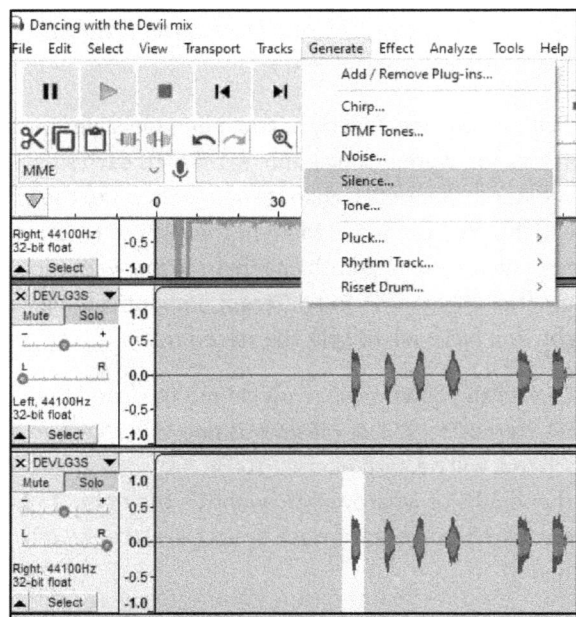

Fig 12-8 Select one of the wave in one of the channels. Then click Generate>Silence>OK.

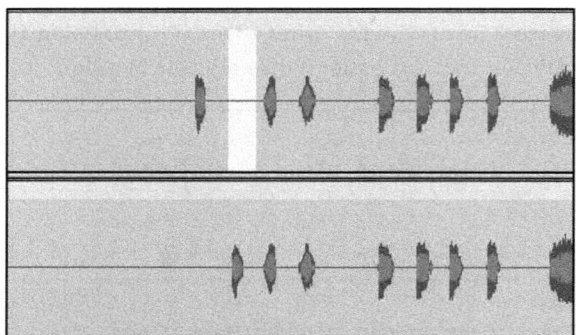

Fig 12-9 Now we repeat the silence but this time to opposite channel on the second wave. Notice how the wave disappears.

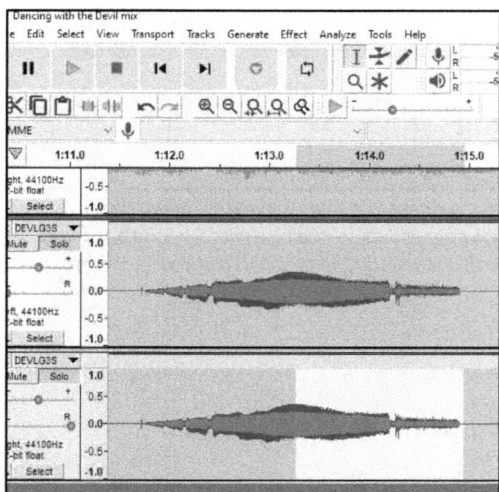

Fig 12-10 Now we are going to split a wave. Zoom in until you one single wave marks the point are going to split it at. Since it is going to start on the right and end on the left. We select the back half and then click Generate>Silence>OK.

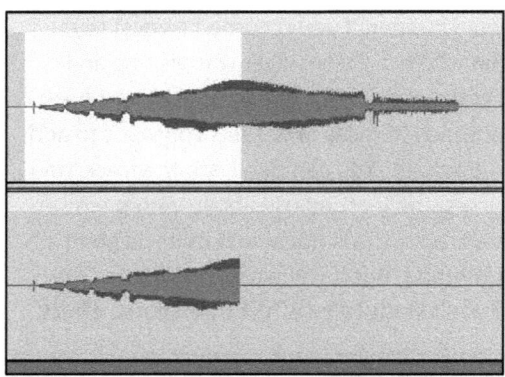

Fig 12-11 *Now we select the front part in the Left track and silence it.*

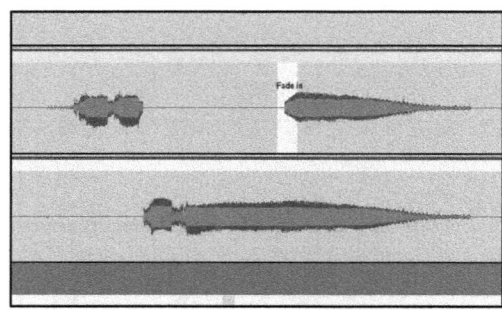

Fig 12-12 You can also cut from one channel to another channel back to both channels with a slight overlap. A good idea would be to add a fade on the channel that is switching over. This will create a circling effect of the sound. It is fine is short amounts like tom-toms going quickly from one channel to another. But do not overdo it, having everything do this all the time. It becomes predictable and boring to listen to

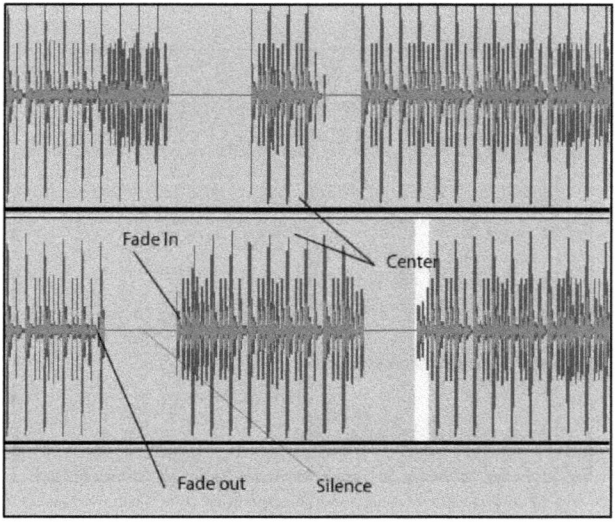

Fig 12-13 *this will create a sound that moves from one side to the center to the other side and the back to center. Use this sparingly or it will get boring real quick.*

Now you added these tracks with your other tracks you likely have a huge amount of tracks, and it is hard to control. And since you have added the effects the all the individual track you wanted it added to now is time to mix these tracks down in a subgroup. Meaning we are going to mix all the drums together and that will be a group and the guitars together and that will be a group, all the vocals and so on each will be a separate group that will have a special place in the mix.

BOUNCING TRACKS

Overdubs on top of overdubs have been a staple since the beginnings of multiple track recordings. This was done by bouncing tracks. Example we have four tracks; track 1 vocals track 2 guitars, track 3 bass now we have track 4 empty, but we still want to add a piano, bass and backing vocals. We mix tracks 1-3 and record them on track 4, these tracks are all one track-track four. This leaves track 1-3 to record the bass, piano, and back vocals. However, we have decided we want to add a distorted lead guitar, but we **don't have** any empty tracks. With bouncing we can record all the track on a single track and open up the three tracks again. And we can add the lead guitar and maybe Rock organ. The thing is you can keep doing this. The problem is sound begins to fade a little with each bounce, so you can only do so much.

Audacity is at its best around 30 track recorder, before it gets so blogged down that even the fastest computer can keep it running quickly. Unlike other true Multiple track recorders there is no bounce function in Audacity. But you can create one. This is good to use when you have lots of multiple tracks open, not only does the program run slowly it gets hard to find the right track you want to use.

What we do is create a-*subgroup*. A subgroup is a group of tracks that have a similar function or group. For example, we have separate tracks for drums; kick, snare, tom-toms, hi-hi-hats **and cymbals' that is six tracks.** We are going to mix these tracks together to create one single drum track.

You should have already applied all the compression, reverb and EQ effects to each individual tracks and these will remain when the tracks are joined together.

Now copy all the drum tracks for your project. Click File>New. A new project page will open. In the new file Click Tracks>Add New depending on the type of tracks you copied click either Mono or stereo. Do one for each of the tracks you copied and paste them into place.

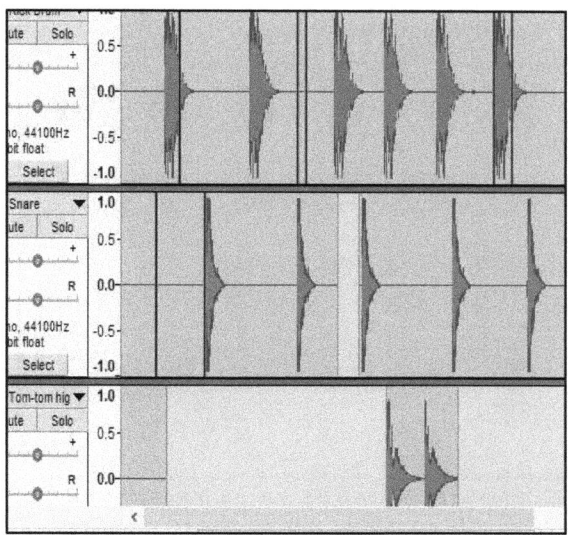

Fig 12-14 First step in creating a subgroup is copy and pasting the track to be joined. Here are the drum tracks.

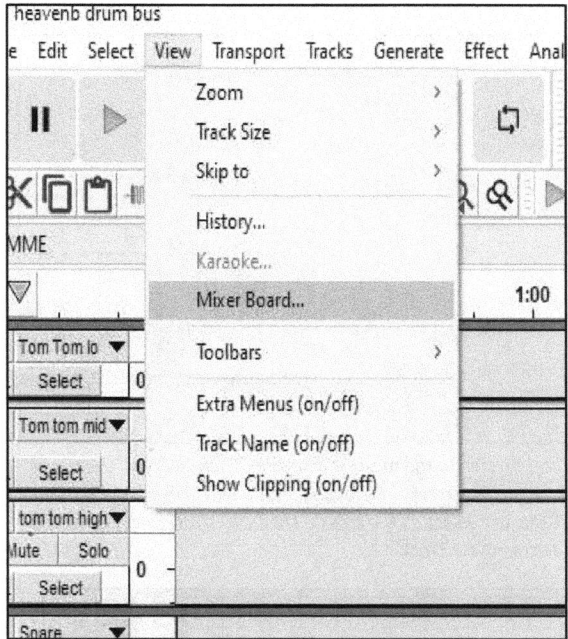

Fig 12-15 Click on View>Mixer board

181

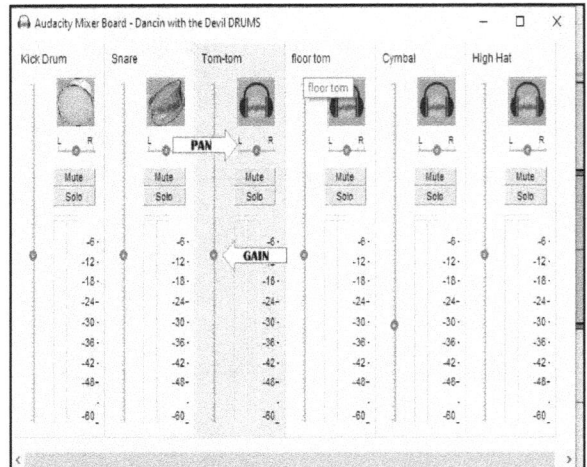

Fig 12-16 Mixing board, this is the chance to place each track in its stereo field and the gain levels. Press on space bar to play and click on the stop button to stop. Once in place and sound levels are right. Close the mixer board by clicking the X in the upper right hand corner.

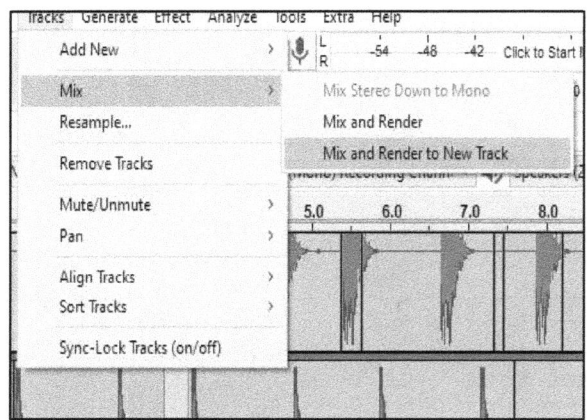

Fig 12-17 Listen to the mix one last time. Then select all the tracks. Click on the first track and holding Shift down Click on the bottom track this will select all the tracks. Then click Tracks>Mix>Mix and Render to a New Track.

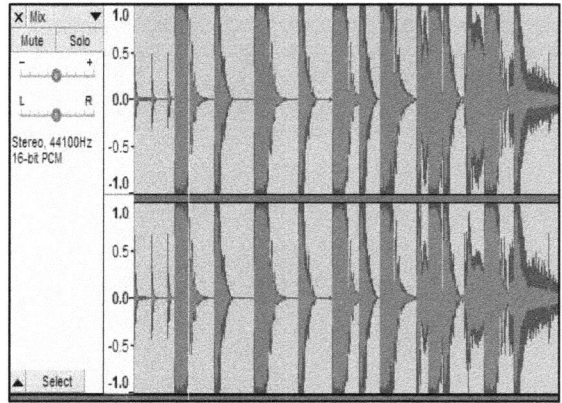

Fig 12-18 This will create a new track at the bottom called mix, this will be a mix of the selected tracks, that are mixed according to your mix. Rename the track copy the track and paste into your original project giving it a different name.

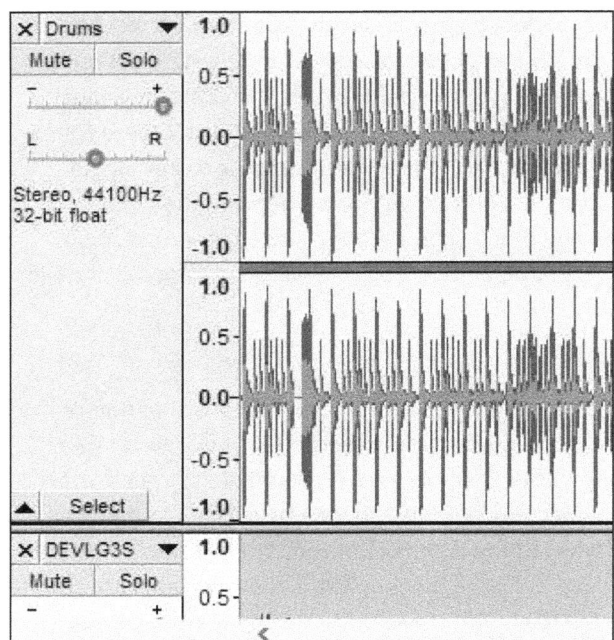

Fig 12-19 Remove the original tracks that you created this one from and play back, check how it sounds. With this we removed 6 separate tracks and combined them into one. The same thing can be done with multiple vocal tracks blending four lead vocal tracks into one, four separate backing vocal into on stereo track.

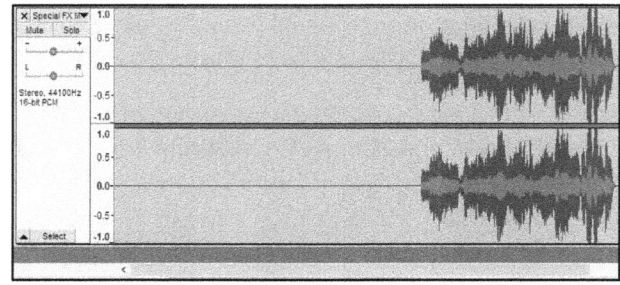

Fig 12-20 Here we mixed down ten different special effect tracks. On the song Angels Cry into one single stereo track and it includes all the special stereo switch from side to side that we had in the separate tracks.

Creating subgroups saves a lot of room and makes it easier for the final mix. For example, on our song *Angels Cry* we have tracks with a grand piano, rock organ, Strings, clean electric guitar, acoustic guitar, 6 drums, bass, O.D. guitar, distorted guitar, Lead VOX, backing vocals and choir vocals and ten channels of special effect all together 30 channels. By combining we got it down to 10, still quite few tracks but easier to work with than 30.

SPECIAL EFFECTS

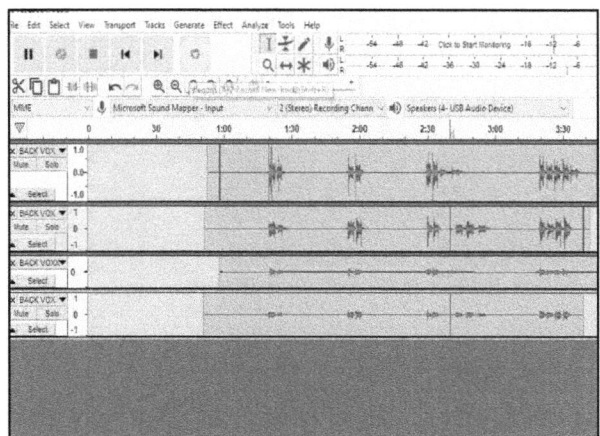

Fig 12-21 We have created two backing vocal tracks, each one having a slightly different tone. Compare the waves in track one and track two, and how different they appear. We then add a wet track (reverb) to each one.

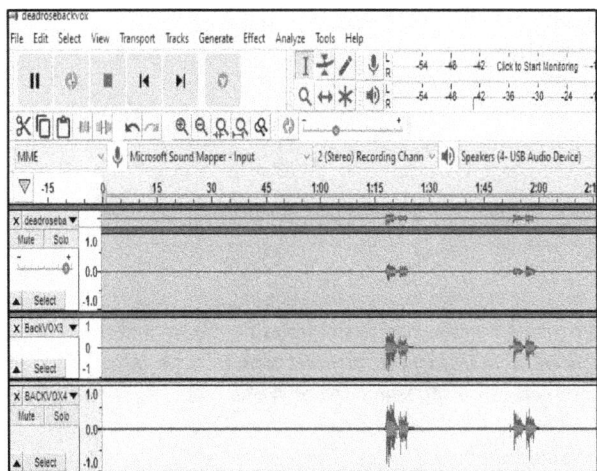

Fig 12-22 Now we add two more backup vocals to the subgroup of backup vocals we already have. Now we mix this down to a single stereo track. And created a heavenly choir for the song Angels Cry.

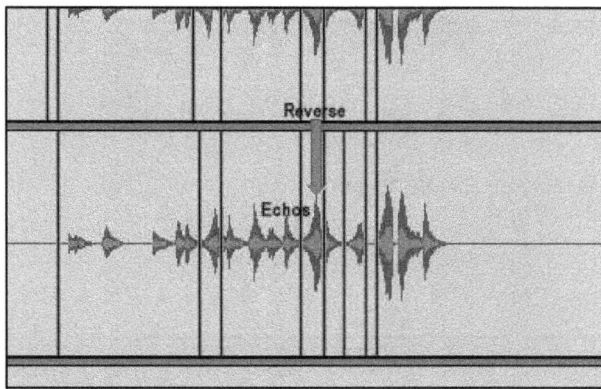

Fig 12-23 Adding echoes and Reverse to a voice and really change the sound. Here we added echoes to a deep laugh, and turned a voice track backwards, but allowed the echo to remain forward.

In the 1960's with the introduction of stereo taking over, bands learned that they could create a long-playing song with some strange sounds, that would not normally come from instruments and voices. They would sound spooky, and out of this world. Audacity lets you do this also. You can create all can of effects by pushing other effects to limit.

Reverse

One of the first special effect was playing something backwards. We have all heard the tales of the 'devil speaking on records in reverse. Form every band that tries this. And this still a good effect, if it is used wisely. Do this only in small amounts as a single phrase or word, or sound. Do it in deep tone, also helps. Also sounds a laugh played back backwards becomes something from the under words. We tried this in our song Angels Cry with reversing the words "is God laughing and we found the made-up nonsense words sounded better the reverse laugh. And the made-up words sound better, and if someone tries to play it back forward, they will get nothing, and their will hear what they want to hear.

We have been discussing vocals for reversing but don't forget about instruments a cymbal reverse creates an awesome out of this world sound. As does slightly tapping on the guitar string and putting it into reverse. Also mate the reverse with other effect like echo and fade in and out. To create even better effects.

How to Add Reverse: Choose a track you want to add this too and then zoom in to individual -waves, you only need to add this to a small amount to get the best result.

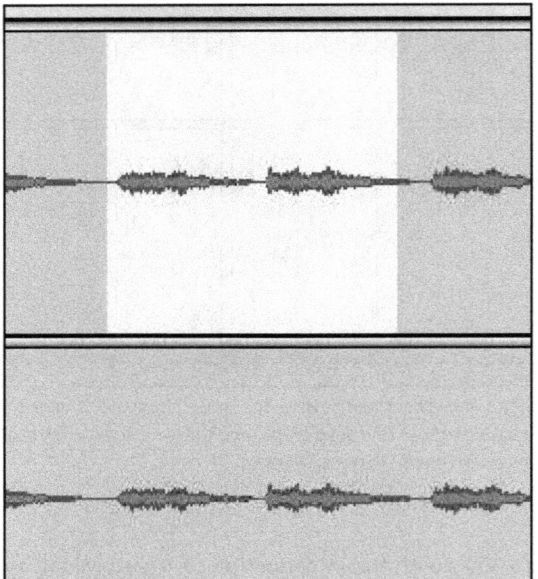

Fig 12-24 Select a small sample then click Effect Reverse. And the section will turn 180 degrees and will play backwards. Avoid long stretches of backwards playing as it gets boring too quick.

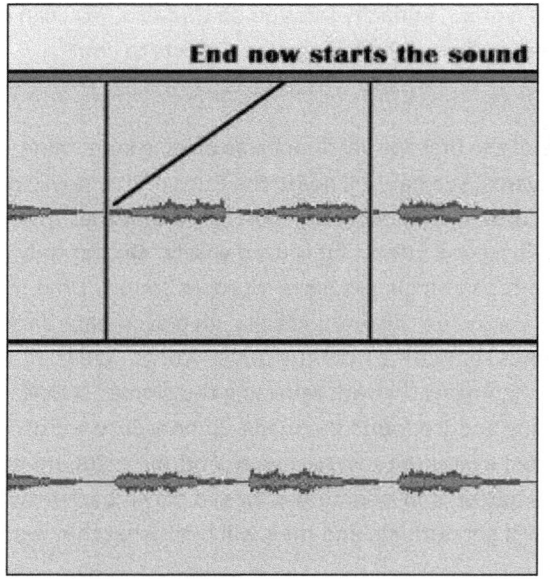

Fig 12-25 The wave will turn around and compare the two upper waves with the ones at the bottom that are forwards.

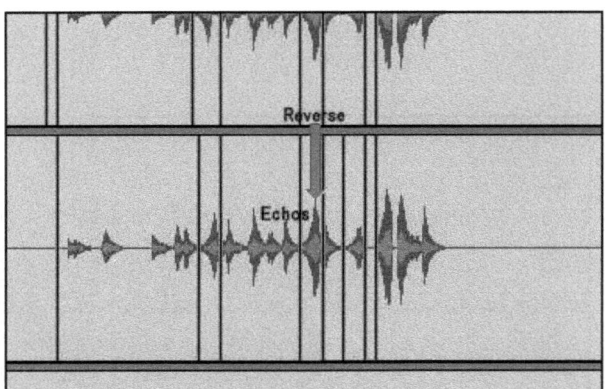

Fig 12-26 Adding echoes and Reverse to a voice-really changes the sound. Here we added echoes to a deep laugh, and turned a voice track backwards, but allowed the echo to remain forward.

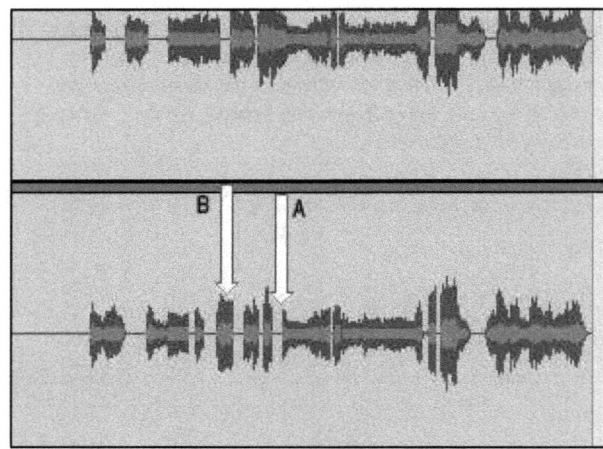

Fig 12-27 When adding special effects, think outside of the box. Here we ran an electric keyboard through a Phaser guitar effect pedal, pushed to nearly to the max and then took the wave of the different channels removing some on one A and reversing the sound on one channel B. We also use a fade out and then reverse it, which gave a unique sound.

Select a small section such as a single cymbal strike or a single phase that is spoken. Next click Effect> Reverse and the wave will automatically reverse. To give it a stranger sound add an echo.

Echo and Delay: It is best to plan for these effects ahead of time, and the work best with other effects like fade out and fade in. In our song Angels Cry, we took the words *"waho, waho"* that were repeated quickly over and over again, added the delay feature with four echoes, and add a fade in at the front and a fade out at the back, pushing the fade in to one side and then in to the center and the fade out on the opposite channel. There are no set rules to use, it is just up to you. Again, like reverse applying this only a small amount works best, when it is applied a whole line, it gets over whelming, applying it to only a couple notes or words is better.

How to Add Echo or Delay: Choose a track to apply this too and zoom in until you see individual waves and apply it to a small amount of that track. Click Effects>Echo or Effects>Delay. If you want more than one echo, and the bouncing effect you hear on records, choose delay. Fill in the information and click okay and it will be applied to the track.

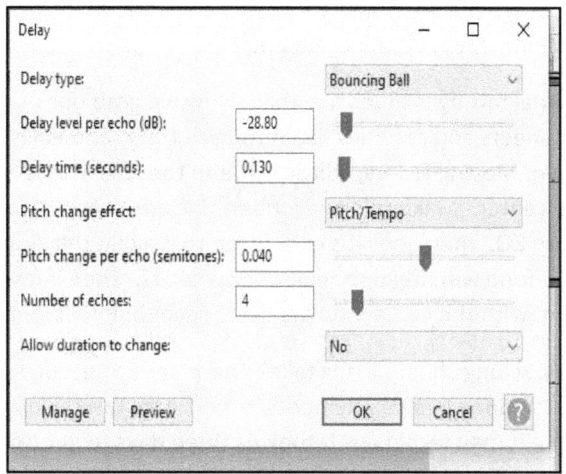

Fig 12-28 the 'Delay' tool. We choose short delay and 4 echoes to get the sound we wanted.

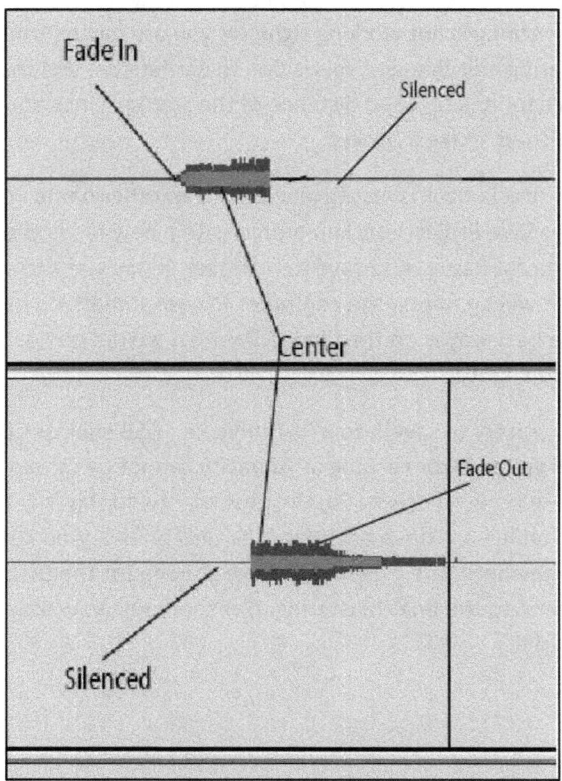

Fig 12-29 An example we used we added a delay of 4 echoes in a bouncing pattern to the entire wave here that is a **'wa-hooo'** sound. Then added a fade in and fade out. Then broke the wave to different channels. Then add a deep reverb. When applying to SPFX you can go deeper than you would a normal vocal.

Vocoder: Want to turn your voice into a futurist sounding robot like voice this effect can do, it also recreates an old sound- the voice box effect. This splits a guitar and the vocal, while it stays exactly the same. Note tempo has a lot to do with this, a fast tempo song does not work well as it comes as mostly noise, but a slow to moderate temp works okay.

First thing you must know is you have to have stereo track for the effect to work. But you also must have two different tracks. One of vocals the other of a guitar fig 12-30. Then select both and make them into a stereo track, fig 12-31 by clicking the down arrow on one of the tracks **and click 'Make Stereo track'**. The two tracks will be combined into one single track. Select the track, and then click *Effect>Vocoder*.

The effect box fig 12-32 will pop up. You will have to play around with the sliders to get the sound you want, by moving one a little and previewing, then moving another and previewing again. Note that when sliders are pushed to the right there is less effect and to the left, there is more of the effect. When you find it write down the numbers and click OK. It will apply to the selected part of the track. Just like any other effect a little goes a long way.

It can be also used to change the voice, to make it smoother, but it takes a lot of changes to get it sounding right and not sound unnatural. We suggest you start out with the minimal amount and work your way up, if you do this.

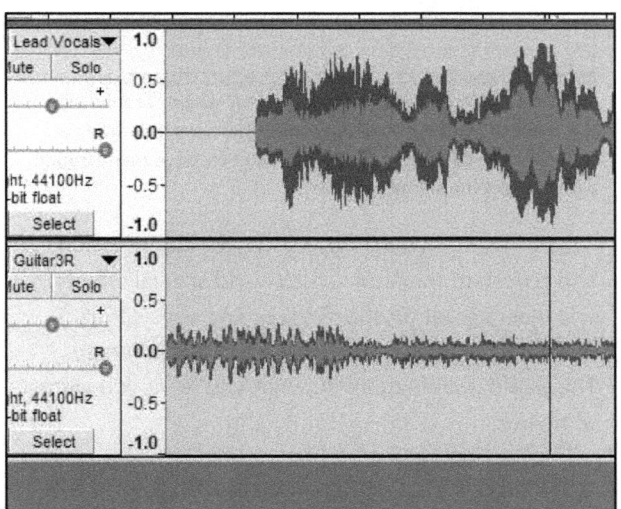

Fig 12-30 to create the voice box effect you need a vocal and a guitar track. It sounds best when there is a little over drive on the guitar.

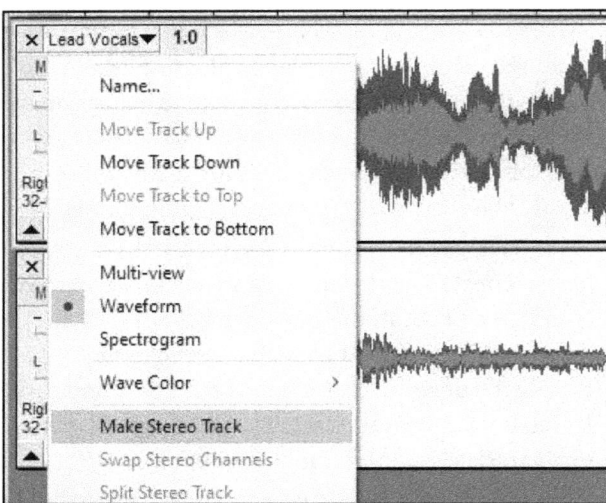

Fig 12-31 Make the two separate track a stereo track.

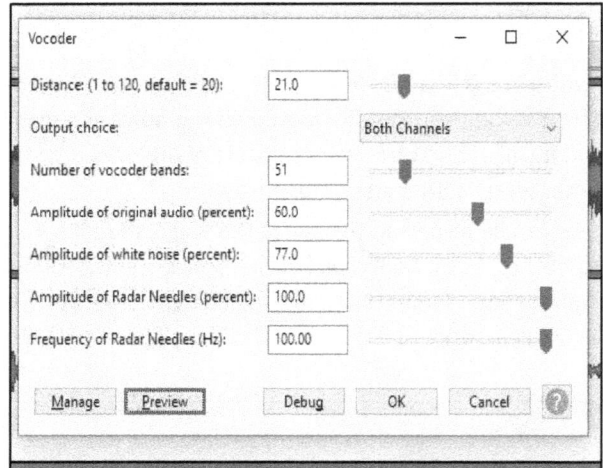

Fig 12-32 The Vocoder effect box. It takes playing around with the slider to get the sound you want. These are the setting we found for the talk box. But you may want to move them around a little to get the sound you want.

Other Effects: Pushing effects like compression and reverb to the limit can also add special effects, and works great on short waves and vocals that make no scenes to begin with. Like *"Waho waho…"* The world is wide open do what you want you want to hear.

FINAL MIX:

Going to take you back to your school days or is that dazes? For me that was swigging down coffee and eating sugar wafers (only the chocolate and strawberry-didn't like the plain vanilla) all the while going over everything we had learned over the whole semester. Reviewing all the underlines in the book, notes that were taken, and everything the teacher said. It was 3 a.m. and class was at 8 a.m. but no time for sleep, oh the pressure.

Final mixing is much like that. Now we grab our notes, and log sheets and carefully listen to each track, and each song again. Moving faders, a little more to the left, a little more to the center. Make this one louder, this one softer. Add a little more EQ. then once it's over listen to it again this time, if it was done with headphones, use speakers. Then if it was loud, with the volume down. Once again but now in mono.

How long should a mix take? There are no set rules. Some can be done in a couple hours; others may take all day, for some it may take days. It took us three days to get Angels Cry mixed. The thing is do not rush through it. If you get tired don't do what we did in school and keep studying, it doesn't work in this class. You should take a break, especially if something is not working right. Or you are having trouble hearing any changes, this is due to ear fatigue, and the only cure for it is rest and distance of the sound. Once you are satisfied, make a backup.

A simple back is just to give the file another name. Click File>Save Project>Backup then create a new file and give it a different name. And save it. However, if you want to save it so it will be not on the computer in case something happens. The best way is on the Cloud. Do what we did above but save on the Cloud.

If you try to save it to a FAT drive i.e., USB stick or CD you will get an error reading as Audacity cannot be stored on these types of drives. So, the best way to do this is with a portable hard drive and place the files on this. And keep it somewhere safe. Now you have studied for the test, and it is time to the final-Mastering. Get some rest you are going to need it.

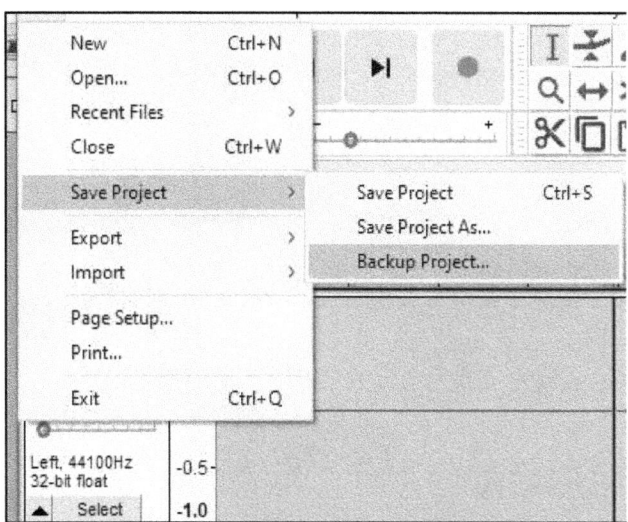

Fig 12-33 easiest way to back up a project is saved it is a different file with a different name.

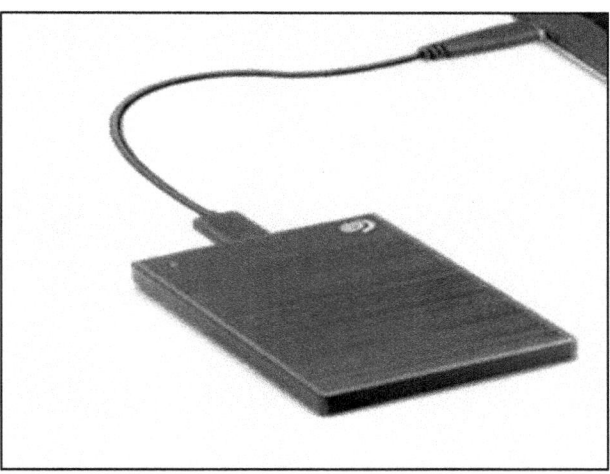

Fig 12-36 A portable hard drive is good for aback up offsite.

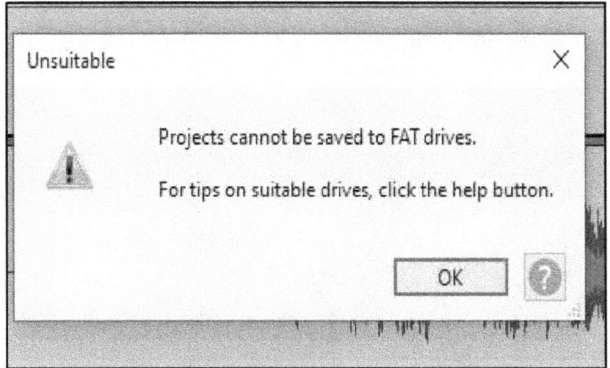

Fig 12-35 If you try to back up to a FAT drive i.e USB stick or CD this is what you will get. You can modify it to work if the file is under 4Gb but most song files will be over this. And even then we *don't* recommend this as problems will happen as it cannot run fast enough.

For the next section you are going to need a list of all the material that is going to be on the record, list of songs, the running time and be thinking of a title. As the next section is Mastering.

PART IV MASTERING

Chapter 13 Do the Master Mix

This is what you have been waiting for, to make all those songs into a full album. However, it isn't just merely just loading them all on to one file and giving it some name. Care must be used to how songs begin, how they end, and in what order are they to appear in. This also the chance to boost those low-level songs up and tap the extra loud down a little to where the same sound level is on all songs.

If you haven't yet, do take some time away from the songs. DO NOT go from mixing to mastering, your ears need some time away, at least a week two. Then you will come in with fresh ears and hopefully a new look on them. You may find that what you though sound great two weeks ago, now **doesn't cut** it and you may find yourself back to mixing.

But if you are ready to master, now you really must wear your producer hat. And if you are really wearing this hat the right way your musician half is going to have problems with you. And you are going to go through these points.

CREATING A MASTER TRACK: Even with after creating subgroup you have several different tracks, and you can upload them or **create a** '*Master.*' You must have a master to do this. A master is the final recording and sounds like the album that will be released, and it will be the last time you can clean up and change minor things before it is ready.

The first thing you must do is convert the Audacity program files into a wav file, this will create the master song. To do this open Audacity and then open your file for your first song. Fig 13-1

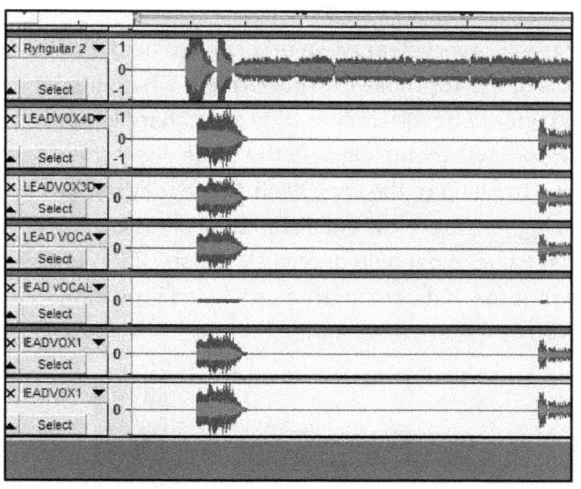

Fig 13-2 Select all the tracks

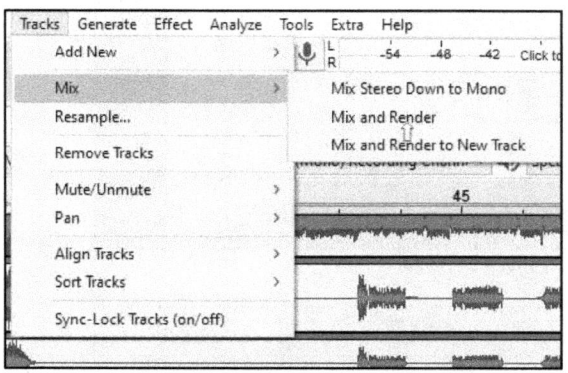

Fig 13-3 Click Track>Mix>Mix and Render.

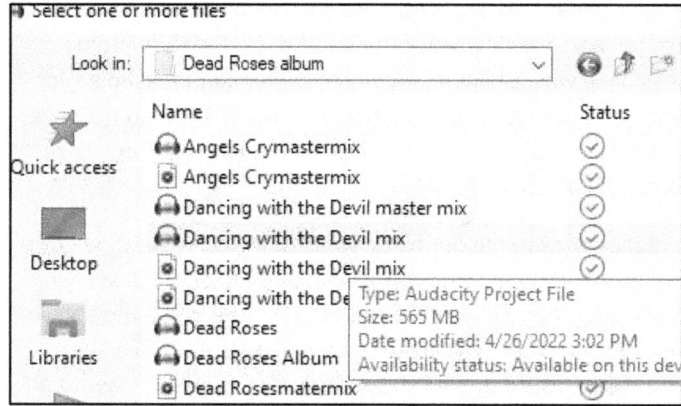

Fig 13-1 Open your mix.

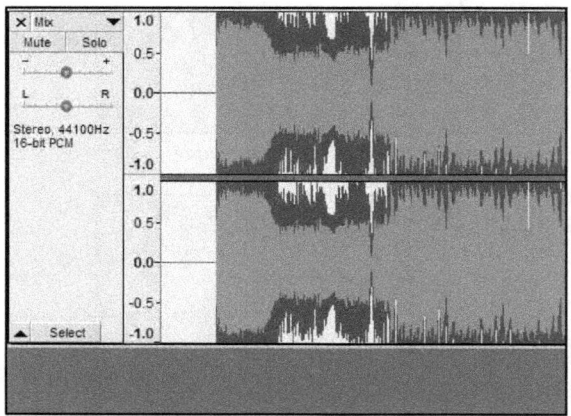

Fig 13-4 A single stereo track will be created.

Next select all tracks, click *Select>All or Control A, fig 13-2 Now click Tracks>Mix>Render and Mix. Fig 13-3* this will create a single stereo track Fig 13-4 with all your changes you made in the individual tracks. Now save into another file, noting these are still not uploaded files, that will come later. Now repeat this process again for each of your songs.

Too Soft or Too Loud

Some songs may overpower while others need help. One of the best tools to use for those overpowering is a hard limiter. This is found under Effects>Limiter, then select hard limiter under the drop-down menu. Fig 13-5 the value you put in the boxes is going to be up to the song itself. Some may require 2 or 4 or even higher. Start low and listen then come back and up in a higher value, did it help or make it worse. If it is worse than go down some. If it helped, try pushing it a little bit more until you find that sweet spot.

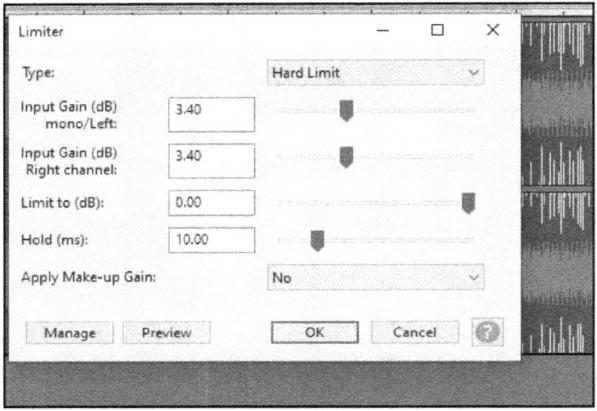

Fig 13-5 Example of a hard limiter.

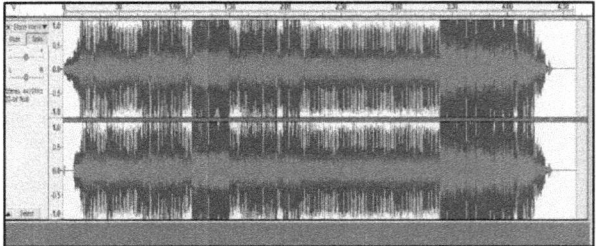

Fig 13-6 The song Storm Warning without hard limiter

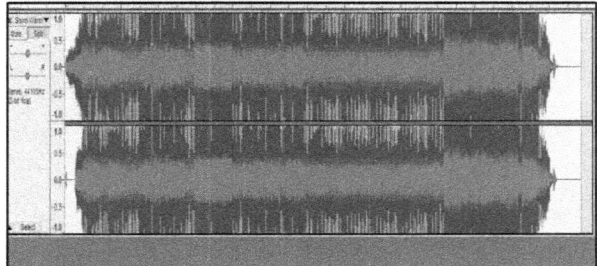

Fig 13-7 Storm Warning after hard limiter.

Compression

Unlike, the use of compression before the use of compression here will affect ALL THE instruments and voices. So, if you use it, use it in small amounts and listen carefully to how it effects the other instruments and voices.

They key is not the amount of compression as it was earlier but the attack and release time. One of the great uses for compression here is how the song pumps. A fast attack is usually used in pop, hip hop, and rock and will react with the drums. With a fast release the drums are more subdued, while a longer release will cause the drums that have that **'thump-thump" sound that can drive a song-**if that is the sound you want.

The ideal use of compression in master is to use low amount (under 5dB) of compression with a slow release. The more the meter bounces the more notice compression will be. Slow-release times are the most inaudible, while fast release time will be the most audible. However fast attack and release helps to reduce transients-short lived sounds. Slow attack will react to vocals but have little effect on drums. See fig 13-8.

The thing is used small amounts and work up to the point the sound is being damaged, then go back down. Note, if you the quiet passages of a song is too loud, this a true sound of being over compressed.

Now a little bad news: If you are hearing noise and the track is clipping badly no matter what you do, it is likely you over compressed it. Compare a nice full marshmallow that is **so big you can't eat it. If you compress it just** enough, you can put it in your mouth, and it still has all the taste and texture of the marshmallow you know. Now smash the marshmallow flat and try to eat it. The flavor changes because the texture has changed, it is not the same. And no matter what you do **to the marshmallow you can't get it to be the fluffy item it** was once was. Likewise, if you have over compressed a song **you can't save it. You will have to go back** and redo it all over again from the raw unaffected track, and if you **didn't** -save it- you will have to go back and rerecord.

Take for example our track *Dancing With the Devil,* we over compressed the overdriven guitars and ended up destroying the tracks. And in haste we did not save the original track, so back to the studio. Mistakes happen to all of us, even **professionals, so don't feel bad if this happens.** Just write it up to experience and move on.

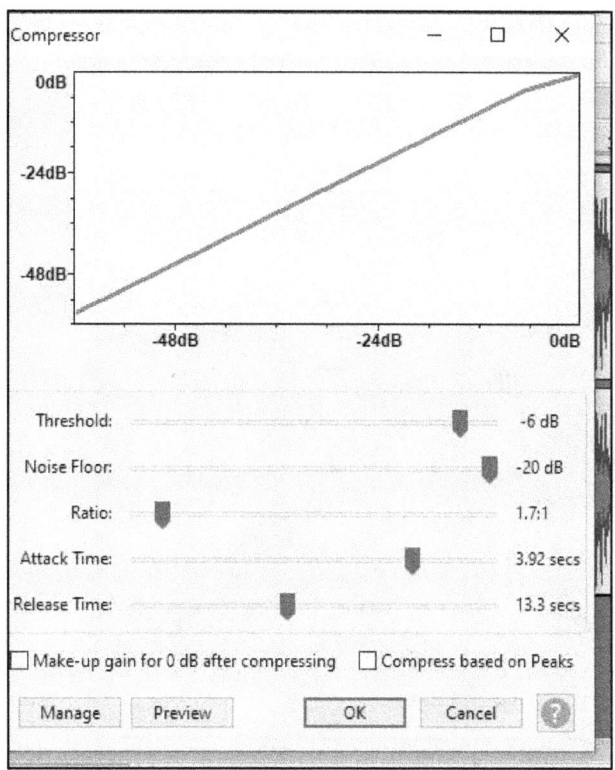

Fig 13-8 Here we used a slow attack time to bring out the vocals and the sliding bass of the song Another Love Song

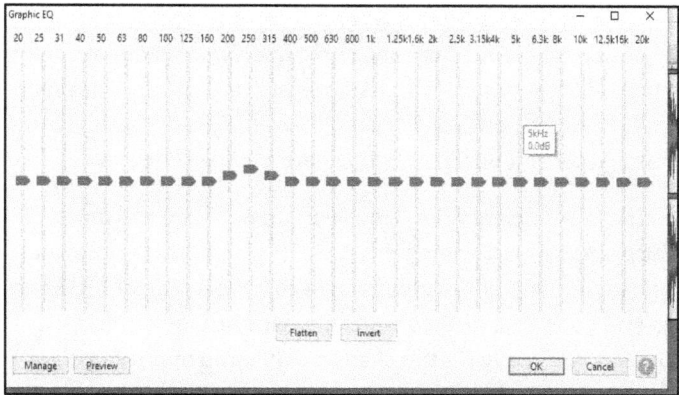

Fig 13-9 An example of feathering (balancing) frequencies in EQ.

Balance the Frequencies- Kenneth

On October 4, 1986, while walking along Park Avenue to his apartment in Manhattan, the well-known CBS news anchor Dan Rather was attacked and punched from behind by a man who demanded to know "Kenneth, what is the frequency?. In 1994 the group R.E.M. released a song entitled "*What's the Frequency, Kenneth?*" on their album Monster.   So, we take a creative approach to the use of EQ in mastering.

Do not apply EQ in mastering like you apply butter to a piece of bread. Don't just apply one that applies to all the tracks. So instead of applying one lump sum to one frequency, you feather it out. See fig 13-9. Instead of applying 3 dB at 250 Hz, you apply 1.5 dB at 250 Hz, then +.5 Db at 200 and 300 Hz. This will result in smoother sound. Don't start out big, use small amounts like .25 or .5 dB at first. Also do not be afraid to split the stereo signal and add the small amount of EQ to only one channel.

To Fade Out or Not to Fade Out That is the Question

If Bill Shakespeare had been a musician that might have been the words he wrote. Ever listen to a record and notice some songs end in a hail of glory while others slowly fade out. The big question why? Uh there really is no answer it depends on the song.

A hard rocker that ends in a hail of glory, does not need to be faded out, it would kill the mood of the song. But a flowing song that repeats repeatedly and then just ends would be a natural for a fade out. You don't want an album that has nothing but fade outs, nor do you want one that has nothing but hail of glory endings. Not even one that is recorded live. How can you fade out a live album you ask.

While you can't fade out the music on a live album, you can fade out the crowd and applause, and into a another song. Doing this way will make it sound more natural that the band went into that song, even though they played another song originally. So how do you decide?

By listening. Some songs just seem to naturally want to be faded out while others need a strong ending. For example, our song *Dancin' with the Devil*. Ends the same way it begins with a blood curdling scream from the vocalist, and the guitarist pulling on the tremolo arm, that would not work with a fade out. So, in this case, we just allow the distorted rhythm guitar to decay out naturally.

However, our song '*Let Son of a Poor Man*' is softer rock with piano base that drives it, and ends with the singer singing over and over '*Let the son of a poor man, ooh the son of a poor man, Yeah the son of a poor man take you home tonight."* So, this song we faded out.

But it isn't because this was not a hard rocker that we choose a fade out. Our song *"I am the Night."* Repeats over and over *"I am the Night...I am the nig-ht!"* and yet this fades out. However, our song *"I Need 2 Love U"* also repeats with a hard guitar riff. But ends with a hard ending suddenly.

There are no set rules. However, do not have too many fade outs or hard ending in a row. This is unprofessional and annoying. One of the great places to have a fade out is when to you go from a mellow song to a hard fast one, that fade out get you ready for the change. While the opposite going from a hard ending can get the listener ready for the upcoming ballad.

Creating a Great Studio Fade Out: **Select** the part you want to fade, then Click Effects>Studio Fade Out and Audacity does the rest right? No big deal! Right? The number one mistake beginners make in mastering is with the fade out they create one that is too quick, and it does not sound natural, it sound amateurish. See fig 13-10.

To use it select the portion you want to fade out. Then click *Effect> Studio Fade Out* fig 13-14. Select enough that will create a proper fade out of the song. You may even want to have it fade out before it comes to an end. Fig 13-13.

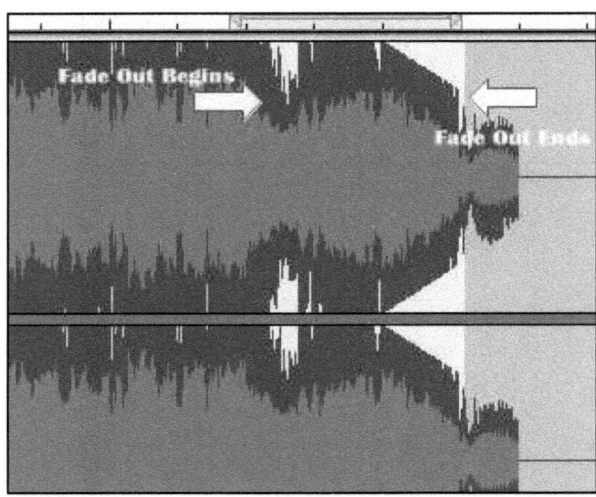

igF13-13 Select only a portion of the ending for the fade it will sound more natural then doing it until the very end.

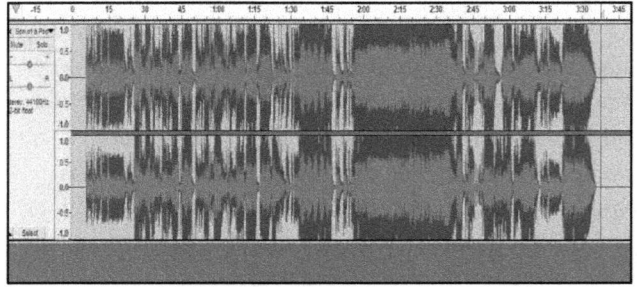

Fig 13-10 Using a short fade out creates an unnatural sounding fadeout.

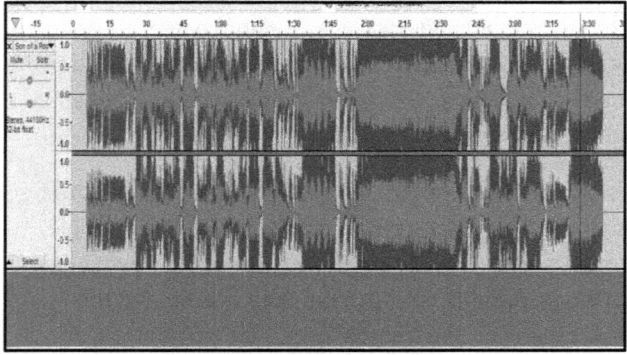

Fig 13-11 This the original take on the *'Let the Son of a Poor Man'*. Notice the short ending it is not long to create the right ending sound.

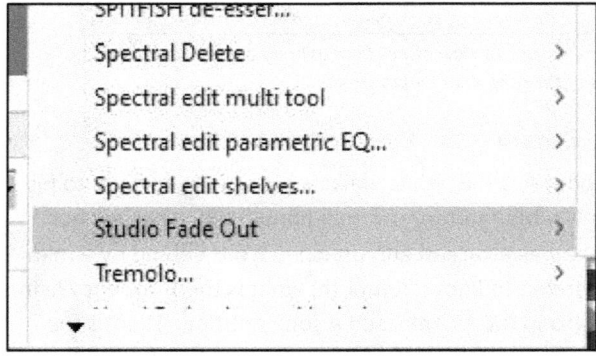

Fig 13-14 Click Effect>Studio Fade out

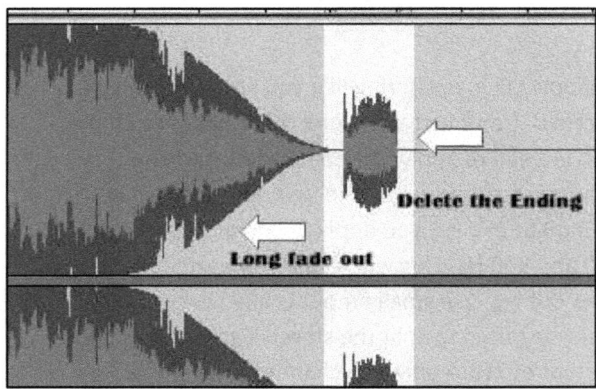

Fig 13-15 Now we have a 3.25 second fade, that ends before the original ending of the song. Now delete the original ending that is after the fade out.

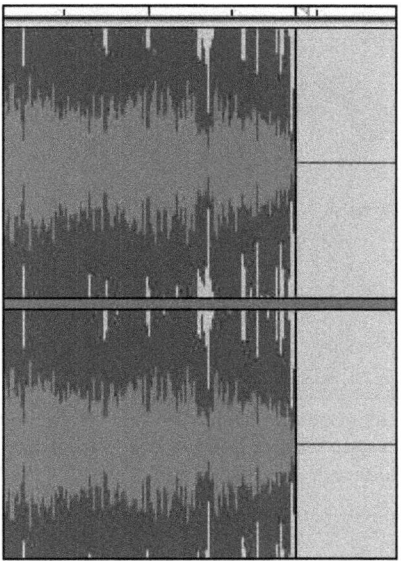

Fig 13-16 Originally our song I am the Night was too short to have a proper fade out which we wanted.

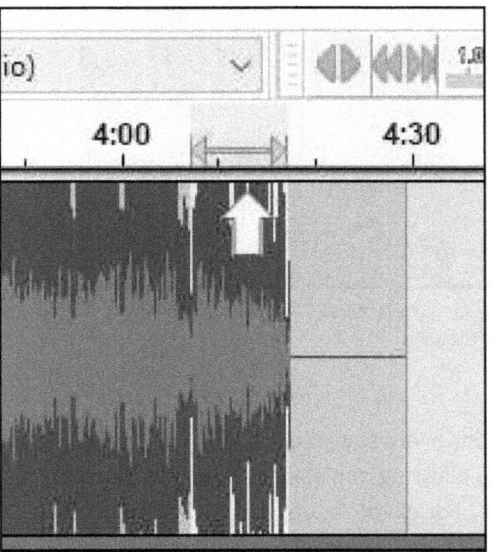

Fig 13-17 Select and copy a portion of the song that repeats. In our example it it's the chorus.

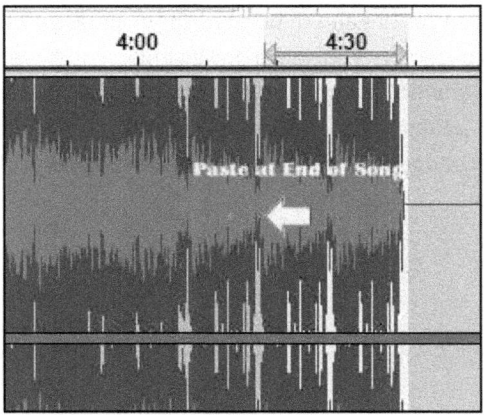

Fig 13-18 Paste at the end of the track, be sure to leave more than enough to fade out properly. Then create your fade out.

What happens if you don't have a long enough song at the end to create a fade out? Fig 13-16. Well, you can go back and rerecord the ending making it longer. Or in some case you can copy, Fig 13- 17 and paste at the end fig 13-18. And then fade it out like above.

To Fade In or Not to Fade In That is Another Question

Some songs don't need a fade in but others can benefit from it. If you had a hard rocking or hard rap song, then go into softer song. And the hard song does not have a fade out then a soft fade in at the beginning of the softer tone song could be useful. Another use if you have a long music intro, it can allow the listener to be drawn into the song, or if SFX are used.

For example, our song *"Strom Warning"*, fig 13-19, uses a tornado warning siren as its introduction. A sudden blast of a screaming siren, does not make the same impact as it does when it is fade in. At the end of the song, we let the siren die down as the end of the song. Sometimes a short fade in is better when going from a fast-moving song to a slower one. For *Another Love Song* we use a short fade in. Fig 13-20

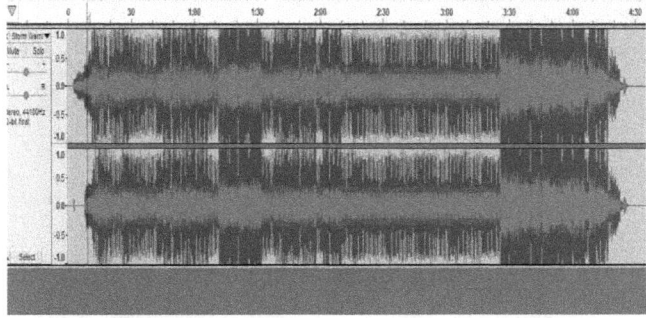

Dig 13- 19 *For the song 'Storm Warning' it begins with a tornado warning siren, which could be a shock to the listener's ears. So, we used a long fade in. Where there is a sharp sound suddenly starts use a longer fade in rather than a short one.*

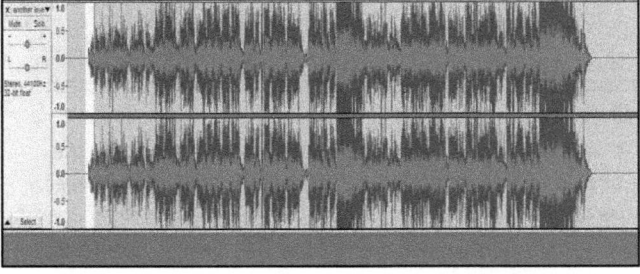

Fig 13-20 *'Another Love Song' begins with soft electric piano so here we use a short fade in. Just enough to temper the sound changing form the last song before it. While we allow it to end naturally with one sustain piano chord.*

How to Do a Fade In: Select the amount you want at the front of the song fig 13-21, then click Effects>Fade In. Listen to are you fade in and fade out arrangements and change, if necessary, by undoing.

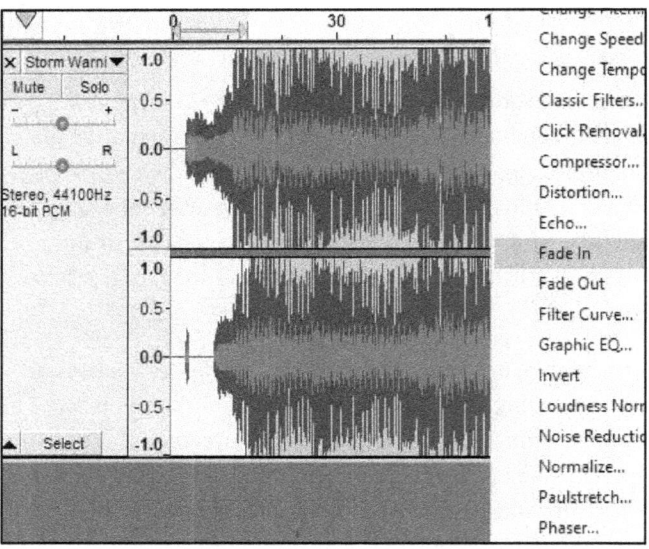

Fig 13-21 We choose a long fade in for the siren in the Song Strom Warning.

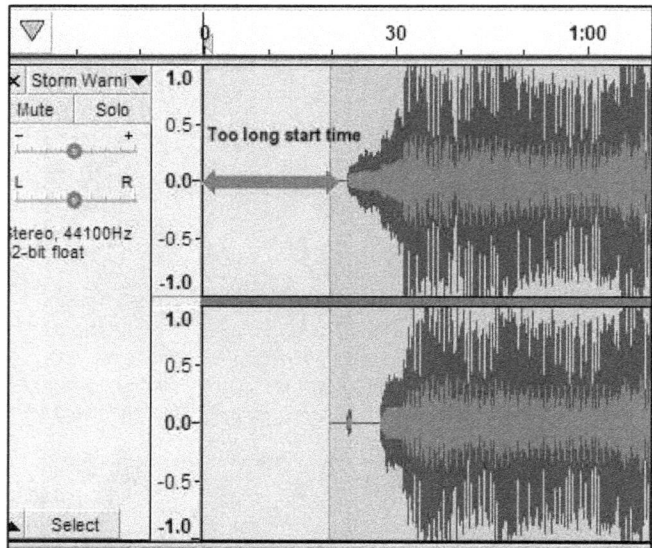

Fig 13-22 We purposely added time to this track to show you how trim it. As you can see there is a long start time. We want to the song to start almost immediately. A too long of a start time over 5 seconds could make the listener think the album is over when it isn't.

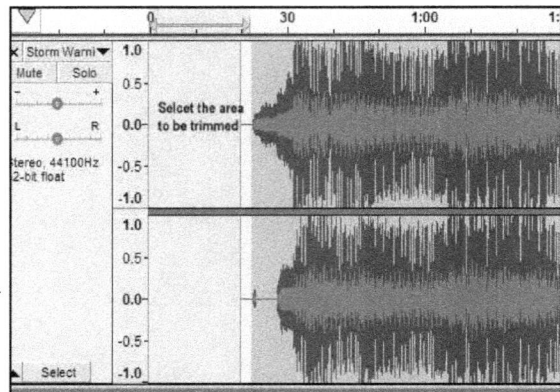

Fig 13-23 Select the area to be trimmed, be careful not to cut off any wanted sound. Then type Ctrl X, this will cut the area selected. If you have stereo tracks, just be sure you cut them both the same amount.

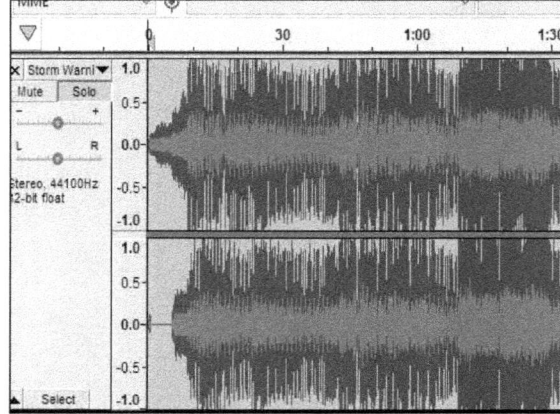

Fig 13-24 Now our song starts quickly. This can also be done if the is a gap of time at the end of the song.

How to Add or Remove Time Between Songs:

You don't want every song starting right after the next one, but sometimes allowing one song to flow into another can create a mood. For example, you have a song about a cheating lover that has been told to hit the road, flowing into song that is about the heartbreak of being all alone can bind the two songs together. But do not over do this, as it can get predictable and make the album boring. Other times you will want a longer space between songs, for example you have had a hard rocker with distorted guitars blazing, then go to soft ballad with acoustic guitar taking a few seconds (but no more than 5 seconds) of silence between each song can help create the mood.

How To Add/Remove Space Before a Song

Removing is pretty simple - select and then delete it fig 13-23. To add space, click on the *Timeshift tool* (fig 13-24) and use it to pull the track where you want it to be. Fig 11-25. This is also helpful in the final layout of the album.

To Normalize or Not to Normalize

Although it might have been used in single tracks, we do not recommend it be using in the mastering section. Normalization looks for the highest peak and then adjust the rest of the file to match this level. The reason it is not used, it destroys the natural sound. It is useful in the use of podcast, but not so much in music.

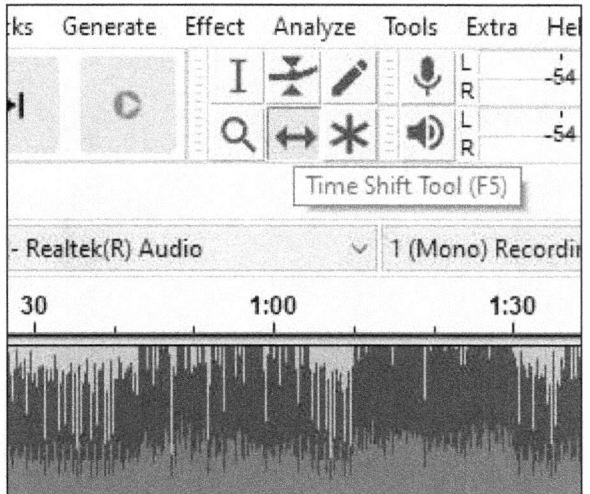

Fig 13-24 to add space in front of a master song track. Click on the time shift tool.

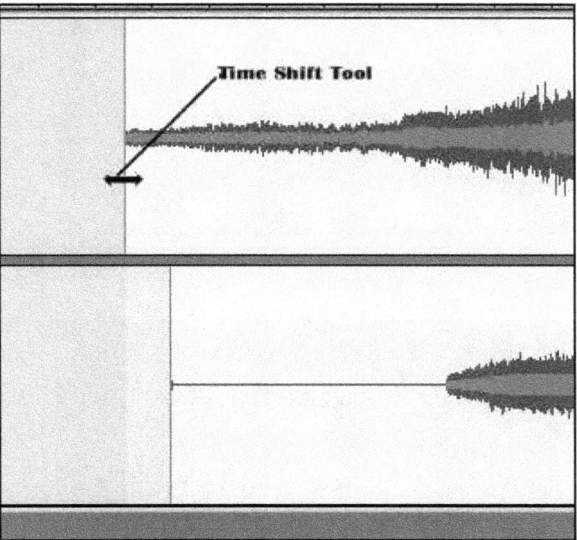

Fig 13-25 Use time shift tool or grab the edge of the track and move it back or forwards, to change the time. If you want both tracks to change the same amount, be sure to select both tracks. It is helpful to zoom in the enlarge the time line at the top to get a better understanding of how much time is changed.

Chapter 14 Making an Album

HOW MANY SONGS ON AN ALBUM?

When I started as a writer, the number one question I got asked was how pages are in a book? The answer is just as many as it takes to tell the story. When I started this project, I got asked 'how many songs on album." The answer is a little bit different, 'however many will fit."

With a vinyl record you only have so much space that it will hold. In short, a record can hold roughly 50 minutes of material, with 25 minutes each side. That said it also depends on the type of music that is going to be used. Also, the length of the songs, and style. If most of your songs are 2-3 minutes in length you could get 12-14 songs on an album. But if they are closer 4 minutes then around ten. So, most important is not the number of songs but the length of the song and type of song that will most likely determine the amount.

If you are going for Jazz, you can get 25 minutes per side, easily this is because the drums and bass can be roll off more. Bass grooves are wider on a vinyl record and thus use up more space, thus rock and roll and country rock, is limited to about 48 minutes or 24 minutes per side. Dance music is even more restricted to about 36-40 minutes or 18-20 minutes preside. But again, number of songs does not matter.

Take for example you have an epic song like Iron Butterfly's "*In-A-Gadda-Da-Vida*" which lasts 17.05 seconds. This album only had six songs on it. Five on one side and legendary song on the other.

If you have a bunch of songs, you can put out a double album which can give you more room like the album "The Beatles" known as the '*White Album*" fig 14-1 which had 30 songs. But they were masters of how to write and record hits. With short very catchy numbers at were made just for playing on the radio. Warning if you are going to put out a double album be sure to have plenty of songs to do this have a least 20. If you have ten or twelve long songs, it doesn't work to make it a double album, the buyer will feel cheated that it has the same number of songs that a normal single album is, yet they have to pay more for a double album. And that is because that production cost will double on you.

Fig 14-1 If you have lots of songs think about trying a double album like the Beatles did with the so-called White album.

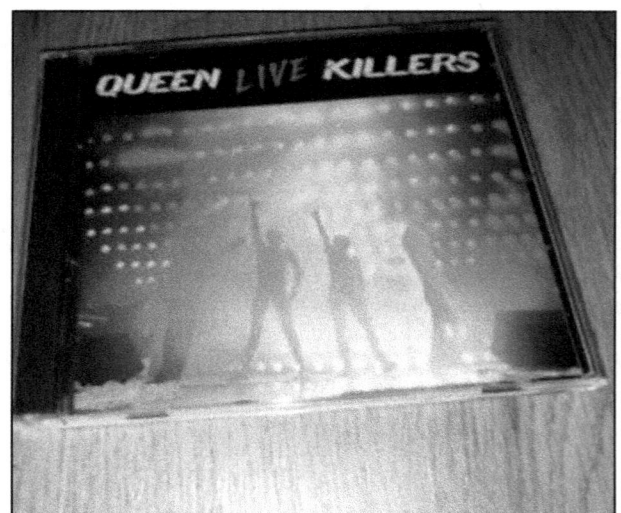

Fig 14-2 With the introduction of CD the amount of music went up to about 80 minutes of music. However, the formula for vinyl records still needs to be kept. Shown is a Live Killers by Queen.

In the days of CD's fig 14-2 and downloadable music there is not the restrictions of time as much, there is also not a side 1 and side 2 as it was it was in the glory days of vinyl. However, the same format for the vinyl is still being used even with CD's and downloads. This is because it creates a recognizable format that has become so familiar.

Even though you have more time on a CD it still is recognizable that the time for an album should be around 36-50 minutes with 18-25 minutes per side. And these should be still the recommend setting you should use. At the time of the writing of this vinyl records were the bestselling medium and frankly nothing can beat the sound that vinyl produces.

So now comes the point of what songs and what order they will go on your album. Make a list of how your song will go along with their time and style. Here is a list of our songs and the way they go on the album.

SONGS		
	Time	Notes
Dancing with the Devil		
Starts off powerful never lets up	5.03	Hard/Rock
Another Love Song		
Driven by electric piano But could be a single	3.56	Soft rock
I AM the Night		
Strong from start to finish	3.55	Heavy Rock
The Angels Cry		
A mix goes from soft piano to acoustic guitar to over driven guitar, to special effects bridge, then to dist. Guitar then ends with acoustic guitar	14:16	Exper. Heavy rock.
Visit Heaven		
Pop mix but has hard edge in chorus	4.34	
(Here comes the) Pain		
Strong all the way	3.48	Heavy Rock
Need 2 Love U		
Strong all the way through Simple but get in your head chord structure possible single	5.02	Heavy Rock
Strom Warning		
Starts out with siren strong hard song	4.25	Heavy Rock
Dead Roses		
Soft acust then hard rock end then soft again	3.20	Hard rock
Son of a Poor Man		
Soft rock	3.35	
Keep On Rockin'		
Drum/Bass/ dist. Guitar at end	2.09	Hard rock
Gamblin' Woman		
Simple driven with O.D. guitar	3.45	Blues driven
More than Beautiful		
Mild	4.54	Sounds more CW
8 Nights a Week		
Driven by Acoustic Guitar	3.24	Soft rock
Total time	1 hours. 5 minutes. 58 seconds.	

So, we don't have any problem with too few songs. We have the problem too many songs and over one hour of music. So, what happens if you have too much song and not enough time? You have a few choices. You could write more songs and create a double album, format it only for CD where more time is allowed or get the blue pencil out and delete some songs and cut others down. See I told you were going to get in a fight with yourself. So, we are going to have to cut.

The First Cut Is the Hardest

First question for the producer to ask the performer part of yourself is "Which of these songs do not fit your style?" Our style is hard rock. So, we go through our list. *"More Than Beautiful "* has more Country and Western edge to it so we slice the blue pencil through it. Now we have 13 songs; this right here could cause problems especially if any in the band or a buyer is superstitious- yes even little things like that can affect your record.

We are still over time so more cutting is needed. *8 Nights a Week,* sounds too much like *Eight Days a Week* by the Beatles. So, we will cut that and while we are at it we will cut *Gamblin' Woman* even though it is a blue sounding song with harmonic we will save for another album.

That gives us 10 songs but are still over 50 minutes at 53 minutes and 58 seconds. Now we can cut *Visit Heaven* as it has a more pop sound, but that is still going to get us barely under the 50-minute range and do to the heavy bass and drums of the hard rock sound that is pushing it limits we need more cuts. So, we will cut *Another Love* song.

Now we have new problem, all the songs are pure hard rock, which makes for a bad mix on album, and all the songs on the album start to sound the same. You must have some softer sounding songs in between all those hard-edge songs. Likewise, must place a fast-moving sound in between all those slow heartbreaking songs. And here you though it was because all the hard rockers were just trying to show the softer side to get girls. Maybe but there are different reasons for that and putting nothing but one type of song on an album can make you a one sound artist.

Now the producer in you is going to suggest we keep *Visit Heaven* and *Another Love Song* and cut *Angels Cry* we could save over 14 minutes. Now the performer is going to scream. "It took two weeks to record and a solid week to mix to create those 30 tracks with Special effects, backward tracks and stereo tracks that switch channels back and forth. "NO!" You scream. "Not after all that work!"

Some where the producer part of you and the artist part of you are going to have to agree. So, you start looking over the songs. You notice that some songs have an extra-long guitar solo or drum solo in the middle. While this is great for live shows, this is where cuts can happen in the studio. We also notice long ending and long intros, these two can be cut.

That wonderful very long guitar solo has got to go, and we are going to cut it to 15 seconds. Now that hurts, don't it? To be able to do this you have to make a cut somewhere in the middle of the solo where it will not be noticeable. Listen for a point where the solo stops for a fraction of a second. Maybe where the musician moves their hand up or down the fretboard or keyboard. After you make the cut be sure to *crossfade the clips*, to make the cut less noticeable. Now play it back and see if it sounds okay. If it does not, you may have to undo the changes and more a different cut. Or you may have to punch in a new shorter solo and remove longer one. This will require you to cut the other tracks (you will have to go back to the original multiple track layout) to match the new solo. **Then save it as new file name example 'song title short solo'**. Then convert it to a *wav* file.

Other places to cut are long endings and long intros. Take our song *Dancing with the Devil* we repeat the chorus four times before the song ends with a scream and the whammy are on the guitar. This gives us two separate blocks to work with the repeating chorus and the screaming ending. We can remove two of those choruses and end with two choruses and he scream and save some seconds. Listen for something like this in your song.

Listen carefully and have the mouse pointer positioned above the stop button. When you hear the place, you want to stop quickly stop the playback and notice the time scale at the top of the track, note you may have to zoom in to be sure you can read fractions of seconds. Now start play back again, with the mouse pointers positioned over the stop button again. When it comes to the other point stop playback. Note that time. Now select that span and delete it. Next crossfade the clips. And listen back to see if you are satisfied with the cut.

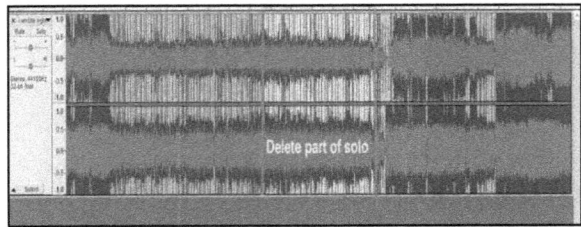

Fig 14-3 Listen to where the instrument lets up a little maybe before it starts a different octave. Then select this part or the other part to keep and remove the rest of the solo. Doing this we were able to cut the solo down and save several seconds

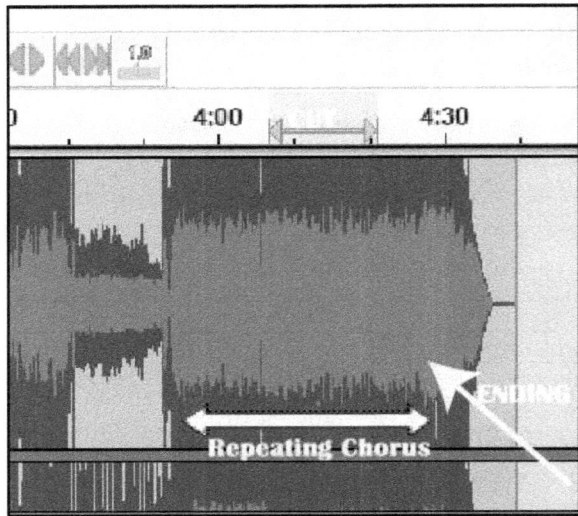

Fig 14-4 Here we remove the two middle repeating choruses, for it makes for a better cut then trying to remove to two beginning or two ending ones.

With the cut in the solo and the cut at the repeating ending we were able to cut Dancing with the Devil down from over 5 minutes to just 4:16 seconds. Now we move on to other songs.

Another place to look for is extra verses, do you have four verses when three could be used. However, before you cut a verse listen carefully. Make SURE the cut does not harm the song. Listen as both the producer and the artist. Take for example our song *Dead Roses*.

It tells the story of a once glamorous star who is now sitting **at Mason's bar sipping gin that went stale. And hides her face** behind a veil as she holds on to Dead Roses. Then goes on to be accused of murder. And is defended by Mason (yes as in Perry Mason). So, we thought of cutting this verse:

Now she remembers when her beauty charmed them all-
Mason is gone, he hangs upon the wall-
Now the mourning has no end-
Wondering will love ever begin-
And in her heart, she holds-
Dead Roses de-ad roses © *Herd Paul A. 2022 BMI*

This is the verse before the song switches to a harder rock sound with these lyrics

Now it is withered up like dried thrones-
And it cuts the flesh to the bone-
And the blood flows down over..
Dead Roses, Dead Roses-
For a love that never came true-
For all that tis left of me and you-
Are...
Dead Roses.... © Herd Paul A. 2022 BMI

In removing this verse, it would not let the story come to an end that was being told before the song becomes a personal feeling. So, we must keep it. My musician side won over the producer side, and it remains untouched. You must decide which half of you wins in each song Producer or Artist.

Now we went through and cut down songs and made a compromise with our two halves on Angels *Cry* we kept it but toned down that seven-minute solo. It now runs 10 minutes and 51 seconds.

Our play list now looks like this:

Time Cut Play List	
Title	New time
Dancing with the Devil	4:14
Dead Roses	3:53
I am the Night	2:53
Angels Cry	10:51
Another Love Song	3:57
Pain	3:49
Storm Warning	3:34
Visit Heaven	4:31
Keep On Rockin'	2:09
Need 2 Love U	4:15
Total time	46:04

With 46 minutes and 4 seconds this will give us enough time on a vinyl record plus be able to leave gaps in between songs. That brings to arranging the album

ARRANGING THE SONGS' PART 1

Ever noticed that when you play an album, that the songs make you feel different ways? Maybe almost taking you through a range of emotions? It is not done by accident; this is carefully planned out.

Take REO Speedwagon's *Hi Infidelity* album, it may seem just like a collection of songs but it plays out a story. It opens with the rocker song of *"Don't Let Him Go."* A song that the song writer Kevin Cronin has described as a plea to the band's girlfriends.

Then we go into the more laid back *Keep on Loving You*. Which is about still loving her even though she has cheated. Third song *Follow my Heart* now we are having second thoughts should we stay with her and love her and follow our heart or follow our head who is saying get the-hell out.

Fourth song *In Your Letter,* we see that she has left, or it could be taken from the other side that the guy she is cheating with is wondering why won't you leave him and be with me.

Last song on side 1 is *"Take it on the Run"* the opening lines set the mood of the songs. This is about the woman that still cheating. And even though he hears the tales going around the town, he is still doesn't want to believe it.

It is almost like reading a romance novel at this point and you just have to go to side 2 to see where it is going to go. *"Tough Guys"* is another hard rocker that opens side 2. This where the woman who has left her love has now comes see she doesn't like who this other person is.

Next, we have *Out of Season* Where the one that has been left is now feeling all alone. Then comes '*Shake it Loose Tonight"* Sort of like a one-night stand, ready to do the deed but not fall in love. *Someone Tonight,* loneliness maybe wanting the someone. And it ends with, *I Wish You Were There*. The one you love is not there, in fact the one you love is not yours to love anymore.

When albums have song that all connect, they are called a '*concept album'*. It does not have to tell a story; it is just that the songs on the album have a connection with each other. It could be childhood memories, things that are all along on route 66, in REO's case it had to Infidelity. They took a twist of the name High Fidelity that had to do with stereos at the time and create this record that put them solidly into the annals of rock and rock history.

Do all your songs have something in common? Maybe you have a concept album, this can be useful in naming the album. Again, if you have songs about all the places on Route 66, you could call you album '66 High'. But we will get into naming the album a little latter. First let's get the songs arranged.

Arranging the Songs Part 2

Once again listen to your finished songs, Have the list of the songs you created. Now you will have to have to have another hat to wear the one as listener. Pretend you have never heard these songs before. It could also be good if you have a good friend to come in a listen to the songs, not to tell what they think, *but what they feel.* As they listen have them jot down a piece of paper what each song makes them feel like. Does it make them feel good, sad, or ready to stand up and dance, take-action or they want to sing along. Note if there is one, they want to sing along to or find themselves sing it later- circle those and target these as your singles.

Now note the length of the songs this is because you want to span out the songs. You don't want a bunch of long songs or a bunch of short songs together.

Next look at the feel of the songs that your friend felt. Do they have general order that they could fit into? For example, you have a song of falling in love with someone you just see across a crowd street. Then another about the first kiss, then one of where you give your heart and soul. And then of heartbreak. By putting the songs in that order, you create a feeling for the listener that will be drawn into it like story. They will feel the heartbreak because it will transfer to their lives. As we all have this, no matter if are in a relationship or not at the time. A song we hear will take us back to that time with former love, or a current love. Songs are not just words and music they are pure emotions, and they take us on journeys into heart. Use that when arranging the songs.

That said, time and tone of the songs also play into how things should be arranged. If these above examples are all slow ballads, you would not want them together, and certainly not starting the album.

No matter what your style, from a Vegas troubadour to a heavy metal band the first song should start off strong and powerful, so it draws the listener into the record. Even if you have a hit that is more mellow do not lead the record off with it. Instead place it at number two or three track. Again, take **REO Hi infidelity's** even though *Keep on Loving You* was going to be the single you released, **you wouldn't want it starting the album.**

Likewise, **Queens' Day at the Races starts off with** Brain May's rip-it up rocker *"Tie Your Mother Down"* not *Somebody to Love*.

Now if your record is going to be named (we will cover later) after one of the songs and it is strong it would make sense to start off the album with this song. The one exception would be if the song is super long (over 5 minutes), you want a short to medium in length under 5 minutes, if possible, to start out the album. Save the long songs for deeper in the arrangement.

So, for our album the one song is perfect to start it off- *Dancing with the Devil*. With the pick rack and scream it will grab attention and show what style of music is on this album.

Second song on an album can be two things, one it can where your single is going to be (remember those songs your friend was singing along with this is where you place it) or it can be where a completely different style of song is. For example, you have hard rock or rap song leading off, then have softer tone song this could go here. Thus, for our album we choose *Another Love Song* for here. With its soft electric piano and lyric like this:

I will never write another love song, that you will ever hear-
How can you write another love, when the one you love is not here-
I will never write another love song, that will hold you till dawn-
How can you write another love, when the one you love is gone...gone...gone..oh my baby is gone- © 2021 Herd Paul A. BMI

....it is perfect for right after the one driven by loud distorted guitars. Now we could add another soft tone here, but too slow or fast and aloud songs together is not desirable. May have a come of fast loud songs, then place in a slower more melodic song then go back to a faster beat song. So the third song should take that route, and if you have an album title after a song this is good place to have that song. We place *Storm Warning* as our song here. The opening with the storm siren place just tells the listener that a big change is coming. And get the listener ready for its muted distorted guitar and these lyrics, it moves the listener back to the hard rock sound.

I hear the thunder in the distance, it is calling your name-
I hear the rain falling and it is doing the same-
Like fingers on the windowpane-
I hearing you begging me to come in-
I say No, I can't face the pain- © 2021 Herd Paul A. BMI

The end of side one is good place which what would be a B side song of a single, it also a good place to place a longer song. As is the case with Led Zeppelin's IV album and *Stairway to Heaven*. Note if you have real long song it should go at the end of side two. Another song you can have at the end of side 1 is another style of your music. For example, in our album we place *Keep On Rockin'* at the end, with its heavy drum and bass through most of the song and the guitar at the end it was perfect to transition to the other side.

One of those chosen singles is another good place to open side two up, it can be a strong song or slower, but it should have some strength to it. Such as "The *Prophet's Song*" from Queen's *Night at the Opera* which begins side two. Again, follow the format of side one not placing too many of the same styles of songs together. Mix it up, but at the same time don't get into a predictable rhythm of fast song, slow song, fast song. You don't want the listener to know what is coming. Maybe instead have fast song, slow song, fast song, fast song, slow song, slow/fast song, Strong song. If you have an experimental song a good place for this at the end of side two. That is where listeners go deep into records and find favorites. Like the Doors original album with the song *The End*.

Also be aware of the length of songs. Just like you mixed up the style. You don't want a bunch of songs the same length together, so have a couple of stronger songs than place in a longer one. Likewise, if you have a bunch of longer songs put a shorter song in between. This is our mix:

LAY OUT
Side 1
Dancing with the Devil	4:14
Another Love Song	3:57
Storm Warning	3:34
Need 2 Love U	4:15
Visit Heaven	4:31
Keep On Rockin'	2:09

Side 2
Pain	3:49
Dead Roses	3:53
I am the Night	2:53
Angels Cry	10.51

CREATING AN ALBUM ON AUDACITY

Now that you have your songs cut down to fit, mixed, master individually and arranged it is time to make a full album. Open the song you want to be your opening song. If there isn't a small amount of silence at the start add a little no more than 3 seconds, there should be only a small time before the sound starts.

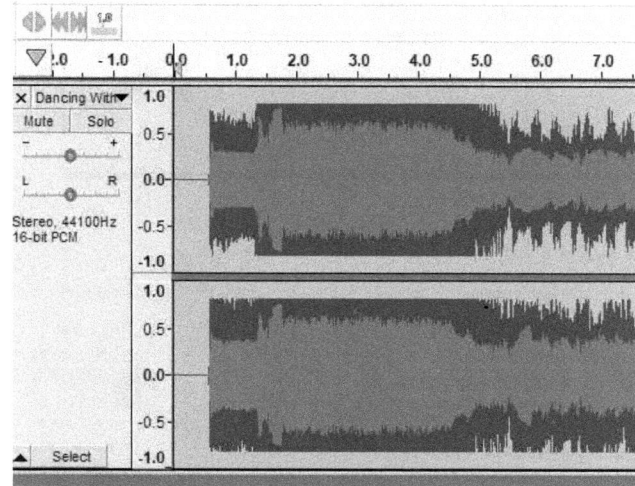

Fig 14-5 We are going to start with Dancing with the Devil, notice that strong powerful opening, this will get attention.

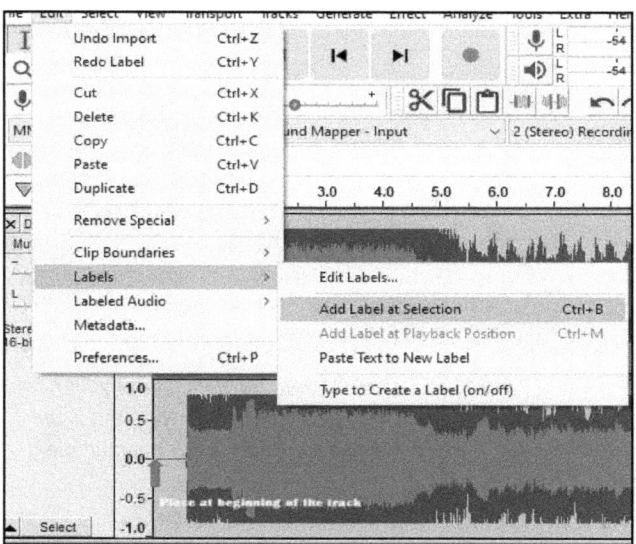

Fig 14-6 We need to Label the song. Click EDIT> LABELS>ADD LABEL AT SECTION.

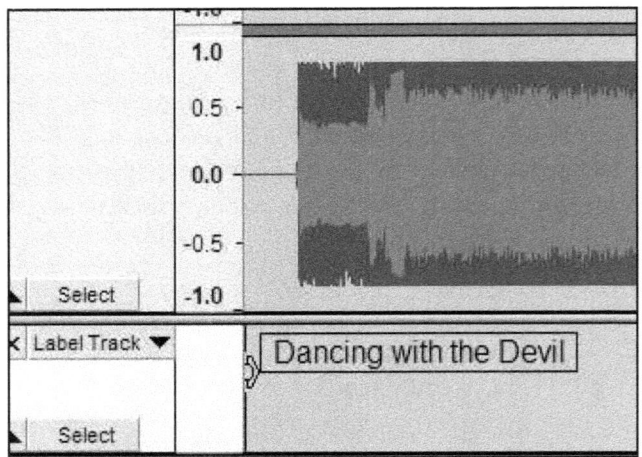

Fig 14-7 Type in the Song title.

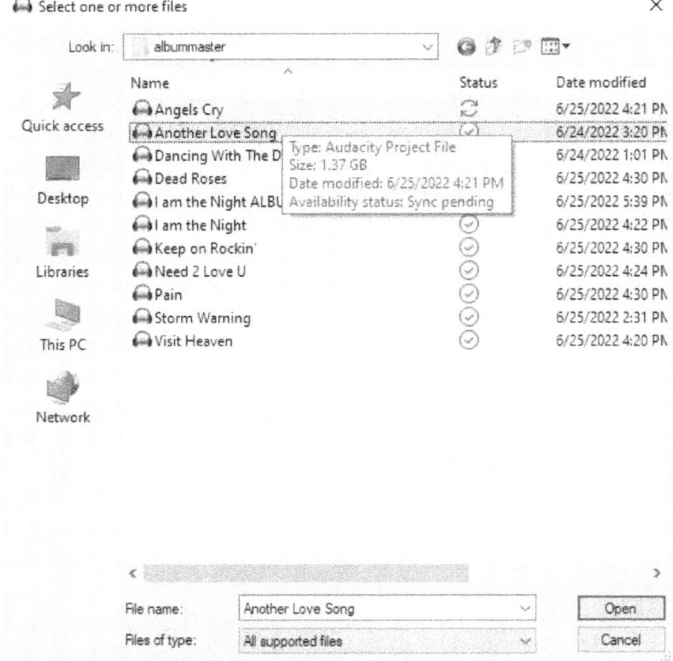

Fig 14-8 Click FILE>IMPORT. Hunt for your file then import your next second song by clicking on the title and then OPEN. Note this is the mixed down project file with a single stereo track not the multiple tracks.

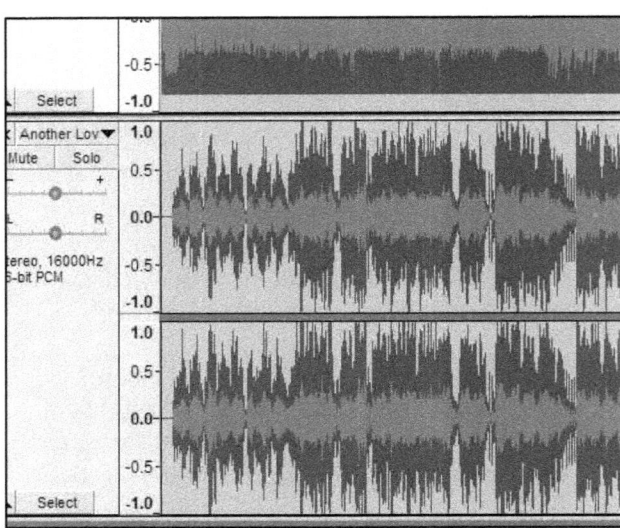

Fig 14-9 Notice the imported song is in another track just below the first one. We can't have two songs playing at the same time. So, select this song, by clicking on the gray area at the head of the track.

Fig 14-10 Now copy and paste the second track behind the ending of the first track on the top track. Notice how Audacity shirks, the first track down. Be sure to leave a blank space between songs to leave between two songs is dependent on the songs themselves. If you are going from a hard rocking song to a mellow ballad you might want to leave a few seconds (no more than five) between each track. But in this case the two songs go together and so there is only a small amount of silence before the next song begins. Then label the track as you did before in fig 14-8

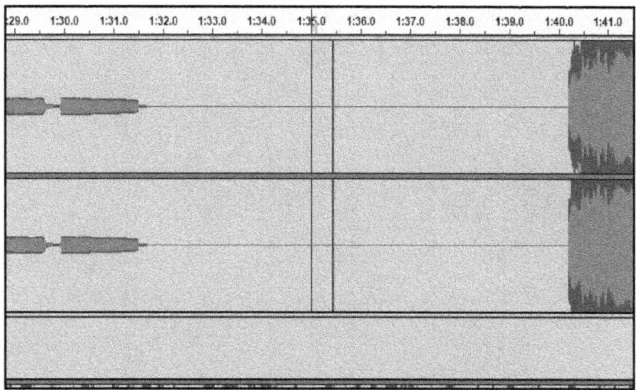

Fig 14-11 Be sure to zoom in to where the time line is in fraction of seconds. For you see what looked like a small amount of silence in the previous photo, is in fact several seconds. And this gap would ruin the sound we were going for.

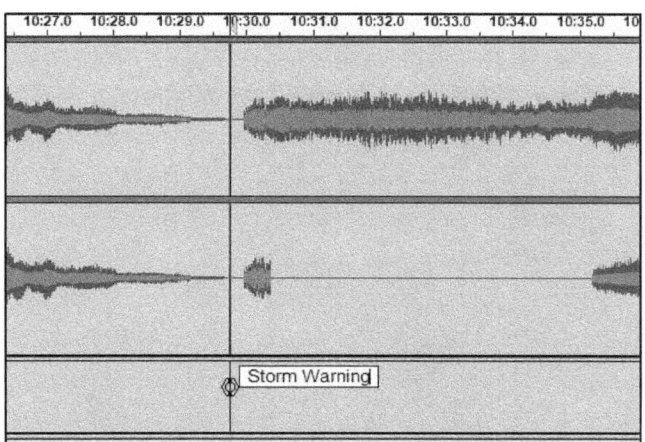

Fig 14-12 Notice the line (arrow) that indicates where one song ends and another track begins. Even though these two different songs are different. The first is softer rock and the second hard as nails, we want a short time between them as the opening tornado siren and carry the first songs as they are both about lost love. The first regret of not being there. And the second trying to get over love. So let the song decide.

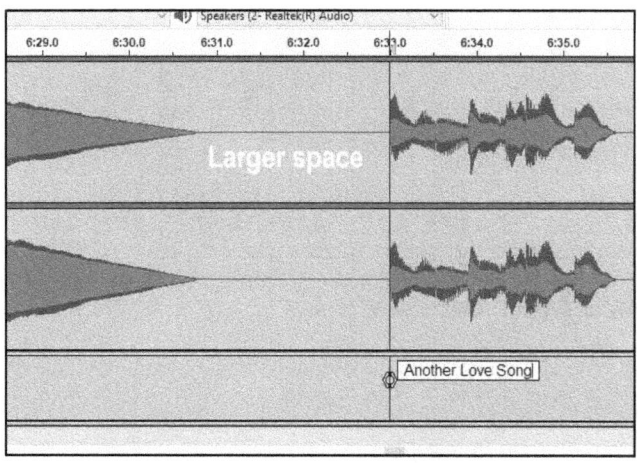

Fig 14-13 Because there is big difference between these two songs there is a larger gap between the songs.

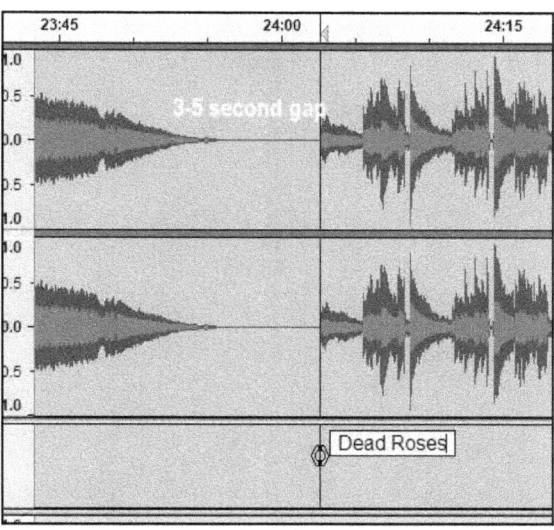

Fig 14-14 Leave a little longer gap between the last song on side 1 and the beginning song on side 2. This will give the illusion of switching sides. If you were using a 3 second gap, use a 5 second gap.

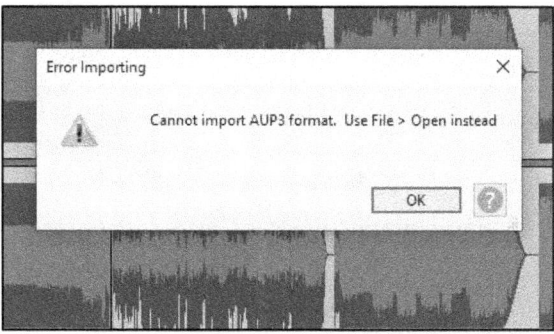

Fig 14-15 If you get this error, just open the file copy and paste into place of the album you are creating.

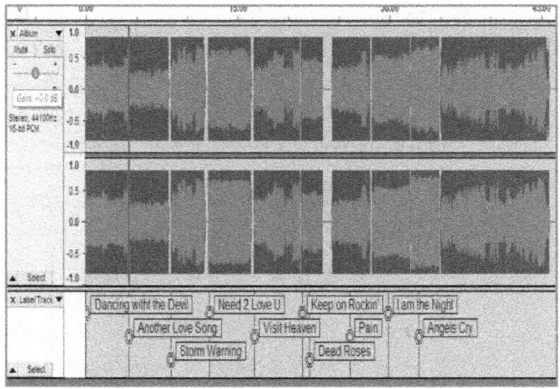

Fig 14-16 a complete album now on one single track.

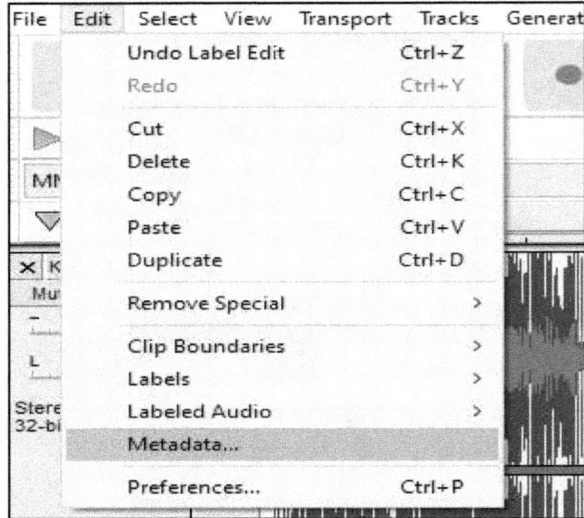

Fig 14-17 Now we use meta tags to define the songs. Select the first song by clicking on it then click EDIT>METAG DATA.

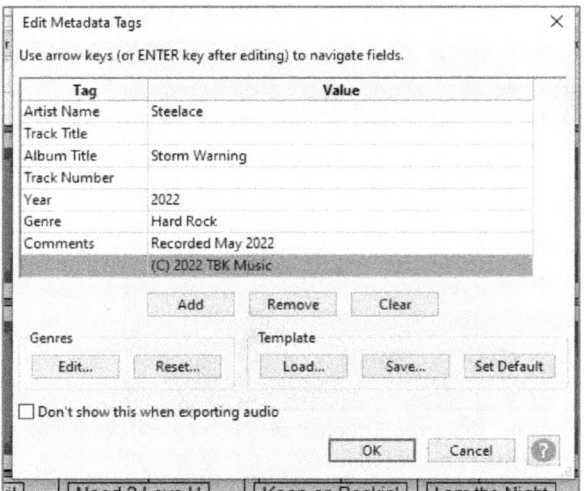

Fig 14-18 When you click OK this box will appear. Type in artist name Album name the year and type of music. Comment section can be used for copyright information or your website. Do not fill in track title or track number this will be fit in later. Click OK and select he next song and repeat, again do not fill track title or track number.

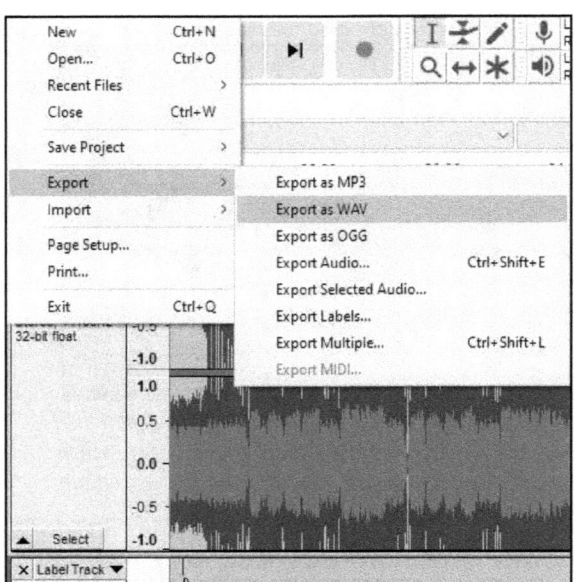

Fig 14-19 When done click FILE>EXPORT> and the type of file you wish to export as. We choose WAV, as that is the most common.

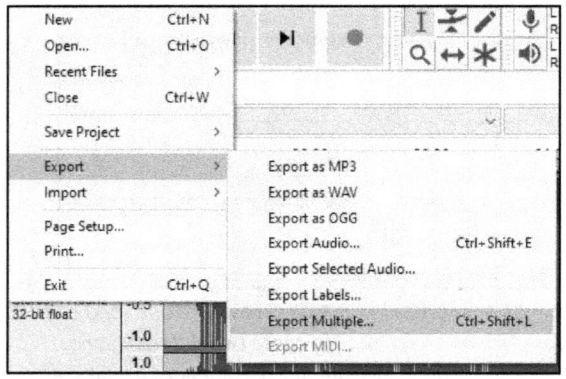

Fig 14-20 Click FILE>EXPORT MULTIPLE

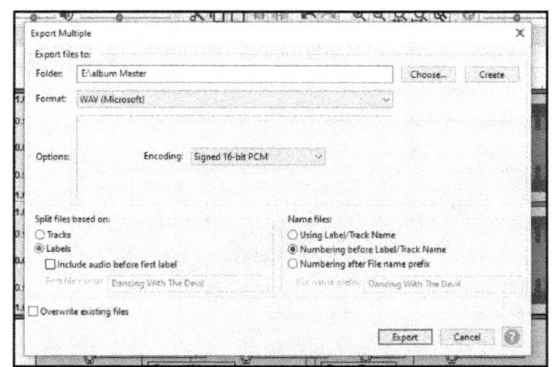

Fig 14-21 Mark boxes marked LABELS And NUMBER BEORE LABEL/TRACK NAME. Click Export.

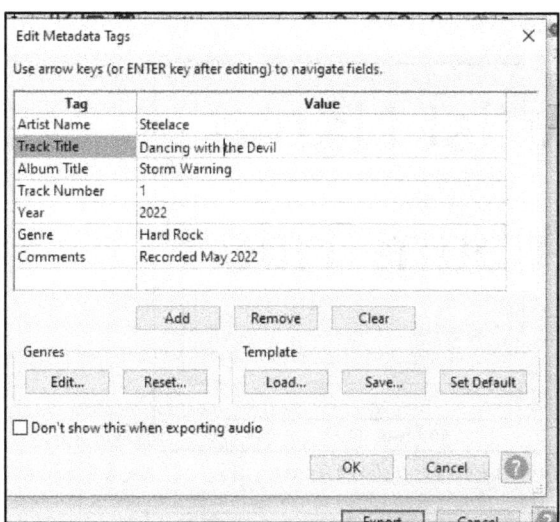

Fig 14-22 See how the song name and it position is automatically filled in. Click OK and it will take you to the next song, and then the next song all the way through the album.

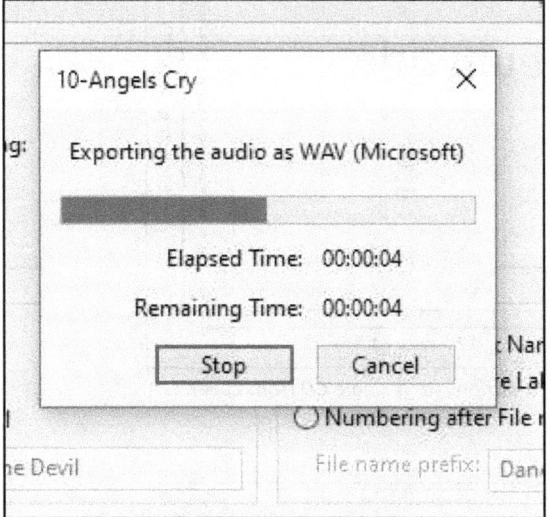

Fig 14-23 this box will pop up as it export each song.

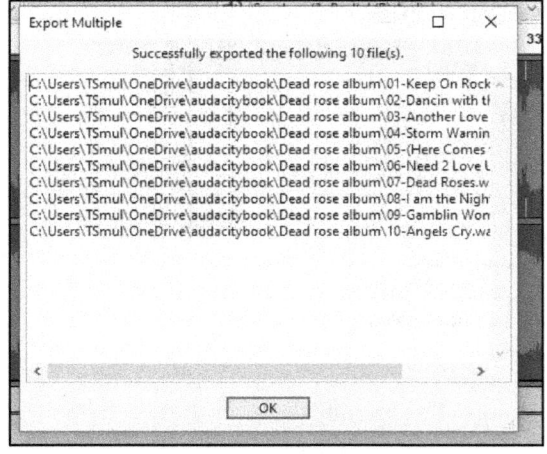

Fig 14-24 After exporting it will show this each song is a separate file but in one folder.

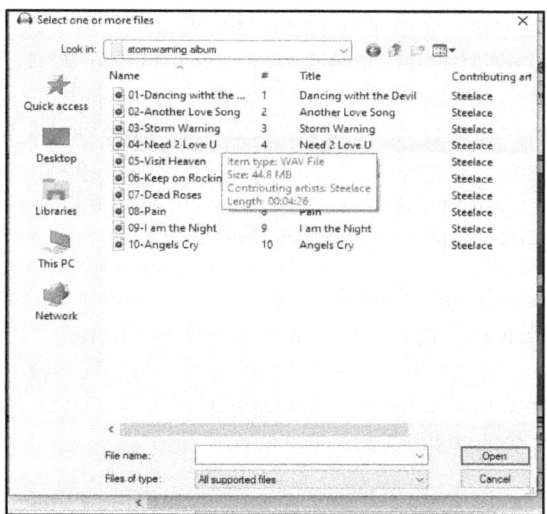

Fig 14-25 And here it is you master album. All the song listed in their order on the album.

NAMING THE ALBUM

What is in a name? A record is a record by any name. The name of the record is like the title of book or a movie. It can make or break it. **Would go see a movie called 'On One Bad Christmas Day',** or would you rather see one called *Diehard*? How about a book called, Dorothy Goes on Trip or is *The Wizard of Oz* better?

The same thought should be used for the naming of your album. Where do you get names? The most common is from a song on the album itself. However, inspiration can inspire the title. Maybe an old movie such as Queen's *Night at the Opera* and *Day at the Races* that were inspired by old Mark Brothers films. Maybe it is something deeper and spiritual to you. Be warned to not go too far out as it might confuse people. Also, if naming an album after a song on the album be sure you select the right one. What would it have been like if Guns and Roses had named their debut album *Appetite for Destruction* after a song on the album and choose "My Michelle", how would it have been seen a heavy metal head banger or soft pop?

Names can be simply the band name this happens with many first albums such as the *Doors*, or *Van Halen*. Also, when **you're** thinking of a name visualize what the cover art might look like.

Is the cover going to wild with graphic art, or just plain like the Beatles-all white album or **Metallica's** Black album? Do it like the professionals do pick three or four titles and sketch up some ideas for the covers and see what each looks like. If you have a band have each member vote on it. Have family members and friends help you pick. Maybe even put it on your band's social media site and have fans vote.

DESIGNING YOUR COVER

You can hire a graphic designer to help you create your cover, maybe someone in your family. Or go to a local college and ask the professor of the art department if there is someone that could help. This will cost you.

If you want to do it yourself there are many programs that help including Photoshop. Adobe Illustrator or In-design. You just need to know dimensions you will be working with. Remember you may be designing more than one cover. So, think in terms of small and large. What might look great on a larger vinyl album, may not look that great on a CD cover

33-1/3   Vinyl record 12x12 front and 12x12 back

45 rpm   Vinyl single record 7x7 front and 7x7 back

CD CASE

Type of CD Cover	CD CASE Dimensions			
	Inches		Millimeters	
	Length	Width	Length	Width
CD Single insert Frt.	4.7	4.7	120	120
CD Single insert Bk.	5.9	4.7	151	120
Double Front insert	9.5	4.7	242	120
Slim CD	6	4.7	154	120

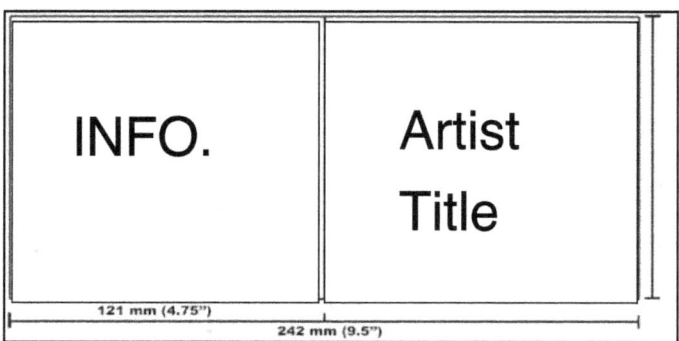

Fig 14-26 Format for double front insert. The back is fold down over the front cover. Additional sheets can be used to create a foldout that will include legal information and lyrics.

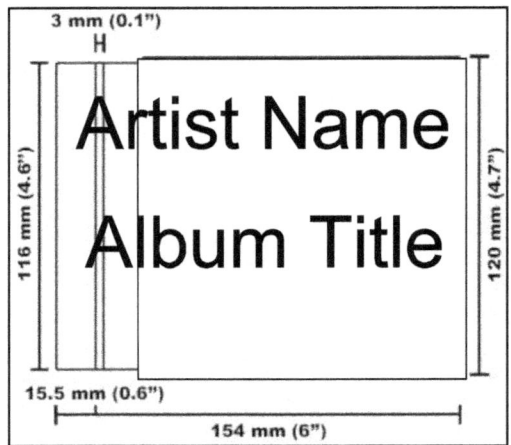

Fig 14-27 Dimensions for a slim CD case

Fig 14-28 Dimensions for a single CD front cover.

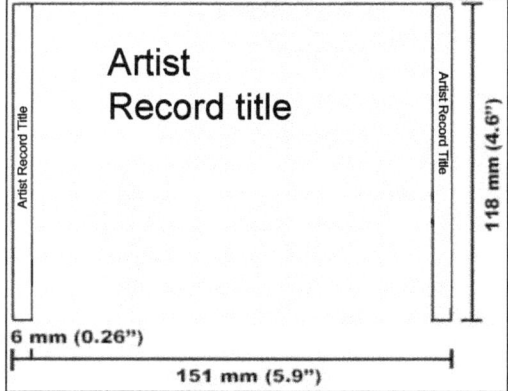

Fig 14-29 Single Cd Back cover

Jewel case are plastic cases they are used to store the CD and the front cover is the same as the front of the album on a 33-1/3 rpm record. With a double sleeve front cover, you can get more information about the record here. If you want liner notes like lyrics, you can just add another inside page and fold it up behind the front cover. There are legal parts that must be placed on every album, and we cover this later.

Paper sleeve — is a type of CD cover which is made from a sheet of paper folded in a special manner with an upper part folded and glued to fix a disk inside the envelope. This is the simplest and the cheapest CD cover. However, it can also be made professionally and using brand identity or desired pictures. You can also insert a piece of folded paper for liner notes and lyrics. The draw back to these type of covers ar they are the least durable type of CD case you will also need a special program like *RonyaSoft CD DVD Label Maker* that will provide you with the templates with proper CD case dimensions to print, fold and glue the sleeve.

For stream services you cover should be 1600 x 1600 pixels to 3000 x 3000 pixels at 300 dbi it should be perfectly square.

Designing the Cover: There are many way you can design a record cover, one of the easiest is using this website https://www.canva.com/create/album-covers/ . They have several formats and photos, or you can do it yourself. Some are free, but the best call for you to pay for the Pro series. However, if you want your own cover design and photos you will have to do it yourself using a digital dark room program and a program like Illustrator or In Design to get the dimensions right.

Do not be surprised that you may want to change you mind on the name you first selected. We did as first we selected *Storm Warning* and instead decided on *I am the Night*. Which caused us have to switch the places of the two songs on the album.

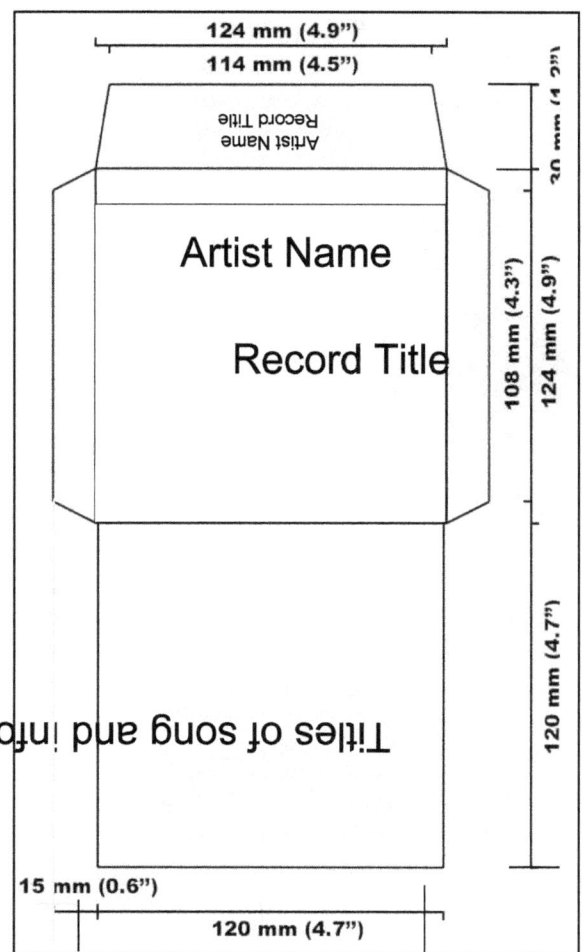

Fig 14-30 Paper sleeve dimensions

Fig 14-31 Sometimes simple as with the one by Led Zeppelin is useful. When selecting a cover design be sure it looks okay in both color and black and white.

Fig 14-31 Example 1 of album cover Storm Warning.

Fig 14-33 Example 3 Dead Roses We like this cover, but it was pink in color and we did not like that. Again, remember color matters.

Fig 14-34 Example 4 Dancing' with the Devil. This brightly colored. But not as attention grabbing as example 2.

Fig 14-32 Example 2 album cover I am the Night this is the one we chose for our cover. We took a shot of a cape draped model dressed in black the place a skull and a transparent face with a "death card" with the band logo.

We created all the covers in *Photostudio by Arcsoft.* Using photos that were in *Commons* or public domain or ones we took then added our touches to. They were saved as JPG photos with high resolution at 600 dbi. The actual cover can be laid out in In Design®. Use the above dimensions in the program to create what you want. Or another design program like Illustrator®. There are templates that can be downloaded online. If you need more pages duplicate the last pages dimensions, then add this on to the length of the strip.

Liner Notes

This is where you can thank your Aunt Lorraine for you giving you your first real guitar. But there are also legal aspects that you have to place in there. Such as giving credit to the artist that created the cover design, list the photographer that took photos of the band. It is looks like this: Cover artwork by John Smith © year Smith, John. Photography by Jill Smith © year Smith Jill

Country of Manufacturer

Your website: or the website of the record company

UPC Barcode can be found at www.gs1us.org

Liner Notes:

Track Numbers and song titles

Credit for the song writer Song Tile Music by J.D. Jones Lyric by M.J. Jones, © year Jones, John D, Jones Martha J. If all the songs are done by one songwriter and do both music and lyrics just use All Song music and lyric by J.D. Jones. You don't have to list it on each song. The names here would be the actual names of the songwriters. If you are doing a cover song, give the credit also to the writers that done it before you.

Give credit to Musicians, producer, engineer, and the label who helped put the album together. Also, management team. While these are your legal obligations are those you are under contact those under. It is nice to thank anyone that has a hand in the making of an album, even the person that brings the coffee.

List the Music publishing company, and ASCAP or BMI etc.

Liner notes also include lyrics which is great for the listener who wants to sing along. There are two ways to list lyrics:

Keep On Rockin

The Squeeze method: *Some days it's just better to go back to bed/ Pull up the covers and hide your head/Forget the words that every fool has said/But I won't give up on you!/ Tell you what I am gonna do © 2022 Herd Paul A. BMI*

And the standard version:
Keep ON Rockin'
*Some days it's just better to go back to bed-
Pull up the covers and hide your head-
Forget the words that every fool has said-
But I won't give up on you!-
Tell you what I am gonna do!- © 2022 Herd Paul A. BMI*

Compact digital logo

The squeeze version takes up less space, but the standard is easier to read. After each song denote the copyright © year {Artist name}. Each song must be covered. Below that ^{P} in a circle like the copyright with the artist's name or record company. This should be used even if you don't have a copyright with the government, it denotes the copyright of the recording. If all the songs are by the same person and the record writes belong to them then the following is place on the album at the end of the lyrics. (P) © Year artist name or record label.

ALL RIGHTS RESEVED: Unauthorized duplication is violation is a violation of applicated laws.

Thanks to: This is where you thank everyone from your mother, girlfriend, wife, and of course your agent, lawyers and such. It can be anything here.
Contact Information: Give contact info for the artist, Fan club, booking agent, and management group.

If you are not including lyrics most of this can go on the back of the album. If you record on a compact disc. Be sure to include the compact disc logo. Also, the record company name and logo. If you are doing your own, it is wise to create a record company name and create your own logo and then register it with the state you live in with as a fictional name business. This will make you look more professional. If you use trademark be sure to us ^{TM} or ® symbols. Use ® only with registered trademarks. TM is used where it has not be registered.

Other Considerations:
If you used cover songs contract them for a mechanical licenses, this is usually the music publishing company that is listed on the record. If you have hired a musician, even if it is your brother, have them sign a work for hire agreement. This shows that they are being paid for their work and they hold no claim to the song. Pay something if is even a dollar.

If you have artwork that you did not create, give credit to the one that did even if it is free on the web. Take a screen shot showing that and then still give credit if there is a name listed or that photo is from Commons or Public domain.
Now that it is done register the album with the copyright office and with ASCAP or BMI, this is how you get paid when a radio station plays your song or downloads it. Also register with SoundScan if you want to attract the attention of record labels or expect lots of sales.

Setting Up for Vinyl

A vinyl record is made up of thousands of grooves, these groves are keyed to the frequency. A single grove of 1 kHz means the stylus would swing side to side 1000 times per second. Carefully watch the stylus arm and watch how it moves as the record plays, and how it reacts to the different sounds. Especially bass! This is the key element to watch for when mixing a master for a vinyl record. A bass heavy record will cause the record to jump and skip. So, if your music will make the metal roof of your car shimmy like the hips of a hula dancer, it is not a good mix for a vinyl record. The bass will have the brough a way down.

Once the master is mixed then a master lacquer is created and sent to the pressing plant. This is a mirror smooth aluminum disc coated with tin and silver nitrate then dipped in a nickel sulfate and electroplated. During the nickel sulfate bath, the lacquer is removed, and the nickel coating is peeled away. The nickel is the metal master and is a negative of the lacquer.

The metal master is then returned to the nickel bath and electroplated once again. This creates a positive copy called the mother master. It could be played but doing so would destroy it.

The mother master is now dropped back into the nickel bath and is electroplated yet again. This is known as the 'stamper' it is a negative copy and this is used to press out the plastic records. It will be good for about 70K pressing before it must be replaced.

Fig 14-35 An example of a vinyl master. One is created for each side of the record.

Fig 14-37 Stamping disc. This will last for about 70,000 pressing. So, several of these are created in case the record become a platinum seller.

Since the master lacquer cannot be played without destroying it. A short play 'ref' disc is also created This can be played 4-5 times before it starts to degrade in sound.

The process of making these disc is beyond the individual. So a specialty company needs to be used. One of those is like Aardvark Record Mastering in Denver, CO. website:
http://www.aardvarkmastering.com/ their prices are very reasonable, and their website will instruction you to their specifications.
For more record pressing company's see appendix.

Mastering for a CD

You must set to the RED BOOK setting. Red Book is the standard for audio CDs (Compact Disc Digital Audio system, or CD-DA) an audio content medium digitized at 44,100 samples per second (44.1KHz) and in a range of 65,536 possible values or 16 bits.

Thus, it allows for 79.57 minutes of digital audio on one disc or 99 tracks. The format was developed by Sony and Philips in the 1980s which became the audio medium standard for decades until the mp3 format was intruded in the late '90s. The CD replaced traditional audio tape and was the rage for its low noise floor with high digital sound quality. If you are going only for CD and not vinyl you have more leeway in having more time for songs. But if you are going for all methods CD and Vinyl then the time limit for vinyl records must be duplicate here.

The Red Book disc is divided into 3 primary sections which are: lead-in, program, and lead out. Every CD has a TOC (Table of Contents) or list of tracks which is stored in the Lead-In area of the CD disc. This records every track on the disc to recall.

The Standards of RED BOOK

1. Time limit of for 79.57 minutes of digital audio

2. Minimum duration for a track is 4 seconds (including 2-second pause)

3. Maximum number of tracks is 99

4. Maximum number of index points (subdivisions of a track) is 99 with no maximum time limit

5. International Standard Recording Code (ISRC) should be included

You may also want to add Copy Control which keeps a disc from being copied. ISRC can accessed at www.isrc.com .

WHAT IS ISRC?

ISRC (International Standard Recording Code) is the globally recognized standard numbering system for audio and music video recordings. It consists of a 12-digit alphanumeric code and functions as a universal identification number for each sound recording.

ISRC codes are primarily used to identify and catalog individual songs (tracks) on an album. The ISRC allows you to get paid for digital music sales by ensuring that your royalties are tracked properly. ISRC codes are necessary to sell your individual tracks via iTunes and other online music distributors. They are also required for any songs that you plan to offer for streaming on Spotify and other streaming services.

Similarly, you need to get ISRC codes in order to have your songs participate in the Billboard charts. To have a chance at making the Billboard music charts, your release must be registered with Nielsen SoundScan using your ISRC codes for the individual tracks. If you do not register then your sales figures are not counted, and you remain invisible to the system. It also required for CD of Church sermons, audio books, and spoken works CD works.

Does it cost? Yes but at the timing of the writing of this guide it was a fee to register and small fee per track.

DITHERING

Dithering or to dither means adding noise to the audio signal. Why would you add noise? So to trade a little bit of low-level hiss for a great deal of distortion. The distortion is first caused by using a fixed number of bits. If you dither, do it ONLY ONCE! It happens when you are down sampling say you have a song that has sample at 32 bits and you are going to 16 bits or the project rate is different. You would run Dither. Audacity has a dither program it is under EDIT> preferences> Quality.

You can choose the type of dither to be used in Audacity when performing operations requiring downsampling, or you can turn dither off altogether by setting it to none.

You might try applying some dithering when downsampling from 32 or 24 bits to 16 bits. s. Dithering isn't needed on 24- or 32 bit files. Dither can make 16-bit recordings sound better. The keep to it is trial and error, if you don't like click undo or Ctrl Z.

"Rectangular", "Triangular" and "Shaped" types of dither are simply different methods for randomizing the rounding process. The rectangular method can be thought of as like the roll of a die - any number has the same random probability of surfacing. The character of rectangular dither noise is low level white noise. The triangular method is characterized as a quieter, more constant, and higher pitched hiss than rectangular noise (sometimes called blue noise). Shaped dither is noise with a carefully contoured frequency content that puts most of the randomization at frequencies we can hear least easily. Shaped dither is the least audible at normal levels of amplification and is the default for the "High-quality conversion" setting.

Dither applied on Export

Dither is only applied when converting from a higher bit depth to a lower bit depth. Exporting to WAV or other uncompressed audio format is virtually lossless in all situations. However, there may be a very small amount of change to the audio data with some types of uncompressed audio export, depending on the settings in Audacity Preferences (see below).

Exporting to 32-bit PCM WAV format is 100% lossless - no dithering is applied.

Exporting to 24-bit PCM WAV format may be dithered with a peak dither level of around -130 dB

Exporting to 16-bit PCM WAV format may be dithered with a peak dither level of around -80 dB

When exporting to 16-bit, the maximum "error" is +/- 3 on a scale of \xe2\x88\x9232768 to +32767. 16-bit audio can at best be only accurate to the nearest digit on this scale.

When exporting to 24-bit, the maximum "error" is +/- 3 on a scale of -8388608 to +8388607. At the present time, state of the art audio electronics exhibits greater inaccuracies than are produced by dithering to 24-bit format.

BURNNG A CD:

You can burn a CD with your computer, but only in short runs. Better is to use a CD burning program. There many of them out there. The best do cost some but fairly reasonable. It works like this:

1. Download the free CD burner on your computer.
2. Insert a blank CD disc into the CD drive on your computer.
3. Run the free CD burner, click "Add File" button. In the open window, select music video files you want to burn and click Open.
4. Edit the music file according to your needs, then click "Burn" button to burn music to an audio CD.

The drawback to this is it does not look professional and may not include the ISRC which means you could have the bestselling album and not be listed on the charts. So, the best method is to send a master to a CD pressing plant. They can create a glass master then create a professional CD with jewel case.

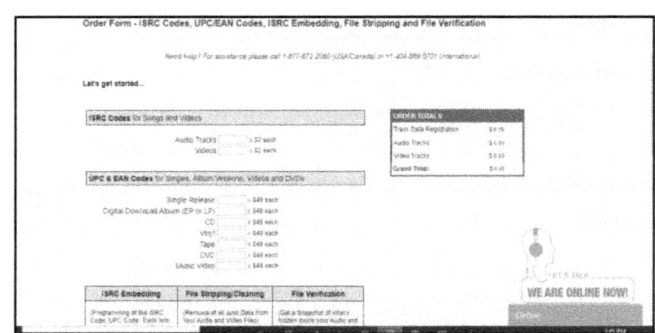

Fig 14-38 Order screen on the ISRC website.

Other Legal Things with Putting Out an Album

There is music and then there is the music business. They are as different as day and night but each need each other. They are like peanut butter and jelly. Separate they do their own thing, but together they create something amazing.

Music is the creation, you're walking along and you hear someone say something like, "There are Dead Roses here." You think 'what great idea for a song'. You start jotting down lyrics, and then strumming it out on the guitar, and then you are recording. At that moment there is copyright protection is place. This also would apply if you wrote the song down.

However, there are still some tricky things here. The best protection is getting a copyright with the U.S. Copyright Office through their website at https://copyright.gov . You will have to set up an account. In doing so you will have to create a password, unlike other accounts. This password is short lived and must be changed every so often. The copyright office will notify you to make the change. Even if you have one copyright and plan no more. You must keep changing this password to keep the account active. If it is not active it is not accessed in case you need to access it later. And since copyrights go on 50 years after your death. This is a lifelong commitment.

You have two choices - you can copyright one song, but if you are going to do more than one song is cheaper to place the songs in an album. And copyright them as a whole album. Each song has the same protection as if they were copyrighted individually but are listed under an album first. You will have to send them a hard copy of the album.

Part V The Business of Muisc

Chapter 15 The Business of Music

Music is not always about the fun of playing and creating it. It is not called show business because it is all show it is also business. And the worse thing that can happen to you is you suddenly go from working your day job to be a hit song writer and or performer. You are opening in *Madison Square Garden* in NYC. But you do not have clue about the business part of this when a six figure check rolls in. You go on a spending spree and then come the end of the year and taxes are due, and you think that just like your former job they took you taxes out…but they don't do that. You should have been paying taxes in with estimated taxes forms four times a year. Now the government wants their money and you don't have it and your next appearance isn't MTV on reality show about fallen rock stars.

SIGNING UP WITH BMI OR ASCAP

To get paid when your song plays on the radio, in an AD, or downloaded you must be either a member of BMI or ASCAP. You can only pick one, and you will sign a contract that will last for at least two years with them. You can sign up as a songwriter or a publisher. To get the most money possible sign up as both. This will, however, cause you to have to create your own music publishing company.

For BMI

www.bmi.com/join

FOR ASCAP

https://ome.ascap.com/

Company	Business Structure	Membership Cost	Music Catalogue	Number of Member Artists	History
BMI	Nonprofit	Free to artists; $150 to publishers; $250 for companies	17 million songs	1.1 million musicians and composers	Founded in 1939 to protect new music like jazz, blues, and country
ASCAP	Member-owned nonprofit	$50 for new artists, no annual dues; self-renewing membership	10 million songs	735,000 member artists	Original U.S. PRO, founded in 1914 alongside copyright laws

CREATING YOUR OWN MUSIC COMPANY

You have the stories of how song writers and musicians lose control of their own songs. How they can't keep someone from using it for political candidate or an advertisement. You may, many do think, that because you own the copyright you own the song. Yes, you do, but all that means is that someone else can claim it to be their song.

It is the music company that owns the rights to use the song, and in turn get a part of the payment. So, you may find yourself a strong independent and a candidate that you hate using your song "I Win Again!" or your song "She Rides on the Wind" being used for a famine hygiene ad, and there is not one thing you can do to stop it. It is the music publishing company that controls that. Now you can get around this by creating your own music publishing company. Before warned, running a music publishing company is a full-time job, and it will suck the living life out of your creative soul, this is the reason that most entertainers choose to not go down this road. You must decide if you want to be the creative side or the business side.

The first thing is this cannot be for beginners for you must have an official release of a song, that is yours or that you represent someone else. Otherwise, the Performing Rights Organization (PRO) will not process your request. The song could be part of a proper record, CD, or digital release; the soundtrack of a motion picture; or a television/radio broadcast.

Create Your Company Name

Every publishing company must have a unique name. Be sure to pick one that will suit your goals and be your calling card when you're pitching music to potential radio plays and TV or film placements. Ask yourself a simple question: Is it descriptive, appropriate, and memorable? Do a quick check on the internet to see if there is another company with this same name.   At the same time dream up a logo for your company. Like Gene Simmons Money Bags logo.

Register as a Business with Secretary of State of your state and file a fictional name of DBA (Doing Business As). If you are going to be doing any kind of sales at all, request also a Sales Tax Number, if you sell an album in your state, you MUST COLLECT the required sales tax, that is for the area that your business is located in.

Next contact the IRS and request EIN this will give you a federal identification number that will be used on your tax returns. If you're going for a sole proprietorship, you will be filing Schedule C while partnership, or corporation will require different forms. We strongly urge you to do your homework and address this question in advance so you're able to find the business type that best suits your needs.

Next do not use your personal bank account. Instead set up a business account with the business name.

Step 5: Choose BMI or ASCAP and submit your application as a publisher

You'll need to join a collection society as a music publisher. If you're already affiliated with one as a songwriter, you'll want to apply it to your publishing company as well. If you're not yet affiliated, take some time to familiarize yourself with all the options that are out there. ASCAP and BMI are the major PROs in the United States.

If you plan to have multiple songwriter clients of your publishing company, and not just yourself, you will need to set up publishing affiliations with all the U.S. PROs, because in order to publish works by a songwriter registered with one of the U.S. PROs, you must have a publishing company registered with that PRO.

This restriction does not apply to songwriters outside of the U.S.: you can publish a songwriter affiliated with any global PRO using any of your U.S. PRO affiliations. I.e., If you're affiliated with ASCAP, you cannot use that affiliation to register songs for a songwriter client who is affiliated with BMI, but you can use your ASCAP affiliation to register songs for a songwriter client who is another country.

Register your company's songs with the Copyright Office if someone infringes upon your work you'll have better legal protection. This can be done online and typically takes a few months to process. If you have already copyrighted songs in your own name, you'll need to transfer those rights to your publishing company. Remember this the music publishing company, not the songwriter owning the copyrights.

Register with U.S. Mechanical Rights Organizations. The final step is to contact The MLC, The Harry Fox Agency, and Music Reports, and register as a publisher. This is done in addition to registering with a collection society. The difference is that these mechanical organizations issue and collect royalties from the mechanical licenses issued for streaming, downloads, and CDs and other physical music. They do not deal with performance royalties, like BMI and ASCAP does.

Like that was stated at first you have to decide if you want to be mostly about business or music. The other part is that you would create the company and then hire people to run it.

TAX, TAX , TAX THAT MUSICIAN

Unless you are just doing this for a hobby. You are going to have to fill out tax forms, and if you make anything over $400.00 this means in many forms. From gigs, royalties to pay to play. You will have to report this as income on Schedule C, and SE so it might be wise to create your own music company and use many of the points in starting your own music publishing company. But just don't contact BMI or ASCAP as a publisher, but a song writer/artist only.

Now though let's say you write one song and never another one you continue with your job as the janitor at the local school. IRS will not see you as a professional song writer, and thus you will have to fill out Schedule E, Supplemental Income, instead. However, if you continue to write songs the government considers you self-employed as a song writer and you would report your royalties under Schedule C, Profit or Loss from Business.

You may have to pay tax, if you file under Schedule C you can also have deductions that may lower your tax. Deductions can include supplies like strings, and effect pedals. But also, can include costumes (if not used anywhere else) travel cost i.e. hotel rooms. Keep all receipts for travel to lessons, recording sessions, and performances, as you can claim the mileage come tax time. Instrument upkeep and repairs, and the cost of consumable goods like rosin, and picks are also deductible expenses. The costs associated with registering for a business license, maintaining insurance, and if you have a true home office or studio in your home you can deduct part of the rent/house payment plus utilities cost of your home. To do this the space must be used solely for that purpose. Other deductions can include fees associated with maintaining your website, like domain registration and monthly hosting, and even a computer if it is used solely for business. The big thing is that it is a business so you must treat it like one.

Things have changed on deducting records and CD cost. Use to be you spent 10K for getting a record made you could deduct that amount. Now, with some many want to be musicians getting into the business. You can only deduct the part of the cost that you sell. For example, With the 10K invested you have 5K records meaning each one cost $2.00 each you sell them for 10 dollars each. Last year gigs you only sold 500 records. You made $5,000.00 and the cost is 1000.00 you can deduct only that $1000.00. And you must report the inventory of the remining records. You will not be paying tax on the $5000.00 but only on the $4000.00. Big thing is when you buy a bag of picks you keep that receipt, and when you go home write up a purchase order for it. It may only be a few bucks, but make sure you do it every time.

One last thing is in doing this, you may find that your county or state may tax you on all the equipment you use, this will include instruments and recording equipment. Note you will have to have three years of profit out of five years of doing business for the IRS to define it as a business and not a hobby. Business you get deductions, with the hobby no deductions and you pay! Never assume tax people will see something one way. For example, writing this guide about music placed the author in a new category and taxes were issued on the music equipment, because it was being used to make profit, even if it is not directly used for music. It was classified like the computers and furniture of the business. And every area differs, so make sure you ask all the questions you can.

Well there you have it, we have taken you through installing Audacity, recording with it, downloading to it, mixing, mastering, and doing business with it. We wish all luck; you can have and enjoy every minute of it. And never look back on life and wonder "What if?" Instead reach for everything, you fail, but least you will know you have tried.

Author R.N. Roller with his 'collection of toys' Behind him his recording desk. He lives in Monett, MO with his wife.

Appendix I Audacity Short Cuts

File menu

Ctrl + N	New
Ctrl + O	Open
Ctrl + W	Close
Ctrl + S	Save Project
Ctrl + Shift + I	Import > Audio
Ctrl + Shift + E	Export Audio
Ctrl + Shift + L	Export Multiple
Ctrl + Q	Exit

Edit menu

Ctrl + Z	Undo
Ctrl + Y	Redo
Ctrl + Shift + Z	(Mac/Linux) Undo
Ctrl + X	Cut
Ctrl + K	Delete
Ctrl + Alt + X	Remove Special > Split Cut
Ctrl + Alt + K	Remove Special > Split Delete
Ctrl + L	Remove Special > Silence Audio
Ctrl + T	Remove Special > Trim Audio
Ctrl + I	Clip Boundaries > Split
Ctrl + Alt + I	Clip Boundaries > Split New
Ctrl + J	Clip Boundaries > Join
Ctrl + Alt + J	Clip Boundaries > Detach at Silences
Ctrl + C	Copy
Ctrl + V	Paste
Ctrl + Alt + V	Paste Text to New Label
Ctrl + D	Duplicate
Alt + X	Labeled Audio > Cut
Alt + K	Labeled Audio > Delete
Shift + Alt + X	Labeled Audio > Split Cut
Shift + Alt + K	Labeled Audio > Split Delete
Alt + L	Labeled Audio > Silence Audio
Shift + Alt + C	Labeled Audio > Copy
Alt + I	Labeled Audio > Split
Alt + J	Labeled Audio > Join
Shift + Alt + J	Labeled Audio > Detach at Silences
Ctrl + A	Select > All
Ctrl + Shift + A	Select > None
Q	Select > Spectral > Toggle Spectral Selection
[	Select > Left at Playback Position
]	Select > Right at Playback Position
Shift + J	Select > Track Start to Cursor
Shift + K	Select > Cursor to Track End
Ctrl + Shift + K	Select > In All Tracks
Ctrl + Shift + Y	Select > In All Sync-Locked Tracks
Z	Find Zero Crossings
Left arrow	Move Cursor to Selection Start
Right arrow	Move Cursor to Selection End
J	Move Cursor to Track Start
K	Move Cursor to Track End
Ctrl + P	Preferences
Cmd + ,	(Mac) Preferences
Tab	Move to and open Next Label
Shift + Tab	Move to and open Previous Label
Alt + Left arrow	Move to Next Label
Alt + Right arrow	Move to Previous Label
Shift + Home	Selection to Start
Shift + End	Selection to End
Backspace or Del	Delete Key
Shift + Left arrow	Selection Extend Left
Shift + Right arrow	Selection Extend Right
Ctrl + Shift + Left arrow	Selection Contract Left
Ctrl + Shift + Right arrow	Selection Contract Right
Left arrow	Cursor Left
Right arrow	Cursor Right
Left arrow or ,	Cursor Short Jump Left (1 second)
.	Cursor Short Jump Right (1 second)
Shift + Left arrow or Shift + ,	Cursor Long Jump Left (15 seconds)
Shift + Right arrow or Shift + .	Cursor Long Jump Right (15 seconds)

View Menu

Ctrl + 1	Zoom In
Ctrl + 2	Zoom Normal
Ctrl + 3	Zoom Out
Ctrl + E	Zoom to Selection
Ctrl + F	Fit In Window
Ctrl + Shift + F	Fit Vertically
Ctrl + [	Go to Selection Start
Ctrl +]	Go to Selection End
Ctrl + Shift + C	Collapse All Tracks
Ctrl + Shift + X	Expand Collapsed Tracks
F11	Full screen on/off
Cmd + /	(Mac) Full screen on/off

Transport menu

Space	Play/Stop
X	Play/Stop and Set Cursor
Shift + Space	Loop Play
P	Pause
Home	Skip to Start
End	Skip to End
R	Record
Shift + T	Timer Record...
Shift + R	Record on New track
Alt + Right arrow	Move Cursor to Next Label
Alt + Left arrow	Move Cursor to Previous Label
1	Play One Second
B	Play To Selection
C	Play Cut Preview
Shift + F5	Play short period before selection start
Shift + F6	Play short period after selection start
Shift + F7	Play short period before selection end
Shift + F8	Play short period after selection end
Ctrl + Shift + F5	Play short period before and after selection start
Ctrl + Shift + F7	

Left Arrow	Short seek left (1 sec)
Right arrow	Short Seek Right during Playback (1 sec)
Shift + Left arrow or Shift + ,	Long Seek Left during Playback (15 seconds)
Shift + Right arrow or Shift + .	Long Seek Right during Playback (15 seconds)

Tracks menu

Ctrl + Shift + N	Add New > Mono Track
Ctrl + Shift + M	Mix and Render to New Track
Ctrl + U	Mute All Tracks
Ctrl + Shift + U	Unmute All Tracks
Ctrl + B	Add Label at Selection
Ctrl + M	Add Label at Playback Position
Cmd + .	(Mac) Add Label at Playback Position
Ctrl + Home	Move Focus to First Track
Ctrl + End	Move Focus to Last Track
Up arrow	Move Focus to Previous Track
Shift + Up arrow	Move Focus to Previous and Select
Down arrow	Move Focus to Next Track
Shift + Down arrow	Move Focus to Next and Select
Enter	Toggle Focused Track
Shift + C	Remove Focused track

Audio track dropdown menu

Shift + M	Open menu on focused track
Shift + U	Mute/Unmute focused track
Shift + S	Solo/Unsolo focused track
Shift + G	Change gain on focused track
Alt + Shift + Up arrow	Increase gain on focused track
Alt + Shift + Down arrow	Decrease gain on focused track
Shift + P	Change pan on focused track
Alt + Shift + Left arrow	Pan left on focused track
Alt + Shift + Right arrow	Pan right on focused track

Device toolbar

Shift + H	Change Audio Host
Shift + O	Change Playback Device
Shift + I	Change Recording Device
Shift + N	Change Recording Channels

Tools toolbar

F1	Chooses Selection tool
F2	Chooses Envelope tool
F3	Chooses Draw tool
F4	Chooses Zoom tool
F5	Chooses Time Shift tool
F6	Chooses Multi-tool
D	Next tool
A	Previous tool

Keyboard focus

Ctrl + Shift + F6	Move backward through currently focused toolbar in Upper Toolbar dock area, Track View and currently focused toolbar in Lower Toolbar dock area
Ctrl + F6	Move forward through currently focused toolbar in Upper Toolbar dock area, Track View and currently focused toolbar in Lower Toolbar dock area
Alt + Shift + F6	Move backward through modeless windows, undocked Toolbars and the main project window
Alt + F6	Move forward through modeless windows, undocked Toolbars and the main project window

Appendix II Studio Log Sheet

STUDIO LOG SHEET

Date: Recording _____ Mixing _____ ; Artist: _____ Personnel _____
Song Title _____

TRACK NUMBER:									
Instrument, Tuning/Voice	Preamplifier			Compressor			Real-time Recording Effects		
	Polarity:	Gain:	High/Low:	RNC _____ Other: _____					
Microphone Type	Basic track settings			Thresh	Attack	Rls	Gain		
Patt: Targ: Dist:	Pan:		Gain:						

MIXDOWN INFORMATION												
Basic mix settings	Noise reduction	Amplification		Primary EQ			Reverb		Compression			
Pan		Db		Band	Hz	dB	Pre-delay	Hz	Thr	Gain	Ratio	Attack	Rls
Gain (mixer)	Sensitivity	Pitch Change Freq.		1			Decay						
Gain (processed WAV)				2			Damping						
				3			Room sz						
Filters	Bands	Start	To	4			Wet/dry						
Hz	Roll off												
Low Pass	Tremolo						Limiter						
High Pass	Type		Hz				Type:		L	R	Limit	Hold	
	Start						Gain						
	Wet												
	Freq.												

Notes:

Appendix III Sound Booth Plans

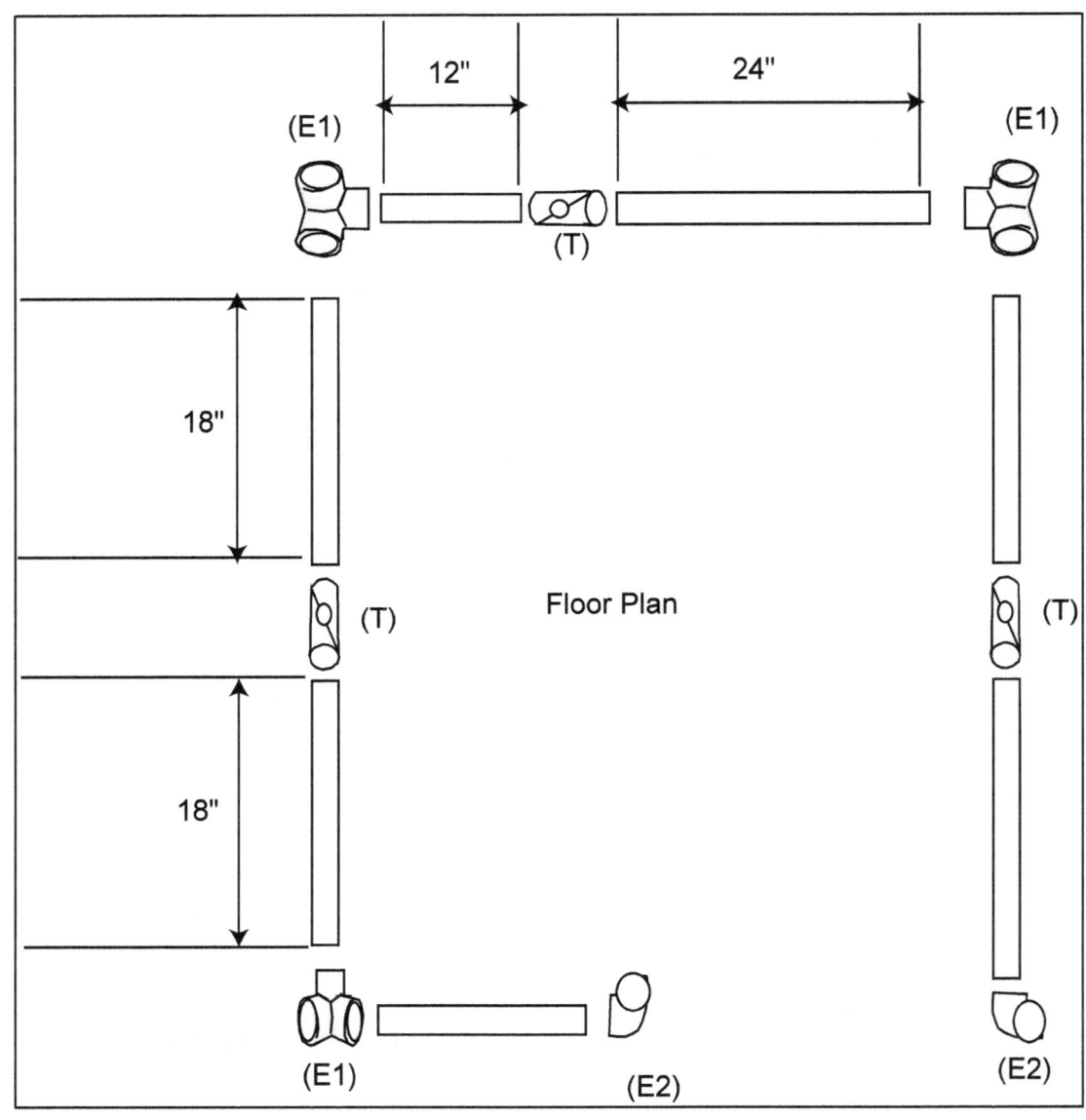

Floor Plan

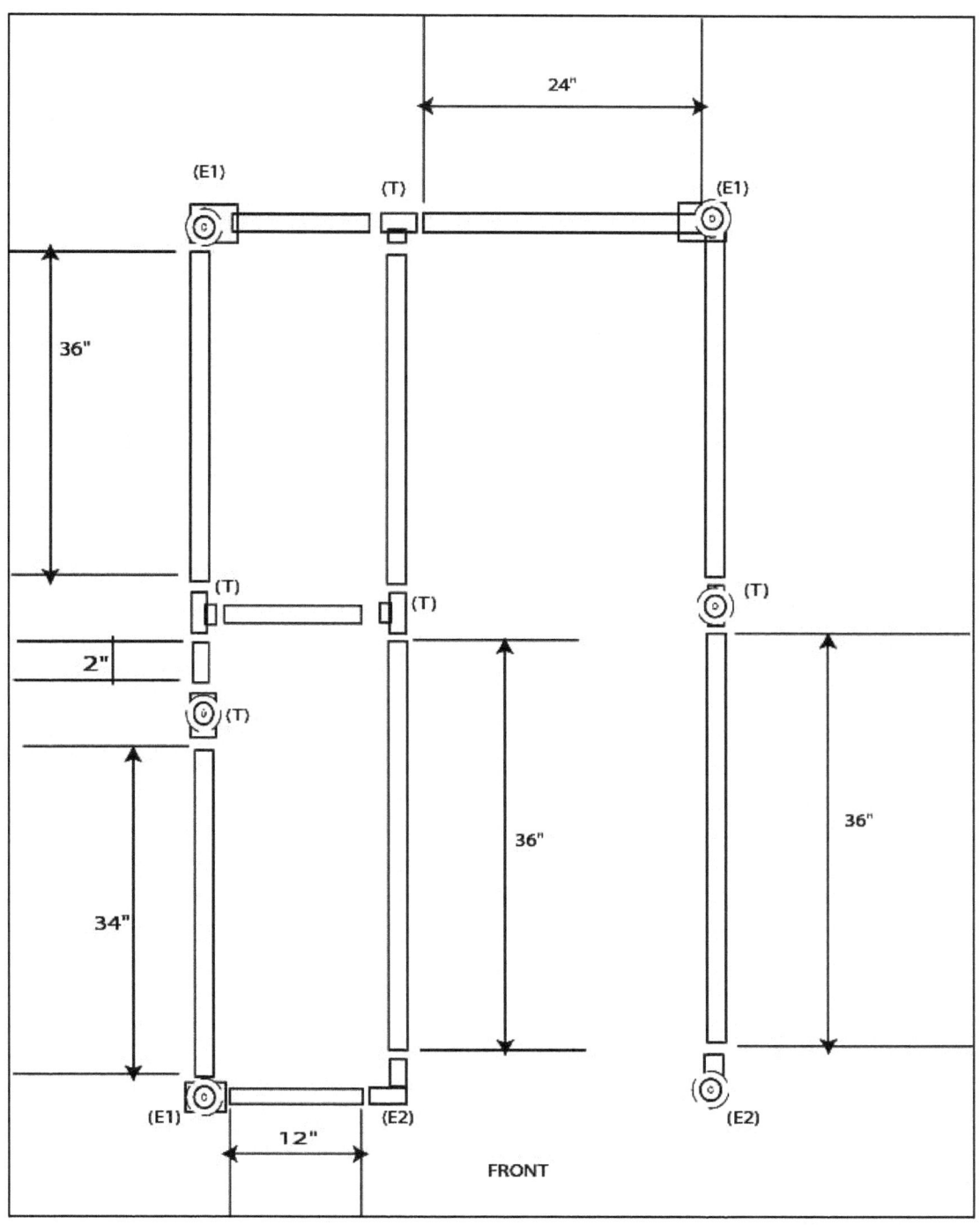

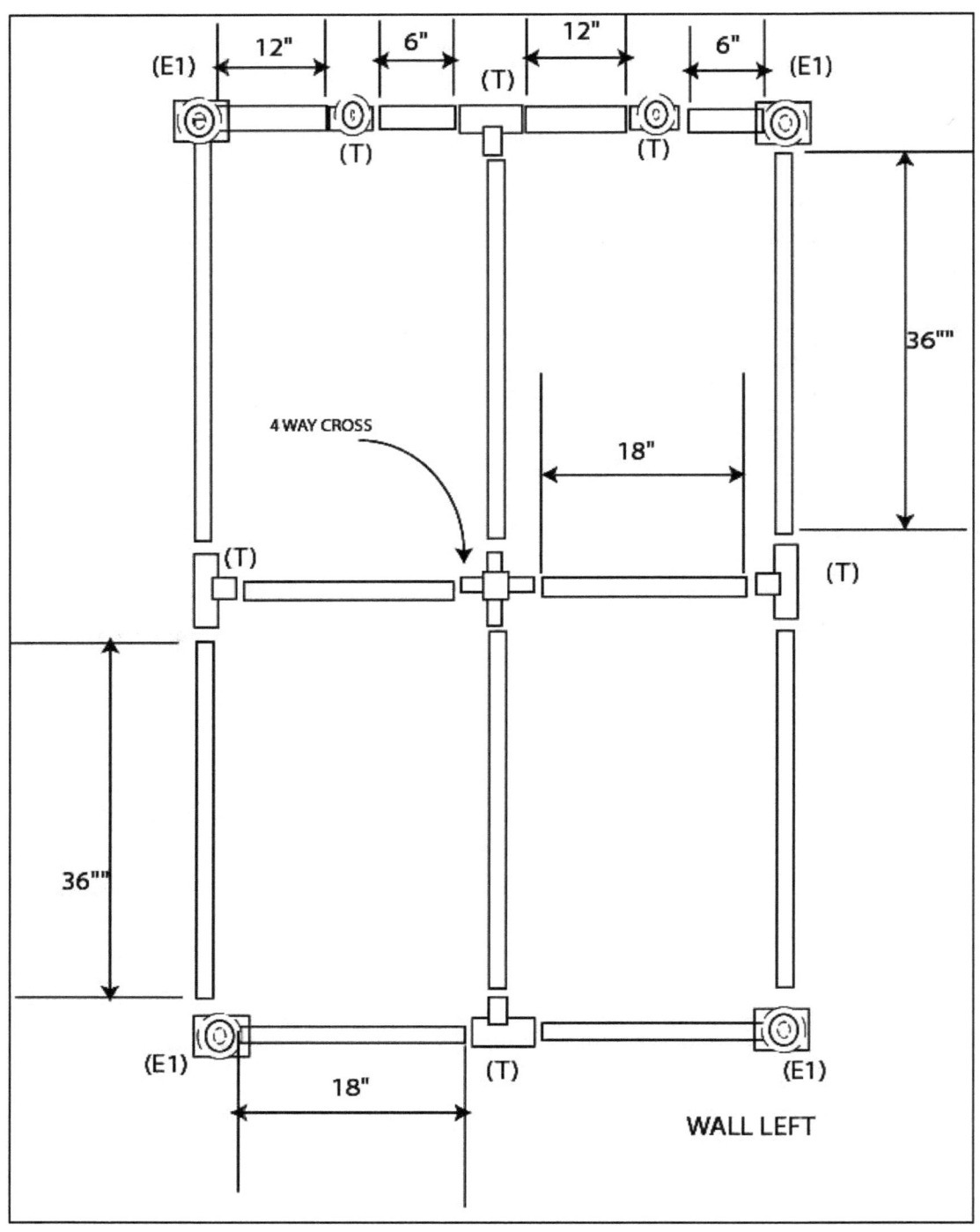

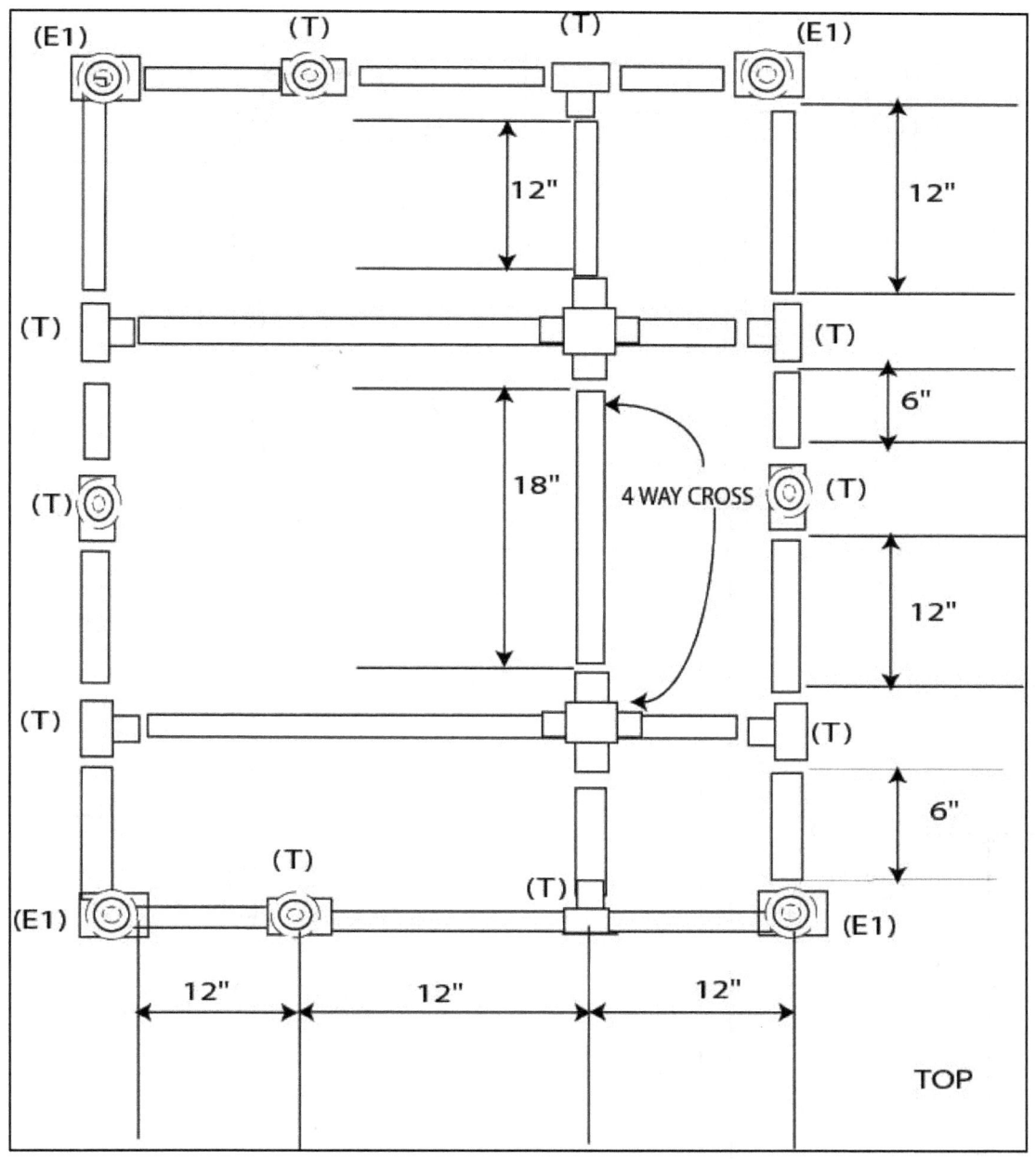

TOP

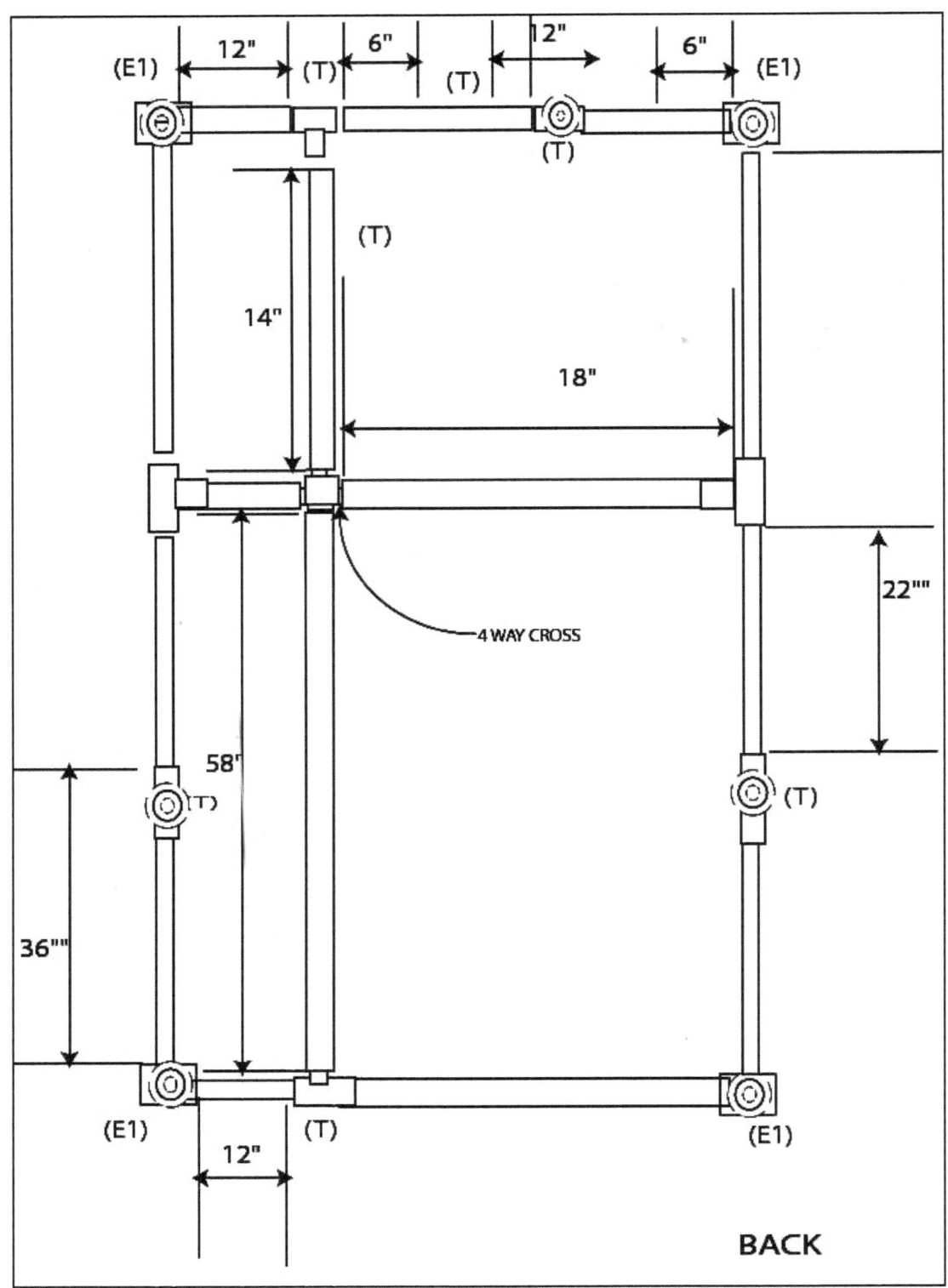

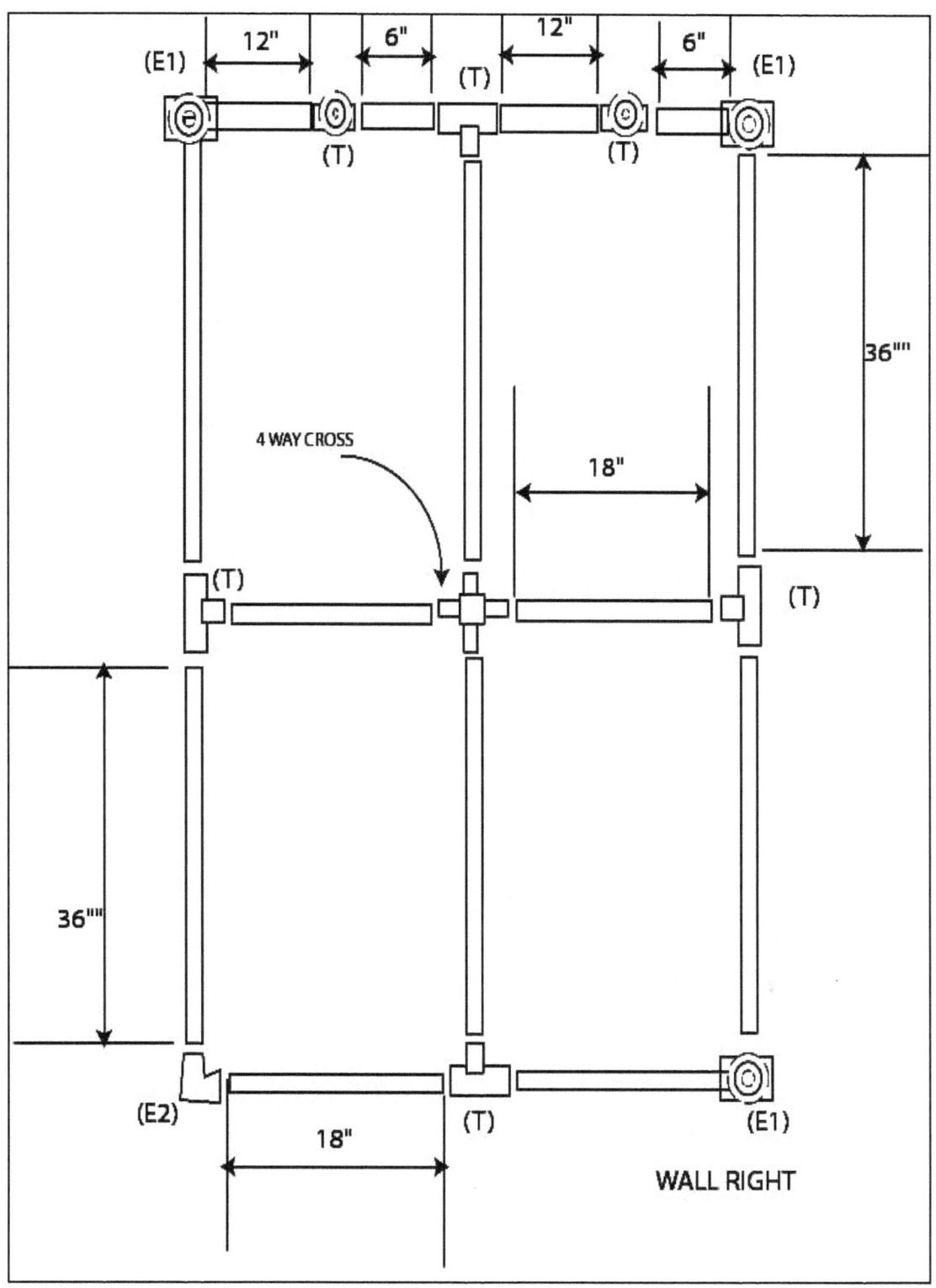

Appendix IV Record Pressing Plants

Archer Record Pressing 7401 Davidson Detroit, MI 48212 313-365-9545 7" & 12" Black & Color	Brooklyn Phono 270 42nd Street Brooklyn, NY 11232 718-788-5777 fern@brooklynphono.com	Burlington Record Plant 660 Pine Street Bay 5 Burlington, VT 05401 802-540-8188	Cascade Record Pressing 16735 SE Ken's Ct., Suite A Milwaukie, OR 97267 503-974-9393 info@cascaderecordpressing.com
Clampdown Record Pressing #102 - 3686 Bonneville Place Burnaby, BC V3N 4T6 778-708-0526 clampdownrecordpressing@gmail.com	Erika Records 6300 Caballero Blvd. Buena Park, CA 90620 714-228-5420 7", 10" & 12" and odd Sizes from 5" to 12" Black, Color1, Picture1 & Shape1 ken@erikarecords.com	Furnace Mfg. 2719-B Dorr Ave. Fairfax, VA 22031 703-205-0007	Gold_Rush Vinyl 1321 Rutherford Lane Suite 130 Austin, TX 78753 512-298-1346
Gotta Groove Records 3615 Superior Avenue #4201 A Cleveland, OH 44114 800-295-0171 7" & 12" Black & Color	Hand Drawn Records 16420 Midway Road Addison, TX 75001 844-438-4695 vinyl@handdrawnrecords.com	Kindercore Vinyl 147 Fritz Mar Ln. Athens, GA 30607 256-338-5928 bill@kindercore.com	Le Vinylist 5264 Wilfrid-Hamel Blvd Quebec City, QB G2E 2H2 418-576-6651 info@levinylist.com
Memphis Record Pressing 3015 Brother Blvd. Memphis, TN 38133 info@memphisvinyl.com	Microforum 1 Woodborough Avenue Toronto, ON M6M 5A1	Musicol Inc. 780 Oakland Park Ave Columbus, OH 43224 800-240-5963 7" & 12" Black & Color	New Orleans Record Pressing 1336 Montegut St. New Orleans, LA 70117 504-507-8621 info@NewOrleansRecordPress.com
Palomino Records 2818 Highway 44 E Shepherdsville, KY 40165-6310 502-543-1521 7" & 12" Black & Color travis@dosado.com	Quality Record Pressings 543 N. 10th St. Salina, KS 67401 785-825-8609 12" only	Record_Technology Inc. 486 Dawson Camarillo, CA 93012 805-484-2747 12" only Black & Color	RIP-V Inc. 685 Mercille Street Lambert, QC J4P 2M1 450-671-7676 12" only
Smashed Plastic 4200 W Diversey Ave Unit #14 Chicago, IL 60639 john@smashedplastic.com	Scftwax Record Pressing 2332 Fernon Street Philadelphia, PA 19145 776-343-7478 softwaxrecordpressing@gmail.com	Sunpress Vinyl 14097 NW 19th Ave Opa-locka, FL 33054 786-577-0983 info@sunpressvinyl.com	The Vinyl Lab 1414 3rd Avenue South Ste. 103 Nashville, TN 37210 916-549-2430 scott@thevinylab.com
Third Man Records 441 West Canfield Street Detroit, MI 48201 313-209-5206 tmporders@thirdmanrecords.com	United Record Pressing 453 Allied Drive Nashville, TN 37211 615-259-9396 7", 10" & 12" Black & Color	VinylRP 95 Levy Road Atlantic Beach, FL 32233 904-853-5128 info@vinylrp.com	

Jackets, Labels, Film Work, and Supplies

Bags Unlimited (800) 767-2247 Paper sleeves, all sizes	Bowers Record Sleeve 5331 North Tacoma Avenue Indianapolis, IN 46220 (800) 876-8881 Paper sleeves and mailers, all sizes	DoradoPkg - Music Packaging 10742 Burbank Blvd. North Hollywood, CA 91601 (818)761-9295 Record Jackets, Vinyl Album Covers
G & M Label Printing 6211 Santa Monica Blvd Los Angeles, CA 90038 (213) 466-1307 Labels 3", 3-5/8" & 4"	Hamlett Printing 405 Humphreys Street Nashville, TN 37203 (615)256-7429 hamlettptg@aol.com Labels 3-5/8" & 4" Printed Sleeves	NiPro Record Plating 7 Marconi Irvine, CA 92618 (949)215-1151 sales@niprooptics.com Record Plating & Stampers
RAE Products 2003 Nolensville Road Nashville, TN 37204 (615) 254-7556 Bubble Mailers for Cassettes and CDs	Ross Ellis 8300 Tampa # J Northridge, CA 91325 (818) 993-4767 Record Jackets, CD covers etc.	Stoughton Printing 130 North Sunset City of Industry, CA 91744 (800) 961-3678 Fax (626) 961-6505 Record Jackets, CD covers etc.
Welcome to 1979 110 48th Ave N Nashville, TN 37209 (844)679-1979 chris@welcometo1979.com Record Plating & Stampers		

Introducing Our newest line TBK Hillcrest Is a line of instructional book written in simple to understand format

Appendix V Sound Examples

Go :   www.pahpublishing/sounds   For example with and without Amplify, Pitch Change, Reverb and how SPX

INDEX

A

Aardvark Record 216
Accordion 109
Acoustic Guitar 133
Adjustable, Fade 48
Album, Copyright 218
Album, Designing Cover 211
Album, Liner Notes 214
Album, Making 200
Album, Mastering For A CD 216
Album, Setting Up For Vinyl 215
Alesis® 104
Amplify 24, 25, 34, 53, 54, 134, 162
Angels Cry .. 186, 187, 188, 190, 201, 202, 203, 206
Another Love .. 9, 135, 171, 195, 198, 201, 202, 203, 205, 206
Appetite For Destruction 211
Arranging Songs 205
ASCAP 221
Audacity 1-5, 7, 9, 10-14, 20-22, 24-25, 27, 34, 37, 40, 46, 52, 54-57, 64-66, 68-69, 75-76, 79-81, 83, 105-106, 108, 110, 112, 114, 119, 122-124, 126, 127, 128, 130-134, 136, 139, 140-141, 143-144, 146, 149, 150, 153, 156, 163, 167, 174, 175-177, 180, 182, 185, 187, 190, 193, 196, 208, 217, 223- 235
Audacity, Connecting Up 75
Audacity, Creating An Album On 206
Audacity, Open 12
Auto Duck 25

B

Backup Singers, Creating 181
Baffles, Sound 86
Balance, Frequencies- 195
Banjo 110
Basics Of Mixing 152
Bass And Treble 24, 26
Bass Guitar 114
Bass Guitar, Microphone Placement. 114
Bass Track 128
Beatles 7, 24, 152, 200, 201, 202, 211
BMI 221
Bohemian Rapsody 139
Bouncing Stereo, Creating 183
Boundary Microphone 98
Brain May 135, 205

C

CD, Burning 218
Change Pitch 27
Change Speed 29
Change Tempo 30
Clarinet 110
Classic Filters 31
Click Removal 32
Click Track 122
Clip Fix 51
Clipping, Hard 35
Clipping, Soft 35
Comporession, Drum- Kick Drums 178
Compression, Bass 178
Compression, Drums-Snare Drums ... 178
Compression, Guitar Acoustic 178
Compression, Guitars Electric 178
Compression, In Master 194
Compression, Using 176
Compression,Backing Vocals 177
Compression,Lead Vocals 177
Concept Album 204
Condenser Microphone 97
Connecting ,Guitar 106
Connecting Instruments 106
Connecting, Drum Machine 109
Connecting, Electronic Drums 109
Connecting, Keyboard 108
Contrast 72
Cross Fade Clips 51
Cross Fade Tracks 51
Cutec 8

D

DAE 10
Dancing With The Devil, Song ... 129, 149, 161, 102, 203, 205, 206 .... 136, 195
DAW 9
Dead Rose, Song 122, 123, 134, 154, 178, 179, 180, 201, 203, 206, 214, 218
Def Leppard 10
Delay 53
Delay Setups 174
Diehard, The Movie 211
Digidesign 10
Distortion 34, 35
Dithering 217
Dominic Mazzoni 10
Don't Let Him Go, Song 204
Draw Tool 62
Drum Kit 110
Drum Kit, One Microphone 111
Drum Kit, Two Microphones 111
Drum Machine 127
Drum Track 124
Drums, Overhead Microphones 112
Dynamic Microphone 96

E

Echo 37
Echo And Delay, How To Use 188
Edsion, Thomas 6
Effects 24
Electric Guitar 113
Electric Lead Guitar 132
Electric Rhythm Guitar 131
EQ 19, 24, 38, 54, 57, 58, 65, 67, 105, 128, 141, 157, 164, 165, 166, 167, 168, 169, 170, 171, 173, 179, 180, 183, 185, 190, 195
EQ Settings Drum Machine 168
EQ Settings , Kick/Bass 167
EQ Settings , Singing Voice 166
EQ Settings Trombone 173
EQ Settings, Acoustic Guitar 170
EQ Settings, Bass Guitar 169
EQ Settings, Drum And Percussion 164
EQ Settings, Electric Guitar 170
EQ Settings, Electric Keyboard 171
EQ Settings, Guitar 165
EQ Settings, Harmonica 171
EQ Settings, Keyboard 166
EQ Settings, Piano 166, 171
EQ Settings, Saxophone 172
EQ Settings, Speaking Voice 166
EQ Settings, Trumpet 173
EQ Settings, Tuba 173
EQ Settings, VOICE 165
EQ Settings, Woodwinds 172
Expand And Compress 35

F

Fade Out, Studio How To 195
Fade, Adjustable 48
Fade, Cross Clips 51
Fade, Cross Tracks 51
Fade, Out 38
Fade, Out Studio 60
Fade. In 38
Fiddle 112
Fiddle, , Microphone Placement 112
Filter Curve 38
Filter, Chebyshev Type II 31
Filter, Notch 56
Filter, Pop 102
Filters, Chebyshev Type I 31
Filters, Classic 31
Filters, High Pass 54
Filters, Low Pass 54
First Instrument To Record 122
Fliters, Butterworth 31
Flute 112
Flute, , Microphone Placement 112
Follow My Heart 204

G

Graphic EQ 38
Guitar Track 129
Guns And Roses 211

H

Hand Claps 115
Hand Claps ,Microphone Placement. 115
Hard Limiter 35
Harmonic, Even 35
Harmonic, Odd 35
Headphones 14, 76, 79, 108, 109, 135, 136, 143
Herd Paul A. 203, 205, 206, 214
Hi Infidelity 204
High Pass Filters 54
Humming ,Microphone Placement ... 120

I

I Am The Night... 138, 196, 197, 203, 206, 213
I Wish You Were There 204
If Guns And Roses 211
Import 79
In Your Letter 204
In-A-Gadda-Da-Vida 200
Interface 78
IRSC 217
Invert 39

K

Keep On Loving You 204
Keep On Rockin' 124, 202, 204, 206
Keyboard 135
Kick Drum, Microphone Placement... 111

L

Labeling Tracks 141
Laying Down A Track 121
Led Zeppelin 213
Let Son Of A Poor Man 196
Leveller 35
Limiter 179
Limiters 54
Line Ports 76
Loudness Normalization 39
Low Pass Filters 54

M

Macros 63
Mastering, Recording 193
Metallica's 211
Microphone 95
Microphone Cords 101
Microphone Placement 106
Microphone Placement, Banjo 110
Microphone Placement, Accordion ... 109
Microphone Placement, Clarinet 110
Microphone Placement, Drum Kit 110
Microphone Placement, Guitar 113
Microphone Placement, Hnad Claps . 115
Microphone Placement, Harmonica.. 115
Microphone Placement, Humming ... 113
Microphone Preamp 105
Microphone, Boundary 98
Microphone, Cardioid 100
Microphone, Condenser 97
Microphone, Dynamic 96
Microphone, LDC 100
Microphone, Microphone 96
Microphone, Omnidirectional 99
Microphone, Polarity Patterns 99
Microphone, SDC 100
Microphone, Shotgun 100
Microphone, Will Not Recognize 146
Microphones, How Many 100
Mircophone, Figure 8 100
Mix, Final 190
Mixing Boards 104
Mixing, Getting Ready 149
Music Company, Creating 221

N

Need 2 Love U 196, 201, 204, 206
Night At The Opera 211
Noise Gate 55
Noise Reduction 40
Normalization, Loudness 39
Normalize 39
NOTCH FILTER 56
Nyquist Plug-In Installer 68
Nyquist Prompt 68

O

Out Of Season 204
Overdrive, Medium 35
Overdrive, Soft 35
Overdrive,Hard 35
Overdub 138

P

Pain 201, 203, 206
Paul, Les 6
Paulstretch 40
Pectral Edit Multi Tool 56
Perry Mason 203
Phaser 42
Photograph, Def Leppard 10
Piano 116, 135, 171
Piano ,Microphone Placement 116
Pop Filter 102
Ports, Line 76
Ports, Mic In 76
Ports, USB 76
Position, Sound 152
Preamp, Microphone 105
Pro Tools 10
Problems With Playback 143
Prophet's Song 206
Ptich, Change 27
Punch In Punch Out 137

Q

Queen 7, 128, 135, 139, 201, 206, 211

R

Record Only for a Short Time............ 146
Recordin, Electric Lead Guitar........... 132
Recording Church Services................ 140
Recording Sermons 140
Recording Studio 82
Recording, Acoustic Guitar 133
Recording, Bass Track 128
Recording, Click Track....................... 122
Recording, Drum Machine 127
Recording, Drum Track 124
Recording, Electric Rhythm Guitar 131
Recording, Guitar Track 129
Recording, Keyboard 135
Recording, Overdub.......................... 138
Recording, Piano 135
Recording, Rhythm Section 122
Recording, Voice 135
Rectifier Distortion............................. 35
Red Book 216
Regular Interval Labels 70
REO Speedwagon's........................... 204
Resetting the Latency 143
Rest Configurations 66
Reverb.. 42
Reverb, Setting up 175
Reverse 44
Reverse, How to use 187
Rhythm Section 122
Ribbon Microphone........................... 96
Roger Dannenberg 10

S

Saxophone 118
Saxophone ,Microphone placement . 118
SD Card 9
Shake it Loose Tonight..................... 204
Shock Mount................................... 102
Sliding Stretch 44
Snare Drum, Mircophone placement 111
Somebody to Love 205

Sound Position, Backing Vocals......... 153
Sound Position, Bass........................ 154
Sound Position, Guitars 154
Sound Position, Lead Vocal 153
Sound Postion, Percussion 154
Sound Postion, Drums 155
Sound Postion, Hamonica 155
Sound Postion, Horns 154
Sound Postion, Keyboards 154
Sound Postion, Piano....................... 154
Sound Postion, Strings 154
Sound Postion, Woodwinds.............. 155
Sound Tools 10
Sound, Depth................................... 156
Sound, Height 156
Speakers,will not recongnize 146
Spectral Delete 56
Spectral Edit Parametric EQ 57
Spectral Edit Shelves.......................... 58
Speed, Change 29
Spitfish 180
Stand, Microphone 103
Storm Warning .. 194, 198, 203, 205, 206, 213
Strom Warning 197
Studio Fade Out................................. 60
studio monitors 79

T

Take it on the Run 204
Tambourine 118
Tambourine, ,Microphone placement
.... 118
TASCAM 7, 8, 14, 108, 124, 146
Taxes, for Musicians 222
Tempo, Change.................................. 30
the Doors 7, 206, 211
The End. 206
The Wizard of Oz 211
Tie Your Mother Down 205
Time, Add or Remove 199
Time, Cutting Songs Down 202
Too Loud 194
Too Soft... 194
Tough Guys...................................... 204
Track, Clarity 162

Track, Clean up 158
Track, Doubling................................181
Track, Removing 161
Tracks, Bouncing..............................185
Tremolo 60
Trombone..114
Trombone Microphone placement....114
Trumpet...114
Trumpet, Microphone placement 114
Truncate Silence 45
Tuba 114
Tuba, Microphone placement 114

U

USB ports..76

V

Van Halen, Eddie................................24
Violin...112
Violin, Microphone placement.........112
Visit Heaven........ 175, 201, 202, 204, 206
Vocal Isolation 60
Vocal Reduction 60
Vocal Isolation Booth........................88
Vocal Isolation Booth, Building 88
Vocals..118
Vocals ,Microphone placement........118
Vocoder 61

W

Wah Wah..46
Wave Colors 142
We Will Rock You.............................135
Whistling ,Microphone placement 120
White Album 200
Will Not Recognize Microphone........146
Wind Screen 102

X

Xrum Kit, Multiple Microphones 111
Xylophone 120
Xylophone ,Microphone placement ..120

www.ingramcontent.com/pod-product-compliance
Lightning Source LLC
Chambersburg PA
CBHW081220170426
43198CB00017B/2675